21世纪英语专业系列教材

英语写作：毕业论文写作

（第三版）

主　编：李正栓　焦绘宏
副主编：魏晓红　白凤欣　尹　静　梁文霞　张媛媛
参编者：张亚蜀　杨　丽　周英莉　王　琪

图书在版编目(CIP)数据

英语写作：毕业论文写作/李正栓,焦绘宏主编.—3 版.—北京：北京大学出版社，2015.6
（21 世纪英语专业系列教材）
ISBN 978-7-301-25857-6

Ⅰ.①英…　Ⅱ.①李…②焦…　Ⅲ.①英语 – 毕业论文 – 写作 – 高等学校 – 教学参考资料
Ⅳ.①G642.477②H315

中国版本图书馆 CIP 数据核字（2015）第 101546 号

书　　　名	英语写作：毕业论文写作（第三版）
著作责任者	李正栓　焦绘宏　主编
责任编辑	刘　爽　叶　丹
标准书号	ISBN 978-7-301-25857-6
出版发行	北京大学出版社
地　　　址	北京市海淀区成府路 205 号　100871
网　　　址	http://www.pup.cn　新浪微博：@北京大学出版社
电子邮箱	编辑部 pupwaiwen@pup.cn　总编室 zpup@pup.cn
电　　　话	邮购部 010-62752015　市场营销中心 010-62750672　编辑部 010-62759634
印 刷 者	北京溢漾印刷有限公司
经 销 者	新华书店
	787 毫米 × 1092 毫米　16 开本　18.5 印张　300 千字
	2006 年 2 月第 1 版　2013 年 1 月第 2 版
	2015 年 6 月第 3 版　2024 年 12 月第 10 次印刷
定　　　价	46.00 元

未经许可，不得以任何方式复制或抄袭本书之部分或全部内容。
版权所有，侵权必究
举报电话：010-62752024　电子邮箱：fd@pup.cn
图书如有印装质量问题，请与出版部联系，电话：010-62756370

"21世纪英语专业系列教材"编写委员会

（以姓氏笔画排序）

王守仁　王克非　申　丹

刘意青　李　力　胡壮麟

桂诗春　梅德明　程朝翔

总　序

北京大学出版社自2005年以来已出版"语言与应用语言学知识系列读本"多种，为了配合第十一个五年计划，现又策划陆续出版"21世纪英语专业系列教材"。这个重大举措势必受到英语专业广大教师和学生的欢迎。

作为英语教师，最让人揪心的莫过于听人说英语不是一个专业，只是一个工具。说这些话的领导和教师的用心是好的，为英语专业的毕业生将来找工作着想，因此要为英语专业的学生多多开设诸如新闻、法律、国际、经济、旅游等其他专业的课程。但事与愿违，英语专业的教师们很快发现，学生投入英语学习的时间少了，掌握英语专业课程知识甚微，即使对四个技能的掌握并不比大学英语学生高明多少，而那个所谓的第二专业在有关专家的眼中只是学到些皮毛而已。

英语专业的路在何方？有没有其他路可走？这是需要我们英语专业教师思索的问题。中央领导关于创新是一个民族的灵魂和要培养创新人才等的指示精神，让我们在层层迷雾中找到了航向。显然，培养学生具有自主学习能力和能进行创造性思维是我们更为重要的战略目标，使英语专业的人才更能适应21世纪的需要，迎接21世纪的挑战。

如今，北京大学出版社外语部的领导和编辑同志们，也从教材出版的视角探索英语专业的教材问题，从而为贯彻英语专业教学大纲做些有益的工作，为教师们开设大纲中所规定的必修、选修课程提供各种教材。他们把英语专业教材的出版看作是第十一个五年计划期间组织出版国家"十一五"重点出版规划项目——"面向新世纪的立体化网络化英语学科丛书"的重要组成部分。这套系列教材要体现新世纪英语教学的自主化、协作化、模块化和超文本化，结合外语教材的具体情况，既要解决语言、教学内容、教学方法和教育技术的时代化，也要坚持弘扬以爱国主义为核心的民族精神。因此，今天北京大学出版社在大力提倡专业英语教学改革的基础上，编辑出版各种语言、文学、文化课程的教材，以培养具有创新性思维的和具有实际工作能力的学生，充分体现了时代精神。

北京大学出版社的远见卓识，也反映了英语专业广大师生盼望已久的心愿。由北京大学等全国几十所院校具体组织力量，积极编写相关教材。这就是说，这套教材是由一些高等院校有水平、有经验的第一线教师们制订编写大纲，反复讨论，特别是考虑到在不同层次、不同背景学校之间取得平衡，避免了先前的教材或偏难或偏易的弊病。与此同时，一批知名专家教授参与策划和教材审定工作，保证了教材质量。

当然，这套系列教材出版只是初步实现了出版社和编者们的预期目标。为了获得更大效果，希望使用本系列教材的教师和同学不吝指教，及时将意见反馈给我们，使教材更加完善。

航道已经开通，我们有决心乘风破浪，奋勇前进！

胡壮麟
北京大学蓝旗营
2007年2月

前　言

英文写作是英语教学的重要目标,对于绝大多数英语学习者而言,写作是一个人英语水平高低的全方位体现。具体而言,英语写作训练有着以下几种主要功能和特点:第一,是英语学习者英语水平的表达,写作需要调动学习者所能够获取的所有相关的英语材料进行实践,比口语训练强度更大;第二,是英语学习者净化英语的过程,在写作的过程中,学习者会逐步将不规范的英语用法和习惯抛弃;第三,是英语学习者精确化的过程,写作是反复推敲的过程,它能使学习者寻找最精确的表达方式。基于此,我们总结了英语写作教学的特点和教材建设的编写经验,重新修订了英语写作系列教材。

普通高等教育"十一五"国家级规划教材,《英语写作:毕业论文写作》(第三版)、《英语写作:应用文写作》(第二版)、《英语写作:基础写作》(第三版),经过多年的使用及修订,得到了教师和学生的认可,更加体现了鲜明的时代性和特殊性,以期让各院校成体系地完成英语专业本科阶段的英语写作教学,学生通过学习本套教材,能够较全面地掌握英语写作技巧,为以后的工作和学习打下良好的基础。

鉴于时间仓促和编者水平有限,本套教材难免有疏漏与不足之处,欢迎广大读者批评指正。

编者

2015.4

目 录

第一章 毕业论文写作概述 ……………………………………………… (1)
- 第一节 什么是毕业论文 …………………………………………… (2)
- 第二节 毕业论文的撰写原则和基本要求 ………………………… (6)
- 第三节 毕业论文的研究和写作过程 ……………………………… (9)
- 第四节 毕业论文的等级评定标准 ………………………………… (10)

第二章 毕业论文的格式 ………………………………………………… (12)
- 第一节 毕业论文的整体格式 ……………………………………… (12)
- 第二节 三种国外流行的学术论文格式 …………………………… (17)
- 第三节 引文的格式 ………………………………………………… (22)
- 第四节 注释的格式 ………………………………………………… (33)
- 第五节 参考文献的格式 …………………………………………… (35)

第三章 毕业论文的选题 ………………………………………………… (39)
- 第一节 影响选题的因素与选择的重要性 ………………………… (39)
- 第二节 选题的原则和方法 ………………………………………… (40)
- 第三节 选定论文题目和拟题 ……………………………………… (41)

第四章 毕业论文资料的准备和利用 …………………………………… (63)
- 第一节 毕业论文资料的准备 ……………………………………… (63)
- 第二节 毕业论文资料的利用 ……………………………………… (66)
- 第三节 各专业丛书书目 …………………………………………… (67)

第五章 毕业论文的具体撰写 …………………………………………… (90)
- 第一节 如何拟写论文提纲 ………………………………………… (90)
- 第二节 如何撰写文献综述 ………………………………………… (95)
- 第三节 如何撰写开题报告 ………………………………………… (105)
- 第四节 如何撰写初稿 ……………………………………………… (108)
- 第五节 如何修改论文定稿 ………………………………………… (134)

第六章 毕业论文的答辩 ………………………………………………… (136)
- 第一节 论文答辩的准备 …………………………………………… (136)
- 第二节 论文答辩的一般程序 ……………………………………… (141)

第七章 毕业论文实例 …………………………………………………… (143)
- 第一节 语言学类 …………………………………………………… (143)
- 第二节 文学类 ……………………………………………………… (166)
- 第三节 教学法类 …………………………………………………… (190)
- 第四节 翻译类 ……………………………………………………… (221)
- 第五节 商务英语类 ………………………………………………… (245)

附录1 《中国图书馆图书分类法》基本类目表 …………………………（269）
附录2 《中国科学院图书馆图书分类法》基本类目表 ………………（270）
附录3 科学技术报告、学位论文和学术论文的编写格式 ……………（272）
附录4 修改符号 Correction Symbols（摘自美国汤姆森集团
    出版的 *Discoveries of Academic Writing*）………………………（281）
参考文献 …………………………………………………………………（284）

第一章 毕业论文写作概述

教育部财政部关于实施高等学校本科教学质量与教学改革工程的意见(教高〔2007〕1号)指出:"加强和改进高校本科教学工作评估,以评促建,以评促改,评建结合,重在建设,促进学校强化教学管理、深化教学改革、提高教学质量。"高校本科教学工作评估是当前高等教育的主要任务,是提高教育质量的关键举措。其基本内容包括7个一级指标和1个特色项目。一级指标下设19个二级指标,19个二级指标中有11个重要指标,毕业论文或毕业设计是其中之一。本科教学工作水平评估的一项重要内容是抽查学生毕业设计(论文)。

根据教育部办公厅关于加强普通高等学校毕业设计(论文)工作的通知(教高厅[2004]14号):"毕业设计(论文)是实现培养目标的重要教学环节。毕业设计(论文)在培养大学生探求真理、强化社会意识、进行科学研究基本训练、提高综合实践能力与素质等方面,具有不可替代的作用,是教育与生产劳动和社会实践相结合的重要体现,是培养大学生的创新能力、实践能力和创业精神的重要实践环节。同时,毕业设计(论文)的质量也是衡量教学水平,学生毕业与学位资格认证的重要依据。"

《中华人民共和国学位条例》第四条规定:"高等学校本科毕业生,成绩优良,达到下述学术水平者,授予学士学位:

(一)较好地掌握本门学科的基础理论、专门知识和基本技能;

(二)具有从事科学研究工作或担负专门技术工作的初步能力。"

英语专业本科毕业论文写作是高等院校英语专业教学计划中一个重要部分和实践环节,是判断学生是否具备毕业条件的一种方式。其目的是检测大学生自身专业水平和完成学业的情况。毕业论文写作的优劣是决定学生毕业时可否被授予学士学位的一个重要依据,毕业论文经过答辩并通过后,学生即将其作为获得相应学位的一个凭证。此外,学生在撰写论文的过程中,培养了综合运用所学的专业知识和理论的实践能力以及初级的科学研究能力,掌握了基本的论文写作程序和技法,并且在提出自己观点的同时,在一定程度上培养了创新能力,为以后的进一步学习和工作打下了一定的基础。

本科生毕业论文应充分体现出对学生四年学习的专业基础知识和研究能力、自学能力以及各种综合能力的检验。通过毕业论文设计的形式,进一步巩固和加强对学生的基本知识和基本技能训练,加强学生创新能力和获取新知识能力的培养,鼓励学生运用所学知识独立完成课题。培养学生严谨、求实的治学方法和刻苦钻研的科研精神。

毕业论文的基本教学要求旨在培养学生调查研究、文献检索与阅读、资料收集、消化整理和分析能力;培养学生综合运用所学知识,独立发现、分析和解决实际问题以及创新能力;提高学生正确撰写毕业论文的能力。

第一节 什么是毕业论文

毕业论文是高等院校毕业生提交的一份有一定学术价值的文章。它是大学生完成学业的标志性作业,是大学生从事科学研究的最初尝试,是在教师指导下所取得的科研成果的文字记录,也是检验大学生掌握知识的程度、分析问题和解决问题基本能力的一份综合答卷。

毕业论文就其内容来讲,一种是解决学科中某一问题,用自己的研究成果加以回答;一种是只提出学科中某一问题,综合别人已有的结论,指明进一步探讨的方向;再一种是对所提出的学科中某一问题,用自己的研究成果,给予部分的回答。毕业论文注重对客观事物作理性分析,指出其本质,提出个人的学术见解和解决某一问题的方法和意见。

毕业论文就其形式来讲,具有议论文所共有的一般属性特征,即论点、论据、论证是文章构成的三大要素。文章主要以逻辑思维的方式为展开的依据,强调在事实的基础上,展示严谨的推理过程,得出令人信服的科学结论。毕业论文虽属学术论文中的一种,但和学术论文相比,又有自己的特点,即具有指导性。毕业论文是在导师指导下独立完成的科学研究成果。毕业论文作为大学毕业前的最后一次作业,离不开教师的帮助和指导。

英语专业本科毕业论文属于研究性论文的范畴。学生经过调查、评论和创造性地利用其他研究者的观点、思想和信息等研究活动之后,将这种研究的结果和结论以研究性论文的形式呈现出来。换而言之,研究性论文是学生研究结果和结论的呈现。但是,一篇研究性的论文绝不是对已有出版物的简单的评述和从中提取一些章句,也不是对他人作品的简单概述,而是在融合吸收的基础之上得出自己的结论,创立并呈现自己的观点。同时,研究性论文是一种书面交流形式,要求清晰有效地呈现信息和观点。

毕业论文通常有一定的长度要求,集中阐述一个学术论题,目的是向相关领域的读者提供关于此论题、目的、方法、结果、结论以及建议等方面的信息。在实验、事实、数据和分析的基础上表达作者对于论题的理解。尽管作者的个人观念、理解力和经历会影响整个写作过程,但论文应该是客观的。

英语专业本科毕业论文作为研究性论文的一种,又叫学位论文,是大学生在教师指导下完成的总结性作业。本科学生毕业论文要有一定的深度,要触及问题的实质,并力求有一定的社会指导意义。根据《中华人民共和国国家标准 UBG 001. 81 GB 7713-87 科学技术报告、学位论文和学术论文的编写格式》(Presentation of Scientific and Technical Reports, Dissertations and Scientific Papers):"学位论文是表明作者从事科学研究取得创造性的结果或有了新的见解,并以此为内容撰写而成、作为提出申请授予相应的学位时评审用的学术论文。"

1. 写毕业论文的意义

学习研究调查、评论、创造性地利用其他研究者的想法、信息和观点等在学生的发展过程中发挥着重要作用。在学生的教育经历中,创作研究论文的各种活动——识别、查找、评估和融合他人的研究以及随后清晰明了、富有说服力地形成和表达自己的观点,处于核心地位。

学习如何撰写研究性论文就会帮助学生为将来的职业生涯做准备,因为无论学生在毕业后从事什么职业,都会不可避免地要查询某个特定事物的资料,将信息和自己的观点相结合,有效地表达和呈现自己的想法、研究结果和得出的结论。

研究可以增长学生对于一个话题的知识,加深对其的理解。有些研究会证实,有些又会质疑和修改之前的想法和观点,但是总是会影响学生的思维。

毕业论文是高校英语专业教学的重要组成部分,是对学生学习成果的综合检验。撰写毕业论文最基本的意义在于它能为学生顺利完成本科学业、取得学士学位提供凭证。除此之外,撰写毕业论文还具有如下意义:

(1) 毕业论文的撰写可以总结、运用和提高学生各方面的专业知识和技能。撰写论文与英语专业课程教学是密切联系、相辅相成的。英语专业的本科生在近四年的专业学习中,已经学习并掌握了本专业各门课程,如语言学、文学、翻译、教学法等的基本知识和一些相关资料。这些知识和材料的储备为他们撰写毕业论文打下了一定的物质基础,但是这只是一个被动的接受过程。而撰写毕业论文是将所学的知识消化、吸收、总结和运用,并主动调动写作能力、总结能力、分析问题能力和解决问题能力的一种创造过程。所以说,毕业论文是对学生学习成果的综合检验,同时更能反映出学生的实际能力和水平,是对学生写作能力和知识运用能力的综合训练和提高。

(2) 毕业论文的撰写可以促进对专业知识,特别是对某一课题的认识的深化。学生在撰写毕业论文前首先要进行选题,查阅和收集相关资料和信息,阅读和整理这些资料和信息,并在此基础之上写出提纲,继而完成全文。这个发现问题、分析问题和解决问题的过程也就是学生的认识由浅入深的过程。

(3) 毕业论文的撰写可以培养和提高学生的思维能力,特别是逻辑思维能力。与一般作文相比,学术论文内容丰富、逻辑性强、前后连贯、说理透彻。学生撰写一篇毕业论文,需要层层深入地科学论证和逻辑分析,最后提出自己的观点;或者是先提出自己的观点,然后再层层论证。因而,完成一篇毕业论文可以帮助学生进行严谨的逻辑思维训练,从而提高学生的思辨能力。

(4) 毕业论文的撰写可以提高学生的英语写作水平。撰写毕业论文是要写规范的学术文章,这就有一个如何表达的问题。学生要用所学的英语词汇、语法知识、写作方法与技巧写出文章,表达要清楚、准确、有说服力,这将对学生四年来所学的知识来一个总考核。如果基础不扎实,写出的文章就会词不达意、语不成句、思维不清、结构混乱。所以说,撰写毕业论文既是学生驾驭英语语言能力的一次考核,也是一次提高语言运用构造篇章能力的训练和提高。

(5) 毕业论文的撰写可以培养学生初步的科研能力。由于本科学生撰写毕业论文是他们初次撰写学术论文,大体水平不高,但是在撰写毕业论文时,学生基本上掌握了规范的写作方法和技巧,提高了英语写作水平,培养和提高了逻辑思维能力,确立了科学的研究态度和钻研精神,而所有这一切正是科学研究者所应具备的能力。这也为他们今后进一步的科学研究和撰写更高一级的学术论文奠定了基础。

2. 毕业论文与学年论文的区别

学年论文是高校在校学生在大学二三年级以后开始练习撰写的考查学习成果和科研能力的论文。它是学生通过一段时间的基础课的学习之后,在教师的指导下,运用自已掌握的基础理论知识及写作方法与技巧,独立地提出问题、分析问题、解决问题,就某一学术问题进行科学研究而写成的论文。学年论文的写作也是了解学术论文写作的步骤和方法,培养和锻炼学术研究能力的一种尝试。学年论文写成后一般不进行论文答辩,由指导教师审核后,写出评语、评定成绩。

学年论文和毕业论文都要求学生运用所学的专业知识,就某一学术问题提出观点、分析论证、得出结论,在性质上是一样的。但二者又有所区别。也可以说:学年论文在广度、深度、难度等方面都只是论文的雏形,它只是在自己的学习过程中,对某一观点进行分析研究,并提出自己的见解,是一种探索尝试性质的作业;而毕业论文则要求能更充分地展示出作者的分析能力与综合概括能力,要比学年论文更规范、更系统,其论点更加深刻,内容更充实、更具有综合性,是大学本科四年所学之大成,是学生各种能力的最佳发挥和综合的体现。

此外,毕业论文需要答辩。在论文答辩会上,老师提问、学生回答和争辩,师生对话,双向交流,给学生们充分的阐述自己的观点和见解的权利。毕业生参加论文答辩会,认真听取老师提问和同学的答辩发言,对照联系自己的论文写作,会获得许多科学研究和论文写作的经验和其他在课堂上难以得到的教益。

当然,优秀的学年论文经过导师的指点,经过学生的进一步拓展、加深,也可以成为一篇优秀的毕业论文。

3. 毕业论文的分类

毕业论文是学术论文的一种形式,为了进一步探讨和掌握毕业论文的写作规律和特点,需要对毕业论文进行分类。由于毕业论文本身的内容和性质不同,研究领域、对象、方法、表现方式不同,因此,毕业论文就有不同的分类方法。

(1) 按学位等级分

在学习结束时,学生要按一定的要求就某一学术问题撰写论文,并就论文所研究的问题进行答辩,这样的论文称之为学位论文(thesis)。本科生写的是学士论文,硕士研究生写的是硕士论文,博士研究生写的是博士论文(dissertation)。大学英语专业本科生的毕业论文实际上就是学士学位论文。本书所说的是学士论文,基本上不涉及硕士论文和博士论文。

(2) 按学科门类分

毕业论文属于学术研究文章。从学术研究的内容来看,有自然科学研究和社会科学或人文科学研究两大范畴。前者包括理学、工学、农学、医学等;后者包括文学、史学、经济学、哲学、法学、教育学等。英语专业的学生毕业论文是属于人文科学领域的学术论文。

(3) 按研究性质分

毕业论文可分为开创性课题研究论文和发展性课题研究论文两个大类。开创性课题毕业论文指的是开创学科新领域、新理论或填补研究空白的论文。发展性课题论文是指对已有的学术观点作深化、补充或修正、纠谬的论文。英语专业本科生所撰写的毕业论文只是学术论文的一种初级形式,对于创新和发展的要求不高,但在撰写毕业论文时学生应尽可能地使自己的论文具有创新性和发展性。

（4）按研究方法分

对一个问题，论文作者可以从不同的角度，用不同的方法进行探讨和研究。所以按照研究方法，毕业论文可分为分析评论型、扩展研究型、综合论述型、自主命题型等论文。分析评论型论文可以就某位作家、某部作品、某种语言现象或教学方法进行理论性的探讨或分析，并在此基础上推导出自己的结论。扩展研究型论文首先在学习研究他人在某一问题上已作出的研究成果或结论，在此基础上做进一步的拓展研究，并有所创新，得出自己的结论。综合论述型论文要求作者在大量阅读有关文献的基础上，研究学者们在某一方面所做出的结论，然后对其进行综合性介绍和客观评论。自主命题型论文则要求作者主要根据自己的知识积累、学习体会和感受，对某一学术问题进行探讨，表明自己对这一问题的观点，并进行说明和论证。英语专业本科生在撰写毕业论文时可以选择任意一种类型的论文进行尝试性写作。

（5）按内容性质和研究方法分

按内容性质和研究方法的不同可以把毕业论文分为理论性论文、实验性论文、描述性论文和设计性论文。英语专业大学生一般写的是理论性论文。理论性论文具体又可分成两种：一种是以纯粹的抽象理论为研究对象，研究方法是严密的理论推导和数学运算，有的也涉及实验与观测，用以验证论点的正确性。另一种是以对客观事物和现象的调查、考察所得观测资料以及有关文献资料数据为研究对象，研究方法是对有关资料进行分析、综合、概括、抽象，通过归纳、演绎、类比，提出某种新的理论和新的见解。

（6）按议论的性质分

按议论的性质不同可以把毕业论文分为立论文和驳论文。立论性的毕业论文是指从正面阐述论证自己的观点和主张。一篇论文侧重于以立论为主，就属于立论性论文。立论文要求论点鲜明，论据充分，论证严密，以理和事实服人。驳论性毕业论文是指通过反驳别人的论点来树立自己的论点和主张。如果毕业论文侧重于以驳论为主，批驳某些错误的观点、见解、理论，就属于驳论性毕业论文。驳论文除按立论文对论点、论据、论证的要求以外，还要求针锋相对，据理力争。

4. 毕业论文的选材范围

不同类别的高等院校，由于学生学习的是不同领域的知识，所写的论文涉及的内容也不一样。作为高等院校英语专业本科学生的毕业论文，主要是涉及英语语言、文学、教学法或翻译研究等选材范围。

大学期间一般外语院系都开出60门以上的课程（含必修课和选修课），有些学校甚至更多。因此，英语专业的毕业论文可写的范围非常广泛，大体可分为几类：文学类、翻译类、语言学类、教学法类和特殊用途英语（其他）类。

（1）文学类论文

这类论文主要研究英国、美国、澳大利亚及其他以英语为母语的国家的文学及文学作品，或对不同地域、不同时期、不同形式、不同体裁的文学作品进行评议；或对作品产生的背景，作家的风格、派别，或是作品的主题思想以及作品对社会进步产生的作用等进行分析评论。

这些年来，比较文学研究比较活跃，在这方面也可大有所写。如："陶渊明与华兹华斯的自然观""古希腊悲剧《美狄亚》与中国古典悲剧《窦娥冤》之异同"等等，学生可根据自己的实际情况来选论文题目。

(2) 翻译类论文

翻译方面的材料相对多些,所以要写这类论文的学生较多。这类论文一般要求学生在翻译完一篇原文材料后,还要用英文写一篇与上述材料相关的论文(此类论文一般要求1500字左右)。翻译课(含英汉互译)是语言专业学生的必修课程。写此类论文一方面是测试学生对英语句型的分析和理解能力、对原文整体的把握能力和汉语的表达能力,另一方面是检测学生的英语写作能力。

另外学生也可以就如翻译理论、翻译方法、翻译实践中的系列问题、翻译与文化的关系等等进行研究与写作。这些年来,关于翻译研究的论文不少,如:"文化差异与不可译性""翻译中的虚实观""翻译中的形象转换""语域与翻译""翻译中的常用技巧(省略、增强、词性转换等)""文章标题的汉英翻译""冗余信息与翻译中的省略"等。学生也可以从中外翻译史,对于某一作品的不同翻译版本进行比读评论,甚至可以尝试提出自己的译本等方面来写。

(3) 语言学类论文

这类论文包括词汇学、语法、当代语言学的各个分支及其理论,以及语言学对其他学科,如语言学对翻译等的影响及作用。

(4) 英语教学法类论文

英语作为世界上应用最为广泛的语种,已越来越受到各国的重视,在全世界掀起了"学英语"热,英语教学则越发显得重要。国内外学者也在探讨与研究各种英语教学的理论与实践方法,英语专业本科学生特别是师范院校的学生可以从不同的方面,如英语教学法理论、英语教学法发展史、或具体某一课程的教学、课程设计等进行研究与写作。

(5) 特殊用途英语(其他)类

这方面的论文有:经贸英语、科技英语、新闻英语、法律英语类的用词、句法及语篇特征的分析等。

当然撰写毕业论文的内容还不止以上所述。学生在写作毕业论文时,应根据自己的特定条件以及自己院系的具体要求从大到小、由宽到窄进行思考和筛选。也就是说,学生选题要从大的选材范围着眼、小处入手,尽量做到所写的论文具有完整性、学术性和科学性,写出一篇论点明确、论据充分、材料充实、论述深刻的论文。

第二节 毕业论文的撰写原则和基本要求

毕业论文无论在内容或形式上都有一定的要求,这也是考核论文成绩的基本依据之一。毕业论文的撰写要遵循一定的原则和符合一定的基本要求。

1. 毕业论文的撰写原则

撰写毕业论文的目的在于训练学生从事学术研究的基本能力。通过撰写毕业论文,使学生了解和掌握进行科学研究和撰写学术论文的基本程序和方法,提高学生发现问题、分析问题和解决实际问题的能力,特别是使其养成勤于思考、善于思考以及乐于思考的习惯,为毕业后走上工作岗位从事教学、科研或其他工作打下初步、扎实的基础。因此学生在撰写毕业论文时应严格遵循下列原则:

(1) 学习原则

毕业论文写作的过程是对几年来所学知识融会贯通、综合运用的过程，要求学生将所学知识系统化。学习原则即是学生在总结前面所学的基础上，还要学习更多的知识，掌握更多的学习方法和提高科学研究的能力。对于过去学习的知识是一次总结、一次检验，对将来从事的工作和研究是一次演练。学生在撰写毕业论文时，必须运用所学的专业知识，理论联系实际，在相关的领域合理选题，并运用科学的方法对所论问题进行深入的研究和思考。通过论文的写作，可以充分调动学习积极性，并发现学习方法上的问题，加以改进。在选题和搜集资料的过程中，学生可以学到四年本科阶段没有学习到的某一专业领域的理论知识；在毕业论文的撰写、修改和定稿的过程中，学生可以学习和掌握撰写学术论文的基本方法和技巧，所以撰写论文是一个总结、积累和不断深化的学习过程。

(2) 独立原则

毕业论文的写作是学生自主学习、独立写作的过程，符合大学生独立自主的学习特点。毕业论文写作是一个在教师提示指导下，学生发挥自己的主动性、独创性的过程。它是科学研究的起步阶段。独立原则要求学生要相信自己，破除依赖思想，要自己动手选题和查找资料，在大量占有资料的基础上，通过归纳、综合比较找出规律性的东西来，得出结论。当然在撰写过程中，可以借鉴别人的成果、征求别人的意见。特别是在每一个阶段要主动争取教师的指导，这是必不可少的。但是，毕业论文写作的完成还是学生自己努力和思考的结果，否则就达不到毕业论文撰写的目的，失掉这一重要训练机会。

(3) 科学原则

毕业论文作为一种规范性的学术论文，本身就带有一定的科学性，所以毕业论文的撰写也必须遵守科学原则。科学原则是指研究的内容准确、思维缜密和结论合乎逻辑。首先选题是一个周密的科学研究过程，材料的收集、整理、分类以及最终的取舍都要求运用科学的方法和态度，以便做到论文的内容真实可信，得出的结论符合专业发展的客观规律，并能正确引导以后的研究方向。其次，毕业论文的撰写要运用科学的写作方法和技巧才能最终得以完成。另外，毕业论文的科学原则也包括理论、知识的完整系统性，支离破碎、不合逻辑的论文不能作为毕业论文。毕业论文的撰写要用科学的思想作为指导，运用科学的方法对资料进行分类、筛选和优化，得出真实、准确、可信的结论。

(4) 学术原则

本科毕业论文虽然是一种水平较低的学术论文或学术论文的雏形，但是它也是学生经过选题、收集整理材料、撰写等过程之后，表达自己的研究成果的论文。因此，本科毕业论文的撰写同样要遵循学术原则。遵循这一原则，就要求学生必须能对某一专业领域中繁杂零乱的文献资料与理论研究状况进行分析、归纳，能够从中找出以往研究所存在的问题和不足，并能够提出自己的想法与相应的对策。虽然本科毕业论文的写作对这一原则的要求可以相对低一些，但学生在写作时，要尽可能多地使自己的论文带有一些学术性，以便为将来的进一步研究和写作打好基础。

(5) 创新原则

创新是学术论文的生命，没有创新，学术就不能发展。所以在写作毕业论文时要大力提倡创新。遵循创新原则，就要求：第一，坚决反对抄袭已有文献资料和研究理论，反对人云亦云，反对资料搬家；第二，鼓励学生敢于发挥创造，把毕业论文写得更深刻、更新颖,但也要防止新奇怪谬的倾向。所谓新意就是要在前人论述的基础上有所拓展、有所延伸。或赞成前人的某一理论观点;或者反对某个观点,与别人商榷争鸣;或对某一阶段、某一方面学术领域的研究状况做综合归纳,予以综述;或是纠正前人研究出现的错误或是弥补其不足。毕业论文必须要有属于自己的一些独立的见解。如果停留在前人的成果上亦步亦趋,人云亦云,提不出创新的见解来,论文写作就成了一种重复劳动,因而失去了撰写论文的意义,更重要的是,有可能犯抄袭剽窃的错误。

(6) 规范原则

本科毕业论文或学士论文是规范性学术论文的一种形式,所以它的撰写必须遵循规范原则。规范原则首先体现在毕业论文的写作要遵循学习、独立、科学、学术、创新等原则,即上述几种原则的总和构成了毕业论文写作的规范性原则。其次,毕业论文写作的规范原则还要求整个写作的最终结果——论文,要符合一些基本的要求,如篇幅、格式、文献、内容、装帧等各个方面的要求。结构零乱甚至混乱的文章根本谈不上是学术论文,它所反映的不仅仅是文章结构格式上的不合规范,更严重的是它反映了论文作者不严谨的学术态度。因此本科毕业论文的撰写必须遵循规范原则。

(7) 理论联系实际的原则

撰写毕业论文必须坚持理论联系实际的原则。理论研究,特别是社会科学的研究必须为现实服务,为社会建设服务,为两个文明建设服务。理论来源于实践,又反作用于实践。科学的理论对实践有指导作用,能通过人们的实践活动转化为巨大的物质力量。科学研究的任务就在于揭示事物运动的规律性,并用这种规律性的认识指导人们的实践,推动社会的进步和发展。因此,毕业论文在选题和观点上都必须注重联系社会的实际,密切注视社会生活中出现的新情况、新问题。坚持理论研究的现实性,做到理论联系实际,就必须迈开双脚,深入实际,进行社会调查研究。只有深入到实际中去,同客观事物广泛接触,获得大量的感性材料,然后运用科学的逻辑思维方法,对这些材料进行去粗取精,去伪存真,由此及彼,由表及里的加工制作,才能从中发现有现实意义而又适合自己研究的新课题。

2. 毕业论文的基本要求

本科毕业论文是大学本科毕业前撰写的学位论文,是学术论文的初级形式,是为将来进一步的专业研究做准备,因此它在形式和内容上都应符合一定的要求,按照一定的写作程序进行,体式完整规范。

(1) 毕业论文的篇幅要求

学士毕业论文正文部分应不少于 8000 字,引文不超过论文正文的 30%。论文单面打印。论文写作的参考文献(中英文专著或文章)应不少于 20 本(篇)。

(2) 毕业论文的格式要求

按科学和规范的写作原则,本科毕业论文的撰写要符合一定的体例格式,其中包括整篇论文的格式、注释注解格式、引文格式和参考文献的体例格式等。这一部分将在第二章"毕业论文的格式"中详细阐述。

(3) 毕业论文的内容要求

本科毕业论文的内容大体包括论点、论据以及论证方法三个方面。在论点这一方面毕业论文要做到言之有理,即论文中要有作者鲜明、准确、有创见性的观点和判断,或是对某一专业问题提出可行的解决方案或是为某一课题的研究指出一个新的研究方向等。

在论据方面，毕业论文的写作要做到言之有据，即论文观点、判断、解决方案以及新方向的提出要有充实准确可靠的理论和事实依据，不能空穴来风，建空中楼阁。论文言之有理、言之有据，才能言之有物。

毕业论文写作在论证上要做到言之有法和言之有序。言之有法即指写作要依据一定的论证方法来完成，如立论法、驳论法或立与驳相结合的方法以及归纳、演绎、类比等方法，不能信手写来，毫无章法。言之有序要求论文写作要有次序性，行文连续流畅，合乎逻辑，使文章浑然一体，无懈可击。

(4) 毕业论文的装帧要求

对于毕业论文的装帧要求，各院校都有自己的具体规定，但总的来说，不外乎以下形式：

① 纸张大小一般要求为 A4

② 装订顺序

封面(包括院校名、姓名、题目、导师姓名、专业、完成日期等信息)

扉页

英文摘要(包括关键词)

中文摘要(包括关键词)

目录

正文

注释

参考文献

致谢

第三节　毕业论文的研究和写作过程

包括英语专业本科毕业论文在内的学术论文的撰写主要有以下六个环节：

1. 选择题目（Choosing a topic）
2. 准备书单（Preparing a working bibliography）
3. 搜集资料（Collecting information）
4. 编写提纲（Outlining the paper）
5. 撰写论文（Writing the paper）
6. 终稿样张（Elements of research papers）

此六个环节可以归纳为论文写作的两大阶段：准备阶段和执笔阶段。准备阶段包括选题、收集资料(其中包括阅读、整理、分析和评价资料)和写出论文大纲。选题涉及选择研究方向或领域、界定题目、缩小范围和初步提出论题或拟题。选定题目后，就可以利用各种综合性的索引、专题性的索引、计算机检索以及网上查阅等方式选择一些与论文题目相关的文献，即参考书单，了解与题目相关的文献情况。根据参考书单，搜集、阅读、评价资料，通过做笔记、复印或电脑录入等方式记录有用信息。阅读整理材料的同时可以根据要求的类别和格式编写提纲,内容包括论题的表述、论文的结构等。

学生经过准备阶段的选题、搜集资料、阅读整理筛选相关的资料,并写出开题报告和论文大纲之后,就要把自己对于论题的思考诉诸文字,使之语言化,这就是论文写作的执笔阶段。执笔阶段主要是撰写论文,主要包括撰写初稿、修改润色、编辑文字、论文格式和校对定稿几个环节。或可以概括为三个阶段,即拟写初稿、修改和定稿。

拟写初稿时,要注意资料、结构和语言三方面的问题。资料是否充实,结构是否合理,语言是否准确达意等问题都应在这一过程中得到解决。但在这一过程中最好能做到一气呵成,以便保持思路的连贯性,即使在以上所提三方面有欠妥之处,也应留到修改过程去完善。

修改是对论文初稿的精加工、深加工。在这一过程中,除了作者自己要认真阅读修改之外,还要征求和获得导师的指导和同学的意见,对论文的语言、结构甚至论点等方面进行修改、润色和调整,最后定稿。

定稿后的论文要符合一定的样章要求,主要内容应包括论文封面、目录、首页、正文、注释和参考书目等。

第四节　毕业论文的等级评定标准

学士毕业论文写作经过准备和执笔两个阶段后,最后定稿完成。完成之后要交给导师评定论文的质量、水平如何,最后提交答辩委员会,对论文作者是否可以毕业并获得学士学位做出评定。以下是某高校的本科毕业论文评定标准:

1. 分数等级:一般采用五级记分制,即学士论文的成绩分为优秀、良好、中等、及格和不及格五个等级。

2. 评分原则:评分时应基本参照以下评分原则。

(1) 初稿质量占总分的60%,终稿占总分的40%。

(2) 有令人信服的独特见解的论文可优先考虑评优秀。定稿后的论文中有重大政治思想错误或在论文写作过程中有抄袭他人作品的,评不及格。

(3) 优秀论文的比例一般控制在论文总数的10%左右。对于不及格的论文要严格控制、慎重对待,不应降低要求。

另外一些学校还要求把介于优秀、良好、中等、及格、不及格五种等级之间的难以明确成绩等级的论文,根据学生答辩时的具体表现最终确定成绩等级。

3. 评分标准:给分时可参照以下某高校的毕业论文评分标准。

毕业论文评分主要评估论文内容(50%)、论文结构(10%)、语言文字(30%)和论文格式(10%)四方面。其具体标准分别为:

(1) 优秀论文(90—100分):选题好,内容充实,能综合运用所学的专业知识,以正确观点提出问题,能进行精辟透彻的分析,并能紧密地结合我国经济形势及企业的实际情况,有一定的应用价值和独特的见解和鲜明的创新;材料典型真实,既有定量分析,又有定性分析;论文结构严谨,文理通顺,层次清晰,语言精练,文笔流畅,书写工整,图表正确、清晰、规范;答辩中回答问题正确、全面,比较深刻,并有所发挥,口语清晰、流利。

(2) 良好论文(80—89分):选题较好,能运用所学的专业理论知识联系实际,并能提出问题,分析问题。对所论述的问题有较强的代表性,有一定的个人见解和实用性,并有一定的理论深度;材料真实具体,有较强的代表性。对材料的分析较充分,比较有说服力,但不够透彻;论文结构严谨,层次清晰,行文规范,条理清楚,文字通顺,书写工整,图表正确、清楚,数字准确;在答辩中回答问题基本正确、中肯,口语比较清晰。

(3) 中等论文(70—79分):选题较好,内容较充实,具有一定的分析能力;独立完成,论点正确,但论据不充足或说理不透彻,对问题的本质论述不够深刻;材料较具体,文章结构合理,层次比较清晰,有逻辑性,表达能力也较好,图表基本正确,运算基本准确;在答辩中回答问题基本清楚,无原则性错误。

(4) 及格论文(60—69分):选题一般,基本上做到用专业知识去分析解决问题,观点基本正确,大体清楚,但前后有些矛盾之处。基本独立完成,但内容不充实,缺乏自己见解;有观点,无例证;或有事例,无观点。材料较具体,初步掌握了调查研究的方法,能对原始资料进行初步加工;内容安排混乱,读者能勉强看明白大意;论据能基本说明问题,能对材料作出一般分析,但较单薄,对材料的挖掘缺乏应有的深度,论据不够充分,不够全面;文字表达基本清楚,文字基本通顺。在答辩中回答问题尚清楚,经提示后能修正错误。

(5) 不及格论文(59分以下):论文观点不清楚,前后矛盾或内容有重大政治思想错误。结构安排混乱,读者不得要领。语言文字、句子结构受汉语影响。英语词使用不当,拼写、标点、大小写错误很多。有论点而无论据,或死搬硬套教材和参考书上的观点,未能消化吸收,使读者看不明白内容。离题或大段抄袭别人的文章,并弄虚作假。论文有提要、提纲、注释和参考书目,但格式混乱,缺乏实际调查资料。总体而言,就是内容空洞,逻辑混乱,表达不清,语句不通。在答辩中回答问题有原则性错误,经提示不能及时纠正。

指导教师根据评分标准及原则写出评语,评语内容包括:

1. 学习态度是否端正,是否认真对待论文的写作,是否虚心学习、刻苦钻研。
2. 指出论文在内容、结构、文字表达及格式等方面的优点并如实指出论文的缺点及需要改进之处。
3. 论文是否具备独立见解和创新意识,对学生获取知识的能力、运用知识的能力、分析问题的能力予以实事求是的评价。
4. 按照评分等级给出论文的实际评分。

指导教师给出论文初评分的,一般还要经过全系的联评。联评主要是为了统一评分的标准和尺度,尤其是对优秀论文和不及格论文予以公正一致的评判。

不同高校对学士毕业论文的评分标准的具体掌握有所不同,但大体上是一致的。以上所选大学的毕业论文评分标准仅供参考,各高校学生可参照本校的具体评分标准。

第二章 毕业论文的格式

本科毕业论文是学术论文的基本形式,在内容上不一定会有很高的学术价值,但是在论文的结构与格式上,却有极为严格的要求。毕业论文的格式是否规范也是毕业论文的等级评定的一个重要方面。这就要求毕业论文撰写要严格按照写作程序进行,层次分明、结构清晰、体式完整。本科毕业论文的撰写应严格遵循规范性原则,必须按固定的完整体式进行写作。毕业论文的整体格式以及相关的引文、注解和文献格式可以参照中外流行的学术论文格式,我国在1987年公布了《中华人民共和国国家标准 UDG 00881 GB 7713-87 科学技术报告、学位论文和学术论文的编写格式》。而当前国际上主要有芝加哥格式——Chicago Manual, The Chicago Manual of Style, 美国心理学会格式——APA, Publication Manual of the American Psychological Association, 现代语言学会格式——MLA, The Modern Language Association Style。

第一节 毕业论文的整体格式

根据我国1987年制定的国家标准《科学技术报告、学位论文和学术论文的编写格式》,本科毕业论文的整体格式应为:

前置部分
- 封面、封二(学术论文不必要)
- 题名页
- 序或前言(必要时)
- 摘要
- 关键词
- 目次页(必要时)
- 插图和附表清单(必要时)
- 符号、标志、缩略语、首字母缩写、单位、术语、名词等
- 注释表(必要时)

$$\text{主体部分}\begin{cases}\text{引言—1}\\ \text{正文—2}\begin{cases}2.1\\ 2.2\\ 2.3\begin{cases}2.3.1\\ 2.3.2\\ 2.3.3\begin{cases}2.3.3.1\\ 2.3.3.2\\ \cdot\end{cases}\\ \cdot\\ \cdot\end{cases}\\ \text{图1(或图2.1)}\\ \text{图2}\\ \cdot\\ \text{表1(或表2.1)}\\ \text{表2}\\ \cdot\end{cases}\\ \text{结论}\\ \text{致谢}\\ \text{参考文献表}\\ \text{致谢(Acknowledgement)}\end{cases}$$

$$\text{附录部分}\atop\text{(必要时)}\begin{cases}\text{附录A}\\ \text{附录B}\begin{cases}B.1\begin{cases}B.1.1\\ B.1.2\text{—}B.1.2.1\end{cases}\\ B.2\\ \cdot\\ \text{图B1}\\ \text{表B1}\end{cases}\end{cases}$$

$$\text{结尾部分}\begin{cases}\text{可供参考的文献题录}\\ \text{索引(必要时)}\end{cases}$$

封三、封底

根据欧美的流行格式和我国的国家标准,我国高校本科毕业论文的写作格式一般采用以下通用格式,各高校学生可具体参照本校的格式要求加以适当的调整:

1. 前置部分

封面(Cover)

空白页(Blank Page)

题名页(Title Page)

摘要(Abstract)

目录(Contents)

2. 正文部分

引言(Introduction)

正文(Body)

结论(Conclusion)

3. 文尾部分

注释(Notes)

参考文献(Bibliography)

致谢(Acknowledgement)

以下将对各部分的具体格式加以说明。

1. 前置部分

封面。一般高等院校都要求本科毕业论文要加装封面,提供论文的相关信息,并起到美化和保护内部文章的作用。论文封面应标注的内容,没有统一的规定,各高校有各自的要求。可参考下表:

××××× 大学
本科生毕业论文

题目：＿＿＿＿＿＿＿＿＿＿＿＿＿＿＿＿＿

姓名：＿＿＿＿＿＿＿＿＿
班级：＿＿＿＿＿＿＿＿＿
指导教师：＿＿＿＿＿＿＿＿＿
专业：＿＿＿＿＿＿＿＿＿
院系：＿＿＿＿＿＿＿＿＿
完成日期：＿＿＿＿＿＿＿＿＿

题名页。题名即是论文的题目、标题,通常是用概括恰当的语言反映论文的内容,要求做到精炼明确。题目可以分为正标题和副标题,之中也可以有小标题,位于居中位置。题目的字号与字体没有统一规定,作者可按本校的具体要求来进行选择。可参考下表:

> A Model of Women
> ——An Analysis of Jo in *Little Women*
>
>
> By
> ×××
>
>
> Prof. ×××, Tutor
>
> A Thesis Submitted to the Foreign Languages
> Institutes in Partial Fulfillment of the Requirements
> for the Degree of Bachelor of Arts at
> ×××× University
> April   2014

摘要。摘要是论文内容的简短概论,是一篇独立完整的短文。它应包括文章所研究的问题、研究方法,所使用的资料和最终的结论。英语专业本科毕业论文的摘要要求中英文各一份,字数一般在 200—300 字之间。读者一般是先读摘要后读正文,一些参考书或计算机摘要类数据库也可能收入一些论文的摘要,所以撰写摘要非常重要,应做到言简意赅,准确清楚,包含正文的核心内容,并且自成一体。关键词是从论文中选出的最能表达全文主要内容、主要论点和结论的单词或词组。一般要求关键词为 3—5 个。

目录。目录中所涉及的一个重要问题是论文所采用的序号形式。英语专业本科毕业论文的序号形式可以采用国家标准所规定的用阿拉伯数字的形式,也可以采用文字与英文字母、阿拉伯数字相结合的形式,如:

Introduction
Chapter One
  A
  B
  C
    1
    2
    3
Chapter Two
  A
  B
  C
Conclusion
 或

1. Introduction
2.
   2.1
   2.1
   2.3
3.
   3.1
   3.2
   3.3
4.
   4.1
   4.2
   4.3
5. Conclusion

2. 正文部分

引言。一篇论文的正文总是以引言开始的。引言要概括说明论文所研究的具体问题,描述研究方法以及在相关领域中前人的研究工作及结果,还要说明论文将会得出的相关结论或对本领域未来研究的展望或建议。

正文。正文是论文的核心部分,可以分成几个章节来写。它可包含论文的研究对象、提出的问题、回答问题所用的资料以及由此得出的结论。正文的论证方法要科学,内容要充实,结论要具有说服力。

结论。结论是整篇论文经过论证之后得出的观点、见解,而不应该是文中各章节的重复叙述。结论还应该明确精炼地概括论文写作所使用的材料来源、所使用的论证方法、所提出的观点等以及在哪些方面有所突破和创新,在本研究领域还有哪些方面应进一步研究等等。

3. 文尾(后)部分

注释和参考文献。毕业论文作为学术论文的一种形式,也和学术论文一样要确切地指出论文中所引资料的出处,这是学术基本要求。引用分为一级引用(Primary Quotation)和次级引用(Secondary Quotation)两种形式。一级引用是指直接引自论题本身的文章,如引用约翰·邓恩的爱情诗的诗句等。这种引用是必须有出处的。二级引用是指引自一些评论家、学者等对于同一论题的评论、数据等,这种引用必须注明出处。

注释和参考文献是注明引用出处的两种方式,前者是注明论文中被引用材料的确切来源或作者对所引用材料的解释,后者则列出对论文的撰写有过指导、影响的所有参考资料和文献。注释和参考文献的格式较为复杂,放在本章第四节和第五节分别加以论述。

致谢。致谢是接在正文之后对在论文的撰写过程中给予过自己帮助、启发的人或单位的感谢。致谢首先要具体,应该是表达对自己的导师、同学、朋友和家人等的感激之情;其次要准确,不能只是泛泛地提到"某些人""一些人"的帮助启发,还要具体、准确指出一个人或几个人的名字来;还应强调指出论文中如果出现某些错误之处,作者本人应承担责任而不应指责所提及的人。这样做的目的除了表达作者的感谢之外,还可以避免抄袭剽窃之嫌,并证明论文中的观点等有一定的理论基础,不是空泛之谈。有的学校把致谢部分放在摘要前。作者应尽量遵循本校的规定。

第二节 三种国外流行的学术论文格式

撰写毕业论文时,学生需要引用其他专家学者的论述,并且要按照严格的格式规定及要求列明参考书目,既方便读者参考,也尊重他人的著作权,避免抄袭剽窃之嫌。目前国外有三种流行的学术论文格式,分别是芝加哥论文格式、美国心理学会论文格式、现代语言学会论文格式。以下就对这三种格式逐一加以简要介绍。

1. 芝加哥论文格式(Chicago Manual Style)

芝加哥大学出版部于1906年出版了《芝加哥格式手册》(*The Chicago Manual of Style*)一书,经过了近百年的增补修订,建立了学术论文写作与书目格式的权威地位。《芝加哥格式手册》格式部分详述撰写论文时需要注意的细节,包括标点符号、人名与数字的写法、引文的写法、图表的制作、数学公式、缩写以及注释与书目的编制方法等。其中第二部分的第15与第16单元正是书目格式指南(Documentation),可以说是撰写论文时,编写注释与参考书目的重要参考。

另外,芝加哥大学出版部也出版了《学期论文、学位论文及博士论文写作手册》(*A Manual for Writers of Term Papers, Theses, and Dissertations*)一书,可说是《芝加哥格式手册》的缩节版,内容精简,尤其适合大学生写作期末报告或研究生撰写论文时的参考。

2. 美国心理学会论文格式(American Psychological Association Style)

《美国心理学会写作手册》是社会科学领域的学术期刊普遍采用的书目格式。1928年,一些心理学与人类学期刊的主编一起讨论有关期刊稿约的问题,并拟订了一份说明简介,供有意投稿的作者参考。这份简介成为投稿者准备稿件与期刊编辑审核稿件的依据。这次会议最后拟订出一份七页的写作指南,于1929年刊登在美国心理学会出版的《心理学学报》(*Psychological Bulletin*)上,这就是《美国心理学会写作手册》的前身。1944年美国心理学会的编辑委员会将内容扩充至32页,鼓励年轻学者从事专业写作,1952年正式以《出版手册》(*Publication Manual*)的名称出版。到1994年,此书已出版至第四版。全书共分七章,分别阐释稿件的内容与组织、观念与表达、美国心理学会的编辑格式、稿件的准备与范例、稿件的接受与出版、美国心理学会期刊的政策与编辑对稿件的管理等。其中第三章说明美国心理学会的编辑格式,当中对书目的写作与引用有详细的介绍,具有很大的参考价值。

3. 现代语言协会论文格式(Modern Language Association Style)

现代语言协会格式是人文学科领域广泛采用的一套书目格式指南。《现代语言协会研究论文手册》(*MLA Handbook*)是为高中生与大学生撰写研究报告而编制的。美国现代语言协会于1977年出版《现代语言协会研究论文手册》,为学术期刊与大学出版社所广泛采用。1995年出版第四版,内容包括六部分:研究与写作、写作要点、研究报告的版式、编制参考书目、著录文献来源、缩写,一步一步引领作者认识论文写作。1999年出版的第五版,加入了网络资源的引用格式。

《现代语言协会格式手册及学术出版指南》(MLA Style Manual)则是为研究生与专家学者撰写学术论文而编制的,于1985年出版,1998年出版的第二版详述出版程序,从稿件的准备到与出版相关的版权和法律问题,都有详尽说明。此外,详述了网上资源的注释格式,具有很大的参考价值。

以上三种论文格式有关注释和参考文献的具体要求,请参看下表。

内容\格式	注释	参考文献
芝加哥论文格式 (Chicago Manual Style)	尾注或脚注(Endnotes or Footnotes)	Munro, Alice. Lives of Girls and Women. New York: Vintage Books, 2001.
美国心理学会论文格式 (American Psychological Association Style)	夹注 (Parenthetical Citations)	Munro, Alice. (2001). Lives of Girls and Women. New York: Vintage Books.
现代语言学会论文格式 (Modern Language Association Style)	夹注(Parenthetical Citations)	Munro, Alice. Lives of Girls and Women. New York: Vintage Books, 2001.

另外,国内一些重要外语类期刊论文也都有自己严格的格式要求,下面仅以《外语教学与研究》格式要求和《中国外语》来稿要求为例,加以介绍。其他外语类期刊,如《外语界》《中国翻译》《上海翻译》以及《外语与外语教学》等格式,学生可根据个人需要进行查阅。

一、《外语教学与研究》格式要求

1. 稿件构成

- 论文中文标题、中文提要、中文关键词、论文正文(含参考文献)
- 论文英文标题、英文提要(另页)
- 附录等(如果有)
- 作者姓名、单位(中英文)、通讯地址、电话号码、Email地址(另页)

2. 提要与关键词

论文须附中、英文提要;中文提要200—300字,英文提要150—200词。另请择出能反映全文主要内容的关键词2—4个。

3. 正文

3.1 结构层次

正文分为若干节(section),每节可分为若干小节(subsection)。

3.2 标题

节标题、小节标题独占一行,顶左页边起头。

节号的形式为1、2、3……,节号后加小数点,然后是节标题;或一、二、三……,节号后加顿号,然后是节标题。

小节号为阿拉伯数字,形式为 1.1、1.2、1.3……,1.1.1、1.1.2、1.1.3……。小节号后空 1 格,不加顿号或小数点,然后是小节标题。

小节之下可以采用字母 A. B. C.,a. b. c.,(a)(b)(c)或罗马数字 I. II. III. ,i. ii. iii. ,(i)(ii)(iii)等对需要编号的内容加以编号。

3.3 字体

正文的默认字体为宋体五号。

中文楷体用于字词作为字词本身使用,如:

"夯字怎么念?"

英文倾斜字体的使用范围主要是:

(1) 词作为词本身使用,如:

The most frequently used word in English is *the*.

(2) 拼写尚未被普遍接受的外来词,如:

Jiaozi is a very popular food in China.

(3) 书刊等的名称。

图表的字体可根据需要换为较小的字号。

3.4 图表

图标题置于图的下方,表标题置于表的上方。

图号/表号的格式为"图/表+带小数点的阿拉伯数字"。

图表的字体一般为宋体小五;如果需要,可以适当采用较小的字号。

图表的行距为单倍。

3.5 参引

一切直接或间接引文以及论文所依据的文献均须通过随文圆括号参引(in-text parenthetical reference)标明其出处。

参引的内容和语言须与正文之后所列参考文献的内容和语言一致。

作者名字如果是英文或汉语拼音,不论该名字是本名还是译名,参引时都仅引其姓。其他民族的名字或其译名如果类似英文名字,参引时比照英文名字。

转述某作者或某文献的基本或主题观点或仅提及该作者或该文献,只须给出文献的出版年,如:

陈前瑞(2003)认为,汉语的基本情状体分为四类,即状态、活动、结束、成就。

直接或间接引述某一具体观点,须给出文献的页码,格式是"出版年:页码",如:

吕叔湘(2002:117)认为,成做动词时,有四个义项:1) 成功、完成;2) 成为;3) 可以、行;4) 能干。

如作者的名字不是正文语句的一个成分,可将之连同出版年、页码一起置于圆括号内,如:

这是社交语用迁移的影响,即"外语学习者在使用目的语时套用母语文化中的语用规则及语用参数的判断"(何兆熊 2000:265)。

圆括号内的参引如果不止一条,一般按照出版年排序。同一作者的两条参引之间用逗号隔开,如:Dahl (1985, 2000a, 2000b);不同作者的参引之间用分号隔开。

文献作者如果是两个人，参引时引两个人的名字。中文的格式是在两个名字之间加顿号，如"吕叔湘、朱德熙(1952)"；英文的格式是在两个姓之间加 & 号，表示"和"，如 Li & Thompson (1981)。

文献作者如果是三人或三人以上，参引时仅引第一作者的名字。中文的格式是在第一作者名字之后加等字，如"夸克等(1985/1989)"；英文的格式是在第一作者的姓之后加拉丁缩略语"*et al.*"，如"Quirk *et al.* (1985)"，*et al.* 为斜体。

3.6 随文圆括号夹注

除了用于参引外，随文圆括号夹注主要用于提供非常简短的说明、译文的原文以及全名的缩写或全称的简称，如：

对于莎士比亚学者来说，最重要的词典有两部：一部是十九世纪七十年代德国人 Alexander Schmidt 以德意志民族特有的勤奋及钻研精神编纂的两卷本巨著 *Shakespeare Lexicon and Quotation Dictionary* (1874/1902/1971，以下简称 *Lexicon*)，另一部是 *Oxford English Dictionary* (1884—1928/1989，通常简称 *OED*)。

随文夹注的字体同于正文的默认字体。

3.7 附注

一般注释采用附注的形式，即在正文需注释处的右上方按顺序加注数码 1、2、3……，在正文之后写明"附注"或"注释"字样，然后依次写出对应数码 1、2、3……和注文，回行时与上一行注文对齐。

3.8 例证/例句

例证/例句宜按顺序用(1)(2)(3)……将之编号。每例另起 1 行，左缩进 1 个中文字符。编号与例句之间不空格，回行时与上一行例证/例句文字对齐。外文例证/例句可酌情在圆括号内给出中译文。

4. 参考文献

每一条目首行顶左页边起头，自第 2 行起悬挂缩进 2 字符。

文献条目按作者姓氏(中文姓氏按其汉语拼音)的字母顺序排列。

中文作者的姓名全都按姓＋名的顺序给出全名。英文仅第一作者的姓名(或汉语拼音姓名)按照姓＋名的顺序给出，姓与名之间加英文逗号，其他作者的姓名按其本来顺序给出。英文作者的名仅给出首字母。

中外文献分别排列，外文在前，中文在后。

同一作者不同出版年的文献按出版时间的先后顺序排列，同一年的出版物按照文献标题首词的顺序排列，在出版年后按顺序加 a, b, c 以示区别。

外文论文(包括学位论文)的篇名以正体书写，外文书名以斜体书写。篇名仅其首词的首字母大写，书名的首词、尾词以及其他实词的首字母大写。

篇名和书名后加注文献类别标号，专著标号为[M]，论文集为[C]，论文集内文章为[A]，期刊文章为[J]，尚未出版之会议论文为[R]，博士论文和硕士论文为[D]，词典为[Z]，网上文献为[OL]。

期刊名称后的数字是期刊的卷号，通常是每年一卷，每卷统一编页码。如没有卷号只有期号，则期号须置于圆括号内；如有卷号但每一期单独编页码，须在卷号后标明期号并将期号置于圆括号内。

每条顶左页边起头,回行时悬挂缩进 2 个中文字符。

二、《中国外语》来稿要求

(一)来稿组成和体例要求

1) 中文标题

2) 中文摘要(200 字以内)

3) 主题词(3—5 个)

4) 正文,字数以 6000 字左右为宜,一般不超过 8000 字

5) 注释

6) 参考文献

中外文参考文献不混排,先外文后中文,按作者姓氏(中文姓氏按其拼音)字母序排。参考文献序号用[1][2][3]……表示,序号之后依次为作者姓名、文献题名、书/刊名、文献类别标识、出版地、出版者、出版年月(或期数)、版次及起止页码。外文书/刊名以斜体书写,实词首字母大写;外文论文篇名以正体书写,仅篇名首字母大写。文献类别标识分别为:专著[M],论文集[C],论文集内文章[A],报纸文章[N],期刊文章[J],未出版之会议论文[P],博士论文[D],硕士论文[MA],报告[R],其他[Z]。网上参考文献应注明相关网址。例:

British Association for Applied Linguistics. Recommendations on Good Practice in Applied Linguistics. http://www.baal.org.uk/index.html, 1994.

Halliday, M. A. K. *Explorations in the Functions of Language*[M]. London: Edward Arnold, 1973.

Jackendoff, Ray. Review of Fodor's. The Mind Doesn't Work That Way [J]. *Language*, 2002(1): 164—170.

Lakoff, G. Cognitive semantics [A]. In Eco, U., et al. (eds). *Meaning and Mental Representation* [C]. Bloomington, Ind.: University of Indiana Press, 1988.

黄子东.评介 Pinker 的《语言本能》[J].《现代外语》,1998(1):93—107.

连淑能.《英汉对比研究》[M].北京:高等教育出版社,1993.

7) 英文标题、摘要(200 词以内)和主题词(3—5 个)

8) 作者信息页(请另页填写)

请详细写明作者信息:姓名、出生年、性别、籍贯、工作单位、学历、职称(职务)、联系方式(含邮编、电话、E-mail 等)及研究方向、主要学术成果(如篇名、书名、期刊、出版社、年代、获奖情况)等,可下载或参照所附《中国外语》作者联系表填写。

(二)其他事项

1) 论文请用 Word 格式排版,正文使用 5 号宋体字,A4 纸打印,并随稿附该文电子文件,邮寄到所列地址;或直接发送 email 至所列信箱。

2) 稿件文责自负,编辑部可对拟采用稿件作必要的修改和删节,不同意者请在来稿中声明。

3) 来稿请勿一稿多投;来稿恕不退还,请自留底稿。凡三个月内未得采用通知者,稿件可自行处理。

4) 稿件一经发表,即付稿酬,并赠样刊 2 本。

第三节　引文的格式

正确规范地引用作品原文以及一些专家学者的论述是写好英语毕业论文的重要环节。引用时既要注意引用部分与论文内在的逻辑关系，又要注意引文格式的规范性。注明所引文字的作者和出处丝毫不会影响论文的独创性。相反，注明引用文字的出处可以让读者了解文献来源，评判作者对文献内容的理解。提供关于文章论题的更多的资料，说明论文的资料来源充足，有据可查，真实可靠，以避免抄袭剽窃之嫌。

抄袭剽窃（Plagiarism）指的是在没有给予恰当合适的标明和感谢的情况下使用他人的观点或文字。他人的观点或表达这些观点的文字归属于第一次提出它们的人，因此，当论文的作者在自己的论文中或以直接或以间接的方式纳入其他作者的观点或文字时，需要准确完整地表明文献来源。引而注为引用，引而不注则为抄袭剽窃。

通常情况下，需要表明引用出处的内容有他人的观点以及文字、只有一个出处或出处数量有限的资料、数字数据等，而一些基本常识或一些众所周知的习语谚语等则无须说明出处。

引述别人的观点，可以直接引用，也可以间接引用，这两种引用方式都要加上相应的注释，用来注明所引文字的作者和出处。

（一）直接引用

直接引用指逐字逐句，一字不差，一字不漏地引用。直接引用可以证明观点或文字的权威性，可以保留所引内容的原始文字，也可以强调所引内容的准确性。直接引用时，引文要尽可能简短，如果引文过长，即超过半页，要把引文放到附录部分，并在文中说明。

使用直接引用时要注意：

（1）引用散文形式的文字时，如果引用的文字不超过40字（大约印刷文字的四行），则直接放在论文之中，用双引号引出，例如：

According to APA style, "Incorporate a short quotation (fewer than 40 words) into text, and enclose the quotation with double quotation marks." (*Publication Manual of the American Psychological Association*, Fifth Ed. p.117)

如果引用文字超过40字，则不用引号，另起一行，从左边缩近5个空符，字体用斜体或小一字号正体，隔行打印。例如：

The APA style of quotation of more than 40 words is just as follows：

> *Display a quotation of 40 or more words in a freestanding black of typewritten lines, and omit the quotation marks. Start such a block quotation on a new line, and indent the block about 1/2 in. (1.3cm, or fire spaces) from the left margin (in the same position as a new paragraph). If there are additional paragraphs within the quotation, indent the first line of each on additional 1/2 in. The entire quotation should be double spaced.* (Publication Manual of the American Psy-

chological Association, *Fifth Ed*. *p. 117*)

或：

The APA style of quotation of more than 40 words is just as follows：

> Display a quotation of 40 or more words in a freestanding black of typewritten lines, and omit the quotation marks. Start such a block quotation on a new line, and indent the block about 1/2 in. (1.3cm, or fire spaces) from the left margin (in the same position as a new paragraph). If there are additional paragraphs within the quotation, indent the first line of each on additional 1/2 in. The entire quotation should be double spaced. (Publication Manual of the American Psychological Association, Fifth Ed. p. 117)

(2) 引用诗歌时，如果引用的是诗歌中的一行或两行，则可以在论文正文中直接用引号引出，用"/"分开各行，斜线前后要各空一格，保持原诗的大写格式，例如：

In the holy sonnet "Oh, to vet me, contraryes meete in one," Donne laments his "inconstancy" as if it were extraordinary... (Achsah Guibbory, "John Donne," *English Poetry-Donne to Marvell*, Ed. Thomas N. Corns p. 130)

In his "Hymn to Intellectual Beauty," Shelley personifies the immaterial, spiritual world: "The awful shadow of some unseen Power / Floats though unseen amongst us." (Carole Slade, p. 59)

如果引用的诗歌超过两行，则须另起一行，从左边缩进10格，不用引号；如果一个诗行必须分成两行打印时，被分出来的后半部分要左边缩进5格，例如：

For he both attempts to control God (thus preserving his individual separateness and autonomy) and seeks an intimate union with God that would erase his separate identity：

> Burne off my rusts, and my deformity,
> Restore thine Image, so much, by thy grace,
> That thou may'st knew mee, and I'll turne my face.
> ("Good Friday, 1613: Riding Westward," lines 40—42) (Ibid., p. 142)

In "Song of Myself," Walt Whitman uses the diction and rhythm of natural speech.

> A child said What is the grass? Fetching it to me with
>   Full hands;
> How could I answer the child? I do not know what it
>   Is any more than he.
> I guess it must be the flag of my disposition, out of
>   Hopeful green stuff woven. (Ibid., p. 61)

如果从一个诗行的中间开始引用,把第一个词大致放在它在原诗诗行的位置上,例如:

>   When yet a child
> I oft have dried my tears when thou has smil'd.
> Thou seem'dst my sister:hand in hand we went
>   From eve to morn across the firmament. (Ibid.)

(3) 引用戏剧文字时,比如引用戏剧中的对白,人物的名字要从左边顶格算起,左缩进 10 格,加下划线。如果名字较长,第一次引用全名,之后再次引用时可以用缩略形式。名字之后加句点,与话语之间空 2 格。如果引用的对白连续几行,从第二行开始,从人物名字的第一个字母算起,左缩进 10 格。舞台提示放在括号内,斜体或加下划线,大致与原文相同。例如:

In a flashback, Miller demonstrates that the Loman family has a memory of better times.

>   [*Linda enters, as of old, a ribbon in her hair,*
> *carrying a basket of washing.*]
> Linda. [*With youthful energy*] Hello, dear!
> Willy. Sweetheart!
> Linda. How'd the Chevvy run?
> Willy. Chevrolet, Linda, id the greatest ca ever
>   built. [*to the boys*] Since when do you
>   let your mother carry wash up the stairs? (Ibid., p.62)

直接引用时还需要注意以下几个问题:
(1) 导入引用的方式
为了行文的流畅,在引用时要采用恰当的导入引用方式。导入中应该包括原文的内容和引用的理由,特别说明原文与所写论文之间的关系,如论文作者是否同意引文中的观点,或所引的内容与其他引用内容的区别等等。引文的导入应该是论文语言和引文语言之间流畅自然的过渡。例如:

The idea of translation as an organic process is also clearly present in the thinking of Ezra Pound, who, like so many poets and translation theorists before and after was concerned to try and categorise what happens when a poem is rendered from one language into another.

Pound stresses the importance of the target language for translators. Discussing medieval poetry, for example, he remarks:

The devil of translating medieval poetry into English is that it is very hard to decide HOW you are to render work done with one set of criteria into a language NOW subject to different criteria. Translate the church of st. Halaire of Poitiers into barocco? You can't, as anyone knows, translate it into English of the period. The

Plantagenet Kings' Provencal was Langue d'Oc. (Pound, 1934)
(Susan Bassnett & Andre Lefevere, p. 64)

另外,引文导入中应该包括引文作者的名字——第一次引用时用全名,以后再提到时只用姓氏,和作者的职业或社会关系、地位等——第一次引用时必须说明,以后再引时,必要或需要强调时说明,否则可省略。例如:

James Holmes[第一次引用时用全名], a great translator of poetry across several languages and distinguished scholar of translation [作者的职业或社会关系、地位], attempted to produce a basic set of categories for verse translation. He listed a series of basic strategies used by translators to render the formal properties of a poem. The first such strategy he calls "mimetic form"...
The second strategy outlined by Holmes [再引时只用姓氏]involves a formal shift... (Susan Bassnett & Andre Lefevere, p. 62)

关于直接放在论文之中的引用部分,导入引用的句式见以下例子中的粗体字:

例 1: **As Reuben Brower has indicated**, "The average reader of a translation in English wants to find the kind of experience which has become identified with 'poetry' in his readings of English literature. The translator who wishes to be read must in some degree satisfy this want." (James Holmes, p. 14)

例 2: "I felt before I thought," **Rousseau explains.** (Carole Slade, p. 64)

例 3: **In the introduction to his translation of the** *Kalevala*, **Friberg (1988) overstates the case when he writes**: "The Finnish people through the Kalevala actually sang themselves into existence." (Susan Bassnett & Andre Lefevere, p. 78)

例 4: **In Bentley's translation she says**: "If no one had *wanted* to be free, the king wouldn't have had any fun." (B58/B[entley]25) (Ibid., p. 110)

例 5: **He starts out by stating the audience's resistance to Brecht as follow**: "We have never driven anybody out of the theatre, as we did occasionally with this play" (Blau, 1964: 7a), and then goes on to explain how the actors tried to overcome a similar reaction. (Ibid., p. 114)

关于另外起行的引用文字,导入引用的句式见以下例子中的粗体字:

例 1: **The fact that** this version of womanhood is an active social construction, and one invented by men in the interests of maintaining hierarchies, **is displayed in** Carew's "A Married Woman":

When I shall marry, if I doe not find
A wife thus moulded, I'le create this mind:
Nor from her noble birth, nor ample dower,
Beauty, or wit, shall she derive a power
To prejudice my Right; but if she be
A subject borne, she shall be to me...

... （Carew, *Poems*, pp. 115—116）
（Thomas N. Corns, p. 45）

例 2: ... and later, in a consideration of the Wessex setting, **Ellis directly articulated this idea**:

It would almost seem that in the solitary lives on these Dorset heaths we are in contact with what is really a primitive phase of society... [and] that those qualities which we have found to be distinctive of his heroines, the absence of the moral feeling, the instinctiveness, had a direct relation to the wild and solitary character of their environment. （Cox, p. 130）
（Dale Karmer, pp. 95—96）

例 3: By 1801 Coleridge was changing his mind about Tooke's politics, but according to McKusick, "his admiration for Tooke's scholarship remained unaffected by these feelings." Unaffected? **Here is an entry from** Coleridge' *Table Talk* for May 7, 1830:

Tooke affects to explain the origin and whole philosophy of language by what is, in fact, only a mere accident of its history. His abuse of Harris [...] is most shallow and unfair. Harris, in the Hermes, was dealing—not very profoundly, it is true—with the philosophy of language, the moral and metaphysical causes and conditions of it, &c. Horn Tooke, in writing about the formation of words only, thought he was explaining the philosophy of language, which is a very different thing.
（Stuart Urran, p. 111）

例 4: Roland Barthes's account of textuality and its strategy of quotation is most appropriate to this episode. A multivalent text, **he writes**,

can carry out its basic duplicity only if it subverts the opposition between true and false, if it fails to attribute quotations... to explicit authorities, if it flouts all respects for origin, paternity, propriety, if it destroys the voice which could give the text its ("organic") unity... For multivalence... is a transgression of ownership.
（Derek Attridge, p. 157）

例 5: **As Breen and Mann (1997: 141) point out**:

Learners will generally seek to please me as the teacher. If I ask them to manifest behaviours that they think I perceive as the exercise of autonomy, they will gradually discover what these behaviours are and will subsequently reveal them back to me. Put simply, learners will give up their autonomy to put on the mask of autonomous behaviour. （Phil Benson, p. 52）

无论是直接放在论文之中的引用部分,还是另外起行的引用文字,需要注意的是,这些例子中的句式并非一成不变的定式,学生在写作时应该根据具体行文的需要适当加以变通。

(2) 直接引用中字母的大小写

论文中的引文要合乎论文的整体逻辑,符合论文句子和段落的语法要求。因此,直接引用时,学生要正确使用句子中的大小写,必要时要使用括号等,以便准确表明引文的来源。

如果原文的一个句子在引用时成为论文中一个完整独立的句子,无论在原文中句子的第一个词的第一个字母是否大写,引文中一定要大写,例如(注意粗体字母):

原文句子:To begin with, **h**ow can things so insecure as the successful experiences of this world afford a stable anchorage?

引用句子:William James asks, "**H**ow can things so insecure as the successful experiences of this world afford a stable anchorage?" (Carole Slade, p. 67)

相反,如果原文的一个句子在引用时成为论文中某个句子的一部分,原文句子的第一个词的第一个大写字母要变为小写,引用部分可以用引号,也可不用,例如(注意粗体字母):

原文句子:**E**very war propels some obscure city or town into the limelight.

引用句子:Harrison E. Salisbury has observed that "**e**very war propels some obscure city or town into the limelight," pointing out that the identities of Guernica, Coventry, and Stalingrad emerged largely in connection with war. (Ibid.)

或者:Harrison E. Salisbury has observed that **e**very war propels some obscure city or town into the limelight...

当然,如果有必要保持原文的大写形式,通常情况下,可以用不同的引用导入形式。或者在引用文学作品、经典作品或哲学文章时,保持原文的大写是非常重要的,这时无论大写形式是否符合论文的要求,都要保留。例如上文中的例子可以改为:

Harrison E. Salisbury has observed in these terms/words:

Every war propels some obscure city or town into the limelight.

或者可以用方括号把小写或大写的字母括起来,表明它在原文中是大写或小写:

Harrison E. Salisbury has observed that "[**E**]very war propels some obscure city or town into the limelight," pointing out that the identities of Guernica, Coventry, and Stalingrad emerged largely in connection with war.

William James asks, "[**H**]ow can things so insecure as the successful experiences of this world afford a stable anchorage?"

(3) 直接引用中的引号、感叹号和问号

直接放在论文之中的引用部分要括入双引号,双引号放在逗号或句号之后,冒号或分号之前:

Oscar Wilde wrote that "unselfish people are colorless"; however, most would agree with William Gladstone that "selfishness is the greatest curse of the human race." (Carole Slade, p. 69)

感叹号和问号的位置分两种情况:如果标点符号属于引文,放在引号之前;如果标点符号属于所写的论文,则放在引号之后。

在引用时,还应特别注意:

(1) 引用要准确。在引用时,不能随意改变引文中的拼写、标点、格式等,要与原文保持完全一致。但如果为了行文流畅,语法正确,个别词的首字母的大小写要做相应变化,具体可参考第 7—38 页。

(2) 引文中的引号要从始至终保持一致。有的格式用双引号,有的用单引号引出引文,但是无论采用哪一种,前后要保持一致,不能一会儿用单引号,一会儿用双引号。

(3) 引号后要标注,或用夹注、脚注或尾注来注明所引部分的确切出处,相应格式参照第四节"注释的格式"。

(二) 间接引用

在引用别人的作品来阐释自己的观点时,作者首先要判定是直接引用还是间接引用更为有效。使用直接引用时,如果引用太多而评论太少,就会造成读者注意力的分散,他们就很可能会跳过不读这些长长的引文。

间接引用是不引用别人的原话,而用自己的话转述别人的主要意思,也叫转述。这种引用不能用引号标示。间接引用是用最恰当的词句以释义(paraphrase)和概括(summarize)的方式援引原作者的概念、观点和表达。释义是用不同的表达方式阐述原文含义,使之更加简洁、明了。常用的方法有删除次要信息;使用同义词、反义词等;采用注释性说明;改换说法,如改变陈述角度或顺序等。概括是将整篇文献概括为几句话,甚至一两句话。如:

According to Alun Rees (1986), the writers focus on the unique contribution that each individual learner brings to the learning situation.

It may be true that in the appreciation of medieval art the attitude of the observer is of primary importance (Robertson, 1987).

Ancient writers attributed the invention of monochord to Pythagoras, who lived in the sixth century BC (Marcuse, 197).

国际通用的三种间接引用格式如下:

1. Chicago Manual 格式

Romanticism is here prophetic of an abysmal modernity that leaves poetry operating "under a steady threat of extinction" even as it is the only available vehicle of a certain kind of hope.

"International Structure of the Romantic Image," in *The Rhetoric of Romanticism* (New York: Columbia University Press, 1984), pp. 7, 6, 17.

2. MLA 格式

Even Einstein recoiled from the implication of quantum mechanics that reality is an illusion(Gribbin, 2).

3. APA 格式

Even Einstein recoiled from the implication of quantum mechanics that reality is an illusion(Grbbin,1984,p.2).

可以看到,Chicago Manual 格式采用的是加脚注或尾注的方式,即通过阐释、描述或者转述的方式间接引用别人的观点,不同引号,而在间接引用结束以后用数字编序的方式进行注解说明材料的出处。MLA 格式是在引文后面的括号内标注作者和引文页码,即（Gribbin,2）。而 APA 格式则是在引文后面的括号内标注作者、出版年和引文页码,即（Grbbin,1984,p.2）。

间接引用的具体格式为:

1. 正文中没有出现作者姓名

a. 在括号中标出作者的姓氏和出版年代,中间用逗号隔开。如:

It has been regarded that teachers' role is to provide students with optimal conditions which can facilitate learning so that students can achieve similar results (Bloom,1994).

b. 两位作者,中间用 & 或 and 连接,中国姓氏用汉语拼音。如:

The disadvantage of the multiple regression analysis is that it cannot show the complex interrelations between... (Bryman & Cramer,1990)

c. 多位作者,只需写上第一作者的姓氏,后面加上 et al.。如:

Modern literary studies have their origin in classic studies... (Graff et al., 1989)

2. 正文中已经出现作者姓名

a. 在作者姓氏后的括号中标出出版年代。如:

Fries (1981) attempted to provide evidence that...

b. 涉及一篇以上文献,中间用分号。如:

... some scholars (Sapir,1825；Bowell,2002；Mockery,2004) have also studied the aspectual meanings of these nouns.

间接引用的常用句式有:

1. In an article/a study by X...
2. As X points out that...
3. A study/research by X indicates that...
4. X claims/argues/finds/discovers/states that...
5. According to X,...
6. As is found by X,...

使用间接引用时必须注意:

1. 必须清楚易懂;
2. 必须涵盖原文中所有的要点;
3. 不能出现原文没有表达的任何观点或信息;

4. 不能重复原文作者的句子结构和重要词汇;
5. 要与论文的上下文有机地融合在一起,即要合乎逻辑,如:

　　The narrator's constant references to "malicious code and obsolete data" detract from a more fundamental issue—that we are dumping "the burden of human history" onto computer hard drives. It is this vision of the future that is most alarming:"If (when?) we run out of sources of electricity," she asks, "will we forget who we are?"

6. 要合乎语法,特别要注意融合时态和代词,如:

　　原文:Mr. Moll took particular pains to say to you, gentlemen, that these eleven people here are guilty of murder; he calls this a cold-blooded, deliberate and premeditated murder.

　　引文:According to Darrow, Moll had told the jury that the eleven defendants were "guilty of murder" and had described the murder as "cold-blooded, deliberate and premeditated."

7. 如果对原文略有改动,必须把所改的部分放在括号内,如:

　　Mr. Graham has resolutely ducked the issue, saying he won't play the game of rumormongering, even though he has "learned from [his] mistakes."

间接引用除了指转述别人的话之外,也指引用二手的材料。如果找不到原文的原始出处,作者可以间接从别人的文章中引用过来。这种情况下要用"quoted in"来表明材料的原始出处。如:

Costello, Bonnie. 1981. *Marianne Moore: Imaginary Possessions*. Cambridge, MA: Harvard University Press.
In Louis Zukofsky's "Sincerity and Objectification," from the February 1931 issue of Poetry magazine (quoted in Costello 1981)...

由此可以看出,引用二手的材料时,引文的标注要包括两条信息:
第一条:一手材料的相关信息,如:

Costello, Bonnie. 1981. *Marianne Moore: Imaginary Possessions*. Cambridge, MA: Harvard University Press.

第二条:二手材料的相关信息,如:

In Louis Zukofsky's "Sincerity and Objectification," from the February 1931 issue of *Poetry* magazine (quoted in Costello 1981)...

这两条信息告诉读者:论文的作者在他的论文中引用了 Louis Zukofsky 的文章 "Sincerity and Objectification" 的某些内容,这篇文章发表在 the February 1931 issue of *Poetry* magazine 上，但是出于某些原因，论文的作者没有或是不能直接找到这份杂志，他的引文来自于 Bonnie Costello 在 1981 年出版的 *Marianne Moore：Imaginary Possessions*，该书由 Harvard University Press 出版。

再看一个例子：

> Trying to support his wife and child, and Estelle's two children from her first marriage, Faulkner also considered himself responsible for his dead brother's family (Dean had been killed while flying in 1935), and for his mother' well-being.[4][①]

这里有[4]而没有引号，说明此处是一个加了注释的间接引用。下面是文章后面的注释：

4. As Faulkner wrote in May, 1940：

Beginning at the age of thirty, I, an artist, a sincere one and of the first class, who should be free even of his own economic responsibilities... began to become the sole, principal and partial support—food, shelter, heat, clothes, medicine, kotex, school fees, toilet paper and picture shows—of my mother... brother and his wife and two sons, another brother's widow and child, a wife of my own, and two step children, my own child; I inherited my father's debts and his dependents, white and black. (Quoted in Blotner, *Faulkner*, p.417)[②]

括号中的 Quoted in Blotner, *Faulkner*, p.417 告诉读者以上这些话是转引自 Blotner 的 *Faulkner*，关于这本书信息是：Joseph Blotner, *Fualkner：A Bibliography*. New York：Random House, 1984.

如果要给①②加上出处，则为上文所论的直接引用了：

① Linda Wanger-Martin 主编.《〈去吧，摩西〉新论》(*New Essays on Go Down, Moses*). 北京：北京大学出版社，2007，第 1 页.

② Linda Wanger-Martin 主编.《〈去吧，摩西〉新论》(*New Essays on Go Down, Moses*). 北京：北京大学出版社，2007，第 16 页.

（三）关于电子、网络材料的引用格式

在当今的电子时代，除了纸质的书籍、期刊和报纸等文献之外，还有很多电子和网络在线材料可供参考。如何引用这类材料也是学生在完成毕业论文设计时应该注意的问题。下面主要介绍芝加哥论文格式关于电子、网络在线材料的引用格式，其中包括电子版书籍、在线期刊文章、网络材料、博客条目/评论、电子邮件或文本信息以及商业性数据库的条目等。

芝加哥论文格式关于电子、网络在线材料的引用格式要求包括三个信息：

1. 资源定位符（URL）或数字元件索引号（DOI）；
2. 材料的全部出版信息；
3. 材料的网络发表日期和网络最近修改日期。

URL 是 Uniform Resource Locators 的缩略形式。可译为资源定位符、网站链接、网址、链接等，通常以"http://"开始。例如，http://www.microsoft.com/ 为 Microsoft 的 URL 地址，http://www.chicagomanualofstyle.org/ 是芝加哥论文格式的 URL 地

址。利用 URL 地址，读者可以直接进入材料的来源。但是只有 URL 地址是远远不够的，因为 URL 地址所指向的材料的来源往往已经到了另外一个地址或者已经完全消失了。

DOI 是 Digital Object Identifier 的缩略形式，可译为数字元件索引号，用来标识在数字环境中的内容对象。DOI 可以用来揭示有关该数字对象的一些信息，包括从 INTERNET 哪里可以找到它等。随着时间推移，数字对象的位置信息可能会有变化，但是 DOI 不会改变。DOI 是一个永久性的标识号，由 International DOI Foundation 管理。知道了文章的 DOI 号，通过 DOI 解析器就可以找到该文章电子版的地址了。只要将下面的 URL 地址加在已知的 DOI 前面就可以得到该文献在 DOI 系统中的 URL 地址：http://dx.doi.org/。例如：在 DOI10.1086/529076 前面加上 http://dx.doi.org/就可以得到 http://dx.doi.org/10.1086/529076，这个地址指向标题为"Before Democracy：The Production and Uses of Common Sense"的文章，作者为 Sophia Rosenfeld，发表在 *The Journal of Modern History* 的 2008 年第三期上，其网址为 http://www.jstor.org/discover/10.1086/529076?uid＝3737800＆uid＝2＆uid＝4＆sid＝21100865096951。网络截图为：

DOI 号除了便于网络文章的引用外，还可用于文章检索。

在印刷文本中，如果 URL 或者 DOI 必须在一行的结尾处换行时，应该在冒号（：）或双斜线（//）之后；在单斜线（/），波浪字符（～），句号，逗点，连字符，下划线（_），问号，数码，或百分号之前；或者在等号或 ＆ 号之前或之后皆可，切不可加连字符(-)。在电子发表的文献中，则没必要拆开 URL 或 DOI。如：

http://press-pubs.uchicago.edu/founders/
http://www.jstor.org/stable/2921689
http://www.time.com/time/magazine/article/0,9171,920400,00.html
http://wardsix.blogspot.com/2008/07/two-atlantic-essays.html

"材料的全部出版信息"这部分的格式参考前文的相关论述。

日期问题包括材料的网络发表日期或得到该文献的日期和网络的最近修改日期。如前所述,电子和网络文章是不固定的,随着时间的推移会有所改动甚至完全消失,因此,在引用这类文献时,表明得到文献时的日期和文献的最近修改日期是非常重要的,分别用 accessed＋日期和 last modified＋日期表示,放在网址之前。如：

"McDonald's Happy Meal Toy Safety Facts," McDonald's Corporation, accessed July 19, 2008, http://www.mcdonalds.com/corp/about/factsheets.html.

"Google Privacy Policy," last modified March 11, 2009, http://www.google.com/intl/en/privacypolicy.html.

Evanston Public Library Board of Trustees. 2008. "Evanston Public Library Strategic Plan, 2000—2010: A Decade of Outreach." Evanston Public Library, accessed July 19, http://www.epl.org/library/strategic-plan-00.html.

另外,不同的文件形式,具体的要求也有所不同：

1. 电子版书籍

参考引用网络在线书籍时,要列出 Uniform Resource Locator—Internet 的 WWW 服务程序上的信息位置,如果有相关的规定要求,还应包括该信息材料的存取日期。

2. 在线期刊文章

参考在线期刊文章时,要列出数字元件索引号。如果有相关的规定要求,还应包括该信息材料的存取日期。

3. 博客条目/评论

博客条目或评论可以在行文中引用,如有需要,还应包括该信息材料的存取日期。

4. 电子邮件或文本信息

电子邮件和文本信息可以在行文中引用,或者使用注释的形式,但几乎不列在参考文献部分。例如在行文中引用："In a text message to the author on March 1, 2010, John Doe revealed..."如果使用比较正式的注解则为：John Doe, e-mail message to author. February 28, 2010.

5. 商业性数据库的条目

对于从商业性数据库中获取的条目,要在出版信息的后面列出数据库的名称和该条目在该数据库的编号。下面的例子中,所引用的材料来自名为 ProQuest 的数据库,编号为 AAT 3300426：Choi, Mihwa. "Contesting *Imaginaires* in Death Rituals during the Northern Song Dynasty." PhD diss., University of Chicago, 2008. ProQuest (AAT 3300426).

第四节 注释的格式

注释大体可以分为三种形式：夹注、脚注和尾注。

1. 夹注(parenthsis),也称段中注、文中注或随文注,即在需要注释的文字后面直接加圆括号,引出所引用文字的出处,如第三节中所引用例子的注释形式。《MLA 文体手册和学术出版指南(第二版)》指出:"除了必须向读者说明你从哪些作品中获得了原始资料之外,你还必须说明你从每一个出处获得了什么样的资料和你是从该作品的哪个地方找到上述资料的。提供这类信息的最实用方法是每当你在论文中采用别人的词语、事实和思想时,就做一个圆括号注释。通常作者的姓和一个页码就足以确认原始出处在你所借用材料中的特定位置了。"(吉鲍尔迪,271)参看下例:

  Lynn White (1996) stresses the significance of religion to cope with the ecological crisis.

  Contemporary Canadian women writers are aware of themselves as inheritors of a female literary tradition which includes both European and Canadian predecessors (Howells, 1974).

  Eco-feminism is "a perspective that combines the social systems which control people of subordinate status, especially women, with the control of nature" (Warren, 1994:1).

这种注释形式清晰、准确、简便,但是圆括号中所提供的信息内容,必须与后面参考文献中所列的作者书目相一致。

  2. 脚注(footnote),也称页末注或页下注。顾名思义,脚注出现在需要注释的文字本页的正下方,用一条横线隔开。"脚注出现在各页的底部,与文本的最后一行之间约有四行(或两个双行)的空隙。脚注本身不空行,但两个脚注之间空一行。"如:

  [美]约瑟夫·吉鲍尔迪著,沈弘、何姝译.《MLA 文体手册和学术出版指南》(第二版). 北京:北京大学出版社,2002. pp. 343—344.

  3. 尾注(endnote),也称集中注或篇尾注。"正如各自名称所暗示的那样,尾注出现在文本的后面,另起一页,页码还是按全文顺序排。将注释的题目放在正中离页端一英寸处,空一行之后从左页边处缩进 1 英寸(或 5 个空格),然后在同一行略微向上的地方打上注释号码,不加标点符号。空 1 格后即可打上注释内容。假使注释有两行以上,下面的行数就从左页边开始。逐个连续地打上注释,每行之间空行,并将所有的纸标上页码。"如果注释的第一行没写完,需移到第二行时,第二行要悬挂缩进 2 个字符。

  如果将上述引文用尾注的形式加以注释,形式如下:

注 释

1. [美]约瑟夫·吉鲍尔迪著,沈弘、何姝译.《MLA 文体手册与学术出版指南》(第二版). 北京:北京大学出版社,2002. pp. 343—344.

  同脚注一样,尾注中所包含的信息内容按顺序如下:

  (1) 作者姓名——西方作者先名后姓,中国作者先姓后名。如果用英文表示,则编者、编纂者、译者的姓名前分别用"eds.""comps."和"trans."表示;如果用中文表示则在姓名之后分别用"编""撰"(或省去)和"译"表示。

  (2) 书名——英文名加下划线或斜体,中文名则用《》表示。标明版次,英文用一个序数词和 ed. 表示,中文直接写第几版。

（3）出版信息——包括出版地点、出版社和出版年份。这几项也可单独用句点隔开，也放在圆括号内用，格式为（出版地：出版社，出版年份）。

（4）卷号——英文用 Vol. ...，中文用"第……卷"表示。

（5）页号——单页缩写为 p. ...，多页为 pp. ...—...。

所以尾注的格式为：作者姓名. 书名(版次). 出版地：出版者, 出版年份, 卷号, 页号或者作者姓名. 书名(版次)(出版地：出版者, 出版年份), 卷号, 页号。例如：

1. Gerald Prince. *A Dictionary of Narratology*. (Lincoln & London: University of Nebraska，1987) 23.
2. Prince 23. 或 Ibid. 23.
3. Stacy Alaimo. "Cyborg and Eco-feminist Interventions: Challenges for an Environmental Feminism." *Feminist Studies* 20，no. 1（Spring 1994）: 133-52.

选择论文中采用的注释形式时，还应注意以下几点：

（1）无论最后采用的是夹注、脚注还是尾注，要通篇保持一致，即自始至终只用一种形式，不能忽而夹注忽而脚注或忽而尾注；

（2）注释所采用的注码一律使用阿拉伯数字，从 1 开始，按顺序编号，位置在所注释部分的右上方，不用斜线、圆括号或方括号。标码还应放在除破折号之外一切的标点符号之后。例如：

"In writing a literary essay, you will almost certainly at some point want to incorporate someone else's words."[3]

（3）各个高校的院系对于自己毕业生的毕业论文都有自己的具体规定，所以学生在撰写论文时要查阅并参照本院系的具体格式要求或往届毕业生的论文。另外校内的一些专门为打印论文服务的打印店也是很好的咨询地点。

第五节　参考文献的格式

科学研究取得的新成果通常是在前人成果基础上的新进展，它体现着科学技术的继承和发展。如果在涉及前人成果的地方再把已有成果的具体内容抄到论文当中，不但占去论文的篇幅，冲淡论文的主题，而且抄写这些已发表过的、读者可以查找到的内容是毫无意义的。所以，在论文涉及已有成果的地方，不去重抄已有的成果，而是指出登载这个成果文献（出处），这种做法叫做引用参考文献。所以，对于一篇完整的学术论文，参考文献的录入是不可缺少的。参考文献可以反映论文作者的科学态度和论文具有真实、广泛的科学依据，也反映出该论文的起点和深度。

参考文献所列的是一些书籍、文章的相关信息，这些书籍、文章必须是论文撰写过程中参考和引用过的。参考文献的录入要完整、规范，符合一定的体例。根据英语专业本科毕业论文的选题方向，现将不同方向的参考文献要求及格式分别列出。

(一) 著作
(1) 语言学、教学法和翻译方向的著作

此类参考文献中每一个条目所包含的信息、顺序以及所使用的标点符号如下:作者姓名(英文作者姓在前,加粗,名在后。姓与名之间用逗号隔开。中文作者先姓后名). 出版年份. 著作名称. 出版地:出版社. 例如:

Benson, P. & P. **Voller**. 1997. *Autonomy and Independence in Language Learning*. New York:Addison Wesley Longman.

Chomsky, N. 1965. *Aspects of the Theory of Syntax*. Boston,Mass:MIT Press.

Munday, Jeremy. 2001. *Introducing Translation Studies*, *Theories and Applications*. London and New York:Routledge.

(2) 文学方向的著作

此类参考文献中每一个条目所包含的信息、顺序以及所使用的标点符号如下:作者姓名(英文作者姓在前,加粗,名在后。姓与名之间用逗号隔开。中文作者先姓后名). 著作名称. 出版地:出版社. 出版年份. 例如:

Albert, J Guerad, *Introduction in Heart of Darkness*. New York:New American Library Edition,1950.

Kline, Gloria C. *The Last Courtly Lover*:*Yeats and the Idea of Woman*. Michigan:UMI Research Press, 1983.

(3) 中文著作

此类参考文献中每一个条目所包含的信息、顺序以及所使用的标点符号如下:作者姓名(中文作者先姓后名). 著作名称. 出版地:出版社. 出版年份. 例如:

詹·乔·弗雷泽.《金枝》. 徐育新,译. 北京:大众文艺出版社,2009.

蒋道超.《德莱塞研究》. 上海:上海外语教育出版社,2003.

王嘉陵(编著).《毕业论文写作与答辩》. 成都:四川大学出版社,2003.

(二) 期刊上的文章
(1) 语言学、教学法和翻译方向的文章

此类参考文献中每一个条目所包含的信息、顺序以及所使用的标点符号如下:作者姓名(英文作者姓在前,加粗,名在后。姓与名之间用逗号隔开。中文作者先姓后名). 出版年份. 文章标题. 期刊名称. 期刊号,页码. 例如:

Brown, P. & S. **Levinson**. 1978. "Universals in Language Usage:politeness phenomena". Cambridge:CUP.

Canale, M. & M. **Swain**. 1980. "Theoretical Bases of Communicative Approaches to Second Language Learning and Testing". *Applied Linguistics* No. 1,147.

Kempson, R. and R. **Quirk**. 1971. "Controlled Activation of Latent Contrast". *Language* 47.

(2) 文学方向的文章

此类参考文献中每一个条目所包含的信息、顺序以及所使用的标点符号如下:作者姓名(英文作者姓在前,加粗,名在后。姓与名之间用逗号隔开。中文作者先姓后名). 文章标题. 期刊名称. 期刊号,出版年份及页码. 例如:

Childs, M. W. "From a Distinguished Former St. Louisan". *St. Louis Post-Dispatch* (October 1930).

McCarten, John. "Revolution's Number One Boy". *New Yorker* (January 1938): 13.

(三) 中文期刊上的文章

此类参考文献中每一个条目所包含的信息、顺序以及所使用的标点符号如下: 作者姓名(中文作者先姓后名). 文章标题(用双引号). 杂志名称. 出版年份. 期刊号(加圆括号): 页码. 例如:

聂珍钊. "文学伦理学批评与道德批评". 外国文学研究,2006(2):8—17.

李红. "学习自主性与中国英语教学". 外语与外语教学,1998(1).

张政. "机器翻译难点所在". 外语研究,2005(5):61.

参考文献中各个条目的排列按英文作者姓氏的字母顺序排列,中文作者按汉语拼音顺序排列。如果连续引用同一作者的多部作品,则按作品标题的英文字母顺序排列。在作者处用三个连字符代替,再加入作品名称和出版信息。每个条目从第二行起要悬挂缩进2个字符。例如:

Nida, Eugene A. *Toward Science of Translating, with Special Reference to Principles and Procedures Involved in Bible Translating*. Leiden: E. J. Brill. 1964.

———. "Science of Translating." *Language* 45. pp. 483—498, 1969.

下面就各项内容分别加以说明:

1. 作者。英文作者的姓名按姓在先名在后的顺序,中间用逗号隔开,后面加句点。中文作者姓名也是先姓后名,中间不用标点符号,后面加句号。例如:

Seyfer, Harlen.

王首程.

如果一篇文章或书有两个或三个作者时,英文作者只把第一作者的姓与名顺序颠倒,第二、三作者则保持不变,例如:

Bassnett, Susan and André Lefevere.

Berlin, Derent, Dennis E. Breedlove and Peter H. Raven.

如果是多个作者,可以只列出第一个作者,其他的人可用 et al. 代表,例如:

Schultzc, Brrigitte, et al.

2. 作品名称。如果参考文献中录入的是一本书籍的名称,英文作品要用斜体或加下划线,中文作品则用《》标注。如果录入的是一部作品中的某个章节,或某份期刊或报纸中的一篇文章,则先用""录入文章标题,后面再录入期刊或报纸的名称。例如:

Dryden, John. "The Three Types of Translation." *Readings in Western Translation Theories*. ed. Zhong Weihe.

在这个例子中,*Readings in Western Translation Theories* 是由 Zhong Weihe 编的,所以后边加上了"ed. Zhong Weihe."。同样,如果所列条目是节选某些作者翻译或编辑的作品,也应录入 trans., 译者或 comps., 编辑者这样的信息。

3. 出版信息。出版信息包括出版地、出版社和出版年份。格式是出版地: 出版社, 出版年. 例如:

成都: 四川大学出版社,2003.

Shanghai: Shanghai Foreign Language Education Press, 2001.

另外,在网络上有许多资料可以参考,在参考文献中应该录入以下信息:

(1)作者姓名;(2)作品或材料标题,用下划线或斜体;(3)编者、编纂者或译者姓名;(4)出版信息;(5)访问网站的日期和网址。例如:

Austen, Jane. *Pride and Prejudice*. Ed. Tenry Churchard. 1996. 10. sept. 1997 〈http://www.Pemberley.com/Jane-Info/pride j.html〉

写作学位论文过程中,阅读或运用过某些文献所列出的书目清单,置于正文之后,另页开始。参考文献的著录按原文献语种为原则。

(1)文献目录应另页书写,外文文献排前,中文文献排后。外文文献书名须用斜体。

(2)文献目录一律按作者姓氏汉语拼音或外文字母顺序排列。

(3)每条文献必须顶格写,回行时空两字或五个英语字母。

(4)将各文献的类型代号(即文献类型英文名的首字母)注明在文献之后:专著〔M〕,学位论文〔D〕,论文集〔C〕,报纸文章〔N〕,期刊文章〔J〕,报告〔R〕,专利〔P〕,专著、论文集的析出文献〔A〕,其他未说明文件〔Z〕,电子文献中光盘图书〔M/CD〕(MONOGRAPH ON CD),网上期刊〔J/OL〕(serial online)。

4. 文内所引文献:要求附夹注,应在引文后加括号注明作者姓名(英文只注姓)、出版年和引文页码。若为转引文献,则加 quoted in 字样。

例:(王佐良,1982:38)

　　(Newmark,8:26—33)

5. 参考文献中列出的文献应该与正文中标注的文献一一对应。正文中没有出现的,不应出现在参考文献中。

第三章 毕业论文的选题

所谓选题,顾名思义,就是选择毕业论文的论题,即在写论文前,选择确定所要研究论证的问题。在论述选题问题时,首先应当分清论题、题目两个概念。这二者同属于某一学科中的学术问题,但又有所区别。论题不同于题目,题目是指论文的标题,它的研究范围一般比论题要小。正确而又合适的选题,对撰写毕业论文具有重要意义。通过选题,可以大体看出作者的研究方向和学术水平。选准了论题,就等于完成论文写作的一半,题目选得好,可以起到事半功倍的作用。对于大学英语专业本科毕业论文而言,选题即是选择论题,研究题目,是撰写毕业论文的第一步,它是指大学本科四年级的学生在一定的研究方向内选择的论题或课题,即毕业论文所要重点论述的事项或解答的问题。由于大学本科毕业生在四年的学习中主要是学习专业的基础知识,并没有明确地选择研究方向,所以在选题前还应先大致确定方向以便更好地选择论题。一般而言,英语本科毕业生的方向有英美文学、语言学、比较文学、翻译、教学法(师范类院校)等,学生可根据自己的个人情况进行选择。

第一节 影响选题的因素与选择的重要性

学生选题时不能随意拿来一个论题就写,要考虑诸多因素。首先,大多数院校都提供一些毕业论文的参考选题,以供学生进行选择。除此之外,学生在选题时还应注意本院系对于毕业论文的一些具体规定与要求,要记住时间期限和论文的长度。第三,学生在选题时必须考虑到自身的专业水平与写作能力,题目不能过大过深,否则本科毕业生根本无法完成,文章便会空洞无物;题目也不宜过小过浅,否则无法达到本科毕业论文的水平要求。这两点都会直接影响论文定稿的质量、答辩的结果和毕业。第四,参考资料的多少也会影响学生的选题。资料多,可以为学生提供更大的选择余地,但同时也会增加选题的难度;资料少,论文就会失去基础,如同空中楼阁,一攻即破。

选题是撰写毕业论文的第一步,也是关键的一步,选题的恰当与否会直接关系到毕业论文的质量。

(1)选题即是确定论文的论题和研究方向,选题直接影响到论文撰写能否顺利进行,完成的质量如何,甚至对于学生今后学业的进一步发展也会有很大的影响。正确恰当的选题可避免南辕北辙的错误。

(2)选题主要解决了毕业论文写什么的问题,正确的选题确定了毕业论文的撰写目标和范围,因此可以使学生在一定的范围内收集整理资料,以避免无目的无范围的盲目阅读与研究,可以避免时间和精力的浪费,使学生能在有限的时间内高效率地完成高质量的论文。

(3)选题直接影响论文的质量。选题不好、不恰当会浪费时间和精力,影响撰写速度,有的可能会使论文的撰写走入死胡同,无法向下进行,最终只能草草了事,写出的论文质量不可能高,也很有可能使学生无法顺利完成学业。反之,恰当的选题则为写出高质量的论文打下了良好的基础。

最后,正确选题的重要性最为直接地体现在它能够保障学生写出合格的毕业论文,顺利毕业,拿到学位,这也是撰写毕业论文最为基本的目的。

由于选题直接关系到毕业论文撰写的研究方向、收集资料的范围、学生能否在规定时间完成论文以及论文的最终质量、学生能否毕业等问题,所以学生在进行选题时,一定要有科学认真的态度,遵循一定的选题原则,运用一定的选题方法,以确保选题恰当正确。

第二节 选题的原则和方法

如前所述,选题是毕业论文撰写的第一步,因此学生在选题时应遵循毕业论文撰写的基本原则,如:学习原则、独立原则、科学原则、学术原则和规范原则等。除此之外,学生在选题的过程中还应遵循以下原则:

(1) 选题要切合实际。学生在选题时要从自身的主观条件和客观实际出发,考虑主观因素和客观因素对选题的影响。选题的大小、难易,学生要依据自身的专业水平和能力量力而行,同时还应兼顾时间限制、资料多少等客观因素,以确保论题的可行性与可操作性。切忌眼高手低、好高骛远和草率行事、敷衍了事。尽量使选题符合自身的知识结构、研究能力和写作水平。

(2) 选题要力求创新。选题要切乎实际,要依据主观与客观的条件,并不意味着学生选题时就缩手缩脚、保守不前,而是应在切乎实际的基础之上力求创新。创新是学术与科学研究的生命,是毕业论文写作所应遵循的最为重要的一条原则。学生在选题时应在研究前人成果的基础上,力求找出对某一个领域的研究薄弱甚至没有涉及的方面,或用新的研究方法来研究旧课题,对其进行修改、补充或者是对以前的研究结果进行补充。只有创新才能确保毕业论文的学术价值,使之具有现实意义以促进本学科的发展。

本科毕业论文尽管在创新方面的要求不高,但以长远的眼光来看,本科生在撰写毕业论文,包括选题时,如果总是选别人已经选过无数次的论题,用别人已用过无数次的研究方法,那么写出的文章也就与别人的文章相差无几,便毫无新意可言。这样的文章也可以让学生顺利毕业,但对于学生今后的发展,无论是在科研态度上还是研究方法上都不会有积极的作用,对于论题所属学科的发展也没有益处。因此本科生在撰写毕业论文时应提高对自身的要求,同时各院校、院系也应在创新方面加大对学生的培养与要求,以提高毕业生的质量。所谓"取法乎上,只得其中;取法乎中,只得其下……"便是这个道理。

(3) 选题要具有一定的弹性。学生在选题时对于所选论题的认识并不深刻,或只是肤浅的了解,或只是凭一时的兴趣。随着以后收集整理和阅读思考与论题有关的资料这一过程的深入展开,学生对于选择的论题的认识很可能有相应的由浅入深的改变,这时就应对所选论题做出相应的调整,而不应拘泥于所选论题,影响创造力的发挥,不要"死"在题下。

大学本科生撰写毕业论文,特别是选题时,一般有两种情况:一、导师指定题目或在导师的指定范围内选题;二、学生自己选题。学生在不同的情况下可以利用不同的选题方法。

（1）听取别人的意见。首先学生要去征求导师的意见。导师一般是某一研究领域的专家,有丰富的研究经验,对于本学科的发展情况,特别是本学科发展所需要解决的问题以及今后的发展方向都有较为深刻的认识,学生应主动去找导师了解本学科的情况,帮助自己作出选择。

除了导师之外,学生还可以从以前的毕业生、硕士生处获得帮助,他们可以就论文的整个撰写过程提出许多宝贵的经验。但同时应注意不要过分依赖导师和他人,学生应在获取别人意见的基础上,结合自己的具体情况充分发挥自身的特长。

（2）查阅资料。学生可以查阅图书馆资料和其他信息来源,从中选择自己较为感兴趣并切实可行的选题。可以对别人已研究过的课题进行重新的思考,或用新的材料或用新的论证方法或对他人的观点提出质疑,这样可以避免做重复无价值的研究,可以了解本学科的发展情况,利于创新。但要切忌抄袭他人已有的观点来充当自己的结论。同时,学生在查阅过程中还可以发现就这一论题所作的研究的多寡,是否有足够的资料可供参考。

（3）选题可由大及小,由面及点。选题首先要确定一个大的研究方向,如文学、语言学、翻译等,但大的研究方向中又包含多个次一级的研究分支,如文学中可以有散文、诗歌、小说、戏剧等以及相应的散文作家、诗人、小说家、剧作家等。但每个分支还可以再分,如诗歌包括十四行诗等不同形式的诗歌,也可以分为爱情诗、挽歌等,或可以分为现实主义诗歌、浪漫主义诗歌等,并且不同的诗人对于不同形式、不同风格的写作又有所不同,如莎士比亚的十四行诗与约翰·邓恩、斯宾塞等人的十四行诗等。所以学生在选题时,可由大及小、由面及点,层层缩小选题范围,将选题由一般逐渐缩小到具体的范围。

（4）选择焦点,多角度发散选题。根据第三个方法,选择了某个具体的论述点之后,可以选择从不同角度对同一个论述点——焦点进行写作,如果学生选择了十四行诗作为论述点之后,可以从不同的角度进行研究,如不同诗人——莎士比亚、弥尔顿、邓恩等人的十四行诗的内容、作用等;十四行诗的发展与演变——从意大利的彼特拉克体到莎士比亚体;十四行诗的历史背景——从意大利传入到英国文艺复兴时期等等。第三、四种方法一起,形成选题的由大及小、再由小及大的过程,这样可同时避免选题过大过小的错误。

总之,学生要有充裕的时间来思考、再思考选择的题目。初步的预备性的阅读在评价论题是十分重要：查阅一些相关的书籍、文章、和如百科全书类的一般参考资料。在确定最终的论题之前,确保自己了解研究的广度和深度。

第三节　选定论文题目和拟题

选定论文题目是为论文选择论题,规定为撰写论文的一个大致的研究范围。拟题是在选择好的研究范围之内,在与论题相关的材料的基础上,为论文初步拟定一个标题。

选题只规定了一个大致的研究范围,在与之相关的材料收集好后,下一步更为关键的任务就是初步确定论文的标题。标题有牵动整个论文主旨的作用。好的标题有两个作用：对作者而言,它就像一扇开启宝库的门,使作者在写的过程中步步深入,层层递进,越写越有内容;对读者而言,它就像一扇透视世界的窗,能激发读者的兴趣,使人看后就有不读完不罢休的感觉。论题对一篇论文来说非常重要,一经选定,最好不要轻易更改。

选择论文题目时,总体上说需要考虑以下几个方面:新颖性,题目是否会激发读者的阅读兴趣;独创性,论文所涉及的论题在相关领域是否具有开拓意义,要避免老生常谈;学术性,题目不能一味追求新奇独特,还要包含一定的学术价值;可操作性,撰写毕业论文一般都有时间限制,所搜集的有关某一论题的资料也不可能彻底全面,这就需要考虑论题是否能在有限的时间内和有足够资料的前提下充分展开。选择论题可从以下几个方面入手:

(1) 逐级限定,选好切入点

一个好的论题不是空穴来风,切不可主观臆断,草率行事。应当按照由研究方向到论题再到标题的顺序逐级限定。研究方向指的是一个大致的研究领域,比如语言学、文学、翻译、教学法等;论题主要指论文要论证的命题,比如语言学中的委婉语研究、跨文化方向的称谓比较研究、教学法方向的交际法研究等;而论文题目则是对论题的具体阐述,应求全面深刻,将其缩小到一个更为具体的范围内或落实到某一点。切入点选好的话,论文写起来会很顺利,否则,进行起来很艰难。如:《呼啸山庄》的研究;《呼啸山庄》中的意象研究,《呼啸山庄》中的人物性格的研究;英语中修辞的研究:英语中比喻的研究,英语中隐喻的研究,英语中隐喻的含义、作用及分类;一个流派的研究:一个作家的研究、一部作品的研究、一个人物形象的研究等等。

这样通过逐级限定,把论文定格在一个"有话可说"的点上,就某个问题进行深入的探索和研究。

(2) 大小适宜,小题大做

论文的题目不能太大。英语专业本科生的论文要求在5000字左右,而硕士研究生的论文也不超过20000字,这就表明在有限的字数内不可能就一个非常大的论题进行深刻的阐述。而过于泛泛则是写毕业论文的大忌。比如,有位学生选了这样一个题目《论〈简·爱〉的艺术特点》。这个题目就太大了,可写的内容很多,比如人物特点、语言特点、结构特点等等。如果方方面面都涉及,必然会只及皮毛,难以深入。在导师的指点下,他把题目改为《论〈简·爱〉中三重结构的表现手法》,这样不仅使论文可写的内涵加深,而且很有新意。再比如,有位学生想写艾米莉的《呼啸山庄》,她初步拟的题目是《〈呼啸山庄〉的透视研究》,在开题报告时被导师们否定,他们认为论文题目过大,这样写出的论文肯定是诸多方面的泛泛而谈,不会有太大的学术价值。经过自己的认真思考和导师的指导,她决定把题目改为《论〈呼啸山庄〉中诗的一般魅力》。这样一来,论文就会对一个问题进行专门的研究。同样,论文题目也不能过于窄小,太小的题目会束缚人的思路,使论文无法展开、深入。比如有位学生选了这样一个题目《〈苔丝〉中苔丝的外貌特征》,这样的题目肯定无法深入展开,而且没有多大的研究价值。总之,论文的题目一定要大小适宜,我们要对那些有研究价值的问题进行"小题大做"。

(3) 深浅适度,难易适中

选定论文题目应该难易适中,既不可太难,也不可太容易。每个人知识面的广度和深度差别很大,在选定论文题目时要根据自己的实际情况来选定。如果选定的题目非常生涩难懂,自己在短时间内没有足够的时间和能力去搞清楚所要涉及的问题,这样的题目再新颖、再有价值,也要避而远之。比如有的同学想选取比较文学方向,比较 *Martin Eden*, *The Adventure of Huckleberry Finn* 和 *The Great Gatsby* 三部作品中所描绘的人类寻求自由、追寻梦想的主题。如果事先没有对这几部作品进行过仔细研读,是不可能写出立意深刻、分析全面的文章来的。当然,题目也不能过于肤浅,这样既无法检验出自己的真实水平,也无法提高自己的业务能力。

(4) 力求新颖,避免怪异

论文要求我们不断发现新的问题,进行新的探索。如果论文只涉及前人提过的问题或者只重复别人的观点,内容上毫无创新,就没有写的必要。但是,如果论文题目一味追求新颖,不顾论题的具体要求和实际情况,就会显得怪异别扭,读来令人生厌。论题的新颖独特,并非只是文字上的新奇,只有作者的思想新颖,才能赋予论题新的意义。有些论题进行了开创性的研究,使论文非常新颖别致。比如,在文学论坛上,对莎士比亚《李尔王》的研究不胜枚举;亚里士多德著名的《诗学》几乎尽人皆知。两部作品分开写很难写出新意。经过反复认真的比较研究,作者把题目定为"The application and reformation of Aristotle's Poetics in Shakespeare's *King Lear*"。这样,用亚里士多德的悲剧理论来分析莎士比亚的《李尔王》,赋予两部古老作品以新的内容,很有开创性。但在力求新颖的同时也要防止物极必反,不可一味追求怪异,玩弄玄虚。

(5) 文字简洁,表意明确

一篇论文的标题,要文字简练,含义确切。要能把全篇文章的内容、研究的主要目的或是所研究的某些因素之间的关系,确切生动地表达出来。标题的文字虽以简练为好,但意义明确更为重要。因此,必要时宁可多用几个字。论文题目要经过反复推敲才能确定下来,要一字一字地推敲,做到多一字无必要,少一字嫌不足,画龙点睛,恰到好处。在推敲过程中要注意能对论题进行准确概括,尽可能包含较多的关键词。如果过于泛泛、空洞则会影响文章主旨的体现,例如 Some Thoughts on Translation 这个题目既令读者不知所云,又难以激发阅读兴趣;相反,结构如果过于复杂繁琐,也会影响读者的理解,比如 Inputting Cross-cultural Information for More Effective English Teaching by Means of Inputting Cross-cultural Communication in General College English Teaching 这个题目就显得异常啰唆,令人费解。如果一些论题确实深刻复杂,三言两语无法概括,完全可以将题目以正标题加副标题的形式出现,上述题目可以改为 Inputting Cross-cultural Information for More Effective English Teaching—Means in General College English Teaching,同时还要避免使用一些看似谦虚但实为不必要的套话,比如 A preliminary research in..., An analysis on..., A survey of...,这种标题既削减了论文力度,又使标题看来冗长拖沓。最可行的方式便是直奔主题,言简意赅。每一个单词的第一个字母要大写,冠词、连词和介词除外,例如:The Paradoxical Images in Robert Frost's Poetry; English Idioms—A Mirror Reflecting British Culture。

拟题,即是在确定的论题范围内初步拟定论文的标题。标题就是对论文中心论点的表达,它具有概括论文中心思想和吸引读者等功能。毕业论文的标题应具备以下特征:

1. 准确。要做到"题与文相符",在一定程度上概括文章基本内容,揭示文章的主题。

2. 醒目。要引人注目,有鲜明的倾向性。鲜明醒目的标题,能吸引读者,给人留下深刻的印象。

3. 新颖。要有新鲜感,给人一种独特的感受。只有作者的思想新颖,论题才能富有新意。

4. 简洁。就是言简意赅,具有高度的概括性。简洁要着眼于论题的内容,有的论题文字虽少,但不能表达中心思想就没有达到简练的要求。一般而言,标题的字数应限制在 20 个字以内。

5. 具体。简洁并不意味着空泛。论文的标题应具体地表达出论文的重要观点与论点,切忌空泛而谈。如"Shakespeare""Sonnets of Shakespeare"这样的标题就过于空泛,如改成"The Metrical Features of Shakespeare's Several famous Sonnets"就较为具体了。

另外,在拟定论文标题时还应注意标题中的选词、拼写等问题。一般来说论文题目较多使用名词或名词性短语、现在分词及不完整的句子。这些词或短语比其他词性的词或词组更能高度概括和准确概括论文的中心观点。另外还可以用一个不完整的句子来作标题。

标题中各词的大小写也有要求。一般情况下实词的第一个字母都要大写,如名词、动词(包括系动词)、形容词、副词和代词。如果一个实词是复合词,则两个词的第一个字母都要大写,如 African-Americans。而连词、冠词和一些介词则第一个字母不大写,但是如果一个词的字母是四个以上,包括四个,则不论它是实词还是虚词都要大写其第一个字母。例如:The Paradoxical Images in Robert Frost's Poetry;English Idioms—A Mirror Reflecting British Culture。

选择一个合适的论题不是一件容易的事情。即使是在学生找到了一个感兴趣的论题之后,很可能还得修改论题,修正方法,或者是在开始研究之后完全改变论题。同样,选题之后拟定文章标题只是在学生对所选论题有大致的了解之后进行的,随着学生阅读资料的增加,他们对于选题的了解也会加深,思考也就越多,所以很有可能在提笔撰写时甚至是初稿完成之后会对选题有了新的认识和思考,这样就有可能会对以前拟定的标题进行修改。所以最初拟定的标题不是固定不变的,它只是指导学生写作的基本方向,并在此过程中得到完善。

合适的选题可以保证写作的顺利进行,提高研究能力。如果毕业论文的题目过大或过难,就难以完成写作任务;反之,题目过于容易,又不能较好地锻炼科学研究的能力,达不到写作毕业论文的目的。因此,选择一个难易大小合适的题目,可以保证写作的顺利进行。以下是一些英语专业本科毕业论文的参考选题,仅供参考:

一、美英文学类
诗歌
1. On the Realistic Significance of *The Canterbury Tales*
2. Chaucer's Art of Humor in *The Canterbury Tales*
3. The Theme of Shakespeare's Love Sonnets
4. The Imagery of Shakespeare's Love Sonnets
5. The Theme of Milton's *Paradise Lost*
6. On the Image of Satan in Milton's *Paradise Lost*
7. Comment on the Biblical Images in *Paradise Lost*, *Paradise Regained*, and

    Samson Agonistes

8. An Analysis of Celia in *The Color Purple*
9. On the Imagery of John Donne's Love Poems
10. William Wordsworth's View on Nature
11. The Images of the Laboring People in Wordsworth's Poems
12. Comment on Wordsworth's Poetic Techniques
13. On the View of Harmony in Wordsworth's Poetry
14. On Wordsworth's View of Nature
15. A Comparative Study of Wordsworth's Nature Poems and Those by Tao Yuanming
16. On the Theme of Byron's *Childe Harold's Pilgrimage*
17. Byron's Rebellious Spirit Shown in His Poems
18. Don Juan, A Satiric Epic
19. The Images of Nature in Shelley's Lyrical Poetry
20. The Bird Imagery in Romantic Poetry
21. On the Theme of "Ode to the West Wind"
22. Social Reality Reflected in "Ode to the West Wind"
23. The Symbolic Meanings of Natural Images in "Ode to the West Wind"
24. The Differences Between Elizabethan Poetry and Metaphysical Poetry
25. A Comparative Study of Romantic Literature and Neo-Classical Literature
26. The Theme of John Keats' "Ode to a Nightingale"
27. The Theme of Shelley's Political Lyrics
28. Robert Browning's Writing Style
29. Mrs. Browning's Sonnets from the Portuguese
30. On the Writing Devices of Tennyson's Lyrical Poems
31. The Theme of W. B. Yeats' Love Lyrics
32. The Theme of Yeats' Lyrics on Nature
33. On the Theme of T. S. Eliot's "The Love Song of J. Alfred Prufrock"
34. A Probe into the Ambiguity and Symbolization of Eliot's Poetry
35. On the Themes of William Blake's *Songs of Innocence*
36. Social Reality as Reflected in the Poetry of William Blake
37. The Contrasting Pictures Between *Songs of Innocence* and *Songs of Experience*
38. The Theme of Robert Burns' Love Lyrics
39. On the Theme of Thomas Gray's Elegy Written in a Country Churchyard
40. The Theme of Edmund Spenser's *The Faerie Queene*
41. Alexander Pope's View on Poetry
42. A Comparative Study of English Nature Poems and Chinese Nature Poems
43. The Sound of Heart-Reverie and Melancholy in Emily Dickinson's Poems

44. Emily Dickinson and Her Unique Poetry
45. On the Theme of Dickinson's Love Poems
46. On the Theme of Dickinson's Nature Poems
47. On the Theme of Emily Dickinson's Death Poems
48. Whitman's Poetical Themes
49. Robert Frost's View on Nature
50. An Analysis of Several Robert Frost's Famous Poems
51. The Aesthetic Interpretation of Ezra Pound's Poetry
52. A Comparison Between Wordsworth's Nature Poems and Those by Robert Frost
53. Edgar Allan Poe and the World Literature
54. An Analysis of Edgar Allan Poe's "The Raven" and "Annabel Lee"

戏剧

1. The Humanist Ideas in Christopher Marlow's Plays
2. Parallelism and Contrast of Shakespeare's Dramatic Language
3. An Analysis of Shakespeare's Tragedy Tradition
4. On the Theme of *Hamlet*
5. On the Hesitation of *Hamlet*
6. Hamlet and His Delay
7. Hamlet: His Characters as a Humanist
8. Hamlet: Character Analysis
9. Comment the Themes of *The Merchant of Venice*
10. A Brief Comment on Shakespeare's *The Merchant of Venice*
11. The Image of Portia in *The Merchant of Venice*
12. On the Image of Shylock in *The Merchant of Venice*
13. Woman's Imagery in Shakespeare's Comedies
14. On the Theme of *Romeo and Juliet*
15. On the Theme of Shakespeare's Some Comedies
16. The Cause of Tragedy in *Othello*
17. The Animal Images Used in *King Lear*
18. *Macbeth*, a Tragedy of Ambition
19. The Satirical Art in Sheridan's *The School for Scandal*
20. On the Theme of Mrs. Warren's Profession
21. On Bernard Shaw's Play Characterization
22. The Art of Inversion in Bernard Shaw's Plays
23. On the Theme of Eugene O'Neill's Tragedies
24. Symbolism in O'Neill's Major Plays
25. On the Image of the Hero in *The Hairy Ape*

小说

1. On the Allegorical Meanings of John Bunyan's *The Pilgrim's Progress*
2. The Art of Satire in *The Pilgrim's Progress*
3. The Social Significance of *Robinson Crusoe*
4. On the Writing Style of *Robinson Crusoe*
5. The Themes of *Gulliver's Travels*
6. Jonathan Swift: A Great Satirist
7. Tom Jones: A Miniature of English Society
8. An Analysis of Tom Jones' Character
9. The Contrast Technique Used in *Tom Jones*
10. On the Language Style of *Tom Jones*
11. The Art of Irony in *Pride and Prejudice*
12. Jane Austen's Art of Irony and Its Rhetoric Effects
13. Appreciation of Literary Language of *Pride and Prejudice*
14. Thought of Marriage in Jane Austen's *Pride and Prejudice*
15. The Impact of Money on Marriage in *Pride and Prejudice*
16. The Character Analysis of *Pride and Prejudice*
17. Three Structures in *Pride and Prejudice*
18. Revelation in Fore Couples of *Pride and Prejudice*
19. Love and Lust—*Pride and Prejudice*
20. An Character Analysis of the Heroine of *Emma*
21. The Imagery of Woman Characters in *Pride and Prejudice*
22. Contrast Technique Used by Jane Austen in Characterization
23. Dramatic Art Used by Austen in *Pride and Prejudice*
24. On the Theme of *Oliver Twist*
25. The Social Significance of Dickens' *Oliver Twist*
26. The Negative Influence of Society on Oliver Twist
27. On the Structure of Dickens's *Hard Times*
28. The Literature Characteristics in *A Tale of Two Cities*
29. On the Humanism in *A Tale of Two Cities*
30. On the Theme of *A Tale of Two Cities*
31. The Art of Humor in Dickens' *Great Expectations*
32. The Art of Satire in Dickens' *Great Expectations*
33. Charles Dickens: The Master of Critical Realism
34. The Optimistic Spirit Displayed by Charles Dickens in His Early Novels
35. On Charles Dickens' Character Portrayal
36. On Child Characters in Dickens' Novels
37. On the Horrible and Grotesque Characters in Dickens' Novels
38. *Vanity Fair*: A Great Satirical Novel
39. The High Class as Seen in Thacheray's *Vanity Fair*

40. How the Brontës Become World Famous Writers
41. Jane Eyre, a Symbol of Feminism
42. *Jane Eyre*: A Great Masterpiece with Prejudice
43. An Analysis of Jane Eyre's Image
44. An Analysis of the Characters in *Jane Eyre*
45. The Colonialist Discourse in *Jane Eyre* and *Wide Sargasso Sea*
46. Jane Eyre's Search for Christianity
47. Exposure and Condemnation of English Educational System in *Jane Eyre*
48. On the Religious Hypocrisy of Charity Institutions in *Jane Eyre*
49. The Growth of a New Woman in *Jane Eyre*
50. A Woman's Struggle for Recognition and Equality in *Jane Eyre*
51. On the Psychological Descriptions in *Jane Eyre*
52. The Functions of Describing Natural Scenes in *Wuthering Heights*
53. A Character Analysis of the Hero in *Wuthering Heights*
54. To Love or to Be Loved? An Analysis of Major Characters in *Wuthering Heights*
55. Deep Love and Deep Hate—A Brief Analysis on *Wuthering Heights*
56. The Modernist Features in *Wuthering Heights*
57. Comment in the Techniques of Emily Brontë's Dual Personalities in *Wuthering Heights*
58. Gothic Features in *Wuthering Heights*
59. Emily Brontë and *Wuthering Heights*
60. Romantic Elements in *Wuthering Heights*
61. On the Narrative Techniques in *Wuthering Heights*
62. An Analysis of Heathcliff's Revenge
63. The Destiny of Women in George Eliot's Novels
64. The Psychological Art Applied by George Eliot in Her Novels
65. The Dream and Disillusionment of Dorothea Brook in Middlemarch
66. On Hardy's Tragedy Narrative Art
67. From Pastoral Stories to Great Tragic Novels: An Analysis of Hardy's Novels
68. A Brief Discussion about Tess in *Tess of the D'Urbervilles*
69. Destruction of Tess in *Tess of the D'Urbervilles*
70. Morals Affect Tess' Fate in *Tess of the D'Urbervilles*
71. *Jude the Obscure* as the Masterpiece by Hardy
72. The Tragic Fate of Tess
73. An Analysis of the Source of Tess' Tragedy in *Tess of the D'Urbervilles*
74. Tragedy and Modernity in *Tess of the D'Urbervilles*
75. Tess: A Rebellious Woman in *Tess of the D'Urbervilles*
76. *Tess of the D'Urbervilles*: A Victim of the Modem Society

77. The Functions of the Description of the Natural Environment in *Tess of the D'Urbervilles*
78. The Conflicts Between the Traditional and the Modern in *Tess of the D'Urbervilles*
79. On the Theme of *The Man of Property*
80. The Art of Satire in *The Man of Property*
81. On the Theme of *Sons and Lovers* by D. H. Lawrence
82. D. H. Lawrence's View on Love
83. Psychological Device Used by D. H. Lawrence in Character Portrayal
84. On the Symbolism of D. H. Lawrence's *The Rainbow*
85. Remarks on D. H. Lawrence's Psychological Analyses
86. On the Symbolism of D. H. Lawrence's *The Rainbow*
87. On the Symbolic Art Used by James Joyce in the Short Story *Araby*
88. The Gothic Elements and the Supernatural Atmosphere in *Rip Van Winkle*
89. On Ralph Waldo Emerson's View on Nature
90. Does Hester Get Rebirth? Reexamination of the Heroine in *The Scarlet Letter*
91. The Symbols in *The Scarlet Letter*
92. Amazing Return—An Analysis of the Character of Hester Prynne in *The Scarlet Letter*
93. A Brief Comment on *The Scarlet Letter*
94. Hawthorne's Theory of Romance and *The Scarlet Letter*
95. The Ambiguity in *The Scarlet Letter*
96. About the Symbolism in *The Scarlet Letter*
97. An Analysis of the Heroine of *The Scarlet Letter*
98. Symbolism in Hawthorne's *The Scarlet Letter*
99. Hawthorne's View on Sin and Evil in *The Scarlet Letter*
100. Hawthorne's Symbolic Art in *The Scarlet Letter*
101. On the Theme of *Young Goodman Brown* by Hawthorne
102. The Symbolic Art Used by Herman Melville in *Moby Dick*
103. The Evil of Mankind Portayed in *Moby Dick*
104. On the Language Style of Mark Twain's Novels
105. Mark Twain: A Humorist
106. An Analysis of the Theme of *The Adventures of Huckleberry Finn*
107. The Realism of *The Adventure of Huckleberry Finn*
108. Mark Twain and Huck Finn
109. The Real Theme of *The Adventure of Huckleberry Finn*
110. Mark Twain—The Pessimist Who Brought Laughter to the World
111. Humor and Realism of Mark Twain's *The Celebrated Jumping Frog of California County*

112. On the Child Image in *The Adventures of Tom Sawyer*
113. *The Adventures of Huckleberry Finn*: A Local Color Novel
114. On the Theme of *The Adventures of Huckleberry Finn*
115. The Art of Humor Used by Twain in *The Adventures of Huckleberry Finn*
116. Mark Twain's Wonderful Characterization of Huck in *The Adventures of Huckleberry Finn*
117. Henry James' Psychological Approach in *Daisy Miller*
118. *Daisy Miller*: A Novel of International Theme
119. *Daisy Miller*: The Embodiment of the Spirit of the New World
120. On the Theme of *An American Tragedy* by Dreiser
121. *Sister Carrie*: A Naturalistic Novel
122. Sister Carrie's Broken Dream
123. The Appearance of New Women: On Carrie's New Image
124. On the Tragedy of Hurstwood
125. On the Double Vision of Fitzgerald in His Fiction
126. *The Great Gatsby*: A Story of the Bankruptcy of the American Dream
127. Symbolism in *The Great Gatsby*
128. Social Significance as Reflected in *The Great Gatsby*
129. Hemingway's View on War in *A Farewell to Arms*
130. Psychological Descriptions In Hemingway's *The Snows of Kilimajaro*
131. Return and Transcendence—Comment on *The Bear* and *The Old Man and the Sea*
132. Reexamination of Santiago—Hero of *The Old Man and the Sea*
133. The Tragic Color of Ernest Hemingway's Novels
134. Love Tragedy and War—An Analysis of *A Farewell to Arms*
135. On the Symbolism of *The Old Man and the Sea*
136. On Ernest Hemingway and His Novel *The Sun Also Rises*
137. Heroism in Hemingway's Works
138. The Cuban Culture Contest of *The Old Man and the Sea*
139. The Philosophy of Life in Ernest Hemingway's *The Old Man and the Sea*
140. The Characteristics of Hemingway's Art in *The Old Man and the Sea*
141. Hemingway and Hemingway Heroes
142. On the Image of Hemingway's Fiction Heroes
143. On Hemingway's Language Style in *A Farewell to Arms*
144. The Symbolic Functions of Hemingway's Description of Nature
145. On the Theme of Indian Camp by Hemingway
146. The Symbolic Meaning of the Story *A Rose for Emily* by Faulkner
147. The Gothic Devices Used by Faulkner in Narration of the Story of Emily

148. A Critical Study of William Faulkner's *A Rose for Emily*: Its Narrative Techniques and Structure
149. The Typical Characteristic of O. Henry's Short Story—Comment on *The Gift of the Maggie*
150. O. Henry's Artistic Animation as Seen in His Short Stories
151. *The Gift of Magi* and Consumerism
152. Naturalism as Reflected in *The Call of the Wild*
153. Love Stories in William Cather's "O Pioneers"
154. On the Author and the Major Characters of *The Pearl*
155. On Henry Heming in *The Red Badge of Courage*
156. Some Features of Steinbeck's Literary Style
157. The Modern American Society and *The Death of the Salesman*

二、语言学类

1. Sexism as Reflected in the Chinese and English Languages
2. Lexical Items as Means of Cohesion in English Texts
3. Lexical Cohesion in English
4. On English Oration as a Variety of Language
5. The Polite Language in the English Language
6. Reflection on the English Taboo Words
7. Remarks on Modern American Slang
8. The Different Usage of American Folk Language and Modern American Language
9. A Comparative Analysis of British and American English
10. An Account of Advertising Language
11. Stylistic Comparison Between Broadcast News and Newspaper News
12. News Headlines: Their Features and Styles
13. Stylistic Features of News Reportings
14. A Comparative Study of Chinese and English Body Languages
15. Influences of Chinese Dialectic Accents over English Pronunciation
16. A Contrastive Analysis of English and Chinese Intonation
17. The Functions of Applied Linguistics on English Teaching
18. On English Borrowed Words
19. How to Teach English Phonetics or Grammar by Using a Comparative Approach
20. How to Guide the Students to Practise Speaking English out of Class
21. How to Make an Objective Appraisal of Your Students Abilities in Reading, Speaking, and Writing
22. Note on Ambiguity of English Language
23. A Comparative Study of English and Chinese Proverbs

24. A Comparative Study of English and Chinese Idioms
25. Cursory Examination on English Onomatopoeia
26. On Commonization of Proper Nouns in English
27. Noun-Verb Conversion in Contemporary English
28. Syntactic Functions of Prepositional Phrases
29. A Comparative Study of English and Chinese Prepositions
30. On the English Verbal Fillers
31. On the English Negative Sentences
32. On the English Verbless Sentences
33. On Simplification of English Sentences
34. A Comparative Study of English and Chinese Existential Sentences
35. Positions of Attributes and Adverbials in English and Chinese: A Comparative Study
36. Studies in English Sentences of Implied Condition
37. Tentative Study of Syllepsis in English
38. The Way of Expressing Emphatic Ideas in English
39. On the Revival of Dead Metaphor
40. Tendency of Modern Linguistics
41. A Comparative Study of English Idioms and Their Equivalents in Chinese Language
42. The Expression of Negation in English and Chinese Languages
43. Krashen's Acquisition Theory and English Teaching
44. Pedagory Theories and English Teaching
45. An Analysis of the Chinese Students' Typical Errors in Learning English
46. A Comparison of English Addressing Terms with Their Chinese Equivalents
47. On the Formation and Functions of the English Verb-adverb Groups
48. On the Voice of the English Verbs and Its Chinese Translation
49. On the Syntactic Functions of the English Adverbials
50. The Historical Development of the English Vocabulary
51. On English Ambiguous Construction
52. On Formal English and Informal English
53. The Different Styles of English
54. On the English Rhetorical Devices
55. How to Improve the Students' Reading Comprehension
56. How to Improve the Students Oral or Writing Ability
57. A Comparison Between a Teacher-centered Class and a Students-centered Class
58. A Comparison Between Traditional Teaching Method and Communicative Teaching Method
59. How to Use a Computer in Managing an English Class

60. How to Help the Backward Students in Their Learning of English
61. How to Prepare an Efficient English Test on the Students
62. Comparison of Different Schools in English Grammar
63. English Writing Styles and Diction
64. On the Relation Between Language and Culture
65. On the Development of English Linguistics
66. On the Theory and Practice of Translation
67. Literal Translation and Free Translation
68. How to Apply Linguistic Theory in Language Teaching
69. On the Functions of Sociolinguistics in Teaching of English
70. Latin's Influence on the English Vocabulary in the History Perspective
71. The Recognition of Componential Analysis and Its Application
72. On English Language Historical Changes
73. On English Vocabulary Acquisition
74. My Study on Complimenting
75. Change of Meaning
76. Personality Equality and Wealth Equality
77. An Exploration of Body Language
78. The Linguistic Characteristics of Advertising English
79. On the Merit and Application of Computer-assisted Instruction
80. Multiple Intelligence Theory and Language Teaching-considering Student-countered
81. Body Language on Nonverbal Communication
82. Analysis of Language Characteristics in Advertising English
83. The Local Reality of the Comprehensible Output Hypothesis
84. The Psychological Reality of the Comprehensible Input Hypothesis
85. An Analysis of the Access Effect Advantages of the Prefabricated Chunks
86. The Presentation of the Second Language's Mental Lexicons of Chinese Middle School Students
87. Ways of Child Language Acquisition
88. The Change of English Word Meaning：Factors and Types
89. The Linguistic Characteristics of Advertising English
90. On the Formation and Use of Parody in English and Chinese

三、教学法类

1. On Sino-Western Cultural Differences and the Structure of Chinese Students' Chinglish
2. The Application of Cooperative Learning Theory in Teaching of English Reading
3. Interaction in Oral English Teaching
4. On Developing English Reading Skills
5. The Strategies of Topic Controlling in Spoken English

6. Communicative Competence and Focused Task-based Teaching Approach
7. Error Analysis and English Teaching
8. Role-play in English Teaching
9. Cultural Teaching in English in Middle School
10. Using Questions in English Reading
11. Research on the Improvement of Middle School Students' Communicative Competence
12. On Bilingual Teaching in Primary School
13. How to Design Questions in the Classroom Teaching
14. New Concepts of Modern English Teaching
15. How to Arouse Students' Potentialities in Learning English by Using Non-intelligence Factors
16. Autonomous Language Learning in CALL Environments
17. On Attitude and Motivation in Second Language Learning
18. Making Use of Resources on the Internet to Assist English Learning
19. Task-based Language Teaching Methodology and Its Application in Reading
20. Using Task-based Method and Internet Resources to Improve Teaching of Classroom Reading
21. The Study of Learner's Motivation and its Influence upon Learners and their Learning Process
22. On Communicative Competence, Exploring the Learning Process in China's Context
23. Interaction and English Language Teaching
24. Teacher's Roles and Their Impact upon Learners' Learning Process
25. The Comparison or Analysis of Different ELT Methods and Its Application in China's Language Classrooms
26. The Students' Learning Autonomy and Language Teaching
27. Teaching the Different Skills Based on the Interactive Approaches
28. The Relationship Between Affective State and Language Learning
29. Errors and Language Learning
30. Teacher's Talk and Students' Learning
31. My Perspectives of Senior/Junior English for China
32. Cognitivism and English Teaching of Listening and Speaking
33. A Survey of Students' Motivation of Learning English
34. Extracurricular Activities and English Teaching
35. A Study on Cooperative Learning in Classroom Teaching
36. Communicative Approach and Grammar Teaching
37. Networked Multimedia and Senior/Junior English Teaching
38. Is Multimedia Effective for Language Learning/Teaching?

39. Improving English Reading through Online Newspapers
40. Reflections on CALL/CAI
41. Network-based English Teaching of Reading/Writing/Listening: What Advantages?
42. Applying Task-based Teaching Principles to Organize Oral Classroom Activities
43. Interactive Theory and the Teaching of Listening Comprehension
44. Effective Ways to Improve Efficiency of Vocabulary Learning
45. Improve Students' Oral Proficiency by Using Communicative Language Teaching Method
46. Teaching English by Student-centered Approach
47. How to Combine Traditional English Teaching Methods with Communicative Language Teaching Method
48. Importance and Feasibility of Improving Students' Communicative Competence
49. Make the Best of Language Learning Strategies to Improve English Learning Efficiency
50. How to Improve Students' Learning Style in Classroom Teaching
51. The Importance of Understanding Mild Tones in Studying the English Language
52. The Role of Cultural Background Knowledge in Studying the English Language
53. On English Vocabulary Acquisition
54. English and Chinese Comparison and Translation
55. Differences Between American and British English
56. A Cognitive Approach of English Onomatopoeias
57. A Brief Analysis of English Movies
58. English Ambiguity and Its Functions
59. The Pragmatic Analysis of the Motivations for Euphemism
60. Influence of Science and Technology on English Vocabulary
61. A Study of Student-centered English Vocabulary Teaching
62. Factors Influencing English Learning and Possible Solutions
63. Computer-assisted English Reading
64. Application of Non-verbal Communication in English Teaching
65. Psychology in English Teaching
66. How to Develop Students' Abilities to Listen and Speak English Effectively
67. How to Make Use of Mother Tongue in English Teaching
68. Principles of English Learning and Teaching
69. Strategies on Intercultural Communication Training in English Teaching
70. Reading Efficiently: An English Classroom Model Focusing on Students' Reading Ability

71. Factors Affecting English Listening and Its Appropriate Measures
72. Intensifying Cultural Awareness in Middle School English Teaching—With a Sample Teaching
73. Apply Communicative Approach to Pleasant Teaching—Analysis of My Sample Teaching Experience
74. The Strategic Difference Between Effective Listeners and Ineffective Listeners
75. On Error-correction Strategy in Oral English Classroom
76. On the Use of Interactive Approach in Writing Classroom
77. On the Reciprocal Method of Teaching English Reading
78. On Developing English Writing Skills
79. Collaborative Learning in Writing Class in English Learning
80. Task-based Teaching in Writing Class
81. The Brain-storming in English Writing
82. Cultural Awareness in English Writing
83. Importance of Free Writing
84. Application of Multimedia Technology in College English Teaching
85. Connection Between College English Teaching and CET-4
86. How to Improve the Students' Listening Ability Effectively in English Teaching
87. Task-based Method of English Teaching in Middle School
88. The Application of Schema Theory in Reading Comprehension
89. Body Language in English Teaching
90. The Diversification of English Language Teaching
91. The Present Situation of Bilingual Education
92. Culture and English Teaching
93. Some Designs on English Learning
94. Creating Learning Environments
95. Collaborative Learning: Group Work
96. How Group Work Helps to Teach English Well
97. The Process of Language Learning and Teaching
98. Motivation for English Teaching
99. Solitariness
100. The Activities Used to Improve the English Teaching Class
101. Practice of Task-based Teaching Approach Based on Construction
102. The Interest of English Learning
103. Teach Reading in Senior Middle School
104. Cooperative Learning in Secondary School
105. A Balanced Activities Approach in Communicative Foreign Language Teaching
106. On Communicative Way in Grammar Teaching

107. Culture Education in School English Teaching
108. Consideration on Bilingual Teaching
109. Cross-culture Communication and English Teaching in Middle School
110. Study of Business Letters
111. The English Teaching Based on Multimedia
112. The Contrast of Middle School Education Between China & West
113. Culture Lead-in in English Teaching
114. Psychological Factors in English Teaching at Middle School
115. The Factors Affecting on Teaching a Language and Relevant Teaching Methods
116. A Thesis Presented to the Department of English
117. Making Use of Resources on the Internet to Assist Middle School Teaching
118. How to Improve Students' Listening Abilities
119. Communicative Language Teaching and the Teaching in English Class
120. Grammar Teaching within a Communicative Framework
121. Cultural Awareness in English Teaching
122. The Impact of Different Interpersonal Relationship
123. How to Learn English Vocabulary Effectively
124. On English Writing
125. The Social Psychological Factors of Foreign Language Learning
126. How to Improve the English Writing Ability
127. The Practice of English Class Teaching
128. On Pair Work and Group Work and Their Use in English Language Teaching
129. Cultural Difference and English Teaching
130. International Communication College Culture and Education
131. Initiation and Situation in English Learning Motivation
132. Cognitive Approach in Oral English Teaching
133. Self-access Learning's Effects on the Application of the Balanced Activities Approach
134. International Communicative Activities into College English Language Teaching
135. The Application of Communication Approach to English Teaching
136. A Comparative Study of Compliments: Cross-culture Perspectives
137. Cross-cultural Communication and English Teaching
138. Increasing Cultural Awareness of English for Middle School Students
139. How to Improve Listening Skills of the Secondary School Students in English Teaching
140. The Application of Phonological/Syntactic/Semantic Theory to ELT in Chinese Middle Schools

141. The Application of Traditional/Structural/Transformational Linguistics to ELT in Chinese Middle Schools
142. The Application of Theory of Behaviorism/ Cognitive Psychology to ELT in Chinese Middle Schools
143. The Application of the Theory of Pragmatics/Discourse Analysis
144. Teaching Grammar Within a Communicative Framework
145. A Study on the Direct-spelling Method

四、翻译类

1. On Foreignization and Domestication of Cultural Factors in Translation
2. Foreignization and Translation of Idioms
3. On Treatment of Cultural Factors in Translation
4. On English Translation of Public Signs in Chinese
5. On Translation of English Names of Commendation
6. The Relationship Between Cultural Difference and Translation Skills
7. An Approach to the Translation of Poetic Image
8. A Study of the Chinese Version of Titles of English Films
9. A Study of the Chinese Version of Titles of English Novels
10. A Comparative Study of the English Version of the Poem "Untitled" by Li Shangyin
11. On Culture Translation Under Foreignization
12. On Faithfulness in Translation
13. On Fidelity and Expressiveness in Translation
14. Interpreting and Interpreting Skills
15. On Literal Translation and Free Translation
16. The Comparison and Translation of Chinese and English Idioms
17. Equivalence and Its Application in Translation
18. Cultural Equivalence in Translation
19. Learning a Foreign Language Through Translation
20. Arts in Verse Translation
21. A Comparative Study of Two English Version of *Dream of the Red Mansions*
22. On Translating the Passive Voice
23. On the Translation of English Long Sentences
24. The Social and Cultural Factors in Translation Practice
25. The Application of Functional Equivalence in English and Chinese Cross-cultural Translation
26. English Proverbs and Their Chinese Translation
27. Exploring English-Chinese Audiovisual Translation
28. On Chinese Translation of Journalistic English
29. On the Criteria of Interpretation

30. On the Unit of Translation
31. The Cultural Differences and Arts of Translation in Advertising Language
32. On Transformation Between Parts of Speech in E-C Translation
33. Exploring Substitution and Ellipsis in Translation
34. On English Proverbs Translation
35. On the Criteria of Translation
36. The Analysis of Translation Style
37. Cultural Differences and Translation Strategies
38. Translation and Foreign Language Teaching
39. Chinglish in C-E Translation
40. A Contrastive Study of English and Chinese Allusions and Their Translation
41. English Neologisms in Newspapers and Their Translation
42. On Translation of Humor in *Pride and Prejudice*
43. On Features of Journalistic English and Its Translation
44. Cultural Discrepancies and Their Influences on Translation
45. English and Chinese Translation Song Lyrics
46. Translation of Address Term Between English and Chinese
47. On the Importance of Context in Translation
48. On the Translation of English Pun into Chinese
49. The Role of Dictionary in Translation
50. Thought Pattern and Its Influence on Translation
51. Lexical Characteristics of Legal English and Legal Lexicon Translation
52. Features of Foreign Trade English and Its Translation Model
53. On Euphemism Translation
54. Translation of Metaphor from English into Chinese
55. Features of Tourism English and Its Translation
56. The Great Translator Yan Fu
57. Translation of Brand Names and Their Cultural Associations
58. Gu Hongming: A Pioneer of Translating the Chinese Classics into English
59. On the Principles of Equivalence in Literary Translation
60. A Brief Comment on E. A. Nida's Concept of Translation
61. Cultural Gaps and Untranslatability
62. Translating and the Background Information
63. A Preliminary Study of Explanatory Translating
64. Translating the English Articles into Chinese
65. Translating the English Plural Nouns into Chinese
66. Translating the Lengthy English Sentences into Chinese
67. On Translating English Book Titles into Chinese
68. A Brief Comment on the Several Chinese Versions of *Jane Eyre*

69. Views on the Chinese Version of *Emma*
70. The Chinese Version of *Jude the Obscure*: An Outstanding Example of Artistic Recreation
71. Translating the Style of Literary Works—A Preliminary Study of Wu Ningkun's Version of *The Great Gatsby*
72. A Comparative Study of Two Chinese Versions of *The Merchant of Venice*
73. A Reading of Fang Zhong's Translation of *The Canterbury Tales*
74. On the English Versions of Some of Du Fu's Poems
75. Translating the Titles of Chinese Classic Poetry
76. Common Errors in Translation: An Analysis
77. English Idioms and the Translation
78. How to Deal with Ellipsis in Translating
79. The Importance of Comprehension in Translating
80. The Translation of Trade Marks and Culture
81. On Poem Translation
82. The Appropriateness and Comparison of Poem Translation
83. The Character of Title and Translation
84. The Social and Cultural Factors in Translation Practice
85. English and Chinese Comparison and Translation
86. On the Faithfulness in Translation
87. Translation for EST
88. On Translation Methods of Numerals in Chinese and English
89. On the Du Fu's Poems Translation
90. The Comparison and Translation of Chinese and English Idioms
91. Loyalty in Translation
92. Equivalence and Its Application in Translation
93. Cultural Equivalence in Translation
94. Onomatopoeia and Its Translation
95. On the Cross-culture Pragmatic Failure in English Translation
96. Remarks on the Translation of Chinese Set-phrase
97. What is an Ideal Translation?
98. A Brief Comparison Between Two Basic Translation Methods—Literal Translation and Free Translation
99. Elementary Comment on Literal Translation and Free Translation
100. Learning a Foreign Language Through Translation
101. On the Translation of English Idioms
102. Arts in Verse Translation
103. On Translating the Passive Voice in Scientific and Technology English into Chinese

104. A Comparative Study of Two English Versions of the *Chang Ganxing*
105. Review on the Translation of Movie Titles
106. Features and Translation of Einglish/Chinese Idioms
107. The Translation of Long Sentences

五、语言与文化类

1. The Analysis on the Differences of Interpersonal Relationship Between Eastern and Western People
2. On Values of Chinese from Perspective of Lexicon
3. Research on Sino-Western Differences of Cooperative Principles
4. The Comparison of Euphemism in Wording of Sino-Western Letters
5. How to Avoid Ambiguity in Different Culture
6. On the Influence of Network Vocabulary on Chinese Language
7. The Cultural Connotation of English Etymology and the Teaching of English Vocabulary
8. An Analysis of the Political Prejudice in VOA
9. A Comparison Between News Report of BBC and VOA
10. English Idioms—A Mirror Reflecting British Culture
11. American Culture Reflected in the Use of Words of American English
12. On Cultural Differences of Body Language Between English and Chinese
13. A Comparative Study on Sexism in both English and Chinese
14. Euphemism—Their Construction and Application
15. Comparison Between English and Chinese Idioms
16. The Cultural Conflict in the Cross-cultural Communication
17. A Talk of Cultural Difference Between China and West
18. On Language and Culture in Translation
19. Family Education Differences Between China and Western Countries
20. The Effect of Context on the Meaning of Words
21. A View on the Differences Between Chinese and English Cultures with Regard to Taboos
22. A View on the Differences Between Chinese and English Cultures with Regard to Etiquette
23. A View on the Similarities and Differences Between Chinese and English Cultures in Terms of Proverbs
24. Exotic Cultures Influence on English Vocabulary
25. The Differences Between Chinese and Western Cultures and English Education
26. The Impact of Economic Globalization on World Culture
27. The Cultural Effect of Civilized English on English Writing

六、中西文化比较类

1. A Brief Discussion on Cultural Difference Between Chinese and English

2. The Euphemism in English
3. Characteristic and Cultural Differences of the English and Chinese Idioms
4. Culture Differences in English Learning
5. Animals in Chinese and Western Culture
6. Cultural Differences in English Teaching
7. Chinese and Western Culture Values in Advertising Language
8. The Impact of Economic Globalization on World Culture
9. A Comparison of Color Words Between Chinese and English
10. The Similarities and Differences Between Chinese and English Culture
11. Deep-structure Transfer in Cross-cultural Communication
12. Cultural Differences in Nonverbal Communication
13. English and Chinese Idioms
14. Proverbs and Culture
15. Body Language Functions in Cultures
16. Difference and Similarities of the Word: Black
17. Culture, Language and Communication
18. Culture Difference and Translation
19. Exotic Cultures Influence on English Vocabulary
20. The Future Emergence of Chinese English
21. Euphemism in English
22. The Differences Between Chinese and Western Cultures and English Education
23. Differences Between American and English on Lexis
24. Similarities and Differences in the Connotation of Animal Words in English
25. The Comparison of Culture and Language Between Chinese and English
26. Differences Between American and British English
27. Cultural Difference in Idioms and Ways of Mastery Them
28. Religious Cultural Factors Affecting the Differences of Meanings of Words
29. Specific Differences Between Chinese and Western Cultures
30. An Informal Discussion on Vocabulary's Cultural Connotation Between Chinese and English
31. The Differences of Family Values Between China and American
32. The Dissertations of the Foreign Language Department in Jiangxi Normal University
33. The Comparison of Chinese and Western Interpersonal Relationships
34. A Comparative Study of Empathy in English and Chinese Poetry
35. A Comparative Analysis of Sentence Structures in English and Chinese Poetry

第四章 毕业论文资料的准备和利用

论题确定之后,下一步要进行的工作是资料的准备和利用,即围绕论题搜集、整理相关资料,经过粗读和细读之后,提炼出新的观点,完成论文。

第一节 毕业论文资料的准备

人类文明经过数千年的发展,特别是经过 20 世纪突飞猛进的发展,已经在各个领域积累了大量丰富翔实的文献资料信息。在浩如烟海的文献资料中,学生为了撰写毕业论文在准备资料时,要清楚应该准备什么,怎样准备,以便能在规定的时限内完成毕业论文。

1. 毕业论文资料的准备遵循的原则

准备资料要有一定的原则:第一,准备的资料要包含在论题的大方向之内。论题是属于英国文学或美国文学的,就要在文学的范围内搜集查找资料,这一点是最为显而易见的。第二,准备资料要力求全面。古语云:"韩信点兵,多多益善。"这句话同样适用于写毕业论文的学生,即学生要在大方向大范围内尽可能多地搜集查找与论题相关的资料,使之更为全面,为写作打下最为坚实的基础,其中应包括所有作品,与作品相关的理论、相关批评等方面的资料以及包括作家生平等方面的背景资料。第三,准备的资料要具有可行性。有人称当今的社会是知识爆炸、信息爆炸的社会,"爆炸"即为在短期内各种知识、信息大量涌现,其中无疑会掺杂一些质量低劣的文献资料。所以,学生在准备资料时要选择那些质量高、可行的资料,这一点可以根据出版社、作者等方面来判断。一些大的权威性的出版机构拥有一批专业水平高的编辑,他们可以从质量参差不齐的来稿中选择最为优秀的出版。在某一研究领域有突出研究贡献和独到见解的知名学者的专著一般而言是可靠的。当然有些青年学者也有一些水准很高的专著问世,学生可以自己去判断、选择。第四,准备的资料要新。所谓"新",即要反映出某一研究领域的最新的研究成果。某一论题的研究中,有一些观点、论点是永恒的,不论是产生于数千年前还是最近,都是站得住脚的,是历久弥新的;而有一些观点则不然,它们会带有明显的时代特性,反映了论点的提出者所处时代的历史背景、科技水平。研究发展对于论点的影响,使得这些观点在时代发展的过程中逐渐显现了它的局限性,这类资料很显然是不能利用的。

2. 毕业论文资料的准备使用的方法

如前所述,现在的文献资料浩如烟海,不但数量多,形式也多,如印刷品资料——图书、报刊等,微缩胶片、磁带、光盘、网络数据等。而本科生在撰写毕业论文时,主要利用的是印刷品型材料和互联网数据。所以,学生应该了解如何利用这些文献资料的方法。

(1) 利用图书馆进行文献检索

高等院校的图书馆是满足广大师生学习、教学、科研等需要的文献情报中心。图书馆里丰富的文献馆藏是学生撰写毕业论文的丰富的资料来源。图书馆经过科学的分类排列使得学生检索文献资料变得简易方便。

学生在图书馆搜集资料时，一般可以应用人工和计算机两种检索方式。人工检索主要有以下四种检索工具：书目、索引、文摘和图书馆目录。

● **书目**　书目又称目录，它是著录一批相关文献并按照一定的次序编排而成的一种文献查找工具。一般按字顺、笔画、主题等方法编排书目。利用书目，学生就可以了解在某个时期关于某个专题有哪些书，所需的某种文献资料可以从哪些书里去查找，同时还可以了解某些学术思想的渊源、流派等信息。

● **索引**　书目主要是检索图书信息的工具，而索引则主要是查找报刊（或论文集）论文篇目的工具。索引揭示与记录文献中的有关事项及概念的位置出处，它一般标明书刊中的刊名、语词、主题、人名、篇名、地名、事件，或是加以注释，记明出处页数，按照字母顺序或分类进行排列。

● **文摘**　文摘是以简明、确切的语言记录文献中的重要内容，报道、传递文献资料的信息和提供文献资料的线索的一种检索工具。文献篇幅短，但是信息量大，既节省时间，又能提供文献的线索。文摘主要包括以下主要内容，即文献的篇名、作者、出处、研究主题、内容、结果及结论等。

● **图书馆目录**　学生在图书馆里查找文献资料除了可以用以上三种检索工具之外，还可以利用某一个图书馆的总目录来查找该图书馆的馆藏文献情况。而要利用图书馆的目录，就应了解图书分类法。我国图书馆最常用的主要有三种分类方法，即中国图书馆图书分类法，简称中图法；中国科学院图书馆图书分类法，简称科图法；以及中国人民大学图书馆图书分类法，简称人大法。其中前两种分类法较为常用，其基本类目录详见附录。

学生在使用图书馆目录查找文献资料时，可以根据分类、主题、题名和著者进行查找。

随着现代科学技术的飞速发展，特别是20世纪50年代计算机技术的发展，各门学科的发展也在加速，文献和科学数据快速增加，也就加大了检索文献的难度。但同时计算机技术在图书馆文献管理和检索的应用又大大提高了信息传递和检索的速度。

计算机检索是根据使用人的需求，通过通信线路和终端设备，从预先编制和存贮在计算机中的数据中选出和输出与需求相符合的数据。计算机检索要求学生在进行检索时要通过通信系统使检索终端（你所使用的计算机）与联机检索系统相连接，如果是单机，则直接进入检索系统，然后选择数据库或文档，键入检索词进行检索。

附：国内外在线图书馆网址
1. 中国国家图书馆（原北京图书馆）：http://www.lib.nle.gov.cn
2. 清华大学图书馆：http://www.lib.tsinghua.edu.cn
3. 北京大学图书馆：http://www.lib.pku.edu.cn
4. 北京师范大学图书馆：http://www.lib.bnu.edu.cn
5. 南京大学图书馆：http://202.119.47.3
6. 复旦大学图书馆：http://www.library.fudan.edu.cn
7. 北京外国语大学图书馆：http://www.bfsu.edu.cn/enet/lib/tsg.htm
8. 厦门大学图书馆：http://210.34.4.20

9. 广东外语外贸大学图书馆：http：//202.116.197.6/gplib.htm

10. 美国国会图书馆：http：//leweb.1oc.gov

11. 英国外语辅助教学图书馆：http：//www.sussex.ac.uk/langc/call.html

12. 美国世界图书馆网络中心：http：//library.usask.ca/ejournals

13. 人文科学在线杂志图书馆：http：//166.111.88.20/index.htm

14. 中国在线图书馆：http：//netsupport.tsinghua.edu.cn/navigation/navindex.htm

15. OCLC 联机计算机图书馆中心：http：//newfirstsearch.oclc.org

16. 语言文学在线资源库（Online MLA International Bibliography）：http：//www.silverplater.com/catalog/mlab.htm

17. 英语和外语教学在线杂志：http：//www.u-net.com/eflweb/home.htms

18. 中国期刊网：http：//166.111.88.20/index.htm

19. Uncover 期刊论文原文传递服务系统：http：//uncweb.carl.org/reveal

20. "美国研究"网页：http：//www.georgetown.edu/crossroads/asw

21. ERIC 英语教学文摘档案库：http：//eric-web/tc.columbia.edu/abstracts

22. 美国 ISI 公司 Arts and Humanities Citation Index (A & HCI)-1975-present：Http：//wos.isitrial.com/help/helptoc.html#abhci

23. 美国 ISI 公司 Social Science Citation Index (SSCI)-1975-present：Http：//wos.isitrial.com/help/helptoc.htmo#ssci

24. 美国 Brown 大学语言学虚拟图书馆：http：//www.cog.brpwn.edu/pointers/liguistics.html

25. 英国 London 大学 Berkbeck 学院应用语言学图书馆：http：//alt.venus.co.uk/VL/AppLingBBK

（2）利用网络进行检索

国际互联网是计算机技术、现代通讯技术和信息技术共同发展的结果，它的电子邮件远程登录、文件传输和万维网等主要功能，已经成为网络检索的基础。网络检索即是通过搜索引擎和传统检索方法相结合，从具有丰富信息资源的互联网上查找使用电子图书、电子期刊、电子报纸、联机数据库和图书馆馆藏目录，搜集有用的文献资料。

网络检索可以直接从已知的网址上查找所需的图书馆目录和数据库目录，也可以用网上的搜索引擎直接搜索相关的网址、网页或资料目录。最为常用的搜索引擎有 Google、百度、北大天网、搜狐的搜狗、Alta Vista、北大方正的方正搜书网等。学生可以用这些搜索引擎在网络上搜集与论题相关的资料信息，既快捷方便，又充分翔实。

附：国内外外语与外语教学类网址

1. Applied linguistics virtual library：http：//alt.venus.co.uk/vl/AppLingBBK/welcome.Html

2. Human language page：http：//www.June29.com/HLP

3. Linguistic resources on the Internet：http：//www.Sil.org/linguistics

4. Universal survey of language：http：//www.teleport.com/~napoleon

5. 中国基础教育网：http：//www.benet.com.cn.

6. 中国英语教师网：http：//www.englishteachers.com.cn
7. 美国全球英语学习网：http：//www.globeenglish.com
8. 21世纪英语教学网：http：//21th century.chinadaily.com.cn
9. 北方教育网：http：//www.northedic.com.cn
10. 空中英语教育读者服务综合网：http：//www.kzyyjs.com
11. 上海外语教育出版社：http：//www.sflep.com.cn
12. 外语教学与研究出版社：http：//www.fltrp.com.cn
13. 中国对外翻译出版公司：http：//www.ctpc.com.cn
14. 清华大学出版社：http：//www.tup.tsinghua.edu.cn
15. 北京大学出版社：http：//www.cbs.pku.edu.cn
16. 高等教育出版社：http：//www.hep.com.cn

第二节　毕业论文资料的利用

经过图书馆查询、借阅、网上下载甚至买书买资料的准备过程，每个学生的手边都会有大量的资料。如何利用这些资料，使其最大限度地为毕业论文的撰写服务就是学生面临的另一大问题了。

毕业论文资料的利用是一个繁杂沉重并至关重要的工作，它直接关系到论文质量的高低。对论文资料利用得当，最后论文质量才会有保证，否则会导致质量不高和抄袭剽窃的结果。

毕业论文资料的利用过程可以分为两个步骤：资料的记录和资料的分析。

1. 资料的记录

（1）记录的信息。记录的信息首先是与论题相关的评论、观点及原文等内容信息。但除此之外，学生在记录时还应注意资料的来源信息，即这份资料从何而来，图书馆、网上还是其他地方，作者的全名，出版信息——出版社、出版年、出版地及版本。这样做第一可以便于学生随时查询，第二也可以为注释、参考文献做准备，第三记录的信息还应包括学生在阅读资料时产生的一些想法、观点。有了想法随时记下来，最后汇总，这样可以避免重复思考，省时省力。

（2）记录的方法。最为传统的方法是记笔记：在自己买回的书上记、在本子上记或用做卡片的方法来记，但这种方法有时，特别是在有时间限制的情况下，会用去大量的时间且比较费力，那么学生就可以用复印的方法——将有关的内容复印下来，可以保持资料的原样，日后用于撰写不会失真走样，也可以省时。随着网络技术的发展，学生也可以用软盘、计算机等记录资料，这一方法特别适用于网上下载的资料——资料从网上下载后，可以存在软盘或计算机上，需要时经过分析编辑，直接复制或粘贴在论文中，既方便又快捷。

2. 资料的分析

无论学生采用哪种记录资料的方法，所记录下来的东西归根结底还是别人的成果，其间还难免有些与论题较远甚至毫不相关的资料，这就要求学生要对记录下来的资料进行分析整理——阅读、选择。

整个资料的利用过程实际上就是学生阅读所准备资料的学习过程,是一个由粗到细、由多到少的过程。阅读首先是粗读——浏览,大致找出与论题相关的资料来。然后要对这些相关资料进行精读,找出其中与自己论题、看法的切合点——这些资料是自己观点的佐证,或是被质疑的问题,或是需要修改、补充的论点。郁达夫在谈到翻译前的准备工作时,曾经提出了"学、思、得"的论点,即对所译材料先要阅读(学习)、思考,然后有所收获,形成自己的观点或受到启发。这一论点同样适用于毕业论文写作的阅读资料过程。阅读之中对所读资料进行思考,做到真正消化了资料,而不是囫囵吞枣,生吞活剥,甚至断章取义曲解原资料。

阅读之后有所得有利于资料的选择取舍。试想没有经过细致阅读、思考,怎么会有所感有所得,又怎么会清楚该取哪些有用的资料而舍去无用的?学生在准备和利用资料时,往往会想把搜集到的所有资料都用到文章当中,求多求全,也可以保证字数。但这些没有经过阅读、分析、选择的资料堆砌到文章当中,只会使文章主次不分,观点不明,甚至前后矛盾,毫无逻辑性可言,造成文章里的许多部分牵强附会,漏洞百出。这种文章是断不能合格的。

论文资料的利用是对论文资料准备的升华,使得已成定调的理论资料得到发展,成为具有现实指导意义的新的理论基础。

第三节　各专业丛书书目

目前,国内有许多大型权威出版社引进了多套国外研究、介绍文学、语言学、翻译及外语教学法的英文原版丛书和国内知名学者在相关领域的最新研究成果丛书,现摘录部分丛书以供参考(资料来源:http://www.sflep.com.cn; http://ctpc.com.cn; http://www.fltrp.com.cn; http://www.pup.com.cn):

1. 上海外语教育出版社
(1) 学术专著总目

语言学及外语教学	剑桥文学指南丛书
其他语言与语言教学研究著作	外国文学史系列
21世纪修辞学丛书	外国现代作家研究丛书
当代语言学丛书	世界文化史故事大系
语言学系列丛书	美国文学史论译丛
剑桥应用语言学丛书	其他论著
牛津语言学入门丛书	人物传论
牛津应用语言学丛书	文化与翻译研究
牛津应用语言学丛书续编	翻译与翻译教学研究
现代语言学丛书	国外翻译研究丛书
外语教学法丛书	文化与国俗对比研究
文学与文学史研究	经贸、营销、新闻传播与管理

(2) 文学——剑桥文学指南

书名	作者	出版日期	定价(元)
D. H. 劳伦斯	Anne Fernihough	2003 年	17.00

书名	作者	出版日期	定价(元)
艾米莉·狄金森	Wendy Martin	2004 年	6.60
爱伦·坡	Kevin J. Hayes	2004 年	17.70
爱默生	Joel Porte & Saundra Morris	2004 年	18.40
奥维德	Philip Hardie	2004 年	25.60
澳大利亚文学	Elizabeth Webby	2003 年	18.80
贝克特	John Pilling	2000 年	17.30
勃朗特姐妹	Heather Glen	2004 年	16.80
查尔斯·狄更斯	John O. Jordan	2003 年	14.50
厄内斯特·海明威	Scott Donaldson	2000 年	20.70
亨利·戴维·梭罗	Joel Myerson	2000 年	15.80
亨利·詹姆斯	Jonathan Freedman	2000 年	17.60
罗伯特·弗罗斯特	Robert Faggen	2004 年	18.80
美国现实主义和自然主义	Donald Pizer	2000 年	19.10
美国犹太文学	Michael P. Kramer & Hana Wirth Nesher	2004 年	19.30
弥尔顿	Dennis Danielson	2000 年	19.80
乔叟研究	Piero Boitani & Jill Mann	2000 年	17.30
塞缪尔·约翰逊	Greg Clingham	2000 年	18.20
莎士比亚	Margreta de Grazia & Stanley Wells	2003 年	18.50
莎士比亚研究	Stanley	2000 年	21.20
特·斯·艾略特	David Moody	2000 年	17.60
田纳西·威廉斯	Matthew C. Roudane	2000 年	18.70
托马斯·哈代	Dale Kramer	2000 年	16.20
威廉·福克纳	Philip M. Weinstein	2000 年	16.70
沃尔特·惠特曼	Ezra Greenspan	2000 年	16.00
希腊悲剧	P. E. Easterling	2000 年	25.00
现代主义研究	Michael Levenson	2000 年	16.90
英国十八世纪小说	John Richetti	2000 年	18.70
尤金·奥尼尔	Michael Manheim	2000 年	17.60
约瑟夫·康拉德	J. H. Stape	2000 年	17.60
詹姆斯·乔伊斯	Derek Attridge	2000 年	20.00

（3）语言学

① 牛津应用语言学丛书

书名	作者	出版日期	定价(元)
第二语言习得概论	Rod Ellis	1999 年	21.00
第二语言习得研究	Rod Ellis	1999 年	49.00
第二语言研究方法	Herbert	1999 年	18.00
话语与文学	Guy Cook	1999 年	19.00
客观语言测试	Bernard Spolsky	1999 年	26.00
口语语法	David	1999 年	18.00
实用文体学	H. G. Widdowson	1999 年	16.00

应用语言学的原理与实践	Guy Cook	1999 年	28.00
英语教学史	A. P. R. Howatt	1999 年	26.00
语料库、检索与搭配	John Sinclair	1999 年	13.00
语言测试实践	Lyle F. Bachman & Adrian S. Palmer	1999 年	24.00
语言测试要略	Lyle F. Bachman	1999 年	26.00
语言教学的环境与文化	Claire Kramsch	1999 年	20.00
语言教学的基本概念	H. H. Stern	1999 年	36.00
语言教学的问题与可选策略	H. H. Stern 著 Patrick Allen 编	1999 年	26.00
语言与理解	Gillian Brown	1999 年	15.00
语言教学面面观	H. G. Widdowson	1999 年	15.00
语言学习认知法	Peter Skehan	1999 年	21.00
语言教学交际法	H. G. Widdowson	1999 年	12.00
词汇短语与语言教学	James R. Nattinger & Jeanette S. De Carrico	2000 年	17.00

② 牛津应用语言学丛书续编

书名	作者	出版日期	定价(元)
第二语言学习的条件	Bernard Spolsky	2000 年	20.00
交际法语言教学	C. J. Brumfit & K. Johnson	2000 年	8.00
论以语言学习者为中心	Elaine Tarone & George Yule	2000 年	16.00
模糊语言	Joanna Channell	2000 年	18.00
文学与语言教学	C. J. Brumfit & R. A. Carter	2000 年	21.00
习语与习语特征	Chitra Fernando	2000 年	20.00
英语会话	徐碧美	2000 年	22.00
语篇中的词汇模式	Michael Hoey	2000 年	20.50
语言领域的帝国主义	Robert Phillipson	2000 年	26.00

③ 牛津语言学入门丛书

书名	作者	出版日期	定价(元)
第二语言习得	埃利斯	2000 年	9.20
历史语言学	Herbert Schendl	2003 年	8.50
社会语言学	斯伯尔斯基	2000 年	8.40
心理语言学	威多逊	2000 年	8.80
语言测试	Tim McNamara	2003 年	9.00
语言学	H. G. Widdowson	2000 年	8.60
语言与文化	克拉姆	2000 年	8.60
语音学	Peter Roach	2003 年	7.70
语用学	尤尔	2000 年	8.80

(4) 教学法(2000 年 10 月出版)

书名	作者	定价(元)
词汇:描述、习得与教学(20)	Norbert Schimitt & Michael McCarthy	21.00
词汇教学技巧(18)	Virginia French Allen	9.50
课程设计(4)	Fraida Dubin & Elite Olshtain	12.00
课堂教学决策(3)	Michael P. Breen & Andrew Littlejohn	17.50

如何教授英语语法(8)	George Yule	19.00
如何选择教材(2)	Alan Cunningsworth	10.00
商务英语教学(15)	Mark Ellis & Christine Johnson	14.00
特殊用途英语(6)	Tom Hutchinson & Alan Waters	11.20
外语阅读技巧教学(16)	Christine Nuttall	16.00
外语自主学习——理论与实践(7)	David Gardner & Lindsay Miller	16.00
学习教学：英语教师指南(10)	Jim Scrivener	13.00
英语教学成功之道(12)	Paul Davies & Eric Pearse	13.50
语言教学的挑战与变迁(1)	Jane Willis & Dave Willis	11.50
语言教学话语分析(5)	Michael McCarthy	13.00
语言教学矩阵(19)	Jack C. Richards	12.00
语言教学中的教师进修(13)	Donald Freeman & Jack C. Richards	21.50
语言课堂中的教与学(14)	Tricia Hedge	24.00
语言学习机制(9)	Pasty M. Lightbown & Nina Spada	12.50
语言学习研究方法(11)	David Nunan	15.00
阅读教学的技巧与资源(17)	Sandra Silberstein	9.00

(5) 翻译

① 翻译与翻译教学研究

书名	作者	出版日期	定价(元)
翻译的理论建构与文化透视	谢天振	2000年	21.50
科技英语翻译理论与技巧	戴文进	2003年	13.50
文体翻译论	冯庆华	2002年	25.00
五四以来我国英美文学作品译介史(1919—1949)	王建开	2002年	25.00
译介学	谢天振	1999年	18.00
英汉语比较与翻译(4)	杨自俭	2002年	30.20
中国现代翻译文学史(1898—1940)	谢天振 查明建	2004年	33.00
中国译学理论史稿	陈福康	2000年	23.60

② 国外翻译研究丛书(2004年4月出版)

书名	作者	定价(元)
当代翻译理论(第二版修订本)(19)	Edwin Gentzler	14.00
翻译、改写以及对文学名声的制控(24)	Andre Lefevere	11.00
翻译、历史与文化论集(23)	Andre Lefevere	12.00
翻译教程(7)	Peter Newmark	17.20
翻译科学探讨(21)	Eugene A. Nida	18.50
翻译理论与实践(22)	Eugene A. Nida & Charles R. Taber	13.50
翻译批评：潜力与制约(25)	Katharina Reiss	9.00
翻译问题探讨(5)	Peter Newmark	12.60
翻译学词典(29)	Mark Shuttleworth & Moira Cowie	14.20
翻译学——问题与方法(6)	Wolfram Wilss	16.60
翻译研究(第三版)(27)	Susan Bassnett	14.00

翻译研究：综合法(12)	Mary Snell Hornby	11.00
翻译研究百科全书(20)	Mona Baker	33.30
翻译与关联：认知与语境(18)	Ernst August Gutt	15.80
翻译与性别：女性主义时代的翻译(17)	Luise von Flotow	8.00
后殖民语境中的翻译——爱尔兰早期文学英译(14)	Maria Tymoczko	18.50
解构主义与翻译(13)	Kathleen Davis	8.00
跨文化交际——翻译理论与对比篇章语言学(2)	Basil Hatim	14.50
路线图——翻译研究方法入门(28)	Jenny Williams & Andrew Chesterman	9.80
描述翻译学及其他(10)	Gideon Toury	18.00
目的性行为——析功能翻译理论(3)	Christiane Nord	10.00
通天塔之后：语言与翻译面面观(11)	George Steiner	30.00
文化翻译：笔译、口译及中介入门(15)	David Katan	15.50
文化构建——文学翻译论集(1)	Susan Bassnet & Andre Lefevere	10.00
系统中的翻译：描写和系统理论解说(16)	Theo Hermans	12.00
译者的隐身：一部翻译史(26)	Lawrence Venuti	22.00
语篇与译者(8)	Basil Hatim & Ian Mason	15.60
语言与文化：翻译中的语境(9)	Eugene A. Nida	16.80
语用学与翻译(4)	Leo Hickey	14.50

2. 中国对外翻译出版公司翻译丛书

书名	作者	出版日期	定价(元)
口译技巧	刘和平著	2001年	12.00
余光中谈翻译	余光中著	2002年	12.00
金融翻译技法	陈仕彬编著	2002年	20.80
工商企业翻译实务	许建忠编著	2002年	18.80
变译理论	黄忠廉著	2002年	17.00
译道探微	思果著	2002年	11.00
英汉翻译津指	陈生保著	1998年	13.60
等效翻译探索(增订版)	金堤著	1998年	11.60
中国翻译简史(增订版)	马祖毅著	2001年	22.30
文体与翻译(修订版)	刘宓庆著	1998年	28.80
翻译与人生	周兆祥著	1998年	7.20
因难见巧	金圣华 黄国彬编	1998年	10.30
汉英科技翻译指要	冯志杰著	2000年	13.60
英汉比较与翻译(修订版)	陈定安著	1998年	14.60
文学翻译十讲	刘重德编著	1998年	9.40
法窗译话	陈忠诚著	1998年	14.20
新编奈达论翻译	谭载喜编	1999年	17.60
英汉同声传译	张维为著	1999年	12.00
当代翻译理论	刘宓庆著	1999年	13.80

书名	作者	出版日期	定价
实用口译手册(增订版)	钟述孔著	1999年	29.80
汉英时文翻译	贾文波著	2000年	11.00
翻译批评散论	马红军著	2000年	11.20
词语翻译丛谈	陈忠诚著	2000年	11.20
词语翻译丛谈续编	陈忠诚 吴幼娟著	2000年	24.50
文化与翻译	郭建中编	2000年	22.00
翻译变体研究	黄忠廉著	2000年	18.00
翻译研究	思果著	2001年	14.20
翻译新究	思果著	2001年	13.00
语篇翻译引论	李运兴著	2001年	12.80
文化语境与语言翻译	包惠南著	2001年	18.80
新译学论稿	萧立明著	2001年	10.80
释意学派口笔译理论	[法]勒代雷著	2000年	11.80
翻译与语言哲学	刘宓庆著	2001年	26.80
影响中国近代社会的一百种译作	邹振环著	1996年	12.00
中译英技巧文集	《中国翻译》编辑部	1992年	10.00

3. 外语教学与研究出版社
文学
(1) 北京外国语大学外国文学史丛书

书名	作者	出版日期	定价
马来文学	王青著	2004年	12.90
墨西哥文学	李德恩 著	2001年	8.90
爱尔兰文学	陈恕 著	2000年	9.90
魁北克文学	孙桂荣 著	2000年	8.90
保加利亚文学	杨燕杰 著	2000年	8.90
法国文学	陈振尧 著	2000年	8.90
斯里兰卡文学	邵铁生 著	1999年	8.90
巴西文学	孙成敖 著	1999年	9.90
阿根廷文学	盛力 著	1999年	9.90
罗马尼亚文学	冯志臣 著	1999年	9.90
捷克文学	李梅 杨春 著	1999年	7.90
美国文学	金莉 秦靖 著	1999年	9.90
秘鲁文学	刘晓眉 著	1999年	9.90
意大利文学	沈萼梅 著	1999年	8.90
波兰文学	易丽君 著	1999年	9.90
西班牙文学	董燕生 著	1998年	5.90

(2) 北京外国语大学外国文学选集丛书

书名	作者	出版日期	定价
德语文学选集	韩瑞祥 编	2005年	45.90
英国文学选集	何其莘 张剑 侯毅凌 编	2004年	49.90

书名	作者	出版日期	定价
意大利文学选集	沈萼梅 编	2000 年	39.90
法国文学选集	张放 晶尼	2000 年	39.90
韩国文学选集	金京善 编	1998 年	39.90
俄罗斯文学选集	张建华 等编	1998 年	39.90
西班牙文学选集	刘永信 等编	1998 年	39.90
拉丁美洲文学选集	郑书九 等编	1997 年	39.90

(3) 英美文学文库

书名	作者	出版日期	定价
重划疆界：英美文学研究的变革	格林布拉特 等著	2007 年	53.90
牛津英国文学史 维多利亚人	戴维斯 著	2007 年	57.90
牛津英国文学史 现代运动	鲍尔迪克 著	2007 年	43.90
牛津英国文学史 英国文学的国际化	King，B 著	2007 年	35.90
牛津英国文学史 英国的没落?	史蒂文森 著	2007 年	56.90
当代非裔美国小说：其民间溯源与文学发展	[美]贝尔著	2007 年	42.90
亚裔美国文学作品及社会背景介绍	金惠经 著	2006 年	33.00
当代美国小说 1970 年以来的美国小说介绍	米拉德 著	2006 年	28.00
1945—2000 年的现代美国戏剧	[英]比格斯比 著	2006 年	52.90
美国梦,美国噩梦 1960 年以来的小说	[美]休姆 著	2006 年	32.90
女权主义理论与文学实践	Deborah L．Madsen	2006 年	29.90
牛津美国文学词典	[美]哈特 [美]莱宁格尔 编	2006 年	69.90
哥伦比亚英国小说史	[英]里凯蒂 主编	2005 年	95.00
从柏拉图到巴特的文学理论	哈兰德 著	2005 年	29.90
牛津英国文学词典(第 6 版)	[英]德拉布尔 编	2005 年	99.90
哥伦比亚英国诗歌史	伍德林 夏皮罗编著	2005 年	65.90
哥伦比亚美洲小说史	埃利奥特 主编	2005 年	79.90
哥伦比亚美国诗歌史	帕里尼 主编	2005 年	79.90
现代英国小说	布拉德伯里 著	2005 年	56.90
当代英国小说导读	卡尔 著	2005 年	27.90
理解诗歌(第 4 版)	Robert P．Warren 著	2004 年	53.90
文学理论导论	Terry Eagleton 著	2004 年	21.90
理解小说(第 3 版)	布鲁克斯 等编著	2004 年	45.90
现代诗歌评介	罗林塔尔 著	2004 年	25.90
文学术语汇编(第 7 版)	艾布拉姆斯 著	2004 年	32.90
论解构：结构主义之后的理论和批评	卡勒 著	2004 年	26.90

书名	作者	出版日期	定价
当代文学理论导读(第4版)	塞尔登 等著	2004年	24.90
文学批评方法手册(第4版)	古尔灵 等著	2004年	37.90
她们自己的文学：从勃朗特到莱辛英国女性小说家	肖瓦尔特 著	2004年	32.90

(4) 北京外国语大学比较文学研究丛书

书名	作者	出版日期	定价
碰撞与融会——比较文学与中国古典文学	周发祥 魏崇新 编	2006年	27.90
他乡有夫子：汉语研究导论(上、下)	张西平 编	2005年	38.90
文学间的契合——王佐良比较文学论集	王佐良 著	2005年	11.90

(5) 五卷本英国文学史

书名	作者	出版日期	定价
英国18世纪文学史	刘意青 主编	2006年	33.90
英国中古时期文学史	李赋宁 何其莘 主编	2006年	29.90
英国19世纪文学史	钱青 主编	2006年	42.90
英国文艺复兴时期文学史	王佐良 何其莘 主编	2006年	39.90
英国20世纪文学史	王佐良 周钰良 主编	2006年	69.90

语言学/应用语言学系列图书

(1) 世界著名语言学家系列讲座

书名	作者	出版日期	定价
吉尔斯·福康涅认知语义构建十讲	[美]福康涅 著	2010年	39.90
伦纳德·泰尔米认知语义学十讲	[英]泰尔米 著	2010年	65.90

(2) 北京外国语大学语言学研究丛书

书名	作者	出版日期	定价
语言测试和它的方法(修订版)	刘润清 韩宝成 编著	2010年	15.90
篇章语用学概论	钱敏汝	2001年	14.90
认知语言学概论——语言的神经认知基础	程琪龙	2001年	11.90
理论文体学	胡壮麟	2000年	7.90
语言的符号性	丁尔苏 著	2000年	5.90
语言测试和它的方法(修订本)	刘润清 等编著	2000年	10.90
语言文化差异的认识与超越	高一虹 著	2000年	9.90
外语教学科研中的统计方法	韩宝成 编著	2000年	9.90
外语教学中的科研方法	刘润清 编	1999年	9.90

(3) 当代国外语言学与应用语言学文库(第三辑)

书名	作者	出版日期	定价
社会、历史背景下的跨文化交际(第四版)	[美]马丁 [美]中山 著	2009年	65.00
牛津计算语言学手册	[英]米特科夫 著	2009年	109.90

书名	作者	年份	定价
语音学教程(第5版)	[美]拉德福奇德 著	2009年	49.90
语用学	黄衍 著	2009年	46.90
朗文英语口语和笔语语法(新版)	[英]拜伯 等著	2009年	119.90
最简句法入门：探究英语的结构	ANDREW RADFORD	2009年	63.90
英语语音学与音系学实用教程	PETER ROACH 著	2009年	39.90
话语分析中的基本概念	[美]杜利 [美]莱文森 著	2009年	22.90
音系学导论	[美]奥登 著	2009年	38.80
语言类型学与普遍语法特征	[英]克罗夫特 著	2008年	38.90
二语习得引论	[美]萨维尔·特罗伊克 著	2008年	23.90
语言教学的流派	JACK C. RICHARDS 等著	2008年	29.90
音系学通解	[英]古森霍芬 [英]雅各布斯 著	2008年	32.00
元话语(Metadiscourse)	[英]海兰 著	2008年	26.00
剑桥学生英语语法	[澳]赫德尔森 [美]普尔曼 著	2008年	35.00
认知语言学入门(第二版)	[德]温格瑞尔 [德]施密德 著	2008年	38.90
语言学：语言与交际导论	[美]阿克马吉安 著	2008年	59.90
功能语法导论	M. A. K. HALLIDAY 等著	2008年	69.90
文学中的语言：文体学导论	[英]图兰 著	2008年	28.90
语言心理学(第5版)	[美]卡罗尔 著	2008年	55.90

注：此系列更多书籍见外研社网站。

(4) 当代国外语言学与应用语言学文库(第一批)

书名	定价(元)
当代国外语言学与应用语言学文库(1)	1666.00
语言研究(George Yule)	28.90
语言学教程(Andrew Radford)	38.90
普通语言学概论(R. H. Robins)	41.90
语言学入门(Stuart C. Poole)	19.90
英语语音学与音系学实用教程	25.90
语音学与音系学入门(John Clark)	38.90
转换生成语法教程(Andrew Radford)	56.90
句法学(Andrew Radford)	26.90
乔姆斯基的普遍语法教程(Vivian Cook)	34.90
语义学(John I. Saecd)	34.90
语义学引论(John Lyons)	35.90
形态学(P. H. Mattews)	23.90
语用学新解(Jef Verschueren)	28.90
语用学(Jean Stilwell Peccei)	13.90
话语分析(Gillian Brown)	27.90

书名	定价(元)
话语分析入门(James Paul Gee)	17.90
词典学词典(R. R. K. Hartmann)	16.90
实用文体学教程(Laura Wright)	22.90
语言模式(Joanna Thornborrow)	24.90
语言类型学与普通语法特征(William Croft)	28.90
社会语言学教程(R. A. Hudson)	24.90
社会语言学引论(Ronald Wardhaugh)	34.90
社会语言学(Ralph Fasold)	32.90
会说话的哺乳动物(Jean Aitchison)	29.90
语言心理学(David W. Carroll)	41.90
跨文化交际(Larry A. Samovar)	28.90
跨文化交际：语篇分析法(Ron Scollon)	25.90
换言之：翻译教程(Mona Baker)	27.90
功能语法导论(M. A. K. Halliday)	41.90
功能语法入门(Geoff Thompson)	25.90
历史语言学(R. L. Trask)	41.90
语料库语言学入门(Graewe Kennedy)	28.90
语料库语言学(Douglas Biber)	27.90
语言研究中的统计学(Anthony Woods)	29.90
语言学教程(Andrew Radford)	38.90
第二语言习得研究概况	36.90
语言学和第二语言习得(Vivian Cook)	29.90
第二语言学习与教学(Vivian Cook)	22.90
英语教学科研方法(Jo McDonough)	26.90
如何写研究论文和学术报告	26.90
谈语言：写作读本(William H. Roberts)	34.90
语言教学的流派(Jack C. Richards)	16.90
英语：国际通用语(Peter Trudgill)	16.90
语言教学教程：实践与理论(Penny Ur)	33.90
怎样教英语(Jeremy Harmer)	19.90
英语测试(J. B. Heaton)	19.90
语言测试的设计与评估	27.90
语言教学课程设计原理(Janice Yalden)	19.90
朗文英语口语和笔语语法(Douglas Biber)	99.90
朗文语言教学及应用语言学辞典	44.90
语言与语言学词典(Hadumod Bussmann)	46.90

(5) 当代国外语言学与应用语言学文库(第二批)

书名	定价(元)
当代国外语言学与应用语言学文库(2)	1978.00
语言论：言语研究导论(E. Sapir)	19.90
普通语言学教程 (F. de Saussure)	24.90

语言论(L. Bloomfield)	49.90
语言学综览(M. Aronoff)	72.90
语言学理论(R. de Beaugrande)	37.90
语言与心智研究新视野	22.90
吉姆森英语语音教程(A. Cruttenden)	33.90
音系学通解(C. Gussenhoven)	28.90
汉语方言的连读变调模式(M. Y. Chen)	49.90
优选论(Renk Kaqer)	42.90
汉语形态学：语言认知研究法	31.90
转换生成语法导论(J. Ouhalla)	43.90
当代句法理论通览(M. Baltin)	76.90
乔姆斯基：思想与理想(N. Smith)	25.90
语言知识：其本质、来源及使用	29.90
当代语义理论指南(S. Lappin)	61.90
关联性：交际与认知(D. Sperber)	31.90
语用学引论(J. L. Mey)	35.90
语用学(S. C. Levinson)	38.90
言辞用法研究(H. P. Grice)	36.90
如何以言行事(J. L. Austin)	18.90
言语行为：语言哲学论(J. R. Searle)	19.90
表述和意义(J. R. Searle)	21.90
言语的萌发(J. Aitchison)	28.90
语言学简史(R. H. Robins)	27.90
英语学习词典史(A. P. Cowie)	24.90
现代词典学入门(H. Bejoint)	26.90
英诗学习指南(G. Leech)	24.90
小说文体论(G. Leech)	37.90
人类语言学入门(W. A. Foley)	45.90
英语：全球通用语(D. Crystal)	15.90
认知语言学入门(F. Ungerer, H. J. Schmid)	31.90
语言的范畴化(J. R. Taylor)	31.90
英语的衔接(M. A. K. Halliday)	35.90
作为社会符号的语言(M. A. K. Halliday)	24.90
英语的功能分析：韩礼德模式(T. Bloor)	27.90
历史语言学导论(W. P. Lehmdnn)	33.90
英语史(A. C. Baugh)	41.90
翻译与翻译过程(R. T. Bell)	28.90
儿童语言发展引论(S. H. Foster-Cohen)	22.90
语言学习与语言使用中的错误(C. James)	29.90
第二语言教与学(D. Nunan)	31.90
英语课堂上的学习风格(J. M. Reid)	26.90
语言学习和语言教学的原则	32.90

根据原理教学(H. D. Brown)	42.90
词汇、语义学和语言教育(E. Hatch)	42.90
语言教学大纲要素(J. D. Brown)	25.90
外语学习与教学导论(K. Johnson)	31.90
语言测试词典(A. Davies)	25.90
语言测试指南(G. Henning)	19.90
第二语言习得与语言测试研究的接口	19.90
评估与测试：研究综述(R. Wood)	26.90
语言学课题(A. Wray)	29.90
用语料库研究语言(J. Thomas)	28.90
语法化学说(P. J. Hopper)	26.90
剑桥语言百科全书(D. Crystal)	79.00
应用语言学百科辞典(K. Johnson)	36.90
社会语言学通览(Florian Coulmas)	46.90

基础外语教学与研究丛书

书名	定价(元)
英语学习策略(程晓堂、郑敏)	7.90
英语教学策略论(王笃勤)	8.90
英语测试的理论与实践(武尊民)	9.90
英语教材分析与设计(程晓堂)	5.90
英语课堂教学形成性评价研究	6.90
英语教师行动研究——从理论到实践	11.90

翻译丛书

(1) 翻译学博士研究论丛

书名	作者	出版日期	定价
联络口译过程中译员的主体性意识研究	任文 著	2010年	49.90

(2) 外研社翻译研究文库

书名	作者	出版日期	定价
巴别塔揭秘：同声传译与认知、智力和感知	[阿根廷]贝尔托内 著	2008年	48.90
翻译与权力	[美]提莫志克 [美]根茨勒 编	2007年	27.90
什么是翻译？离心式理论，批判式介入	[美]鲁宾逊 著	2007年	26.00
跨文化性与文学翻译的历史研究	[德]基特尔 [德]富兰克 编	2007年	16.90
论翻译的原则	[英]泰特勒 著	2007年	24.90

书名	作者	出版日期	定价
变换术语：后殖民时代的翻译	[加]西蒙 [加]圣皮埃尔 编	2007 年	32.90
基于语料库的语言对比和翻译研究	[比]格朗热 等编	2007 年	23.90
跨文化侵越——翻译学研究模式(II)历史与意识形态问题	[比]赫曼斯 编	2007 年	23.90
翻译,权力,颠覆	[西]阿尔瓦雷斯 [西]比达尔 编	2007 年	17.90
翻译与文学批评：翻译作为分析手段	[美]罗斯 著	2007 年	11.90
翻译与帝国：后殖民理论解读	[美]鲁宾逊 著	2007 年	14.90
翻译与语言：语言学理论解读	[英]福西特 著	2007 年	19.90
多元下的统一·当代翻译研究潮流	[爱尔兰]鲍克 等编	2007 年	21.90

社会/文化研究系列图书

(1)《自然》百年科学经典

书名	作者	出版日期	定价
Nature 自然百年科学经典（第 2 卷）（英汉对照版）(1931—1933)	SIR JOHN MADDOX 等	2009 年	368.00

(2) 大中华文库

书名	作者	出版日期	定价
俄译论语(汉俄对照)	杨伯峻 今译 [俄]贝列洛莫夫	2009 年	80.00
论语(汉西对照)	杨伯峻 今译 常世儒 西译	2009 年	80.00
老子(汉法对照)	陈鼓应 今译 吕华法 译 陈鼓应 今译	2009 年	70.00
老子(汉西对照)	汤铭新 李建忠 毛频西 译 陈鼓应 今译	2009 年	70.00
老子(汉俄对照)	[俄]马良文 [俄]李英男 译	2009 年	70.00

(3) 北京外国语大学跨文化交际丛书

书名	作者	出版日期	定价
文化研究选读	王逢振 王晓路 张中载 编	2007 年	9.90
美国价值观——一个中国学者的探讨	朱永涛	2002 年	9.90
英语习语与英美文化	平洪 张国扬 编	2000 年	6.90
跨文化交际面面观	胡文仲 主编	1999 年	26.90
跨文化交际学概论	胡文仲 著	1999 年	8.90
中英(英语国家)文化习俗比较	杜学增 著	1999 年	11.90
跨文化非语言交际	毕继万 著	1999 年	7.90

语料库系列图书
外研社英语语料库研究系列

书名	作者	出版日期	定价
基于语料库的英语语言学语体分析（含 CD-ROM 1 张）	桂诗春 著	2010 年	23.90
中国学生英语口笔语语料库 2.0 版（含 DVD 1 张）	文秋芳 梁茂成 晏小琴	2008 年	50.00
中国大学生英汉汉英口笔译语料库（含 DVD 2 张）	文秋芳 王金铨 编著	2008 年	60.00
中国学生英语口笔语语料库（1.0 版）（CD-ROM 3 片装）	文秋芳 王立非 梁茂成	2005 年	36.00

其他学术专著

书名	定价（元）
英语教育研究（刘润清）	11.90
译事探索与译学思考（许钧著）	12.90
双语教学模式探究（盛德仁）	11.90
英语文体学引论	20.90
攀登（英文）（丁往道）	9.90
刘润清论大学英语教学	14.90
语篇与语言的功能（黄国文）	18.90
英国二十世纪文学史（王佐良等）	33.80
英国文艺复兴时期文学史	26.80
论新开端：文学与翻译研究集	20.00
文本·文论——英美文学名著重读	21.90
二十世纪西方文论选读（张中载）	54.90
当代英国文学论文集（张中载）	12.80
当代美国小说理论（程锡麟等）	11.90
英国文学论述文集（李赋宁）	15.00
周珏良文集	24.90
英译陶诗（汪榕培）	9.90
陶渊明诗歌英译比较研究（汪榕培）	13.90
语言学方法论（桂诗春、宁春岩）	39.90
西方古典文论选读（张中载）	19.90
认知语言学概论	11.90
西方语言学流派（刘润清）	12.80
唐宋绝句名篇英译（邓炎昌）	7.80
文化与语言（王福祥等）	15.90
功能主义纵横谈（胡壮麟）	16.90
威廉·福克纳研究（肖明翰）	18.90
艾略特与英国浪漫主义传统	9.80

4. 北京大学出版社

韩礼德文集（影印版）

书名	作者	出版时间	定价
书论语法	M. A. K. Halliday	2007年	55.00
目语篇和话语的语言学研究	M. A. K. Halliday	2007年	36.00
论语言和语言学	M. A. K. Halliday	2007年	55.00
婴幼儿的语言	M. A. K. Halliday	2007年	55.00
科学语言	M. A. K. Halliday	2007年	36.00
计算机与定量语言	M. A. K. Halliday	2007年	36.00
英语语言研究	M. A. K. Halliday	2007年	46.00
汉语语言研究	M. A. K. Halliday	2008年	46.00
汉语语言研究(汉译版)	M. A. K. Halliday	2007年	45.00
语言与教育	M. A. K. Halliday	2007年	55.00
语言与社会	M. A. K. Halliday	2007年	36.00

西方语言学原版影印系列丛书

书名	作者	出版时间	定价
字面意义的疆域：隐喻、一词多义以及概念理论	M. Rakova	2006年重印	20.00
英语语篇：系统和结构	J. R. Martin	2006年重印	45.00
作为语篇的语言：对语言教学的启示	M. McCarthy	2006年重印	28.00
布拉格学派,1945—1990	Luelsdorff	2005年重印	28.00
认知语法基础(1)	R. W. Langacker	2006年重印	38.00
认知语法基础(2)	R. W. Langacker	2006年重印	45.00
论自然与语言	N. Chomsky	2007年重印	22.00
语料库语言学的多因素分析：小词置位研究	S. T. Gries	2005年重印	20.00
语法化	Paul J. Hopper	2006年重印	28.00
美国社会语言学：理论学家与理论团队	S. O. Murray	2005年重印	28.00
英语教学中的教材和方法——教师手册(第二版)	J. Mcdonough 等	2007年重印	25.00
英语语言文化史	G. Knowles	2007年重印	16.00
分析散文	R. A. Lanham	2007年重印	20.00
古英语入门	B. Mitchell 等	2006年重印	45.00
美国英语入门	G. Tottie	2008年重印	38.00
英语语言史：社会语言学研究	B. A. Fennell	2005年重印	35.00
语言学入门纲要	G. Hudson	2006年重印	65.00
语言的结构与运用	E. Finegan	2007年重印	72.00
语言艺术的学与教	D. Strickland	2006年重印	68.00
认知语言学	W. Croft, D. A. Cruse	2006年	45.00
语篇研究：跨越小句的意义	J. R. Martin D. Rose	2007年	36.00
语用学：多学科视角	L. Cummings	2007年	42.00
语言引论(第8版)	V. Fromkin	2008年重印	68.00

语言学论丛

书名	作者	出版时间	定价
系统功能语言学概论(修订版)	胡壮麟等	2009年重印	45.00
文体学概论	刘世生	2007年重印	32.00
现代语言学流派概论	封宗信	2010年重印	22.00
语言与认知概论	齐振海 张辉	2011年	35.00
语言与语言学概论	彭宣维	2011年	45.00
第二语言研究方法概论	田贵森	2012年	35.00
生成语言学概论	戴曼纯	2012年	35.00
认知语言学概论	李福印	2011年重印	56.00
英语词典学概论	文军	2007年重印	28.00
语义学概论(修订版)	李福印	2009年重印	32.00
音系学概论	史宝辉	2012年	35.00
语用和认知概论	孙亚	2008年	32.00
评价理论概论	Peter R. White 刘世铸	2011年	35.00
语言系统与功能	胡壮麟	2008年	32.00
索绪尔语音理论要点评析	马壮寰	2008年	37.00
普通语言学基础	马壮寰	2010年	22.00
语用学:现象与分析	冉永平	2009年重印	30.00
语篇语言学研究	姜望琪	2011年	38.00
功能语言学与语篇分析新论	常晨光 丁建新 周红云	2008年	59.80
系统功能语法入门——加的夫模式	黄国文 何伟 廖楚燕	2008年	52.00
功能语言学与翻译研究——翻译质量评估模式建构	司显柱	2007年	32.00
社会语言学研究方法的理论与实践	张廷国 郝树壮	2009年	42.00
批评性跨文化阅读的主体间评价研究	唐丽萍	2006年	29.00
语言整合描写与系统词典学	杜桂枝译	2011年	52.00
句子语义与非指称词	薛恩奎译	2011年	52.00
英语语篇中的时态研究	何伟著	2008年	38.00
中近代英语中动名词和现在分词混用现象考	石小军、张晶	2010年	25.00
二语语篇阅读推理的心理学研究	范琳、周红 刘振前	2011年	36.00
普通人类语言学视角下的语音简化性研究	尹铁超	2010年	25.00
第二语言习得导论(英文版)	沈昌洪 刘喜文 季忠民	2010年	29.00

文学论丛

书名	作者	出版时间	定价
白居易与日本古代文学	隽雪艳 高松寿夫	2012年	39.00
翻译构建影响——英国浪漫主义诗歌在中国	吴赟	2012年	32.00
叙述者的元小说操控:《法国中尉的女人》的认知诗学研究	梁晓晖	2012年	35.00

书名	作者	出版年	价格
语境、规约、形式——晚清至20世纪30年代英语小说汉译研究	方开瑞	2012年	42.00
国外英语语言文学研究前沿	张旭春	2012年	38.00
越界与融通——跨文化视野中的文学跨学科研究	何云波 张旭 等	2012年	48.00
灵魂旅伴:英美浪漫主义诗新选	张琼	2012年	38.00
美国战争小说史论	李公昭	2012年	98.00
《红楼梦》英译艺术比较研究	党争胜	2012年	42.00
生态批评与生态主义	王诺	2012年	38.00
俄罗斯文学与文化研究(第一辑)	金正娜 刘锟	2012年	49.00
艺术的危机与神话:谢林艺术哲学探微	杨俊杰	2011年	32.00
现代主义·现代派·现代话语——对"现代主义"的再审视	盛宁	2011年	28.00
走向真理的探索	张杰	2011年	38.00
含混与不确定性:狄金森诗歌研究	刘晓辉	2011年	35.00
超越的可能:作为知识分子的乔叟	丁建宁	2010年	28.00
英语文学与文化研究	易晓明	2010年	48.00
维多利亚时代与后现代历史想象	金冰	2010年	35.00
菲尔丁研究	韩加明	2010年	48.00
20世纪美国女性小说研究	金莉	2010年	48.00
差异之美——伊里加蕾的女性主义理论研究	刘岩	2010年	42.00
哥特小说:社会转型时期的矛盾文学	苏耕欣	2010年	36.00
危机与探索——后现代美国小说研究	刘建华	2010年	36.00
从形式回到历史——20世纪西方文论与学科体制探讨	周小仪	2010年	36.00
弥尔顿的撒旦与英国文学传统	沈弘	2010年	35.00
传记文学理论	赵白生	2010年重印	18.00
跨越边界:从比较文学到翻译研究	张旭	2010年	35.00
叙事、文体与潜文本	申丹	2009年	38.00
萧洛霍夫的传奇人生	李毓榛	2009年	38.00
英美小说叙事理论研究	申丹	2009年重印	35.00
现代戏剧理论	[德]斯丛狄 王建 译	2009年重印	15.00
《圣经》的文学性诠释与希伯来精神的探求	刘锋	2008年	28.00
加拿大地域主义文学研究	丁林棚	2008年	48.00
文艺复兴时期英国诗歌与园林传统	胡家峦	2008年	45.00
厄普代克与当代美国社会:厄普代克十部小说研究	金衡山	2008年	35.00
美国诗歌研究	李正栓	2008年重印	44.50
巴赫金哲学思想与文本分析法	凌建侯	2007年	40.00

书名	作者	出版时间	定价
文学文体学与小说翻译	申丹	2007年	25.00
叙述学与小说文体学研究	申丹	2007年重印	20.00
《克拉丽莎》的狂欢化特点研究	李晓鹿	2007年	30.00
"荒原"之风:T.S.艾略特在中国	董洪川	2007年重印	20.00
异域性与本土化——女性主义诗学在中国的流变与影响	杨莉馨	2006年重印	18.00
权力、身体与自我	黄华	2006年重印	18.00
跨学科文化批评视野下的文学理念	杜昌忠	2006年重印	15.00
基督教文化与西方文学传统	刘建军	2006年重印	25.00
美国西部小说研究	陈许	2005年	15.00
《圣经》的文学阐释	刘意青	2005年重印	20.00
灯下西窗——美国文学和美国文化	陶洁	2005年重印	28.00
文本学——文本主义文论系统研究	傅修延	2005年重印	20.00
诗与思的激情对话	王军	2005年重印	22.00

剑桥美国小说新论原版影印系列丛书

书名	作者	出版时间	定价
《漂亮水手》新论	唐纳德·雅耐拉	2007年	20.00
《永别了,武器》新论	司各特·唐纳德森	2007年重印	20.00
《就说是睡着了》新论	哈娜·沃思-内舍尔	2007年重印	25.00
《去吧,摩西》新论	林达·瓦格纳-马丁	2008年重印	22.00
《向苍天呼吁》新论	特鲁迪埃·哈里斯	2007年	20.00
《海明威短篇小说》新论	保罗·史密斯	2007年	20.00
《八月之光》新论	迈克尔·米尔盖特	2007年	22.00
《土生子》新论	肯奈斯·金娜蒙	2007年	20.00
《兔子,跑吧!》新论	斯坦利·特拉钦伯格	2007年重印	20.00
《只争朝夕》新论	迈克尔·P.克拉默	2007年	20.00
《嘉莉妹妹》新论	唐纳德·皮策	2007年重印	20.00
《觉醒》新论	温迪·马丁	2007年重印	20.00
《麦田里的守望者》新论	杰克·萨尔兹曼	2007年重印	20.00
《尖枞树之乡》新论	裘恩·霍华德	2007年	20.00
《拍卖第49号》新论	帕特里克·奥唐内尔	2007年	22.00
《亨利·亚当斯的教育》新论	约翰·卡洛斯·洛	2007年	22.00
《了不起的盖茨比》新论	马修·J.布鲁科利	2007年重印	20.00
《豪门春秋》新论	黛博拉·埃什	2007年	22.00
《最后的莫希干人》新论	丹尼尔·佩克	2008年重印	20.00
《贵妇画像》新论	简·波特	2007年重印	22.00
《红色英勇勋章》新论	李·克拉克·米切尔	2007年重印	20.00
《喧哗与骚动》新论	诺尔·波尔克	2007年	25.00
《太阳照样升起》新论	林达·瓦格纳-马丁	2007年	20.00
《他们眼望上苍》新论	迈克尔·奥克沃德	2008年重印	20.00
《汤姆叔叔的小屋》新论	埃里克·J.桑德奎斯特	2007年	26.00
《瓦尔登湖》新论	罗伯特·F.塞尔	2007年重印	20.00

书名	作者	出版时间	定价
《白噪音》新论	弗兰克·兰特里夏亚	2007 年重印	20.00
《我的安东尼亚》新论	莎朗·奥布莱恩	2009 年重印	20.00
《小镇畸人》新论	约翰·W. 克劳利	2007 年	20.00
《慧血》新论	迈克尔·克莱灵	2007 年	20.00
《所罗门之歌》新论	瓦莱里·史密斯	2007 年重印	20.00
《白鲸》新论	理查德·H. 布罗德海	2007 年	24.00

英国文学名家导读影印系列丛书

书名	作者	出版时间	定价
莎士比亚喜剧导读	Michael Maugan	2006 年重印	35.00
简·奥斯丁导读	Christopher Gillie	2006 年重印	20.00
弥尔顿导读	Lois Potter	2006 年重印	18.00
华兹华斯导读	John Purkis	2006 年重印	20.00
哈代导读	Merryn Williams	2006 年重印	20.00
莎士比亚悲剧导读	Michael Maugan	2006 年重印	22.00
奥斯卡·王尔德导读	Ann Varty	2006 年重印	24.00
乔伊斯导读	Peter Wilson	2006 年重印	22.00
康拉德导读	Cedri Watts	2006 年重印	22.00
劳伦斯导读	Gamini Salgado	2006 年重印	18.00
艾略特导读	Ronald Tamplin	2006 年重印	20.00
庞德导读	Peter Wilson	2005 年	25.00

北京大学比较文学学术文库

书名	作者	出版时间	定价
比较文学与世界文学(第二辑)	乐黛云	2012 年	35.00
徐志摩与英国的姻缘	王立群	2012 年	36.00
中岛敦文学的比较研究	郭勇	2011 年	38.00
比较文学与中国——乐黛云海外讲演录	乐黛云	2005 年重印	65.00
文学与仪式：文学人类学的一个文化视野	彭兆荣	2004 年	22.00
诠释的圆环——明末清初传教士对儒家经典的解释及其本土回应	刘耘华	2006 年重印	28.00
哈姆雷特的问题	张沛	2007 年重印	22.00
中国口岸知识分子形成的文化特证——王韬研究	王立群	2009 年重印	38.00
中国翻译文学史	孟昭毅	2005 年	52.00

未名译库

当代国外文论教材精品系列(主编：周启超)

书名	作者	出版时间	定价
现代西方文学观念简史	彼得·威德森	2008 年重印	28.00
当代文学理论导读	拉曼·塞尔森	2008 年重印	35.00
文学作品的多重解读	[美]迈克尔·莱恩	2007 年重印	22.00

| 文学学导论 | [俄]哈利泽夫 | 2008年重印 | 42.00 |

文学理论与文学研究系列

书名	作者	出版时间	定价
翻译与冲突——叙事性阐释	[英]Mona Baker 著 赵文静 主译	2011年	25.00
有色人民	[美]亨利·盖茨	2011年	35.00
意指的猴子	[美]小亨利·路易斯·盖茨	2011年	48.00
加拿大英语文学史	威·约·基思 著 耿力平 俞宝发 等译	2009年	38.00
现代戏剧理论	[德]彼德·斯丛狄	2009年重印	15.00
圣经文学导论	[美]利兰·莱肯著 黄宗英 译	2008年	55.00
中世纪作家和作品: 中古英语文学及其背景(1100—1500)(修订版)	[英]J.A.伯罗 著 沈弘 译	2007年重印	18.00

新叙事理论译丛(主编:申丹)

书名	作者	出版时间	定价
小说与电影中的叙事	[挪威]雅各布·卢特	2011年	35.00
英语常用隐喻辞典(英汉双解)	秦涵荣	2011年	89.00
后现代叙事理论	[英]马克·柯里	2005年重印	15.00
虚构的权威——女性作家与叙述声音	[美]苏珊·S·兰瑟	2005年重印	18.00
作为修辞的叙·事:技巧,读者,伦理,意识形态	[美]詹姆斯·费伦	2004年重印	15.00
新叙事学	[美]戴卫·赫尔曼	2004年重印	18.00
解读叙事	[美]J.希利斯·米勒	2004年重印	15.00

其他

书名	作者	出版时间	定价
美国历史文化	常俊跃、夏洋、赵永青	2010年重印	29.00
英国历史文化	常俊跃、夏洋、赵永青	2010年	30.00
跨文化交际	常俊跃、赵秀艳、赵永青	2011年	30.00
澳新加社会文化	常俊跃、高璐璐、赵永青	2011年	29.00
欧洲文化入门	常俊跃、黄洁芳、赵永青	2011年	32.00
中国文化(英文版)	常俊跃等	2011年	27.00
《圣经》与文化	常俊跃、李文萍、赵永青	2011年	30.00
希腊罗马神话	杨俊峰、常俊跃	2012年	30.00
美国社会文化	王恩铭	2011年重印	38.00
美国诗歌选读	陶洁	2008年	32.00
美国文学选读	陶洁	2012年	38.00
美国散文选读	陶洁	2009年	31.00
20世纪美国文学选读	陶洁	2007年重印	32.00
英美文学教程	刘树森	2012年	30.00
20世纪英国文学史	王守仁 何宁	2007年重印	26.00
二十世纪西方文论	朱刚	2011年重印	47.00

书名	作者	年份	价格
西方文化史(第二版)	徐新	2011年重印	45.00
《圣经》与西方文化	王磊	2012年	46.00
外国文学作品导引	项晓敏	2012年	42.00
外国文化史	孟昭毅 曾艳兵	2008年	35.00
新编英国文学选读(上卷)(第三版)	罗经国	2012年重印	35.00
新编英国文学选读(下卷)(第三版)	罗经国	2012年重印	35.00
现代英国文学大家	朱望	2011年	38.00
英诗及诗学文选	袁洪庚 等	2008年	32.00
英诗韵律与诗歌选读	宁一中	2012年	28.00
二十世纪英国戏剧	陈红薇	2009年	46.00
外国文论简史	刘象愚	2010年	42.00
西方叙事学:经典与后经典	申丹	2011年	35.00
《圣经》文学阐释教程	刘意青	2010年	48.00
英语文化	王逢鑫	2010年	32.00
新编英美概况教程(第二版)	周叔麟	2010年重印	40.00
英美小说欣赏导论	师彦灵	2011年	38.00
英语散文选读	赵忠德等	2011年重印	29.80
视觉时代的莎士比亚——莎士比亚电影研究	张冲 张琼	2011年重印	29.00
英美小说与电影	张桂珍	2011年	26.00
英语短篇小说选读	方岩	2010年	28.00
英语小说导读(第二版)	袁宪军	2010年	29.00
美国重要历史文献导读:二十世纪	王波	2006年重印	14.00
美国重要历史文献导读:从殖民地时期到十九世纪	王波	2006年重印	18.00
美国历史与文化选读(英文版)	王波	2010年	15.00
犹太文化史(第二版)	徐新	2011年	48.00
英汉习语与民俗文化	殷莉 韩晓玲	2009年重印	29.80
英语学习背景知识·美国加拿大(第三版)	孟继有	2009年重印	17.00
英语学习背景知识·英国澳大利亚(第三版)	何田	2009年重印	10.00
英语学习背景知识·欧洲概览	来鲁宁	2007年重印	20.00
走进英国	高燕	2009年	29.00
英语人文读本:美国篇	封一函	2008年	25.00
英语人文读本:英国篇	封一函	2009年	30.00
英语人文读本·基督教与西方文化	赵中辉译	2008年重印	15.00
美国日常礼仪	George Y. Tang	2006年重印	18.00
美国文明史英文教程	魏啸飞	2008年	48.00
英美文化与习俗	焦英 钱清	2009年	19.00
英语国家概况	訾缨	2011年重印	39.80
澳大利亚社会与文化	张华	2011年	24.00

书名	作者	出版年	定价
跨文化交际学教程	王玉环	2011年	29.00
美国文明史	魏啸飞	2011年	35.00
世界文学简史(修订版)	李明滨	2012年重印	39.80
欧美文学评论选(古代至18世纪)	汪介之 杨莉馨	2011年	25.00
欧美文学评论选(19世纪)	汪介之 杨莉馨	2011年	32.00
欧美文学评论选(20世纪)	汪介之 杨莉馨	2011年	33.00
外国文学名著批评教程	梁坤	2010年	38.00
20世纪外国文学名著文本阐析	黄铁池	2008年重印	29.80
20世纪外国美学文艺学名著精义(增订版)	赵宪章	2008年	76.00
当代英国戏剧史	王岚 陈红薇	2007年	31.00
西方现代主义文学概论(第二版)	曾艳兵	2012年	45.00
西方文学概观	喻天舒	2007年重印	25.00
心有灵犀:欧美文学与信仰传统	齐宏伟	2006年重印	20.00
欧美生态文学(修订版)	王诺	2011年	25.00
比较文学简明教程	乐黛云	2009年重印	16.00
比较文学原理新编	乐黛云	2009年重印	14.80
比较诗学导论	陈跃红	2007年	25.00
东亚比较文学导论	张哲俊	2007年重印	39.80
中外文明十五论	阮炜	2010年重印	35.00
西方思想经典选读	乔国强 何辉斌	2008年	25.00
中西文化比较导论	辜正坤	2010年重印	36.00
西方哲学文选导读	辜正坤	2012年	20.00
中国文化概要	陶嘉炜	2009年	25.00
译介学导论	谢天振	2007年	29.80
通用口译教程	梅德明	2010年重印	42.00
法律翻译理论与实践	李克兴	2008年重印	34.80
广告翻译理论与实践	李克兴	2010年	28.00
英汉与汉英翻译教程	柯平	2009年重印	10.00
英汉翻译教程(第二版)	杨士焯	2011年重印	38.00
英汉翻译对话录	叶子南	2004年重印	15.00
大学商务英语翻译教程	杨大亮	2010年	26.00
翻译理论与实践——功能翻译学的口笔译教学论	朱小雪 刘学慧 [德]高立希 王京平	2010年	35.00
英汉语言对比与翻译	王武兴 等	2009年重印	17.00
翻译与翻译伦理——基于中国传统翻译伦理思想的思考	王大智	2012年	22.00
本地化与翻译导论	杨颖波 王华伟	2011年	26.00
《语言学教程》纲要与实践	赵永清、姚振军	2011年	42.00
英语词汇学习教程	李冰梅	2006年重印	18.00
跨文化交际教程(第二版)	刘凤霞	2011年重印	18.00
商务英语信函写作	王元歌	2008年重印	32.00

商务英语应用文写作与翻译	林静	2008 年重印	26.00
圣经文学导论	[美]利兰·莱肯 著 黄宗英 译	2008 年	55.00
文化话语研究	施旭	2010 年	26.00
高级英文理解与表达教程	孙瑞禾	2007 年重印	14.00
英语的对与错(修订版)	James St. Andre 苏正隆	2005 年	18.00
英语句型语法大补贴(修订版)	廖本瑞 梁淑芳	2005 年重印	15.00
文化与庆典	Greg Banks	2009 年重印	20.00
英汉对比与英语写作	何伟	2012 年	32.00
英语专业本科毕业论文设计与写作指导	李正栓	2011 年重印	12.00
北大英文写作教程	[美]D. M. 考夫曼	2011 年重印	14.00
科研方法与规范(上)	伍巧芳 向明友	2012 年	37.00
毕业论文及研究论文写作	P. P. Heppner	2009 年	45.00
英语写作技巧	Aitchison	2006 年重印	26.00
英文模范作文新词典(第二版)	张震久 等	2006 年重印	36.00
语言学习与新技术：北京大学第二届英语教学国际研讨会论文集	李淑静	2010 年	70.00
实用英语教学法	蔡昌卓 胡一宁	2009 年	34.00
Internet 与英语教学	王媛 等	2003 年重印	10.00

第五章　毕业论文的具体撰写

第一节　如何拟写论文提纲

1. 拟写提纲的重要性

有的同学在收集了相关内容、确定题目后,直接着手撰写论文。其实,这是非常错误的。毕业论文是学术性比较强的文章,涉及内容广泛,资料繁多,篇幅较长,而且论文各个部分阐述的观点既相互不同,又互相联系,关系错综复杂。为了使论文写作顺利进行,必须撰写论文提纲。有的同学认为写提纲是浪费时间,这是因为他没有认识到提纲对论文成功的重要性。中国有句俗话:"磨刀不误砍柴工。"提纲对论文的重要性就像图纸对建筑师的重要性一样。提纲可以帮助作者(1)树立全局观念,便于总体布局,通盘考虑;(2)组织资料,突出重点;(3)避免前后脱节、重复或矛盾;(4)一气呵成,少走弯路。事实上拟写提纲的过程就是一个构思论文的过程,作者通过理顺各论据与论题之间的关系来增强论文的条理性、逻辑性和完整性。

2. 拟写提纲的方法

拟写提纲的步骤是:先拟标题,再写出总论点,最后考虑全篇总的安排。要考虑从几个方面,以什么顺序来论述总论点。先安排较大的项目,再逐个考虑每个项目所包含的小论点,直到段一级,写出段的论点句(即段落主旨)。要依次考虑各个段的安排,把准备使用的材料按顺序编码,以便写作时使用。最后做全面检查,必要时适当增删内容。

在拟写提纲之前应将搜集到的有关资料归纳总结出主要意思,选择要着重论述的问题,找出它们之间的内在联系,然后按一定的逻辑顺序加以组织。首先要找出能概括中心论点的一句话:thesis statement,需要注意的是中心论点比标题(topic)更为具体详细,它界定了论文的研究范围,说明了写作目的和需要解决的问题及结论。例如一篇论文的标题是 Color Symbolism in *The Great Gatsby*,而中心论点是 This essay is aimed to analyze how color symbolism is conspicuous in revealing the theme—the disillusionment of the American Dream。由此可见论点比标题更为全面深入。

提纲的拟写可分为简要提纲和详细提纲。作为初写毕业论文的同学来说,最好能撰写较为详尽的提纲。撰写提纲首先要弄清提纲应该涉及的内容。一般来说提纲应包含以下几个方面:

(1) 材料问题

最初作者可能发现与论文研究方向相关的材料纷繁复杂,涉及面很广。但是这些材料不可能全部写到论文中去。编写提纲的过程,从某种意义上说就是统筹安排材料、决定取舍的过程。有时为了使论文写得精彩生动而有说服力,必要时要"忍痛割爱",只能选择那些最重要、最贴切、最有说服力的材料。选好材料,给总论点和各个分论点提供最有力的论据,是编写提纲需要做的工作。例如要写《红字》中对罪恶的分析,到底谁是真正的罪魁祸首,应当搜集有关这部作品主题思想的文章资料。而有关《红字》叙事技巧、象征主义手法以及人物性格的刻画,虽然与表现的主题密不可分,却不可用作论点的有力论据。

(2) 论点问题

论文的论点是整篇论文的要旨所在。没有论点,论文就失去了论述的意义。有时为了更清楚地说明总论点,还要设立几个分论点。总论点如何提出,分论点如何围绕总论点展开论述,提纲都要详细地安排好。阐述论点时有两种方式可以借鉴:一是只作分析阐释,倾向性不十分明显,比如有关英语教学法的调查和研究;二是作者提出自己的观点,进行立论,要么先破后立,要么破立结合。总之要论点明确,具有说服力。英语专业毕业论文写作较多采取的是后一种方式,因为这样利于创新,具有挑战性。在提出总论点后,继而要进一步论述,这就是分论点的设立。在这之前最好将着重论述的资料进行分类概述,提炼出主要意思,然后寻找它们之间以及和总论点的联系以确定分论点的论述方式,可供参考的有下列几种方式:

总分式 根据总分的安排不同,又可细分为演绎式和归纳式。前者先总后分,后者先分后总。在撰写教学法方向的论文时,便可采取这两种方法,演绎法适用于定量分析法,即以假设为出发点,用数据和实验验证已有的假设;而归纳法则适用于定性分析法,即以观察材料为出发点,通过个案研究发现规律或模式。

并列式 指分论点从不同角度阐述中心论点,在形式和内容上不分主次。比如要论述委婉语的社会功能,作者就可将其分为禁忌功能、礼貌功能、粉饰功能和幽默功能几方面,分别加以论述。

递进式 指的是分论点层层深入展开论述。例如在一篇阐述 The Cultural Implication of the Chinese Cuisine Naming 的论文中,作者是这样谋篇布局的:

Ⅰ The Characteristics of Chinese Cuisine Naming

   1. Primary Motivation—Straightforwardness

   2. Secondary Motivation—Associativeness

Ⅱ Some Problems of Chinese Cuisine Naming

Ⅲ A Few Recommendations

整篇文章是从分析菜肴名称的基本特点入手,揭示其蕴含的文化含义,继而凸现出菜名文化含义日益复杂怪异的问题,从而提出菜肴的命名应遵从文化的可译性和可接受性,以使更多的外国游客更好地了解中国的饮食文化。如此布局具有较强的逻辑性和深度。

对比或对照式 则是就可比的某些方面突出所比事物的相同点或相异点,以便更好地阐明论点。比如有关比较译学的文章就可以采取这种结构,通过比较两个或多个诗歌译本对诗歌形式标记(格律、形式、句法、词汇和修辞)和非形式标记(诗人气质和作品意境、主题等)的处理,分析怎样才能实现诗歌的风格再现。

因果论证式 通常先提出问题,然后分析问题产生的原因,最后提出解决问题的办法和意义。例如在英语教学中为何和如何进行文化导入,或是分析中国学生在第二语言习得过程中产生石化现象的原因及解决办法等都可采用因果顺序。

时间接续式 顾名思义要对某一事物的缘起、发展、完善等过程层层铺陈。比如对一系列政治、历史、社会等事件或某些学术理论的发展状况的论述。

当然在一篇论文中论点的安排方式并不是单一和互相矛盾的。某些深刻复杂的问题需要将几种结构综合到一起才能对总论点进行较为透彻有力的论证。这里提供的论点的论述方式在应用到实际的论文写作中时还要针对不同论题具体问题具体分析,灵活安排。下面就对论点赖以生存的论文整体框架——结构问题作简单介绍。

(3) 结构问题

一篇优秀的论文应该像一首动听的乐曲,流畅自然,决无生涩之感。为了避免在写论文时各个部分"各行其是",撰写提纲时,就要注意各部分的连接问题。各个部分除了完成自己的"本职工作"外,还要注意和其他部分的联系和过渡。比如,如何开头,如何结尾,各段之间、各部分之间如何过渡衔接,编写提纲时都要考虑。一般是按照提出问题、分析问题、解决问题的顺序谋篇布局的。概括来说应注意下列几点:开门见山,不落俗套;紧扣论点,不偏不倚;统筹素材,逻辑排序;善始善终,首尾呼应。具体而言,篇章的组织安排应根据不同的论文题材而定。英语专业毕业论文的选题尽管多种多样,但都可大致划入三种基本论文模式,进行材料分析的实证研究、批评性理论研究和历史性研究。第一种模式针对进行材料收集和分析的调查性论文,比如教学法方面的论文。这种题材突出调查方法、材料搜集、分析结果和现实意义等方面,较多采用前面提到的总分式结构。第二种模式重在理论分析,需要作者阅读大量文献资料,搜寻翔实充分的论据,在此基础上采取立论和驳论的形式,运用多种论证方式论述中心论点。因此结构安排也就偏向于以论点、论据和论证为基础的分析推理过程,如并列、递进和对比对照等。适合此类模式的题材有文学、语言学或翻译方向的论文。第三种模式则是针对某个历史事件或社会现象发展过程的客观评述。比如对美国政党的研究,此类论文较多采用时间接续式或并列结构。在第四节有关初稿写作部分中,上述三种模式还会得到进一步的论述。

(4) 形式问题

拟写提纲时一般先摆出论点(thesis statement),再将全文分为若干章节,大致由引言(introduction)、论文主体(body)和结语(conclusion)三大部分构成。引言主要是提出论点或引出论题;论文的主体部分围绕论点进行论证分析和立论;结语部分总结全文,重申论点。引言和结论不宜过长,可自成一段,如有必要也可不止一段。但论文正文文体必须分成若干章节,每一章节的题目可以用能概括本章主旨的完整句子,例如:

Ⅰ. Ralph Waldo Emerson expounded a political theory close to anarchism.

    A. He believed that individuals should govern themselves.

    B. He believed that the state should not be concerned with property.

Ⅱ. Emerson disapproved of the educational system.

    A. He found fault with methods of instructions.

    B. He criticized the curriculum.

Ⅲ. Emerson sought to abolish established religion.

这种书写形式只需将句首第一个字母大写即可。而如要用单词、短语、从句等非完整句子作为论文题目,则需将每个单词的首字母大写。

另外一个需要注意的问题是章节前面的序号排列。表示划分章节的符号应该统一,能够体现出层次性。按照国际标准对学术论文写作的规定,有两种基本形式可供参考。一种是字母和数字交替使用的方式,如:

Ⅰ. The two reasons for...
   A. The first reason...
      1. The woman...
         a. They could...
           (1) The time...
              (a) The technology...
                 (i) The latest development...
                 (ii) The plans for...
              (b) The receptive public...
           (2) The place...
         b. They could...
      2. The men...
   B. The second reason...
Ⅱ. The reasons against...

另一种是数字排序,如:

1. The reasons for...
  1.1 The first reason...
    1.1.1 The women...
      1.1.1.1 They could...
         1.1.1.1.1 The time...
         1.1.1.1.2 The place...
      1.1.1.2 They could...
    1.1.2 The men...
  1.2 The second reason...
2. The reasons against...

无论哪种排序形式,同一层次的章节必须至少保证两个,否则便无任何排序的意义。其次还要注意前面已论述过的逻辑排序问题。章节的分类也必须严格按照逻辑顺序进行,否则便是一盘散沙,令读者一头雾水。

值得注意的是,文学方向的论文一般采用第一种方式,而语言学、教学法、翻译等方向的论文采用第二种方式。请参看以下提纲范例。

范例 1

On the Language Style of Mark Twain's Novel *The Adventures of Huckleberry Finn*

Chapter I The Background of Mark Twain and Its Influences on His Language Style

  A. The Experience of Mark Twain and His Works

  B. The Relationship Between Mark Twain's Works and America Society

Chapter II Analyzing Language Style of Mark Twain's Novels

  A. Use of Vernacular

  B. Remarkable Humor

  C. A Combination of Colloquial Language and Satire

Chapter III The Significance of Mark Twain's Language Style

  A. He made colloquial speech an accepted, respectable literary medium in the literary history of the century.

  B. The combination of the descriptive realism and the lyrical romanticism make the novel more concrete and full of imagination and enthusiasm.

  C. Mark Twain's language style has swept American literature and made books before Huck Finn and after it quite different.

Conclusion

Notes

Bibliography

范例 2

Negative Transfer of Chinese as the First Language on English Learning

1. Introduction

2. Literature Review

  2.1 Different Definitions of Language Transfer

  2.2 Categories of Negative Transfer

3. Negative Transfer of Linguistics Aspects

  3.1 Negative Transfer in Phonetics

   3.1.1 Different Phoneme Systems

   3.1.2 Tone Language and Intonation Language

    3.1.2.1 Voice and Unvoice

    3.1.2.2 Accent Change

    3.1.2.3 Changes in the Length of the Sound

  3.2 Negative Transfer of Vocabulary

   3.2.1 Meanings of Words

    3.2.1.1 Conceptual Meaning of Words

    3.2.1.2 Connotative Meaning of Words
  3.2.2 Collocation
  3.2.3 Traditional Idioms
 3.3 Negative Transfer of Grammar
  3.3.1 Plurality and Grammatical Accord
  3.3.2 The Tense and the Voice
  3.3.3 The Word Order
4. **Negative Transfer of Cultural Knowledge**
 4.1 On Different Social Etiquettes
  4.1.1 Greetings
  4.1.2 Compliment and Respond
  4.1.3 Forms of Address and Courtesy
 4.2 On Different Values and Morality Standards
 4.3 On Religions and Beliefs
5. **Conclusion**
Bibliography

同时，提纲写好后，还要对提纲进行推敲和修改。这种推敲和修改主要是推敲题目是否恰当，是否合适；推敲提纲的结构是否符合逻辑；检查提纲的层次是否清晰，是否合乎道理；各层次、段落之间的联系是否紧密，过渡是否自然。最后再进行总体布局的检查，对每一层次中的论述秩序进行"微调"。

第二节　如何撰写文献综述

文献综述是在对文献进行阅读、选择、比较、分类、分析和综合的基础上，研究者用自己的语言对某一问题的研究状况进行综合叙述的情报研究成果。文献的搜集、整理、分析都为文献综述的撰写奠定了基础。

文献综述的格式和内容一般包括：

（1）引言：包括撰写文献综述的原因、意义、文献的范围、正文的标题及基本内容提要；

（2）正文：是文献综述的主要内容，包括某一课题研究的历史（寻求研究问题的发展历程）、现状、基本内容（寻求认识的进步）、研究方法的分析（寻求研究方法的借鉴），已解决的问题和尚存的问题，重点、详尽地阐述对当前的影响及发展趋势，这样不但可以使研究者确定研究方向，而且便于他人了解该课题研究的起点和切入点，是在他人研究的基础上有所创新；

（3）结论：文献研究的结论，概括指出自己对该课题的研究意见，存在的不同意见和有待解决的问题等；

（4）附录：列出参考文献，说明文献综述所依据的资料，增加综述的可信度，便于读者进一步检索。

撰写文献综述时,应该注意以下四点:

一、文献综述不应是对已有文献的重复、罗列和一般性介绍,而应是对以往研究的优点、不足和贡献的批判性分析与评论,是经过作者精心阅读后,系统总结某一研究领域在某一阶段的进展情况,并结合本国本地区的具体情况和实际需要提出自己见解的一种科研工作。因此,文献综述应包括综合提炼和分析评论双重含义。

二、文献综述要文字简洁,尽量避免大量引用原文,要用自己的语言把作者的观点说清楚,从原始文献中得出一般性结论。文献综述的目的是通过深入分析过去和现在的研究成果,指出目前的研究状态、应该进一步解决的问题和未来的发展方向,并依据有关科学理论、结合具体的研究条件和实际需要,对各种研究成果进行评论,提出自己的观点、意见和建议。

三、文献综述不是资料库,要紧紧围绕课题研究的"问题",确保所述的已有研究成果与本课题研究直接相关,其内容是围绕课题紧密组织在一起,既能系统全面地反映研究对象的历史、现状和趋势,又能反映研究内容的各个方面。

四、文献综述的综述要全面、准确、客观,用于评论的观点、论据最好来自一次文献,尽量避免使用别人对原始文献的解释或综述。

请参考下列文献综述范例。

范例 1

The Cultural Contrast of Chinese and English Idiom

Usually, the research of idioms is regarded to begin in 1925, when L. P. Smith published his book *Words and Idioms*, and he was thought to be the representative of the idiom research. His main contribution was that he investigated the origin as well as the structure of idioms, besides, he classified the idioms according to their origin. The basic idea held by him was that, the meaning of idioms was not merely the outcome after plusing the single units in the idioms. He also concerned the internal structure of the idioms, however, he did not study much about the meaning and comprehension of the idioms, and he did not explain the reason why the idioms had those features either.

From the 1930s to 1950s, with the development of constructive linguistics, the theories of lexicon, syntax and semantics based on the constructive linguistics were used to explain the internal structure and semantic features. C. F. Hockett, a representative of this period, emphasized the role context played in identifying and explaining idioms. In 1960s, under the influence of Chomsky's Transformational-Generative Grammar Theory, people universally thought words, including idioms, were a relative stable part in a language, less lively to generate. Thus, the research developed very slowly in this period. From the late 1970s, the comparative study of Chinese and English idioms has developed a lot. According to a rough statistics, from

1979 to 2001, three monographs of the comparative study on Chinese and English idioms have been published, more than sixty academic essays concerning this topic have been delivered and more than fifteen kinds of dictionaries and handbooks about Chinese and English idioms have been issued. (Gao Xia, 2001) Those research dealt with the various aspects of idioms, such as the origin, definition, range, function and so on. For example, Chen Wenbo made comparison of Chinese and English idioms from ten aspects in his book *Comparison and Translation of English and Chinese Idioms*. From the late 1980s, with the rapid development of cross-cultural communication, the comparative study of Chinese and English idioms also benefited from it and had a fast development. What's more, the research of this period stretched out the limitation of the previous research. It not only studied the comparison from the whole, but also compared the two kinds of idioms from concrete aspect. For instance, the comparative study of the idioms related to number in Chinese and English. Scholars also led their research from the aspects of psychology, aesthetics, history and others. The cross-subject research of idioms enables the study of idioms more colorful and interesting.

With more and more people becoming passionate with Chinese, it's widely acknowledged that only having a sound understanding of both the Chinese culture and English culture, can we have a better understanding of the culture connotation and have an effective communication. Nowadays, many scholars tend to make the comparison of Chinese and English idioms from the culture aspect, analyzing the cultural difference reflected by the differences of idioms. Especially, the origins of idioms attracted a great attention. Scholars conducted a wide research between idioms and national psychology, idioms and customs, idioms and history development, idioms and geographic environment and so on. It led the comparative study of Chinese and English idioms leap forwards. Yet even though there are numerous essays on the comparative study idioms, the focus on the origin of the idioms are either few or incomplete.

"It has long been recognized that language is an essential and important part of a given culture and the impact of culture upon a given language is something intrinsic and indispensable." (*Linguistics*, 2003) Bearing this in mind, a general knowledge of the relationship of idioms and culture can be reasoned. Idioms, as the essence of a language, the information they carry reflects a large amount of culture background information, their national features distinct and regional features strong. They highly concentrated the orientation of national value and became the embodiment of national value. In a language, it is idiom that reflects culture. Idioms are the crystallization of language development. As a result, the impact of culture upon idioms is also indispensable.

Both Chinese and English have a long development history and include abundant excellent idioms. The idioms reflect the differences of Chinese and English culture. So the study of idioms is an effective way to know a certain language's culture and value system. People in the world communicate with each other more frequently than ever. The knowledge of cross-culture communication is more and more important. A sound understanding of a nation's culture and the differences from one's own national culture is a key to a successful cross-culture communication. So the research of idioms, an effective and easy way to know culture is necessary. In spite of that, the teaching and learning of idioms in the foreign language education in China is a difficult part for a long time. Students cannot make use of the idioms to learn the target culture, which also helps in their language learning. From this perspective, it is also necessary to conduct a research of idioms. At last, the comparative study of idioms also benefits the translation theory.

All in all, the cultural comparison between Chinese and English idioms has both theoretical and practical meaning.

范例 2

On the Female Image in *Mansfield Park*

The studies of Jane Austen loom so large in west literature. As early as in 1812, when Jane first put her work in public, study about her work had sprung. At that time, Scott wrote the first counted critical paper, "An Unnamed About Emma," which gave an impersonal comment. Since then studies about Jane Austen came in a throng. In the research perspective, the western scholars had a variety of opinions and constantly developed a multi-level connotation of Jane's work. Those who from the perspective of feminism and ecological criticism, considered that Jane's work showed a distinctive view of feminism and worry and concern of ecology; who from the perspective of post-colonialism analysed the influence of English colonial expansion upon Jane's work and reflect in her writing; who from the perspective of psychology unscrambled Jane's theme of the works; who from the perspective of creative techniques discussed Jane's irony in her productions; who from the perspective of reality and nature analysed Jane's creative techniques. All of that made contributions to a more deep understanding of Jane's works.

Attentions from Chinese literary translation and foreign literature studies rose at about in 1980s. Before 1980s, lots of critics commented that Jane's life was narrow and theme was trivial, so Jane didn't get a due attention. Zhu Hong is China's earlier attention to Austen scholar, who compiled *Austen Research* in 1985, which did a comprehensive introduction of Austen and her works and opened a window for Chinese scholars to understand and study of Austen. Meanwhile, Kong Haili, Jin Guojia, Lou Chenghong had also translated some foreign critics of Austen's article in *Literary Theory*. All of that had made the 1980s become a little climax for study of Austen. In 1990s, especially since 2000, Jane Austen and her works had become a hotspot in the literature translation and foreign literature research. Jane Austen's work has been made into movies, TV drama. The domestic press, such as the Yilin Press, Shanghai Translation Publishing House, Nanjing University Press, launched the Jane Austen's novels, essays, comments set; research results are more and more. Kong Zhili seriously and comprehensively translated all the works of Jane Austen. There are also other translators who have made a great contribution to the spread of Austen's works in China. There are Zi Pei, Xiang Xingyao, Kong Zhili, Xi Yuqing, Su Dan, Li Yeyi and Zhang Yunlu who have translated *Mansfield Park*.

Researchers think that *Mansfield Park* got a major breakthrough in the psychological description and narrative skill, and it is "a milepost" in the history of the British novel. This work was written after Jane Austen had experienced two major historical changes. In the works reflected the old aristocratic territory gradually invaded by the new bourgeoisie nobility. This is also Jane Austen's first work reflecting the times background at that time. It makes Austen become a more mature female writer. Researches on the *Mansfield Park* were mainly from fine cut-in point such as the study of language features, the image of Fanny, the structure and spirit connotation, imperialist feelings, moral value judgment, connotation of location, post-colonial cultural criticism, temporal and spatial extension, drama in the novel, social and historical connotation, polyphony performance, absence of narrative to talk about. Papers about this novel includes Fu Wenping's "Analyze Jane Austen's Art of Fiction in *Mansfield Park*," which focused on the grasp of the value of Austen characters, plot in the works, up to the whole structure, shape a perfect moral world. Lei Yun's "Fanny Price's Spiritual Image: Woman's Self-shaping and Self-realization in *Mansfield Park*," which adopted the perspective of feminism, through the analysis of woman's self-shaping and self-realization in *Mansfield Park*, put up with that Fanny, the heroine in the novel, as a female image with rich spiritual, condensate Jane Austen's unique insights on the value of women and female influence. Then it pointed out that this novel got enlightenment significance to the contemporary women seeking self-liberation. Song Xiaohan's "The New Female Image in *Mansfield Park*," through the analysis of Fanny, proved that Jane Austen aired the voice of feminism in the works and deeply questioned British social prejudice against women at that time. Zheng Ke's "Definition and Mood Variation Identity—The Analysis of Fanny in *Mansfield Park*," through the definition of Fanny's identity to analyze her mood variation, further explained that Fanny's ethics code and language expression is affected by the different identity. Lin Wenchen's "As I read *Mansfield Park*," by Fanny and Mary's contradictory love and marriage consciousness, reproduced the rational and emotional consciousness in love and the extremely contradictory condition to reveal the significance and value. She thought that Jane Austen was an artist who wrote life from description of life, and her novel value lies in its perceptual representation of the contradictions of life which the writer are most concerned about.

So far, feminist research on *Mansfield Park* is mostly on her marriage, money concept in the work, while it is still a blank about the female consciousness reflected by the female characters in *Mansfield Park*. This thesis will analyze *Mansfield Park* from the female image in order to explore the the unique female consciousness reflected in the novel.

范例 3

The Application of Situational Teaching Approach to Oral English Teaching in Middle Schools

Spoken language was the most frequently used communication tool for humans. Teachers in middle schools should attach importance to oral English teaching and improve the students' communicative ability. (Zhu Minghui, 2009)

Oral English has some features. Firstly, external language expression and internal language thinking are synchronous. Secondly, spoken language is situational. Even for the same topic and content, there are different expressions. Thirdly, spoken language is loose. In order to make the listener understand easily, people tend to use simple structure. (Zhou Xiaoqing, 2012) Oral English teaching is a curriculum which let students learn spoken knowledge and skills. Oral English teaching is an element of English teaching. Through the teaching students can communicate with others in English. (Guan Xulan, 2011)

Oral English teaching has some theoretical bases. Firstly, cognitive learning theory is to explore the law of learning theory through studying the cognitive process. It insists that human is the subject of studying and learn actively. At first, activity is the medium of people's knowledge of the external world. The purpose of education is to make students create not repeat. (Jean Piaget, 1970) Secondly, second language acquisition is also the basis of oral English teaching. S. D. Krashen's language acquisition theory includes five hypotheses: the acquisition-learning hypothesis, the monitor hypothesis, the input hypothesis, the affective filter hypothesis and the nature order hypothesis. In S. D. Krachen's mind, only when learners get comprehensive input which is a little higher than his or her present language level and learners can focus his or her attention on comprehension of meaning, can the learner gain language acquisition. If the present level of learners is called "i," the input "i + 1" can improve the learners' acquisition. Thirdly, the theory of constructivism is of instructional effect to oral English teaching. Constructivism is a branch of cognitive psychology school. One of its key concepts is schematism which refers to perception of understanding and ways of thinking. Schematism is the origin and core of cognitive structure or the foundation of people getting knowledge of events.

American social linguists Hymes have put forward the concept of "communicative competence" according to Chomsky's linguistics competence. Communicative competence could be understood as the application of potential language knowledge and ability. In Hymes' mind, communicative competence should consider four aspects. Firstly, the speaking should be grammatically correct. That is right in form. Secondly, the speaking should be suitable. Thirdly, the speaking should be appropriate. Fourthly, the speaking should emerge in real life.

In the twentieth century, Baker (1924) has suggested that English teaching should include not only grammar and writing but also language as a tool for communication in the social context. Ortega and Norris both have paid attention to issues about oral production. Ortega has offered a different view of relationship between projecting and second language oral production from the standpoint of art. She calls for multiple sources of data and analysis to make guidance for second language use inside and outside the classroom.

It is remarkable of the number of creative activities designed by many scholars over the last fifteen years. These activities are useful to improve learners' communicative competence and they have changed the teaching of oral skills. (Kransch, 1993) He emphasized the great importance of oral English and appreciated the development of oral English teaching.

According to English scholar Hornby's thoughts (1981), situational teaching approach means that the teachers create some concrete and vivid teaching situations purposefully during the class to help the students gain knowledge and develop skills. He insisted the teachers should introduce new vocabulary and sentence structure to the students first to prepare for understanding the article and then dealing with the article when they apply the situational teaching approach.

In foreign countries, linguists and educators have researched the effect of situational teaching approach on teaching extensively and deeply.

Dewey values situational teaching approach much. He is the first person to use situational teaching approach in education. In his mind, the process of teaching is the process in which teachers should create situations to inspire students' learning motivation. He has developed the theory and practice of situational teaching approach.

Firth and Halliday (1974) researched situational teaching approach in oral English class. They thought that situational teaching is to present teaching materials by object, pictures, acting and multimedia. It makes students get more perceptual cognitions and express and react well outside the classroom.

In recent years, scholars in China have done a lot of researches in oral English. In the 1990s, the scholars have explored the situation and problems of oral English teaching from the perspectives of culture shock, teachers' quality, emphasis degree and students' psychological barriers, etc. (Kang & Lu, 1998) Wen (2001) and Liu (2002) have carried out surveys and gave suggestions for the theory and practice of oral English teaching from the backwash effect of the National Spoken Test. Yang (2002) has called for the evaluation of oral proficiency, careful actions in the design of tasks and the application of communicative strategies as well as for the balance between the time distribution of peer talk and teacher talk, between the center on form and on meaning.

Yu Yao (2003) expressed her idea about situational teaching approach. Her definition about the situational teaching method originates from Firth's linguistic theory "language has its meaning according to language background and context." She has the opinion that the students can express their ideas imitating the similar sentences in the situation, communicate with other students emotionally and master language structures. Zhang Qingying (2005) came up with several features of situational teaching approach. Firstly, situational teaching approach has the characteristic of audio-vision and vividness. Yu Yao (2003) thought "the situation is the concrete scene and occasion where language exists." Secondly, situational teaching approach has the characteristics of symmetry of emotion and perception. Zhang Qingying thought that learning process is the process of interaction of students' emotion and perception. Thirdly, situational teaching approach has the characteristics of putting education and enjoyment together.

In China, the situational teaching approach originates from English language teaching established by Zhang Shiyi in 1948. Zhang Jianzhong has also made contribution to the development of situational teaching approach. Zhang Jianzhong and Yu Hongzhen (2000) thought situation is an important factor that influences the effect of English teaching. Wang Yanping and Zhang Jing (2003) have also explored the situational teaching approach. In the article, "The Integration Between Situated Cognition Theory and English Language Teaching," they pointed out that the students should learn in real environment and learning tasks cannot be far away from true situations. Long Wenzhen (2003) also indicated that in concrete situations students understand the passed information and their desire of expressing their thoughts are inspired. Thus the ability of expressing ideas using English is improved.

范例 4

An Analysis of Trademark Translation from the Perspective of Adaptation Theory

Trademark is the sign of a commodity and a sign used by the producers and operators to distinguish their goods or services from the goods or services of others. As an important part of the trademark, trademark word is carefully selected or created by the individual or the individual enterprises for a special purpose to distinguish the goods and services. Trademarks and the translation of trademarks are the products of the development of the commodity economy. Since the reform and opening up, the English translation of Chinese trademarks and the Chinese translation of foreign trademarks have been in increasingly urgent demand as the booming international trade.

Before entering the new century, the trademark translation is based on translating English to Chinese, in particular, that is the study of the translation of foreign trademarks. Ouyang Qiaolin explored the methods and principles of the trademark translation of imported goods: many of the trademark translation takes the measures commonly used in translating foreign words, such as transliteration, free translation, the combination of transliteration and free translation; the translation of foreign trademark will have to follow: a. to reflect the characteristics of the commodity, and to convey product information; b. to be vivid and have the ability to arouse positive associations; c. to adapt to the aesthetic psychology and traditional practices of the Chinese consumers; d. to be concise, catchy and easy to remember; e. to try to keep the form and features of the original trademark.

In the 21st century, many scholars made a bold attempt to apply new linguistic theory, translation theory to the study of trademark translation, and put forward the principles and methods of trademark translation based on these theories. Li Junfang and Li Yanlin made study of trademark translation from the orientation of the trademark naming: there is a certain orientation of the trademark naming, such as national orientation, cultural orientation, psychological orientation and aesthetic orientation; the translation of trademark should be in line with the orientation of the original trademark, or do some adjustments. (2002: 68)

Zhang Ningning explored the application of the means of association used to the trademark naming and translation, such as the pronunciation association, form association and image association. Dai Rong pointed out that the teleology made an important contribution to the trademark translation: (1) the teleological theory breaks through the limitations of traditional translation, and provides a theoretical basis for translators to translate trademarks flexibly. (2) the teleological theory breaks through the traditional theory requiring faith and equivalent, and holds that the effect of translation can be better than the original effect. (Dai Rong, 2004: 182) Li Youhua applied the cooperative principle to trademark translation; Li Liping, Yang Min used the norm theory of descriptive translation studies to trademark translation and required the trademark translation to achieve its short and easy to remember norm, Rhyme and Rhythm norm and beauty of artistic conception norm. (2005: 116)

Bai Shuxia applied adaptation theory to trademark translation, and put forward the adaptation mode of the trademark translation: to make product performance outstanding, and comply with the expressive function of trademark; to pay attention to the choice of words and adapt to the different political systems; to pay attention to controlling the number of words and adapt to different aesthetic habits; to be aware of cultural differences and adapt to the needs of different consumers; to bring about positive association and comply with the consumer psychology. (2005: 91)

In summary, few people were interested in the trademark translation study in China at the beginning of reform and opening up. After 20 years' development, the trademark translation has become a hot spot, and now has become an integral part of the practical translation subject of translation study. The achievements of trademark translation are gratifying, however, the research in this area still exists many problems and shortcomings.

The structure of research team is irrational. The authors of most of the articles are educational workers from higher schools. The researchers of the teaching profession have certain advantages and height in theory, but it is difficult to use relevant theory and translation methods from the perspective of specific translators and users to verify the translation's credibility and effectiveness because of their lack of the actual trademark translation experience. This also reflects the mismatch between theory and practice from the side.

Research methods are not scientific enough. The vast majority of studies only theoretically discussed the methods and principles of trademark translation, but the results of these studies on the validity of the trademark practice of translation is unknown. The most effective way to resolve this contradiction is to understand the needs of business and society to the theory of trademark translation and the practical application research results of trademark translation through empirical investigation. Only to combine the actual needs of enterprises and trademark translation activities that can promote the trademark translation research work and the practical application of research results in the enterprise, so as to bring tangible benefits to the development of enterprises.

Li Shuqin made groundbreaking empirical research in this regard. She made a survey to 50 export business enterprises or companies in the form of a questionnaire,

> covering basic information and conditions of the trademarks registration, the degree of attention to the trademark design and the constitutes of trademark design team and the trademark translation principles and methods. The result shows that the majority of enterprises invest fewer funds in the trademark design; by contrast, the large-scale import and export companies, especially multinational companies pay much more attention to the trademark naming and translated. It is thus clear that trademarks naming and translation are closely related to the development of enterprises. People learn about a commodity from the trademark name at the beginning, so the input of trademark naming and translation greatly affects the effectiveness of an enterprise.
>
> The research of trademark translation has been wide-ranging, but it does not have the size of the system research. The development trends of trademark translation include that the application of translation theory in trademark translation will be further comprehensive and deepening and the impact of Western and Chinese culture will be the key point of trademark translation studies in the future. These trends will eventually pave the way for the establishment of research system of trademark translation.

第三节　如何撰写开题报告

1. 开题报告的内容
(1) Title（论文题目）
(2) Thesis Statement（中心论点）
(3) Purpose and Significance of the Study（研究目的和意义）
(4) Situation of the Study（研究现状）
(5) Difficulty of the Study（研究难点）
(6) Detailed Outline（详细提纲）
(7) References（参考文献）(at least 10 books)

2. 撰写开题报告应注意的几个方面
(1) 开题报告的封面设计（见附页）
(2) 开题报告的正文
A. 页眉需加论文汉语标题，字体为小五，居中，正文中不要加目录和论文题目。
B. 正文至少要有以下内容：
① 选题的目的和意义；
② 文献综述（国内外同行业中的研究现状，自己的研究基础，研究方法）；
③ 论证过程；
④ 研究的难点和重点；
⑤ 预期的结果或结论。

(3) 正文章节标题或小标题

正文章节标题或小标题独占一行,一律用阿拉伯数字表示,形式为:

1
  1.1
    1.1.1
    1.1.2
  1.2
  1.3
    1.3.1
    1.3.2
      1.3.2.1
      1.3.2.2

(4) 文章中的插图和表格

文章中的插图和表格必须简明扼要、规范整齐;A4 页面,英文字体为 Time New Roman,5号;中文字体为宋体,5号;行距为1.5倍。

3. 开题报告正文写作举例:

I. Introduction

1.1 Research Motives

At this level of my research, I decide to select the following issues as my research motives and objectives: ...

In order to examine these research questions more effectively, I would like to adopt

1) a theoretical perspective to examine these issues in my study.

2) an experimental approach for this research.

3) a summary type of study for this survey.

4) an introspective (thoughtful, deep in thought) way of discussion for this paper.

5) a critical method in this thesis.

6) a reflectional plus experimental survey of the related issues in this work.

7) ...

1.2 Literature Review

In order to have a more complete picture about the issues I am to examine, I decide first to do a state-of-the-art type of study(综述性研究), and then see what has happened in this area over the past 5/10/20/30/ or more years.

Some initial resources I want to use in my literature review include:

1) international academic journals such as...

2) national academic journals such as...

3) important monographs and collections such as...

4) Ph. D. dissertations and influential works like...

5) useful on-line databases and services such as...

6) other available information resources such as...

1.3   Existing Problems

Based on the results of some initial reading and personal reflection, I find that there exist some problems that have not received a due treatment (dealing) in this field. My further pursuit (search) proves that some major problems which merit exploration may include the challenging issues listed as follows:

...

1.4   Research Focuses

At the present stage of my research, I select the following relationships and factors as some potential research focuses for me to concentrate on in my further study of the issues identified so far:

...

II. Outline

2.1 Statement 1

2.1.1 Supporting 1

2.1.2 Supporting 2

2.2 Statement 2

2.2.1 Supporting 1

2.2.2 Supporting 2

2.3 Statement 3

2.3.1 Supporting 1

2.3.2 Supporting 2

III. Conclusion Expected

1) We can hypothesize on the basis of the findings reported her that...

2) We wish to highlight here...aspects of the foregoing discussion.

3) In this study, we aimed to answer the question of how... The evidence obtained in all parts of this study, taken together, points in the direction of...

4) In this paper, I have tried to account for some striking differences between... I have argued that these differences can be accounted for in terms of...

5) My analysis supports the view that...

IV. Notes

...

V. References

...

VI. Appendixes

...

4.开题报告体例说明

1)统一用 A4 纸型打印；

2)内容一律用微软中文 Word；

3)页面行距为1.5倍；

4) 页面上边距为 2.5 厘米，下边距为 2.5 厘米，左边距为 3 厘米，右边距为 2.5 厘米，页眉为 1.5 厘米，页脚为 1.75 厘米；

5) 页码的排列顺序：正文部分（包括注释，参考书目和附录）的页码以阿拉伯数字排列，居中。

附页：The Design of the Cover of the Thesis Proposal

> B. A. Thesis Proposal
> 学士学位论文开题报告

××学院外国语学院
School of Foreign Languages of ×× College

论文题目：_____
Title：_____
专　　业：_____
指导教师：_____
班　　级：_____
学　　号：_____
姓　　名：_____
日　　期：　　　　20　　年　　月　　日

指导教师意见：

　　　　　　　　　　　　　　　　　　　　　　指导教师（签名）：
　　　　　　　　　　　　　　　　　　　　　　日　　期：

第四节　如何撰写初稿

　　撰写初稿就是在提纲的基础上，把论点具体化，用所选材料去论证，使论文初具规模，为修改论文准备好"蓝本"。毕业论文字数较多，篇幅较长，写作时不可能一次完成。但是对那些相对独立，内容完整的部分最好能一次完成。因为写作思路一旦中断，恢复需要一定的时间。而写作时出现的灵感也是稍纵即逝。因此撰写初稿时需注意写作的流畅性和即兴发挥，无需担心细枝末节的格式或形式，因为在以后的修改和校对中还会再详细审视原稿。在撰写初稿之前，应大致了解论文的组成。

1. 毕业论文的组成部分

毕业论文一般有以下几部分组成：

1. The front cover 论文封面
2. Title Page 题名页
3. Table of contents 目录
4. Abstract（中英文）摘要
5. The text of the paper (introduction(绪论)，body(本论)，and conclusion(结论)) 正文
6. Notes (optional) 注释
7. Bibliography 参考文献
8. Appendix (optional) 附录
9. Acknowledgements (optional) 致谢

其中论文封面、首页、目录、附录、注释和参考文献的格式前面已有所介绍，兹不赘叙。这里将要谈及的是如何撰写摘要、致谢和正文。一般来说，摘要在格式上虽位于正文之前，但在其成型之前作者需要对全文有一个宏观的把握。因此应在正文初稿撰写完成后再总结归纳摘要的内容。论文的核心部分即论文正文的撰写。题目的确定、材料的准备以及提纲的拟订，都是为论文的具体撰写服务的，其中正文部分涉及最为实质性的内容。下面就正文中绪论、本论、结论的具体撰写分别加以阐述。

2. 正文的撰写

（1）绪论（Introduction）

我们知道"好的开头是成功的一半"，写毕业论文也是这样。绪论部分要提出问题，明确中心论点；介绍研究本论题的原因、目的和意义；必要时要对前人所做的相关研究做简要的介绍、回顾或评价；作者本人在哪方面做了补充、发展和创新；介绍论文的整体框架，引发读者兴趣。需要注意的是对相关研究背景进行介绍时，不要漫无边际地罗列一系列著作或文章，应当选择侧重点各不相同的重要研究成果，并能够突显自己的研究论题在其中的地位与联系。当然也不可厚此薄彼，以此抬高自己论题的研究价值。总之，绪论部分的撰写忌讳说一些不着边际的废话，而要开宗明义，直指要点，这样才有利于论文本论部分的展开。绪论的撰写没有固定的格式和要求，要根据具体的研究方向和撰写内容采取不同的写法。可用一段或几段的篇幅引出论题，以下几种形式可供参考。

叙述式：通过叙述某件事情引出中心论点。一篇回顾从 1660 年到 1900 年莎士比亚戏剧表演的文章就是以一历史事件开头的：

> After the monarchy was restored, in 1660, London's theatre companies were re-established in a way that determined their organization until the radical changes of the 1843 Theatres Act. Two companies, Sir William Davenant's (the "Duke's") and Thomas Killigrew's ("The King's") were licensed for regular performances. These royal patents, passing from Davenant and Killigrew to their heirs and assignees, were the instruments of governmental control over theatrical performance.

描述式：通过描绘一具体事物或事件引出中心论点。一篇调查美国校园餐饮业服务水准的文章是这样引入正题的：

When I worked as a waiter at a local pizza parlor, the area manager would drop in once every two weeks and inspect the restaurant. He would watch us through the course of an evening and when the crowds thinned he would gather us all around and review our performance. At the onset of every debriefing, as they were called among the crew, the first words from his mouth would always be, "From the moment the customer enters those doors, his dining experience begins. He will form an opinion in his mind about us; and it is your job to ensure that opinion is good! If it isn't, I'll know about it, and then so will you."

Even though my experience at that restaurant lies a year behind me, whenever I eat out, I always recall the customer's opinion—especially when I am the customer. When the students of Wright State University eat at the campus facilities, they form opinions about their dining experience just as any customer would, and whether that experience is good or bad is the responsibility of the food service company. Recently, I conducted a survey to determine the student's opinion of the food service at Wright State. My purpose was simply to determine whether the students were satisfied with the overall performance of Service America, the catering company that handles all of the campus dining facilities.

铺陈式：介绍研究背景，提供相关信息和研究成果。英语专业的学术论文写作大多采取这种形式。一篇名为 Shakespeare and the Traditions of Comedy 的论文开门见山地引出莎氏所借鉴的英国文学史上的不同喜剧传统：

Shakespeare took the traditions of comedy and transformed them. Not all of them: the more urban comedy of manners from classical New Comedy, which Ben Jonson used so strikingly and which emerged again after the Restoration, he never made his chief interest. But the tradition of English romantic comedy coming to him from Lyly and Peele and others, with its roots in medieval literature and even older folklore, this he grasped and transmuted. Shakespeare's voice is as distinctive as Mozart's. He was in the current of Italian traditions, and could make brilliant adaptation of New Comedy in Plautus; but the result is always an unmistakably Shakespeare's harmony。

设问式：提出问题引入论点，吸引读者注意力进行思考。一篇论述 Authorial Ambivalence and Its Interpretive Challenges in *Tess of the d'Urberville* 的论文就是以一个颇具争议性同时反映出作者矛盾心理的问句开头的：

Was Tess raped or was she seduced by Alec d'Urberville? Readers and critics alike have been confronted with this inevitable and yet unsolvable question from the time when *Tess of the d'Urberville* was first published in 1891. Books and articles have been written and published to tackle the issue and a discussion on this novel in a graduate seminar very often turns into a fiery battlefield between the warring students. The question is inevitable in that the nature of Tess's experience with Alec lies in the center of the ultimate problem of the novel: Is Tess a "pure" woman? If the answer is yes, then in what sense is she "pure"? It provides a point of entry into the thematically complex world of this Victorian novel. The question is also unsolvable because the relation between Tess and Alec, especially what happened between them in the Chase, is largely engulfed in heavy fog, darkness, and silence;and we can in no way see clearly and judge with any degree of certainty. This interpretive difficulty is caused mainly by the authorial ambivalence which is abundant in the novel. Indeed the narrator himself seems quite perplexed by the complexity of the human experience exemplified in the short life of Tess, the heroine of the novel. In this paper, I will attempt to unravel this authorial ambivalence in terms of its discursive and ideological determinants and assess the interpretive challenges it poses to the readers.

驳斥式：对某些广为人知的观点提出质疑，从而立论。比如在探讨以学生为中心的教育模式中教师位置时，作者便可以从驳斥全面否定教师作用的观点入手：

Of unquestionable importance for language learning has been the development in recent years of learner-centered models of education. These models, however, do not deny the importance of the teacher, nor imply that there is no role for the teacher in a learner-centered classroom. Quite the contrary. There is a new, more evolved role which can be, if in some ways more challenging, also more exciting and fulfilling. Similarly, learner autonomy is a welcome goal for education, but it doesn't mean the absence of the teacher in the learning process. As Stevick(1980), Lozanov (Lozanov and Gateva 1988), Heron (1989), Aoki (this volume) and others have pointed out, learners must be prepared for autonomy gradually, and their expectations and needs, which at times may be for non-autonomous structures, must be considered.

引文式：以引语开头引发读者兴趣，自然过渡到论点。一篇论述莎士比亚语言艺术的文章就是以引用他的作品《暴风雨》中的人物语言开头的：

My language? Heavens!
I am the best of them that speak this speech,
Were I but where 'tis spoken. (*The Tempest*, I. 2.428—430)

Ferdinand's lines are a useful text for this chapter and not merely because, in this age of global travel, his surprised joy at hearing his own language spoken strikes a familiar chord. Transposed into the third person singular and the past tense, the lines could very well serve to record the received opinion of another kind of traveler: those who have explored the realms of Shakespeare's language, which is of course also the language of Ferdinand and many hundreds of other speaking characters. Shakespeare as an artist in language, it is generally agreed, is a natural genius nurtured by the state of his native speech, when and where it was spoken. Or, to use the language of one of the most experienced travelers in these particular realms of gold.

The extraordinary power, vitality and richness of Shakespeare's language are due in part to his genius, in part to the fact that the unsettled linguistic forms of his age promoted to an unusual degree the spirit of free creativeness, and in part to the theory of composition then prevailing.

(2) 本论（Body）

本论是论文的核心和灵魂。在这一部分作者要展开论题，用最有说服力的论据在最长的篇幅内表明自己的观点和研究成果。它不是简单地堆砌例子和材料，而是采用分析推理的方法论证论点。本论写得好坏直接关系到整篇论文的成败。所以一定要花费最多的时间和精力把论文写得深刻、精辟。

任何论文都包括三部分：论点、论据和论证。英语专业的毕业论文也不例外。下面就从这三方面来介绍论文本论部分的具体撰写。

A. 论点问题

论点最初应该在写提纲时就予以明确，在本论部分就论点的具体展开予以适当的注意。论点应该做到明确、深刻而新颖。一个好的论点会让作者感到有东西可写，有话可说。论点应该在本论的开头提出，以便为以后具体的论证树立目标。在立论上需要注意以下几点：

① 立论要有据可依，不可主观臆断，更不要前后矛盾。比如有人想写汉诗英译方面的文章，在发现很多古诗译本无法达到音、义、形三美的境界后便做出 Poetry is untranslatable 的结论。这不免太过武断，因为优秀的英译汉诗毕竟是少数，正是这些精品向我们诠释了诗歌的可译性和人类进行文化沟通的可能性。如果在诗歌可译性的前提下探讨如何达到音、义、形三美的境界，此论文会更有学术价值和实际意义。

② 论点要明确，不要论证许久，读者却不知在为何而论证，尤其要避免用词模糊而产生的歧义。例如在一篇论述哈代和他的《德伯家的苔丝》的文章里，作者开篇提出正是这部作品使他成为当时最杰出的英国批判现实主义作家，接下来作者并未去证明和阐述这个论断，而是讲述小说的梗概、主人公的性格特点以及象征手法的运用。这样一来便使读者如同雾里看花，难以把握作者的真正意图。

③ 论点要新颖。一方面要会旧瓶装新酒，也就是采用新的角度去分析、挖掘看似平常的材料，从而提出新论点，比如用叙事理论中"陌生化"的概念去探讨诗歌和小说中的情节；另一方面要刻意培养自酿佳酒的本领，也就是敢于选取前人未曾涉足过的领域另立新论，或是进行跨学科研究，提出自己的独特见解，比如用认知语用学中最佳关联性的理论去检验文学翻译中的风格再现。当然要想在论点上有所创新，是具挑战性的，既需要灵感的迸发，更需要平时的大量阅读，厚积薄发。

④ 切入点要深刻。如前所述，选题时应小题大做。"大做"就是要使论点深刻，能反映出事物的本质，经得起对其前因后果和发展规律的推敲和探索。但如果过大，效果也

不会好。一篇名为《论海明威作品中的几个主题》的文章阐述了他的几部作品中所体现的有关战争、爱情和硬汉形象的主题,虽是面面俱到却也如同蜻蜓点水般面面不到。这样的论点不可能做到深刻鲜明,倒不如选取其中一部作品的一个主题深入挖掘,重新立意。

  B. 论据问题

  论据是用来说明论点的可靠依据。可以说没有论点的论文好像一支没有统帅的散兵,而没有论据的论文则像一个没有号召力的"孤家寡人",论点根本无法站住脚。所以论点和论据是密不可分的两个部分。在拟写提纲时,作者已经对所查资料有所选择,但在具体的撰写过程中,要结合论点的逐步展开和深入,进一步对论据进行选择、补充,使之更好地为论点服务。在选择和安排论据上要坚持以下原则:

  ① 论点和论据的统一。论据是为论点服务的,所选资料应该能充分说明论点。如果论据在论证论点时有牵强的感觉,要坚决去掉,否则会让人对论点的可信度产生怀疑。如前面提到的有关《苔丝》的例子,要证明这部作品奠定了作者批判现实主义作家的地位,就需提供相关的论据表现其对传统的道德、伪善的宗教、不幸的婚姻和腐朽社会的批判,而不是大段描写故事情节和人物性格。否则论据和论点相割裂,整篇论文如一盘散沙,难以起到论证作用。

  ② 论据要有说服力。"一是真实可靠,二是典型,三是充分。"所谓真实可靠,就是作者要从翔实的文献和客观的观察、数据中寻找论据,切不可主观臆断,凭空捏造。尤其在写教学法方向的论文时,需要对教学现状进行调查。一些必要的手段如观察、录音、问卷、访谈、个案研究、现场记录、日记等保证了数据信息的有效性和代表性,因此更需要调查人采取实事求是的严谨的科学态度。所谓典型是指论据要具有普遍性,能反映问题实质。比如在比读两位译者的汉诗英译作品时,不能因为某几句诗行再现了原诗的音韵效果,就断定这位译者成功再现了音美,只有他将此手法贯穿用于译本始终,才可证明其翻译的风格。所谓充分,不但指"量",还指"类"。论据如果只是事例的堆砌,不免单一和无力。假如能使用多种论据形式如引用(直接引用、转述、总结),数据,定义等,论点必将更具说服力。

  ③ 论据的提出要有层次。充分的论据会使论文的可信度增加,但在提供论据时不能一味罗列,要注意顺序和层次,根据论点的变化而变化。也就是会"摆事实",讲道理。我们来看一篇名为 Using Written Teacher-Feedback in EFL Composition Classes 的文章中所用的论据是如何分布的。在绪论部分作者阐述了论题的研究背景——教师在作文课上提供书面反馈意见的理论依据,这里所采用的多为引用型论据:

  In recent years the process approach to writing has become the mainstream orthodoxy in EFL composition. This approach seeks to shift emphasis away from an endless stream of compositions assigned by the teacher, written by the learners, and handed in for marking by the teacher, handed back to the learners and promptly forgotten by them as they start on the next assignment. Instead, the emphasis is on the process of writing itself, and involves pre-writing work to generate ideas, and the writing of multiple drafts to revise and extend those ideas. Feedback is seen as essential to the multiple draft process, as it is "what pushes the writer through the various drafts and on to the eventual end product" (Keh, 1990: 294). Various types of feedback are possible, including peer feedback, conferencing, and written teacher's feedback, as well as more innovative methods such as the use of taped commentaries (Hyland, 1990) and computer-based response. In fact, the possible approaches to feedback are so varied and numerous that Lynch (1996: 155) suggests that teachers should "offer learners a range of feedback types...[which] may stand a greater chance of success than reliance on a single technique."

继而作者锋头一转，指出书面反馈的问题所在——教师的作用实际上无异于专家和评价者，使学生的选择余地大为减少。即便是较为敏感的教师也无法扭转这一事实，这里作者采用了事例论据：

Of course sensitive teachers in their role of collaborators would try not to couch their feedback in overtly authoritative or threatening ways, following advice such as that from Diffley and Lapp (1998, cited in White and Arndt 1991: 125) to "respond as a genuine and interested reader rather than as a judge and evaluator." None the less, the fact remains that at the end of the day (or semester, course, etc.) judges and evaluators are exactly what most teachers are, and the students know it. I will illustrate my point using an example of mid-draft feedback presented in White and Arndt's book on writing process (ibid.: 126). The teacher's written response to a first draft on "family new year celebrations in your country" took the form of a letter to the student, which included praise and reader style comments, e.g. "I really enjoyed reading your draft. You have some good expressions..." The letter then proceeds to make suggestions such as "Why don't you begin with that sentence," "Now, at this point, you can tell your reader what might it is," and "Then you can explain what New Year's Eve means in Uruguay, how..." and "You can end by..." The advice given is never threatening, and its content seems to have been very well thought out—exactly the sort of thing any teacher would wish his or her students to take on board.

The student's final draft is then presented to us, incorporated all the suggestions that the teacher had made. This example, along with the many other studies which also show how the quality of texts improves after teacher's feedback (see Ferris, 1995), can be viewed as demonstrating either that because of the knowledge the person giving them in "advice" will eventually be evaluating the paper, or that perhaps simply out of respect for the teacher's greater skill at writing, when reacting to the teacher's feedback on mid-drafts, learners (consciously or otherwise) do not employ their faculty of choice.

那么问题背后的实质是什么呢？教师这样做的目的何在呢？作者使用定义明确了

作文课的主要目标：

> I mentioned above that the overwhelming picture which one gets from the literature on the subject is that the aim of EFL composition classes is a short-term one—to facilitate improvement in drafts. Naturally, teacher's intervention is the most effective way of achieving this. If, however, we reconsider our aims to incorporate long-term improvement in writing ability, the usefulness of this short-term technique becomes less obvious. It is arguable that greater learner's choice, albeit accompanied by less successful results in the short term, will eventually produce learners who are able to function more autonomously and with a greater degree of self-confidence in their writing than would otherwise have been the case.
>
> We could also add to our aims the general educational principle that teachers "have only been really successful when they have made themselves redundant," and that they ought to "encourage learner's autonomy, not teacher's dependence" (Lewis, 1993: 188). Providing mid-draft feedback that has the effect of reducing the necessity of learners having to choose and discriminate would not appear to be the best way of realizing these principles.

从上述三部分所引用的论据可以看出，论点是统帅，不同类型的论据恰是其麾下各支队伍。当需要引出论题，证明其重要性时，就需援引理论或权威作为前锋；当需驳斥对方观点，指出谬误时，就需举出事例或数据作为诱饵痛击要害；当一切就绪，论证充分时，方可合路包抄，明确定义，树起自己的观点。

C. 论证问题

论点和论据只有通过合情合理、有理有据的论证才能使二者融为一体。论述文常见的毛病之一是论点正确，论据也充分，只言片语地论证之后便毫无过渡地仓促下了结论。令读者感到有如腾云驾雾，又似突遇奇峰，总之毫无头绪。如下面的一段文字：

> 但是自幼深受神学影响的哈代，尽管后来摒弃了"仁慈的上帝"，在他的大脑深处仍萦绕着宗教的幽灵。许多作品中时而出现的内在意志力，时而出现的造物主，说明他心灵深处超自然的影响阴魂不散。他总是试图用一种虚无缥缈、不可捉摸的力量来解释世上造成不幸的偶然性，以此把人类的命运看成是造物主盲目行动的必然结果。这种思想也充分体现在他的诗中，例如，他的名诗《会合》。他把一切令人感到困惑的灾难和不幸，归结为这种神秘力量的影响。诗中代表人类最高文明的豪华客轮"泰坦尼克"的毁灭正是这种神秘自然力量的体现。

看到这段论述，读者的第一反应也许是一样的"虚无缥缈""不可捉摸"。因为一般读者对这首名诗也许并不熟悉，他们所期冀的正是从对它的深入分析见出诗人的世界观。而作者却在这里戛然而止，不能不说是令人遗憾。由此可见只有论据而没有论证的过程只能是材料的堆积，毫无生气。那么该如何论证？方法都有哪些？内容决定形式，作者要根据所选论文方向、论点之间的关系来确定具体的论证方法。常用的三种基本论文模式是进行材料分析的实证研究、批评性理论研究和历史性研究。下面便就这三种模式分别论述其论证方法。

在进行材料分析的实证研究中，尤其以教学法方向的论文为代表，较多采用归纳式和演绎式论证。

归纳式论证事先没有形成看法、观点，通过实证研究、分析得出结论。比如一篇名为《中国学生英语关系从句外置结构的习得——显性教学与隐性教学实证研究》的文章采用的就是归纳式论证。在引言部分作者阐明研究目的：探讨在中国英语学习环境下，以汉语为母语的高中二年级学生学习和掌握英语关系从句外置结构的情况。在实证研究部分作者介绍了实验设计，包括变量、被试、材料、测试评分等组成部分；实验过程，包括实验前的测试、教学实验、实验后测试及五周后的测试；结果与讨论，包括三个水平组之间的差异、实验组与对照组的比较。最后得出结论，被试处于学习该目标结构的准备状态而尚未处于习得它的水平，课堂教学有利于增强语言知识，提高语法运用和判断的准确率，但还无法构建完备的目标结构知识。

演绎式论证则以假设为出发点，事先进行预示，通过实验数据进行验证。一篇旨在对中国内地英语学习进行实验研究，调查邻近原则习得的文章《成人二语习得中邻近原则的可及性研究》首先提出了四个研究假设：学习者拥有的以普遍语法形式存在的内部语言结构在二语学习中仍起作用；母语中没有激活的或被应用于不同领域的普遍语法参数在二语习得中不存在母语迁移，母语语法此时不是二语学习者的初始状态；一旦学习者的参数设定为一定的值，理论上依赖于此参数的一系列表面上互不相关的结构在中介语中都可以被习得；如果普遍语法可及，教师组和学生组的语法判断表现应该相似。随后用实验方法、受试、测试材料和测试程序予以检验，通过结果与讨论得出结论：中国英语学习者能成功习得母语中没有激活的或被应用于不同领域的邻近原则，即重设邻近原则的英语参数值。实验结果为外语学习中普遍语法的直接可及假说提供了新的佐证。

在批评性理论研究中，大致可采取两种论证方式：立论和驳论。立论采取各种论证方法从正面阐述论点，而驳论则通过驳斥对方论点、论据和论证来树立自己的论点。这里我们主要介绍立论的几种方法：

① 解读式论证。这种方法适用于文学方向诗歌的评析。由于诗歌篇幅大都不长，可以通过逐行逐句逐词的文体分析探讨其思想、艺术内涵。当然小说或戏剧中的某一场景、对白或章节也可视需要采用这种方法。下面一段探讨 Stopping by Woods on a Snowy Evening 艺术特色的论述采用的就是解读法来分析它所呈现的两个不同世界：

The artfulness of "Stopping by Woods" also consists in the way the two worlds are established and balanced. The world of the woods is a world offering perfect quiet and solitude, existing side by side with the realization that there is also another world, a world of people and social obligations. Both worlds have claims on the poet. He stops by woods on this darkest evening of the year to watch them fill up with snow, and lingers so long that his little horse shakes his harness bells to ask if there is some mistake. The poet is put in mind of the "promises" —he has to keep, of the miles he still must travel. We are told, however, that the call of social responsibility proves stronger than the attraction of the woods, which are "lovely" as well as "dark and deep"; the poet and his horse have not moved on at the poem's end. The dichotomy of the poet's obligations both to the woods and to a world of "promises" the latter filtering like a barely heard echo through the almost hypnotic state induced by the woods and falling snow—is what gives this poem its singular interest.

② 分析式论证。这种方法适用于篇幅较长的论说文,一般是将较为复杂的事物分解成若干部分,一一论述或选取其中之一深入挖掘。就文学方向而论,可以分析一部作品的情节结构、叙事方法、人物性格特征和刻画、象征手法、思想主题、语言修辞等;就语言学方向而言,可以分析某种语言现象的性质、用途和意义,如广告用语的特色和文体风格、前置词短语的句法功能、母语/方言对英语语音学习的影响等;就翻译而言,可选择翻译技巧、翻译标准、风格翻译、文化翻译进行分析;就社会文化方面,可分析某民族的价值观取向与特点,如美国的个人主义价值观、成功意识、家庭、爱情和友谊观、宗教观等。

③ 比较对比论证。有比较才有鉴别,论文写作中常常用比较或对比的手法说明问题,辨明论点。比较是为求似,对比是为求异,但两者都有一个共同的前提:所比事物具有同一性、可比性;对比的方式往往采用整体式或交替式两种方法。整体式指的是先将一事物的特点按照比较对比点列出,再将另一事物的特点也相应列出,纵观全局,得出结论,这一方式比较适用于篇幅短小的议论文;而在学术论文中更多采用的是横向比较,一般是将比较的两个事物的相同或不同点按照比较对比点一一列出,再进行深入分析,如下所示:

比较对比分析的方法	
整体式	交替式
纵向分别阐述所比事物的特点	将所比事物分点进行横向比较
X 事物的所有特点:A. 比较对比点 1 B. 比较对比点 2	比较对比点 1:A. X 事物在这一点上的特点 B. Y 事物在这一点上的特点
Y 事物的所有特点:A. 比较对比点 1 B. 比较对比点 2	比较对比点 2:A. X 事物在这一点上的特点 B. Y 事物在这一点上的特点

比如英汉语言文化对比中的一系列论题:日常生活中的文化差别,成语、谚语和格言差别,比喻和联想的差别,颜色在语言中的运用差别,典故、委婉语、禁忌语、非语言交际等方面的差别。以日常谈话中的文化差别为例,可以从打招呼和告别,各种称呼、祝贺和赞扬,其他社交礼节等方面引出英汉语的不同点,再分析深层原因即价值观的差异。

④ 分类论证。在学术论文写作中为了有效组织材料、逐步展开论述,常常用到分类手法。运用这种写作方式时需注意以下几点:分类原则要明确恰当,具体要由论述的目的和论点决定。如果是论述诗歌翻译的风格再现问题,就要按诗歌文体的风格表现来分为形式标记和非形式标记。形式标记又可细分为音律、形式、句法、词汇、修辞等;而非形式标记则可分为表现手法、作者气质和作品意境等。其次要坚持分类原则的一致性,分

类的事物不能相互交叉覆盖,要具排他性。例如一篇探讨高中英语课六种结尾方法的论文在谈到结尾的基本原则时归纳如下:简洁性原则、启发性原则、趣味性原则、准确性原则、新颖性原则和总结性原则。很显然,最后一个原则有些画蛇添足,它是前几种原则的出发点,不能与之相提并论。最后,分类原则下属的类别要完整、全面。比如本书论述的是如何撰写学术论文,就要包含论文各个部分的撰写方法,不能有所遗漏。

⑤ 比喻论证。这种方法就是用比喻的手法将抽象的道理变得深入浅出,同时增强文章的生动性、可读性。余光中在谈论翻译的直译和意译手法时,曾用过一个惟妙惟肖的比喻:翻译如女人,忠则不美,美则不忠。这不一定完全正确,但就其比喻而言却有一点新意。

⑥ 引证法。顾名思义,引证法就是援引某些理论或权威的话加以佐证。需要注意的是在引证时,要灵活变通,不可大段抄袭,隐没自己的论点。除直接引用外,转述、总结也是不可或缺的化用手段。例如下面两段引文与作者观点融为一体,毫无晦涩生硬之感:

> Since the 1970s Communicative Language Teaching (hereafter CLT) has entered the world of English teaching and learning. Communication, the backbone of CLT, has been set as the goal of teaching language. "Grammar-free," in particular, has become the most popular label in the language classrooms. Victim of this fashion, grammar, which is more associated with the systematic formal properties of language, has been dismissed from language classrooms for many years (Harmer, 1998). However, research in CLT has revealed its weakness (Ellis, N. 1994: 3).

> "More recently, in the light of analyses of the disappointing abilities of graduates from 'grammar-free,' there are again calls for a return to explicit methods."

> Accordingly, "the rejection of grammar" has come to be regarded as the most damaging misconception in CLT (Thomas, 1996). That is to say, the pendulum of grammar teaching has swung back again in the 1990s, but this should not mean a return to traditional memory-based and drill-based explicit methods. Grammar teaching needs to play a new role, namely, to act as a "Facilitator" (a means to an end) rather than as a "Terminator" (an end) to language learning.

⑦ 例证法。也就是最常见的摆事实,讲道理。在语言学和语言与文化方向的论文中较多采用这种方法。关键是要将所举的语言现象与论证完美结合,不可产生"两张皮"现象——事例和结论毫不相干或论证不充分。具体可参照前面谈到的论据问题。

⑧ 因果论证。这种方法就是通过分析原因或结果的方式对中心论点加以论证,也是较为常用的一种论证方式。比如分析跨文化交际中的一些问题,如中美文化冲击产生的原因,或是学生在英语学习过程中遇到的困难,如大学英语听力教学中的障碍因素,便可采取这种方式。关键是要搞清楚原因和结果各是什么。既不能颠倒因果顺序,也不能随意增删原因或结果,因此这方面的论证需要翔实、全面的调查分析,同时还要具备清晰的逻辑和合理的组织结构。

当然上述若干论证方法在论述过程中要百花齐放才可奏出和谐完美的乐章。三种论述模式对彼此的论述方法也并不排斥。比如在历史性研究中,由于作者主要是发现、挖掘事实而不是重新立论,因此在综述某一文学或语言学流派的发展过程中,也会用到因果、分类和举例等论证方法。

一篇论述严谨、推理正确的文章除了运用上述论证方法外,还要注意避免逻辑错误,常见的几种谬见列举如下:

① 前提错误

前提错误指的是推论前提未加任何限制或解释,容易使人挑出漏洞。比如诗歌不可译这个论题。只能说诗歌中的某些因素如格律、句法、形式等难以在目标语中实现完全对等。如果完全不可译,那么文学翻译的理论和实践岂不是毫无存在的价值了?

② 仓促结论

仓促结论指的是从个别或几个例子便得出一般性的肯定结论。在撰写英语教学法方向的论文时,尤其要注意避免这种错误。这也是为什么必须采取实验数据的方法来推断和验证一些教学理论和原则。

③ 因果错误

因果错误指认定两个先后发生的事件必然存在因果联系。比如下述论断:Religion obviously weakens the political strength of a country. After all, Rome fell after the introduction of Christianity. 罗马的衰落与基督教的传入并无必然因果联系,因此所做的宗教削弱政治统治的推断自然无法站住脚。

④ 前提矛盾

用两个互为矛盾的前提是无法作出正确推理的。比如在探讨认知语用学中的关联理论和文化翻译的关系时,作者认为文化翻译涉及的是文本之外的不同的文化、心理、审美等深层现象,因此无法用一个较为科学的翻译标准来衡量,而另一方面又认为关联理论探讨的是人在交际过程中的深层认知活动,是可以用来诠释同样作为深层交际的文化翻译现象的。这样一来论述就剪不清,理还乱,无法进一步展开。

⑤ 人云亦云,盲目论证

人云亦云,盲目论证就是抛开客观论据,还未进行深入论证,便照搬别人的观点,为己所用,这是论文中最忌讳的。比如一篇探讨劳伦斯哲学的文章,作者在介绍完他的哲学——返真主义的含义后,简单提及了几部作品的主题和人物,便论述如下:

> 劳伦斯在其作品中,通过主人公的行动,反映出人生的真相,他不惜将人的表面上的一切修饰与伪装统统剥去,剩下赤裸裸的"自我"。我们知道,劳伦斯认为性爱是改革,是促使社会前进的必要前提,建立一种新的婚姻恋爱观,而不像《查泰莱夫人的情人》中那种垂死挣扎的婚姻生活。他认为性爱有无比强大的毁灭性,它要无情地燃尽英格兰的贫瘠,燃尽英格兰的卑鄙。他认为传统的性爱是坐以待毙的象征,故此必须让每个人的血液都达到沸腾,让从精神的颤动中获得再生的簇新、洁净、裸露的肌体来替代大地间的僵硬和麻木。可以说劳伦斯的性理论正是他哲学返真主义的体现。

对不熟悉劳伦斯作品的读者来说,看到这一段论述只能感到文字上热血沸腾的气势,并不能领会其深层含义,要想真正理解其性理论的哲学含义恐怕还需对文本进行翔实的论证。

⑥ 以"理"压人

以"理"压人就是一味援引权威和专家的话佐证自己的观点。但是即便是权威也会为人怀疑,何况此权威未必是彼权威。这就是为什么在论述时有必要采取多种论证方法。

⑦ 假设错误

假设错误指论断中的假设被曲解,不符合实际情况。在一篇名为"The Innocent Shylock in *The Merchant of Venice*"的文章中,作者谈到夏洛克备受歧视,任人欺凌,但还是时刻维护犹太人的尊严,并不是一个十足的恶棍,确实值得同情时,将安冬尼奥与其作了对比:

> Antonio looks down upon Shylock, but now, he asks Shylock to give some help. What is excessive is that Shylock is very friendly and does not want to take interest, but Antonio still abuses him. Obviously, Antonio is too arrogant. It suggests that Antonio despises Shylock, and Antonio is also a real hooligan from this point. We say Shylock is great because he endures the insults of Christians, and he still helps them.

如果说为夏洛克翻案,还其一定的公道,这无可厚非。但完全脱离原著事实,对其一味美化就很牵强附会了。

⑧ 类比错误

两个性质完全不同的事物自然无法相提并论。前面那个有关翻译和女人的类比之所以成立,是因为,在某些人眼里,它抓住了两者的一些相似本质:在一些人看来,美女性情不专一,而丑女则相对忠诚;同理,在一些从事翻译的学者看来,字句华美的译文与原著相背甚远,而与其亦步亦趋的译文又难登"达、雅"之堂。我们设想一下,如果将翻译和男人一比,上述论证效果就荡然无存了,原因就在于二者风马牛不相及。

⑨ 人身攻击

这种错误在于对反对的观点只字不提,却恣意贬低持有此观点的人。比如下面这个有关汤姆·克鲁斯的例子:

> There were 750,000 people in New York's Central Park recently for Earth Day. They were throwing Frisbees, flying kites, and listening to Tom Cruise talk about how we have to recycle everything and stop corporations from polluting. Excuse me. Didn't Tom Cruise make a stock-car movie in which he destroyed thirty-five cars, burned thousands of gallons of gasoline, and wasted dozens of tires? If I were given the opportunity, I'd say to Tom Cruise, "Tom, most people don't own thirty-five cars in their life, and you just trashed thirty-five cars for a movie. Now you're telling other people not to pollute the planet? Shut up, sir."

⑩ 循环论证

循环论证指将结论作为前提进行循环论证。最著名的一个例子就是有关上帝是否存在的论断：有人说上帝所以存在是因为圣经上这么说的；当被问及我们为什么要相信圣经的话时，答曰："圣经是上帝的杰作，一定是真的。"这里需要证明的恰恰是上帝存在，因此再把它作为论断的前提——"圣经是上帝的杰作，一定是真的"，是无法自圆其说的。

（3）结语（Conclusion）

善始还需善终，本论部分固然重要，但结语也不可忽视，它是论文的意义所在、主题的升华和启迪心智的窗口，绝非仅是全文和论点的简单总结和复述。作为画龙点睛之笔，它应该阐释论题在相关领域中的意义，所作研究的局限性和对未来进一步深入研究的建设性意见。如下面一则结语范例：

> This study looks at poetry with insight on teaching and learning English and of how to extend the literary experiences of EFL students. This study reveals that poetry can be a good resource for teaching English and provides poems and appropriate activities which are proven to work in EFL classrooms. The poems and activities presented in this study were carefully selected for use by EFL teachers to support lessons if they plan to integrate poetry into current curricula.
>
> By employing the poems and activities suggested, EFL teachers can help their students develop language skills because poetry provides authentic language input. Students could improve their speaking skills by reading poems alone or with classmates, and then learn linguistic structures through the activities suggested. Poems can also promote oral and written communicative competence by encouraging students to talk about poems and respond to them in their journals. When students were learning the target language with meaningful materials, they voluntarily participated in classroom conversations which led to further development of their oral communication skills.
>
> Poetry also provides many topics for writing, especially in comparison to other second and foreign language composition classes where literature is not adopted. Most students acknowledge that connecting poetry and dialogue journal writing is effective because it not only develops writing skills, but also enhances communicating through writing. When adopted in EFL classrooms, poetry and dialogue journal writing can help teachers and students effectively complement teaching materials and any writing programs given to EFL students at all levels.
>
> Overall, this study revealed the possibility and potential of integrating poetry and dialogue journal writing into EFL curricula. EFL students are not just interested in accumulating sets of context-free, structurally based linguistic units and vocabulary lists in the target language anymore. Rather, students want to learn a new language through literary work which promotes their language skills and extends their life experiences at the same time. Therefore, I hope that EFL teachers who are trying to integrate poetry into current EFL curricula can find some suggestions and solutions in this study. In addition, I advocate strongly that EFL students have

the right to enrich their lives through good literature.

论文的结语虽无固定模式可以套用,但关于其如何开头,还是有一些较为常用的表达方式可供参照:

In summary,...
To summarize,...
The conclusion is that...
On the basis of the above discussion, we may come to the conclusion that...
Through the analysis of..., we may conclude as follows:
The writer concludes that...
The author finds that...
In this paper, we have explored...
In this paper, we examine...
This paper shows that...
This paper looks at...
This paper reveals that...
This paper concludes that...

3. 如何写摘要和关键词

论文都具有摘要,主要是为了便于交流。摘要是内容的简短陈述,可以使阅览者不用阅读全文就能了解论文的主要信息。

论文摘要为论文独立的单元,通常分中文摘要与英文摘要两部分,出现于每篇论文题目之后、正文之前(但亦有置于文后者),其顺序是中文摘要在前,英文摘要在后。

摘要是整篇文章的缩影,其内容应能反映整篇文章的主旨。摘要的内容应以简短的方式述明整个研究之来龙去脉与结果,包括写作的目的、写作的方法、研究的结果以及所得之结论等等。因此,摘要中不能出现含有历史背景,新旧信息以及未来研究的构想和与本文无关的观点、看法等内容。

摘要的主要内容包括撰写该论文的目的与重要性,撰写时所使用的材料与方法,研究后的结果以及所得的结论。这些内容的顺序一般为:

1. 研究的主要内容,完成的主要研究工作;
2. 研究的目的和重要性;
3. 获得研究的成果和相关的见解;
4. 结论或结果的作用。

我国大部分高校都要求英语专业的学生撰写毕业论文摘要。一般来说,毕业论文摘要的字数要求在200—300个词左右。论文摘要不要列举例证,不写过程,不能用图表,不要照搬论文正文中小标题或论文的部分文字。尽管摘要的具体内容因所选专业和论题而异,其各组成部分的撰写格式还是有一定的规律可循。

(1) 主题句 (topic sentence)

摘要的第一句话往往开门见山,直奔主题,提出研究目的和对象:

The purpose of this paper is...

The primary goal of this research is...
In this paper (article), we aim at...
The chief aim of the present work is to...
This paper discusses (studies, concerns, deals with)...
This paper argues (demonstrates)...
This paper explores (probes into, elaborates on, expounds)...
This paper makes a comparison of (an overview of, an analysis of)...
In this paper, the author attempts to (intends to, proposes, contends, points out, argues)...
Based on (Centering around)..., this paper is to review (prove, illustrate)...

(2) 主体句 (supporting sentence)

在概述了论题后,接下来要进一步涉及研究方法、实验过程、调查或论证分析等具体内容来填充骨架。常用的句式如下:

The method used in our study is known as...
The technique we have applied is referred to as...
The procedure can be briefly described as...
The approach that has been adopted extensively is called...
Detailed information has been acquired by the authors using...
The research has recorded valuable data using the newly developed method.
The underlying concept of this theory is...
The underlying principle of the theory is as follows.
This is a working theory which is based on the idea that...
The fundamental features of this theory are as follows.
The theory is characterized by...
The experiment, consisted of three steps, is described in...
We have carried out several experiments to test the validity of...
Recent experiments in this area have suggested that...
Examples with actual experiment demonstrate...
Special mention is given here to...

(3) 结束句 (ending sentence)

从某种意义上说,摘要就相当于一篇微观论文,其结束句的功能也类似本论中的结论,需要阐明结果、说明应用、点明意义或引发反思:

In conclusion, we state that...
In summing up it may be stated that...
Therefore, it can be concluded that...
The results of the experiment indicate that...
The studies we have performed showed that...
The investigation carried out by... has revealed that...
All our preliminary results throw light on the nature of...

This fruitful work gives explanation of…
These findings of the research have led the author to a conclusion that…
Finally, the paper reflects on the current situation pertaining to…

下面我们来看一篇完整的摘要是怎样将上述要点化零为整的：

　　This study examines cross-cultural contrastive rhetoric in argumentative writing.［主题句］To achieve this purpose, 50 Chinese students from Beijing Institute of Machinery and 30 English students from Exeter University in Great Britain are asked to write an English essay on an assigned topic. In addition, Chinese students are asked to write a Chinese essay on the same writing task.［主体句］The data suggests that L1 Chinese writings are significantly different from L1 English writing in two of selected rhetorical features, e. g. type of the discussed problem and affective appeal. Both English and Chinese students demonstrate similar strategies in terms of the orientation length and citation. Chinese students tend to display similar rhetorical strategies in both L1 and L2 writings.［结束句］

　　此外，还需注意的是，摘要一般在初稿完成后再着手撰写。因为它包含的内容较为全面，如果不对论文有一个整体把握，是难以归纳总结、取其精华的。

　　如果说摘要是整篇论文的缩影，那么关键词就是其提炼出的精华，它们直指中心论题，是论文中出现频率最高的词汇，同时也是论文论述的焦点。关键词就是文章中提到的关键的术语，是从论文的题名、提要和正文中选取出来的，是对表述论文的中心内容有实质意义的词汇。关键词是用作计算机系统标引论文内容特征的词语，便于信息系统汇集，以供读者检索。关键词大多选择名词形式，字数一般在 3—5 个字之间，首字母不必大写，位于摘要底端，如下所示：

Abstract：The paper conducts a preliminary investigation into the relationships between canonical works of translation and the literary canon in order to highlight the impact of the translation canon on the literary canon. The author argues that it is only through translation that a literary work of one country can become a classical work of another country. Through a case study of Chinese classical poems, the author shows how a literary work can gain rebirth through a translation that is rich in intertextual association. Finally, the paper reflects on the current situation pertaining to the translation for modern Chinese literary works—a situation which provides much food for thought.

Key Words：canon　translation　literature　poetry　intertextuality

　　从这篇摘要还可以看出关键词的提取离不开论文的标题，因为后者是全文主旨的高度凝缩，起着高屋建瓴的作用。本文标题是 The Translation Canon and the Literary Canon，关键词中有三个词直接取自其中，其余两个皆为摘要中隐含的重要信息。由此可见关键词、论文标题和摘要中的论题是高度统一的。

不论国内还是国外的论文，关键字的选取都是遵循一定规范的，是为了满足文献标引或检索工作的需要而从论文中选取出的词或词组。关键词包括主题词和自由词2个部分：主题词是专门为文献的标引或检索而从自然语言的主要词汇中挑选出来并加以规范了的词或词组；自由词则是未规范化的即还未收入主题词表中的词或词组。

写关键词的目的是为了便于检索。当你的论文进入文献库之后，输入论文的关键词，就能够把相关的论文检出来。

选择关键词首先要从论文题目中选择。其次从正文中选择那些出现频率最高、最具有代表性、起到核心或主体作用的专业术语。关键词排列顺序是如果大小比较明显，则按照关键词的内涵"从大到小"的规则排列。如果关键词的内涵大小不明显，或者词与词之间的大小缺乏可比性，那就按照在论文中出现的先后顺序，或者按照习惯表达的先后顺序来排列。选择反映你所写的论文特点的词和词的特征明显的用语作为关键词。关键词之间不要重复。不要把句子写成关键词。在不影响词义的前提下，关键词应该尽量精炼，选择最小化的词单位。例子参照上文的摘要。

4. 致谢

致谢词一般独立成页，放在论文主体之后或之前。目的是对自己在撰写论文期间获得的帮助表示感谢，这些帮助可以是导师辛勤的指导和批阅、家人和同事的大力支持或是原著作者对引文的授权许可。致谢的顺序一般是由主要到次要，由个人到集体，主要针对那些提供过直接帮助的个人或机构。此外致谢词要真挚、简练、恰到好处。既不要夸大其词，也不可轻描淡写。下面列举了两则致谢词的范文可供参考：

(1) The author wishes to express his most sincere appreciation to Prof. X, who read the manuscript carefully and gave valuable advice. Tremendous thanks are owed to Mr. X for helping him with the data analysis. The author is also indebted to the No. 4 Middle School for offering some samples.

(2) During the months of research which led to this paper, I have received help and guidance from Prof. X. His great patience and stimulating supervision played a vital part in the completion of this study. I owe to Mr. X for help and advice at the early stage of my research. Thanks should also be extended to Prof. X for interest and practical help, to XXX for friendly and fruitful discussions, and to XXX for careful proofreading. Without their encouragement and help, it would be impossible to carry the work through to its end.

第一篇言简意赅，点到为止。第二篇言辞恳切，翔实具体，富于变化。从中我们可以寻到一些固定的词句作为致谢词的开头格式：

The author wishes to express his/her appreciation to somebody for something/doing something.

The author is (deeply) indebted to... for...

The author's special thanks should be given to...

My gratitude also goes to...

My heartfelt thanks are also due to...

I owe to somebody for something.

I would like to acknowledge my indebtedness to…

I gratefully acknowledge the help of…

I would extend my sincere thanks to my tutor…

My work also owes much to … for his encouragement and great help.

This work was supported in part by…

The above research was made possible by a grant from…

This thesis would not have been possible without the support and assistance that I received from…

5. 论文的语言要求

一篇高质量的论文不仅取决于内容,还取决于流畅的语言表达。毕业论文属于正式文体,因此在语言上应力求正式、准确、客观、严密、简练、富有逻辑性。具体应注意以下几方面:

(1) 用词特点

正式性:避免使用缩写形式,比如 do not 而不是 don't,it is 而不是 it's。表达同一意思时,尽量使用词语而不是短语,因为后者较前者更为口语化,且不够精练,比如用 investigate 要比 look into 更为正式,而用 determine 要比 make up the mind 更为简练。使用标准的表述方式,避免使用口语、俚语,比如使用 escape 要比 go on the lam 更为正规,而 succeed 要比 make it 更为标准。

准确性:使用具体、明确的词语,避免模糊性较强的表达方式,诸如 maybe, sort of, a little bit 等词;学会使用一些限定词,避免主观和绝对化,如 typically, usually, sometimes, for the most part 等。

客观性:在正文中表述自己观点时避免使用第一人称和第二人称(致谢中除外),否则会削弱文章的客观性。最好使用名词、第三人称或无人称结构,如 This article studies/ is aimed to, it gives an analysis of, it is concluded, it can be seen that, it has been pointed out that 等。避免使用带有歧视色彩的词语,最常见的是人称性别歧视,如:As a student learns to read more critically, he usually writes more clearly, too. 可采用的修改办法有三种,其一将单数变为复数,如:As students learn to read more critically, they usually write more clearly, too. 其二将 he 变为 he or she,或者干脆重新措辞,避开人称代词:Critical reading leads to clear writing. 此外在表述职业时还要学会使用一些中性词语:

Biased	Neutral
actress	actor
chairman	chair, chairperson, coordinator, director, bead, leader, president
congressman	congressional representative, member of congress, senator
fathers (of industry)	founders, innovators, pioneers, trailblazers
housewife	homemaker, woman

续表

Biased	Neutral
man (verb)	operate, serve, staff, tend, work
man and wife	husband and wife
man-hour	operate-hour, time, work-hour
mankind	human beings, humanity, humankind
manmade	artificial, fabricated, manufactured, synthetic
manpower	crew, personnel, staff, workers, workforce
newsman	journalist, newscaster, reporter
poetess	poet
policeman	police officer
repairman	repairer
spokesman	representative, spokesperson
statesmanlike	diplomatic, tactful
stewardess	flight attendant
waitress	waiter, service person
craftsman	artisan
deliveryman	courier
foreman	supervisor, lead juror
freshman	first-year student
heroine	hero
layman	layperson
male nurse	nurse

有关更多正确使用非性别语言的具体实例,下列书目可供参考:

American Psychological Association. "Guidelines to Reduce Bias in Language." Publication Manual of the American Psychological Association. 4th ed. Washington: Amer. Psychological Assn., 1994. 46—60.

Frank, Francine Wattman, and Paula A. Treichler. *Language, Gender, and Professional Writing: Theoretical Approaches and Guidelines for Nonsexist Usage.* New York: Modern Language Association, 1989.

International Association of Business Communicators. *Without Bias: A Guidebook for Nondiscriminatory Communication.* 2nd ed. New York: Wiley, 1982.

Maggio, Rosalie. *The Dictionary of Bias-Free Usage: A Guide of Nondiscriminatory Language.* Phoenix: Oryx, 1991.

—. *The Nonsexist Word Finder: A Dictionary of Gender-Free Usage.* Phoenix: Oryx, 1987.

—. *Talking about People: A Guide to Fair and Accurate Language.* Phoenix: Oryx, 1997.

Schuwartz, Marilyn, and the Task Force of the Association of American University Presses. *Guidelines for Bias-Free Writing.* Bloomington: Indiana UP, 1995.

规范性:对于所选的英语拼写类型——美式或英式,全文要始终保持一致,最好选择一本标准的美语和英语词典，如 *The Oxford Guide to English Usage* 或 *The Columbia Guide to Standard American English*。而在一些情况下使用特殊词语时（比如专业术语、古英语、外来词或某些具有中国文化特色的词语），则不仅应保持原词的拼写形式，还要在注释里写明使用原因和含义。除此之外，还要注意单词的大小写、换行时单词的分割原则（见附录 4）、数字、标点符号、作品标题和人名的书写规范。有关这方面的详细内容可参考高等教育出版社出版的《英语论文写作规范》。

简明性：虽然毕业论文中的许多专业术语多为"大词""长词"，但这并不违背其言简意赅的特点，要做到用词恰如其分、恰到好处，需采取一系列语法、词汇手段：

① 不定式或分词短语替换。如定语从句 The research that is being carried out is very successful 就可替换为 The research being carried out...；条件状语从句 If you look carefully, you will discover... 可替换为 Looking carefully, you will discover...；两个并列单句 In our experiment, we used a number of probes. The reason for that was to eliminate the problems and errors. 就可用不定式替换成 In our experiment, we used a number of probes so as to eliminate the problems and errors.

② 前置定语替换。如 the precision of the experiment 可以改为 the experimental precision；the transmission of the data of the network 改为 the network data transmission；he thinks it is never too old to learn 用 his never-too-be-old-to-learn spirit 代替。

③ 副词替换。诸如 It is admitted/supposed/clear/obvious/would appear that/would thus seem that, There is no doubt that 的句式都可用下列副词代替：admittedly, supposedly, clearly, obviously, apparently, seemingly, undoubtedly。

④ 名词或名词短语替换。比如，主语从句 what he has investigated 就可替换为 his investigation；同位语从句 due to the fact that the direct measurement of the radial current distribution cannot be performed at present，可替换为名词短语 due to the lack of direct measurement of the radial current distribution。

⑤ 动词替换。一些名词性结构为了简明起见往往还原为动词结构。例如，By way of piping lines, the crude oil is transmitted from the well to the refinery 如用动词表述就相对简练许多：The crude oil is piped from the well to the refinery；同样，The analysis of this method will be discussed in the following parts 可直接替换为 This method will be analyzed in the following parts。

⑥ 形容词替换。一些动词结构可简略为同义的形容词结构，如 do not know—unaware of, point out faults with—critical of, give much food for thought—thought-provoking。

⑦ 介词短语替换。一些原因或条件状语从句可改写为这种形式，如 Because the weight of the rope and the sand was lost... 替换为 Without the weight of the rope and the sand, ...；If the Internet had not been invented... 替换为 But for the invention of internet...

⑧ 使用省略结构。在并列或从属结构中，相同的词或短语在后面的单句从句中可以省略，最经典的便是培根"Of Studies"中的几个句子：Some books are to be tasted, others to be swallowed, and some few to be chewed and digested；除此之外，在时间、条件

或让步状语从句中,如果主句和从句中的主语一致,从句中的主谓可以省略。

⑨ 专业术语替换。在学术论文写作中如果不熟悉本专业的一些常用术语,常会导致用词啰唆,同时也会削弱文章的说服力。比如 acquaint prospective teachers with methodology 的表述就比 acquaint prospective teachers with how to teach 更具专业水准;而 diction, syntax, textual differences 就远比 word choice, the rules of grammar, differences of (or related to) the text 简练。

⑩ 缩略语替换。前面的用词规范部分涉及了论文写作常用的缩略语,除此之外一些机构或专业缩用语也可使行文简明扼要。比如 EFL, ESL 就比 English as a foreign language, English as a second language 简练许多。

删除冗余用法,如 progressively improve, gradually decrease, completely unanimous, necessary requirement, brief summary 等表述。还有一些常用或典型的结构可参照下表:

Bulky	Concise
in spite of the fact that	although
on a regular basis	regularly
in all other cases	otherwise
bring to a consideration	consider
afford an opportunity to	allow
in conjunction with	with
after this has been done	then
the question as to whether	whether
in view of the fact that	seeing that
on account of the fact that	because
owing to the fact that	since
in view of the foregoing statement	therefore
inasmuch as	since
a number of	several
in regard to	about
in all cases	always
in order that	to
in most cases	usually
a small number of	a few
for the purpose of	for
in the vicinity of	near
in connection with	about
in the majority of instances	usually
each and every one	each
in the foreseeable future	soon
as to whether or not	whether
a great deal	much
with the exception of	except
have no other choice	must
in a hasty manner	hastily

(2) 句法特点

① 句式复杂。由于学术论文的理论性、逻辑性、严谨性较强,所以与此相适应的语言形式也应采取较为复杂的复合句、长句和平行结构等,这样才能更加完整、深刻地论述中心论点。下面这段有关 Chinese and Western Thinking on Translation 的论述就很好地运用了上述句式:

> In short, translational practice is one of the strategies a culture devises for dealing with what we have learned to call the "the Other." The development of a translational strategy therefore also provides good indications of the kind of society one is dealing with. The fact that China, for instance, developed translational strategies only three times in its history, with the translation of the Buddhist scriptures from roughly the second to the seventh century AD, with the translation of the Christian scriptures starting in the sixteenth century AD, and with the translation of much Western thought and literature starting in the nineteenth century AD, says something about the image of the Other dominant in Chinese civilization, namely, that the Other was not considered very important. Nor is China, as was sometimes erroneously believed, alone in that respect. A much more extreme example is provided by Classical Greece, which showed no interest in the Other, did not develop any thinking about translation and hardly translated anything at all.

本段基本上是由复句构成,第三个长句的主语的同位语中又包含三个"with"的并列结构,其后紧跟一个较短的倒装句式,其间又不乏插入语"for instance,""as was sometimes erroneously believed"。总之,长短结合,富于变化,充分论证了中心论点。

② 语态客观。如前所述,学术论文追求客观真实,除了在人称上多选择第三人称以产生客观距离、增强说服力外,在语态上还使用被动以减少主观色彩。例如:

> The word bilingual(ism) **is frequently used and understood** without posing any problem even in Japanese as a loan word. **The word is commonly used** as if **the concept is taken into granted**. However, the concept of bilingualism covers wide range of definitions. It seems to be problematic, as bilingualism is a topic, which amalgamates multidimensional aspects and levels of using two languages. Firstly, **bilingualism is treated** on two levels simultaneously as individual and societal bilingualism or bilingual individuals and bilingual societies. To differentiate this bilevel character, **the terminology, bilinguality, is introduced** to refer to the former and bilingualism to the latter (Hamers et al., 2000). Secondly, definitions of bilingualism range from a native-like competence in two languages to a minimal proficiency in a second language (L2)...

这段论述基本是以被动语态介绍中心论题,通过摆事实讲道理,创造出一种真实可靠的语境。当然被动语态的使用也是有一定的限度,它主要是在主语不被人所知或并不重要的前提下使用。当有明确主语时,被动语态就显得不够简洁有力,需要和主动语态交替使用,作为平衡句式的一种手段。

③ 时态分明。在论述过程中作者往往要采取多种论证方法(如引证、例证等),在分析小说或戏剧时要提供大段原文,在整理调查数据后还要盖棺定论,因此时态问题便凸现出来。时态混乱会导致论述思维不清,进而影响论述的力度和读者的理解。

总体上说,一般现在时的使用较为广泛。除了一般性的论述和分析外,在叙述文学作品中的情节或描述某一作品,作者刻画或再现的人物、事件时,还使用一般现在时便于真实再现、剖析批评:

Sons and Lovers relates a story of Paul's family life and his love fair with Miriam and Clara; more importantly, it gives an account of Paul's struggle to emancipate himself from his mother's tenacious hold on him. Since the Morels' union is founded on a sexual fascination, it turns out to be as complete fiasco after a temporary happy marriage life. Gertrude shares no intellectual, moral or religious sympathy with Morel as a result of the barrier of class and education...

另外学术论文中也经常使用一般过去时。比如在援引著作权威作为论据时:"Ronald Barthes, for example, invited us to reconsider the role and power of the author in the making of a text."

当然如果一些经典之作或大家之言对后世一直有深远影响,也可使用一般现在时:"In an important essay, Gideon Toury discusses 'pseudotranslation,' the text that claims falsely to be a translation."

除此之外,过去时还可用于汇报试验过程或结果:

In April 2002, the research was conducted. The Chinese students were asked to write argumentative essays in English and Chinese of at least 400 words/characters.

In summary, comparison of native language writings showed that some English students were skillful in using more sophisticated rational appeals to analyze...

需要指出的是时态的选择并不是绝对的和单一的。上述实验结果如可作为推而广之的结论,就需使用现在时:"This research suggests that the use of L1 helps the subjects' task rather than impedes their L2 performance."

(3) **语篇特点**

① **层次性**:这里主要指论文的组织结构,绪论、本论和结论一个都不能少;同一层次的章节内容应并行不悖,围绕一个中心论点进行延伸;而大章节对小章节又能起到统帅作用。这一点与起草提纲是一致的,关键是采用合理严谨的论证结构组织全文,具体可参照前面有关论文提纲的论点和章节结构。

② **逻辑性**:主要针对论证问题,论点、论据和论证,三者需紧密结合,高度统一。此外还要采取正确的推理模式和论证方法论述中心论点。有关此方面的详细内容,第五章第四节初稿写作中的论证部分列举了常用的论证方法和常见的逻辑错误,兹不赘叙。

③ **连贯性**:指的是句子、段落或各分论点之间过渡自然、和谐、富有逻辑性。主要存在于两个层面:宏观和微观。宏观,如前所述,指的是文章整体结构要严谨、合理。微观层面的连贯性主要指句子和段落之间的过渡衔接。这主要靠一些词汇和语法手段保持

文章的完整性、连贯性。从下面这个例子我们可以总结出一些规律性的指导原则：

The adoption of a colonial language, such as English, as the lingua franca by a multi-ethnic, multinational developing country may serve the purpose of providing an ethnically neutral language for communication. The access to English by developing countries, irrespective of whether they are former colonies or not, facilitates their economic development, particularly their participation in the world capitalist system, as Fishman (1996) points out. However, it raises the issue of (in) equality at the intra-national as well as international level.

First of all, the term "lingua franca," as Phillipson (2000) points out, is somewhat deceptive. It refers to a common language that people use to communicate with each other, and it implies that the language can be accessed by everybody. This hides the inequality between those who have access to the language and those who do not.

The asymmetrical power relationship among the official language in post colonial countries perpetuates social, economic and political inequality, and favors speakers of the colonial languages, at national, sub-national and supranational levels.

首先，这三段是一个有机统一的整体。第一段提出 topic sentence：However, it raises the issue of (in) equality at the intra-national as well as inter-national level. 后两段作为 supporting details 进一步论证"lingua franca"不平等的深层原因和表现。由此可见即便要实现文章的微观层次也就是篇章的连贯性，也要首先把握其整体性即论点、论据的统一。

其次，为了实现语篇的连贯，作者使用了一些词汇和语法手段：

a. 使用代词代替名词或名词短语：The access to English in **developing countries**, irrespective of whether **they** are former colonies or not, facilitates **their** economic development, particularly their participation in the world capitalist system, **as** Fishman (1996) points out.

b. 使用代名词代替从句或整个句子，如上句中的 as 所示。除此之外，一些代名词还可代替时间和地点状语从句，如 then, there 等。

c. 使用指示代词代替先前提到的事物：如 **the** term "lingua franca"... **This** hides the inequality between those who have access to the language and those who do not. 此外还有 that, these, those, the former, the latter 等。

d. 重复关键词，如文中的 language, lingua franca, English 等。

e. 使用近义词或短语表述相同意思，如：inequality 和 asymmetrical power, facilitate 和 favor。

f. 使用同一个词的不同形式：... it implies that the language can be **accessed** by everybody. This hides the inequality between those who have **access** to the language and those who do not.

g. 以部分代整体或整体代部分：The adoption of a **colonial** language, such as **English**, as the **lingua franca**...

h. 使用一些过渡词：

论文要讲究结构工整规范，必须讲究逻辑结构的合理性。过渡词和过渡句就像文章中的黏合剂，发挥着连接上下文的作用。合理使用这些过渡表达就会使文章连贯、流畅，防止段落的支离破碎。

举例子：such as, for example, for instance, take...for example/for instance, and so on, so on and so forth, as far as...is concerned, as for, with to...;

表强调：particularly, in fact, as a matter of fact, actually, most importantly, chiefly, especially, instead, moreover, the most important, to emphasize, undoubtedly, to be sure, certainly;

表对比或转折：however, on the other hand, whereas, nevertheless, on the contrary, in contrast, though, although;

表次序：at first, first of all, in the first place, first and foremost, in the beginning, to begin with, to start with, first of all, firstly, secondly, thirdly, fourthly, next, last, finally, after, following, as will be seen, in what follows;

表并列：and, as well as;

表对照：in comparison, in contrast, in relation to, likewise, similarly, correspondingly;

表递进：besides, furthermore, in addition, also, further, additionally;

表因果：as a result, consequently, therefore, accordingly, thus, for this reason, in effect, due to, hence, so, obviously, it can be seen clearly;

表推理：otherwise, if not, in that case;

表让步：although, now that, since, considering, still, whereas;

表目的：for this purpose, to this end, in order to, with this goal, in view of this;

表解释：in other words, rather, that is, namely, to put it more, specifically, accurately;

表时间：eventually, in the end, since, so far;

表总结：in all, in short, in brief, in conclusion, to sum up, in summary, in the final analysis, to put it in a nutshell, finally。

i. 保持时态、人称的一致性。这三段使用的都是一般现在时和第三人称，直接明了，客观实际，现实性、说理性较强。恰恰体现了学术论文科学严谨的文风。

当然实现篇章连贯的手段并不仅局限于词汇层次，一些句式的合理运用也会收到同样的效果。比如排比句式就可使行文简明流畅、主旨突出，正如前面谈到的一个例子：

The fact that China, for instance, developed translational strategies only three times in its history, with the translation of the Buddhist scriptures from roughly the second to the seventh century AD, with the translation of the Christian scriptures starting in the sixteenth century AD, and with the translation of much Western thought and literature starting in the nineteenth century AD, says something about the image of the Other dominant in Chinese civilization, namely, that the

Other was not considered very important.

整段话虽仅为一个长句,但并未使人感到拖沓费解,原因就在于排比句式的语用反而增强了文章的层次性和连贯性。总之,要使文章如行云流水般自如,关键是要把握微观、宏观的各种写作技巧,内容、形式并重,方可写出鞭辟入里的佳作。

第五节 如何修改论文定稿

论文写成后,作者需要从总体上进行全方位、多层次的复审、检查和修改,以保证全文论点明确,结构严谨,行文流畅。所以论文的修改是论文写作过程中必不可少的一个环节。

1. 论文修改的内容

论文修改可以从宏观和微观两方面展开。宏观包括内容和结构,微观包括语言和格式。下面逐一对此进行论述。

(1) 宏观修改

论文内容的修改主要涉及:其一检查中心论点和分论点;其二检查论证所用材料;其三检查论证方法。

论文的中心论点是论文的灵魂。修改论文时首先要注意中心论点是否明确,另外要看各个分论点对中心论点的论述是否恰当。如果分论点是从各个侧面来说明中心论点的,就要检查分论点涉及的内容是否全面,是否紧扣主题;如果分论点是逐层深入地来阐述中心论点,就要检查各个分论点是否按照由浅入深,由表及里的逻辑顺序逐层剖析。这种论述方式最忌讳的是论述不深入,修改时要尤为注意。其次还要对自己提出的论点多问几个为什么,是否能站住脚,有没有可能被别人加以驳斥,自己除了搜集论证资料外,也需反复审视论点,采用反面例子加以质询,以确保论点的客观准确和说服力。

论据作为论点强有力的支撑,同样要经得起反复推敲。修改时作者需对材料进一步筛选、过滤。如果论据显得单薄无力,就要补充新的材料;如果论据在论证论点时显得牵强,要毫不犹豫地删掉,及时更换新的材料;如果论据显得啰唆、累赘,就要精简。总之,要掌握一个原则:论据要始终围绕论点,不偏不倚,准确适度,把握质和量。

撰写论文所用的论证方法在修改过程中也要重新审视。对于不同的论题,不同的作者会选用不同的论证方法。无论哪种论证方法一定要做到合乎逻辑,有理有据,水到渠成。要避免由于论证不足而产生的论点、论据"两张皮"现象。

论文结构指论文的整体框架或组成部分,本章第四节已有所论述。修改论文时,要注意论文结构是否和谐,层次是否分明,条理是否清晰,开头、中间和结尾是否各司其职,分工明确又和谐统一。各章节、段落之间过渡是否自然、逻辑性强,是否有重复或自相矛盾之处。这些都是修改论文结构时要注意的问题。

(2) 微观修改

这一方面的修改主要针对语言和格式。论文的语言修改需注意选词、语气和语调、语态、时态、句法和篇章等方面。具体可参照本章对论文语言特点的论述。至于格式的修改,则应注意字母大小写、斜体、缩写、标点符号、数字或序列号等问题;尤其还要注意检查引文和注释的格式和正确性。对引文的出处、参考书目的作者、出版地、出版社、出版时间都要进一步地核对,确保不出差错。这里需要提及一点的是如文章中的直接引文过多,应考虑在修改过程中将其化为自己的语言,否则难逃抄袭之嫌。有关微观修改常用的修改符号可参照附录4。

2. 论文修改的方法

修改论文的方法很多,主要可以归纳为以下几点:

(1) 立足中心,着眼全局

论文要经过好几遍修改才能趋于完善。但是最初对论文的修改一定要立足中心,着眼全局。论点是否明确,前后是否矛盾;论据是否确切;全篇布局是否合理,段落之间的衔接、过渡是否自然;论文是否是一个无懈可击的整体等等。这些问题一定要在最初的修改过程中完成,只有这样才能为论文下一步更为精细的修改打好基础。

(2) 边写边改,趁热打铁

有人称这种方法叫"热处理"。"热处理"适合对局部论文的修改。比如:写成一部分论文后,在思路还没有中断的情况下,马上从头至尾再看一下刚写的段落,是否把要说的内容全包括进去,对论点的阐述是否明确,论据是否充分有力,论证是否恰当。这种修改方法的好处是可以把那些稍纵即逝的灵感发挥得淋漓尽致,使论文新颖别致。

(3) 冷静处理,稍安毋躁

这种方法也叫"冷处理"。"冷处理"适合对论文的总体修改。论文写完后,可以先放一放,搁置一段时间后再拿出来修改。这样,经过一段时间的调整,从论文中走出来,让自己的思路摆脱原来的思维模式,远距离地看一看,便于从总体上把握论文的整体框架。

(4) 求教良师,求助益友

论文在自己修改了几遍后,应该拿给同专业的同学或朋友看一看。有时由于自己知识层次、认识水平和思考角度的限制,对自己论文的某些毛病很难发现,而让别人来看一下,可能会从另一个角度发现论文的不足和缺陷,这样再改一遍,会有意想不到的效果。当然这些改动之后,最好自己再大声朗读一遍,确保万无一失。这些工作做完后,再拿给导师作进一步的定夺。作者要根据导师的建议做最后的修改。这样经过层层过滤,论文会最大限度地体现作者的整体水平和素质,变得更加"纯美"。

(5) 使用电脑,事半功倍

电脑的普及大大提高了我们的学习和工作效率。对于论文的修改,它的作用尤为突出。Word文档中的单词纠错、查找和替换,段落的复制和粘贴,Thesaurus找寻近义词和反义词等功能极大地方便了论文的修改润色。作为即将毕业的大学生,掌握这些基本技巧也是为将来的工作及研究打下必备基础,因而是不可忽视的。但与此同时我们应当看到,电脑毕竟不等同于人脑,它不能进行更为深入的思考。所以有些问题单纯地依靠电脑也是不可行的,比如特定语境下的选词,如果不假思索,一味盲信其自动纠错功能,则根本无法做到准确贴切;再如对文章整体结构的把握,电脑固然可以帮助我们有效地修改某一段落或语句,但由此而涉及的过渡问题和前后语序问题,电脑"却无动于衷",由于屏幕只能容纳短短几十行,我们也不容易发现某个语句或段落牵涉的整体结构问题。遇到这种情况,最好将论文打印出来,在纸上再做修改,方可做到纵观全局,成竹在胸。当然所修改的草稿最好保存下来,留作备用。

第六章 毕业论文的答辩

毕业论文答辩(oral defense)是答辩委员会成员(以下简称答辩老师)和撰写毕业论文的学员面对面的,由答辩老师就论文提出有关问题,让学生当面回答。它有"问"有"答",还可以有"辩"。

毕业论文答辩是审查毕业论文(作业)的一种补充形式。一般来讲,本科以上(含本科)毕业生都要参加答辩。其毕业设计的成绩,是由文章成绩和答辩成绩组成,最后由评审小组、评审委员会鉴别评定。

答辩小组一般由三至五名教师、有关专家组成,对文章中不清楚、不详细、不完备、不恰当之处,在答辩会上提出来。一般来说,教师、专家所提出的问题,仅涉及该文的学术范围或文章所阐述问题之内,而不是对整个学科的全面知识的考试和考查。毕业论文答辩的主要目的,是审查文章的真伪、审查写作者知识掌握的深度,审查文章是否符合体裁格式,以求进一步提高。学生通过答辩,让教师、专家进一步了解文章立论的依据及其处理课题的实际能力。

因此,毕业论文答辩是高等院校审查毕业论文质量、考察毕业生理论知识水平、运用知识能力的一项重要工作,同时也是检验教学效果的一种有效方式。论文答辩关系到毕业论文成绩的优劣,还决定能否授予学位。因此每个毕业生都要积极认真地做好答辩的准备工作。

第一节 论文答辩的准备

学生在做答辩的大体准备工作时可以从下列几个方面着手:

1. 选择这个题目的原因,研究、写作它有什么学术价值或现实意义。
2. 这个课题的历史和现状,即前人做过哪些研究,取得哪些成果,有哪些问题没有解决,自己有什么新的看法,提出并解决了哪些问题。
3. 文章的基本观点和立论的基本依据。
4. 学术界和社会上对与本论文题目有关的某些问题的具体争论,自己的倾向性观点。
5. 重要引文的具体出处。
6. 本应涉及或解决但因力不从心而未接触的问题;因认为与本文中心关系不大而未写入的新见解。
7. 定稿交出后,自己重读审查新发现的需要改进之处。

具体的准备工作如下:

1. 答辩的心理准备

论文答辩要求毕业生就自己的论文内容现场回答答辩委员会提出的问题。这种形式要求学生既要对自己的论文有全面深刻的了解,具备一定的分析、解决学术问题的能力,还要求学生有较强的应变能力。就英语专业的学生而言,答辩还是考察论文作者英语口语表达能力的一个途径。基于以上几点,答辩者应从心理上做好充分的准备,防止两种极端偏激的思想。

(1) 对答辩产生恐惧心理,唯恐自己回答不出老师的问题,或根本理解不了老师所提问题,从而影响自己水平的正常发挥。其实,答辩委员会的老师只是对与论文相关的问题进行提问,不会为难答辩者。既然论文是自己一年心血的结晶,内容熟悉,观点清楚,根本无需给自己增加过多的压力。重要的是,答辩者一定要自信。信心就像能力催化剂,会将人的一切潜能都调动起来,将人体各部分的功能推动到最佳状态。

(2) 另一种偏激的思想是有些答辩者认为论文写成就万事大吉,答辩只不过是走形式,思想上麻痹大意,根本不放在心上。在这种心态的影响下,是根本做不好答辩的,有时甚至会影响学位的获得。其实,答辩是答辩者和答辩老师之间进行的一次学术交流,学生应该把答辩看成是对自己多年学习的一次全面综合的检验,是对自己论文的一次全方位透视,只有经过答辩这一环节,答辩者的水平才能在这种直观互动的环境下得到进一步的提高。

2. 答辩的内容准备

(1) 自述报告的作用

在答辩老师提问前,答辩者首先要对自己的论文进行一个 10—20 分钟的简短介绍。自述报告虽短,却能说明整个论文的结构、内容和论点,可以在答辩时做到语言简洁,思维清晰,给答辩老师留下一个好的印象。需要注意的是,既然是自述报告,就需在答辩前将论文"消化"为自己的思想。能够做到成竹在胸,即使不看文本,也可将大体框架和重点内容很自然地"讲述"出来。只有如此才可避免由死记硬背带来的拘谨和僵硬感。最好的效果是不背,不读,只是口头说。

(2) 自述报告的撰写

注释法 这种方法需要列出答辩过程中每一部分的小标题、主题句和时间限制,以一篇题为 China English and Chinese English 的论文为例:

Content:China English and Chinese English(15 min.)

Greetings and Thanks(30 sec.): Good morning, ladies and gentlemen. First, I would extend my sincere thanks to my tutor... who gave me great help in the completion of this study. The title of my thesis is China English and Chinese English.

Background of This Study(1 min. 30 sec.)—Introduction: Three stages of English in China: (1) Chinese Pidgin English (CPE), (2) Chinese English, (3) China English.

Idea Formulation/Main Argumentation(8 min.)—Chapter 1 begins with an introduction to the definition and classification of China English; **Chapter 2** focuses on the definition and characteristics of China English; in **Chapter 3** the author points out the significances of distinguishing China English and Chinese English.

Conclusion/Summary(2 min. 30 sec.): —The aim of our learning English is not only to learn the culture of its native speakers, but also to communicate our own culture within the world.

Questions and Answers(5 min.)

多媒体辅助法 除了以书面文字为主的报告方式外,多媒体手段的应用也使得传统的口头答辩方式更为有效便捷,尤其当论文里包含大量图片图表时,使用视听辅助手段更是事半功倍。因此在拟写自述报告或答辩过程中就会经常用到或听到下列表述用语:

What I'm going to talk about today can be summed up into the following three points. First of all, let's see the No. 1 slide. Slide please. —**using lantern slides**

It would be very interesting to take a look at the basic characteristics, which are shown in this transparency. —**using an overhead projector**

Now the results of our investigation are listed in this table. We can see from the table that these results are very similar to those obtained by Professor Smith. —**using tables**

在制作多媒体报告课件时还要考虑下列问题:

a. 文字部分清晰准确。一些要点可以采取对比度鲜明的色彩加以反衬,如红白对比,黑黄对比;拼写正确,字号适中,一方面便于听众理解,另一方面展示语言应用能力。

b. 表格图形等表述形式简洁清楚。为吸引听众注意力,这一部分也需使用对比鲜明的背景设置;线条的比例大小要适中,一些抽象概念或公式如有必要可适当添加文字提示。

c. 多媒体演示和口头表述有机结合。报告课件的完成并不一定能保证答辩的成功。因为在答辩过程中往往会出现人机冲突——口头阐述和演示步骤难以协调一致。这时就需预先设想报告效果,要么在演示之前解释论点,要么在演示之后归纳总结。总之,要保证多媒体对论证思路的"辅助"作用,而非将其取代。

d. 重点内容打印分发。所谓重点内容是指学术价值含量较高的分析或调查结果。由于演示时间有限,听众不可能在短时间内把握全部有关内容。因此如果答辩者想让感兴趣的听众对此有更深入的了解或进行保存,可以事先打印若干份分发下去,以保证后续陈述的顺利进行。

(3) 自述报告的"消化"

如前所述,自述报告的撰写只是提供一个可供操作的纲领,下一步更重要的任务是对报告或论文中所要涉及的细节内容进行全面认真的准备,也就是消化吸收。由于答辩委员会是由多名教师组成,他们会从不同角度、不同侧面、不同层次地提问,如:

a. 选题的起因、动机和目的。答辩者要对论文这些内容的前因后果清清楚楚。

b. 论文的中心论点和分论点的内容以及相互之间的关系。论点是一篇论文的灵魂,也是答辩老师重点提问的内容之一。他们会从论点入手来检查作者对问题的认识深度。比如有的同学的论文题目是 The Modernist Tendency in *Sons and Lovers*,答辩委员会的老师可能会提出下列问题:What is the modernist tendency? How is it reflected in theme and structure in this novel? 事实上这就需要作者从中心论点和如何证明论点的角度去回答问题。

c. 论据的使用。论据是支持论点的根本保障。论据的来源及其在本论文中的作用是答辩中会遇到的问题。比如一位同学写了一篇有关文学翻译的文章,主要论述忠实对等原则在红楼梦诗词翻译中的体现,答辩委员会成员可能就会对其所举出的诗歌翻译出处提出这样的问题:Who once translated the poems in *The Dream in Red Mansions* besides D. Hawkes and Yang Hsien-yi ? Whose version do you think is better, D. Hawkes' or Yang Hsien-yi's? 在回答时,作者就需要考虑谁的译本作为论据更能体现出忠实对等原则这一中心论点。

d. 论证方法。论文中所用论证方法在答辩前要进行一次总结分析,务必使其严谨规范,合乎逻辑。答辩老师就其提出问题时能够做到有理有据,自圆其说,最忌讳自相矛盾。具体注意事项可参照第五章对论证方法的论述。

e. 论文的学术价值和现实意义。一篇论文只有具有学术价值或现实意义才值得去研究。论文作者对前人观点的继承以及对相关学科的发展是答辩老师重视和感兴趣的内容,所以答辩者要作出较为详细的准备。比如一篇名为 Relevance Theory and Translation 的论文,将认知语用学中的关联理论用于翻译研究。答辩老师自然会对其中涉及的关联理论的内容、这个理论与翻译的关系及对翻译的指导作用发问。在准备过程中这些"亮点"就需要答辩者下些工夫。

3. 答辩的细节准备

(1) 答辩前首先要对答辩场所有所了解,可以提前去看一下,以免答辩时因地点不熟产生紧张心理。

(2) 答辩时的穿着要大方得体,不要奇装异服,女生要避免浓妆艳抹。

(3) 答辩时要注意调整自己的心态,避免过于紧张,要做到不亢不卑,沉着自信。

(4) 答辩时要带上底稿及答辩提纲。在答辩前再浏览一下答辩提纲,做到心中有数。

(5) 答辩时要带上纸和笔,以便就答辩老师的提问进行记录,更好地进行答辩。

(6) 答辩的开头、结尾注意礼貌问题。对答辩老师的提问、意见和听众的注意表示感谢。

(7) 答辩时如听不清或听不懂答辩老师的提问,不要含糊做答,可礼貌地请老师再说一遍,然后再回答。

(8) 答辩时答辩老师会对某个论点或问题提出异议,此时,不要过于紧张,马上否定自己;也不要过于固执,咄咄逼人。应该采取的态度是有理有据地阐述自己的观点,能够自圆其说,还要让答辩老师信服。

(9) 答辩时对那些较复杂、自己一时回答不清的问题,可请求老师给出短暂的思考时间,然后再有条不紊,逐步深入地作答。

4. 答辩的技巧问题

(1) 答辩时要注意语音语调,尽量做到准确无误,平稳一致;语速要适中,过快过慢都不可取,一般以每分钟 100—120 个词为宜;音量也要掌握好,不可过高或过低;此外重读、停顿和一些肢体语言都要予以考虑,以避免陈述的单调性。这些都需要答辩者从听众的面部表情得到反馈,及时予以调整。

(2) 答辩时所用语言要简洁明了,直奔主题。不要用过于生涩难懂的语言,以显示自己的学问。一些不适合口头表述的专业术语在不被误解的情况下可以用代词或缩写代替。也不要用过于随便的语言,和答辩这种庄重的场合格格不入;必要时可以使用一些幽默的话语,调节紧张气氛,但不要离题万里,毫不相关。下面两则开场白轻松幽默地引入正题,十分巧妙:

Mr. Chairman, ladies and gentlemen,

Good afternoon. Today I'd like to talk about the MIS in China. But don't be mistaken—the "MIS in China" is not a young lady in China. MIS is a short form for Management Information System. It is an integral user-machine system for providing information to support operations, management, and decision-making functions in an organization.

Good afternoon, everyone,

There is a Chinese saying "with a hare under one's garment" to describe the uneasiness for a nervous person. That is how I am feeling at such a moment; and in front of such a big audience, there seems to be a hare under my garment.

Well now, speaking about "nervous," I would like to show you the result of my experiment on the nervous system of a rabbit...

（3）学会使用模糊语言。我们在前面提到论文的书面语言需经过字字推敲，准确无误。但在答辩过程中，时间的紧迫性和临场反应的瞬时性又要求答辩者适时使用模糊语言如：something like, a sort of, it's a kind of thing to, nearly, over, about 以避免绝对化和主观化。一些精确的数字统计一时难以记起，是情理之中的事，只要口头表述与文字部分出入不大，是完全允许的。

（4）答辩过程中出现一些口误现象实属正常，关键是采取一些补救措施将之化解，如下面几个例子：

I am afraid that is cutting a bit of fine—I was saying, there's not enough time left for preparing for the test. (for a moderate tone)

I'd like to talk this over with you later—well, to be more exact, 7:30 tomorrow evening. (for more specific time)

What I have seen is very impressive. Of course, the experimental techniques cannot be called advanced yet—I mean, in regard to the automation and its management. (for minimization of negation)

In the experiment I discovered a new way, or rather, I used a new method to observe the movement. (for honest statement)

（5）在答辩过程中需用到多媒体手段时，为保证口头陈述的连续性，往往需要答辩者使用一些填充话语，如 well, now, let's have a look..., Er—, here you see..., you know...，当然如果前后内容时间间隔很长，还可以采取重复强调主要内容的办法：

(While handling the transparencies)

What I said just now was about the close relationship between language and culture. As to the aim of foreign language teaching, it can be divided into 3 levels, just as the following picture shows.

（6）在回答老师提问时对不同问题要采取不同的回答技巧。如果是没有听清楚问题，

可以直接要求重复:Pardon? / Sorry, I didn't catch what you've said. Would you mind repeating your question? / What was the last sentence, please? 如果是只听懂大意,还想进一步使问题明确化,可以委婉地提出:Sorry, I'm not quite sure of your question, could I understand your question like this... / To the best of my knowledge, you were asking me about..., am I right? / It seems to me that what I have been asked perhaps means..., was that your question? 如果已理解问题,但对自己的答案不甚肯定,在回答时要留有余地:I wonder if I could answer your question like this... / Personally, I suppose it's very likely to... / Perhaps I could give you more examples concerning this. 如果对一些问题无从下手回答,要么采取直接回避的方法:Sorry, I am afraid I know very little about it. I am all ears to your suggestions; 要么采取迂回战术反复强调已陈述过的内容,以此获得时间重新整理思路;或者采用模糊词语,对一些难以精确表述的概念"一带而过";如果所提问题有些纰漏,或和论文意见不同,可以委婉说明理由:I should have thought you misunderstood some of what I said in my talk just now. / I agree with much of what you said, but for the last point, I would say it would be better if you could look at the problem from another side. / I think you have raised a very good question. But, I have to point out that... / Personally speaking, I think what you have said also sounds reasonable. However,...

第二节　论文答辩的一般程序

论文答辩要在答辩委员会主席或答辩小组组长的主持下,按照一定的程序进行。
答辩会的大体程序为:
1. 学生作说明性汇报。(5—10分钟)
2. 论文答辩小组提问。
3. 学生答辩。(一定要正面回答或辩解,一般允许准备10—20分钟)。
4. 评定成绩。(答辩会后答辩小组商定,交系、院学位委员会审定小组审定)

1. 预备工作

正式答辩前有一些预备工作要做。首先,答辩委员会主席或答辩小组组长在答辩前要向参加答辩的学生简要介绍一下委员会成员及答辩顺序,然后确定学生的答辩顺序。

2. 答辩者进行自述报告

自述报告是答辩学生就自己的论文进行的10—15分钟的阐述。自述报告要包括论文的主要观点、论据使用、论证方法;对前人观点的发展、总结及其学术价值。自述报告要做到思路清晰,简明扼要。

3. 正式答辩

论文作者做好自述报告后,答辩老师会就相关问题提问,要求学生现场一一作出论述。答辩学生要认真谨慎地回答老师的提问。

4. 综合评定,公布成绩

答辩进行完后,答辩委员会或答辩小组要就学生的答辩情况进行最后的综合评定,给出成绩或等级,最后由答辩委员会主席或答辩小组组长予以公布。

总之,论文答辩的目的简单说是为了进一步审查论文的格式和内容,即进一步考查和验证毕业论文作者对所著论文论述到的论题的认识程度和当场论证论题的能力;进一步考察毕业论文作者对专业知识掌握的深度和广度;审查毕业论文是否学员自己独立完成等情况。

在答辩会上,答辩小组成员将论文中阐述不清楚、不详细、不完备、不确切、不完善之处提出来,让作者当场作出回答,从而就可以检查出作者对所论述的问题是否有深广的知识基础、创造性见解和充分扎实的理由。

对于答辩者来说,答辩的目的是通过,按时毕业,取得毕业证书。学员要顺利通过毕业论文答辩,就必须了解上述学校组织毕业论文答辩的目的,然后有针对性地做好准备,继续对论文中的有关问题作进一步的推敲和研究,把论文中提到的基本材料搞准确,把有关的基本理论和文章的基本观点彻底弄懂弄通。

毕业论文答辩虽然以回答问题为主,但答辩,除了"答"以外,也会有"辩"。因此,论文答辩并不等于宣读论文,而是要抓住自己论文的要点予以概括性的、简明扼要的、生动的说明,对答辩小组成员的提问做出全面正确地回答,当自己的观点与主答辩老师观点相左时,既要尊重答辩老师,又要让答辩老师接受自己的观点,就得学会运用各类辩论的技巧。如果在论文答辩中学习运用辩论技巧获得成功,就会提高自己参与各类辩论的自信心,就会把它运用到寻找职业或工作的实践中去,并取得成功。

第七章　毕业论文实例

前六章有关论文写作的理论概述及各部分写作实例提高了我们对毕业论文写作的理性认识,但如何将学到的知识综合运用到一篇论文中去,还需要我们通过具体实例进行全面认识。下面选登了语言学、文学、教法、翻译和商务英语方向的几篇毕业论文,仅供参考。这些论文虽然在学术性和创新性等方面还有待提高,但是从内容、格式、语言、论点以及论证方法等方面基本符合英语专业本科毕业论文的设计要求。

第一节　语 言 学 类

××大学

本科生毕业论文(设计)册

题目:英语中问候语的研究

学院＿＿＿＿＿＿
专业＿＿＿＿＿＿
班级＿＿＿＿＿＿
学生＿＿＿＿＿＿
指导教师＿＿＿＿＿＿
完成日期＿＿＿＿＿＿

A Study of English Greetings

By
×××
Prof. ×××, Tutor

A Thesis Submitted to the Foreign Languages

Institutes in Partial Fulfillment of the Requirements

For the Degree of Bachelor of Arts at

×× University

May 2014

Abstract

Greeting is an indispensable part in people's daily life. When people meet, encountered or contacted by phone or letters, they will first greet each other, which are basic human courtesy, and people all around the world have the common etiquette habit. But with the globalization of the economy, people's range of communication has increased significantly. Now not only people need to talk to their locals, but also talk to many foreigners who come from countries all over the world. It is obvious that how to greet correctly is a very important question. Greeting have the function of establishing, maintaining and adjusting varies of relationships. Meantime it guides language to further communication between people. Sometimes greeting can reflect the identity, status and closeness of the relationship between people. Therefore the proper greeting is very important for people in their daily life. However, due to the difference of cultural background between countries, people's habits and customs are different, thus people's greeting is different in content, manner and words, so in cross-cultural communication, people often make varies of mistakes.

Due to scholars' research of greetings, people gradually know more about it. The research reduces many unnecessary mistakes that people make in cross-cultural communication. But it's not enough, and it should get more attention in order to promote the cross-cultural interpersonal communication between countries. So this thesis aims to explore the daily greetings in English-speaking countries based on an English film. This thesis is divided into five parts: The first part roughly describes the purpose, significance of the study and the organization of the thesis; the second part does a detailed review and summary about the research done on greetings abroad and in China; the third part describes the categories of greetings and the functions of greetings based on an English movie, providing a detailed introduction about the use of greetings in people's daily life in English-speaking countries; the fourth part discusses the reasons that affect the use of greetings in English countries; the fifth part draws a conclusion and points out the limitation of this research.

Key words: greeting   intercultural communication   cultural differences   politeness principle

摘 要

  问候语是人们日常社会生活中不可或缺的一部分,人们见面、偶遇或者通过电话、书信联系的时候,首先都会互相问候一下,这属于人类基本的礼貌问题,而且是全世界人民所共有的礼仪习惯。但是随着经济的全球化,人们的交流范围越来越广。现在人们不仅仅需要跟本国人、本地人打交道,而且还经常会跟各种各样的外国人交流。这个时候怎样正确地问候就显得非常重要了。问候语具有建立、维持和调节各种人际关系的作用,同时它也是打开人与人之间进一步交流的先导语。有时候问候语还可以体现出交际双方的身份、地位以及二者之间的亲疏关系等。因此合适的问候语对于人们的生活非常重要。但是由于国与国之间的文化背景、人们的生活习惯、习俗各不相同,人们问候的内容、方式和言辞也不尽相同,因此在跨文化交际中人们经常会发生各种各样的交际失误。

  这些年来也有许多国家的不少学者对此进行过各种各样的研究,人们也从中多多少少了解了一些,从而在跨文化交际中也减少了许多不必要的失误。但是这些还不够,它应当得到更多的重视,以此才能进一步促进各国之间人与人的跨文化交际。因此才有这个以一部英文的电影为基础,对英语国家的日常问候语进行的研究,希望本研究能够为跨文化交际起到积极的作用,也能够在人们日常生活中的跨文化交流中起到一点帮助作用。

  本篇论文分为五部分:第一部分介绍了本研究的目的、意义和论文的组织;第二部分对国内外对问候语方面所做的各项研究进行了详细的回顾与总结;第三部分在一部英文电影的基础上对问候语的分类和功能作用进行了大概的阐述,同时指出了英语国家中人们日常问候语的习惯和方式等;第四部分讲述了影响英语国家这种问候方式的原因;第五部分对全文进行了总结并得出最后的结论,同时指出本论文研究的局限性。

关键词: 问候语 跨文化交际 文化差异 礼貌原则

Contents

Abstract ··
Abstract in Chinese ··
1 Introduction ··
　1.1　Purpose of the Study ··
　1.2　Significance of the Study ··
　1.3　Organization of the Thesis ··
2 Literature Review ··
　2.1　Literature Abroad ··
　　2.1.1　Leech's Politeness Principles ··
　　2.1.2　Brown and Levinson's Face Theory ··································
　2.2　Literature in China ··
3 The Categories and the Functions of Greetings ··
　3.1　The Categories of Greeting ···
　　3.1.1　Greetings According to Time ··
　　3.1.2　Greetings According to Formality ·····································
　　3.1.3　Greetings According to Politeness Strategies ······················
　　3.1.4　Greetings According to Social Settings ······························
　　3.1.5　Greetings According to Content ··
　　3.1.6　Greetings According to Language Origin ···························
　3.2　The Functions of Greetings ···
　　3.2.1　Greetings as Illocutionary Acts ···
　　3.2.2　Greetings as Access Rituals to Further Communicative
　　　　　 Interaction ···
　　3.2.3　Greetings as Interpersonal Functions ·································
4 Main Factors Causing the Use of Greeting in English Countries ··················
　4.1　Social Factors ··
　4.2　Cultural Factors ··
5 Conclusion ···
　5.1　Summary of the Study ··
　5.2　Limitation of the Study ··
Bibliography ···

1. Introduction

1.1 Purpose of the Study

The purpose of this thesis is to find out the features of English greetings through the study of conversation to reflect the importance of greetings in order to help people to know more about differences between American and Chinese greetings, to state the function of greetings in cross-cultural communications, so as to reduce the number of mistakes in daily cross-cultural communication as well as avoid unnecessary misunderstandings.

Greeting is an important part in people's daily life. When people meet, encountered or contacted by phone or letters, they will first greet each other. It is a basic human courtesy, and people all around the world have the common etiquette habit. But with the globalization of the economy, people's range of communication has increased significantly, now people not only need to talk to their own people, but also talk to many foreigners who come from different countries all over the world. So now it is obvious that greeting is very important for people in everyday life. How do people greet correctly? Greeting has the function of establishing, maintaining and adjusting varies of relationships. Meantime it guides language to further communication between people. Sometimes greeting can also reflect the identity, status and closeness of the relationship between the two speakers. Therefore the proper greeting is very important in people's daily life. However, due to the difference of cultural background between countries, people's habits and customs are different, so people's greeting is different in content, manner and words. Thus people often make varies of mistakes in cross-cultural communication.

Over the years, there are many scholars in many countries who conducted a series of studies in greetings, and people gradually know more things about greeting. By studying English greetings, it reduces many unnecessary mistakes that people make in cross-cultural communication. But that's not enough, and it should get more attention, in order to further promote the cross-cultural communication between countries. So there is the study about the daily greetings in English-speaking countries based on an English film, hoping the research can have a positive function in the cross-cultural communication, and do more help in the cross-cultural communication of everyday life.

1.2 Significance of the Study

Greetings are words that used to open communications in everyday life or inform someone that you know their presence. As an everyday behavior, greetings are routine and happen at very low levels of awareness in interactions, which is seemingly an awareness reaction to people. It is a so quick, simple, and routine part of communication that people usually have not thought that what happens during those few seconds. Being a part of culture and people's life, greeting plays a very important part in helping people to reduce the mistakes in cross-cultural communication.

Therefore, the academic study of greetings is no doubt of any hesitation. First, theoretical studies of greeting can help people to better understand a culture and society so that do more help in people's cross-cultural communication. And as a minor part of interaction, greeting has an important function on the establishment, maintenance and management of human relationships. People can establish, maintain, and strengthen their friendship through it, while greetings also can show the rituals of speakers and their social status, or if they are aware of each other, and the roles they play in the communication and so on. Thus a study of greetings is very necessary.

Meanwhile, the study of greetings also can help to develop a situational approach towards the study of culture in the background of globalization. Generally speaking, greeting is a reutilized situational frame transmitted in a given social cultural community. Like many other situational frames such as parting, complementing, apologizing, wedding etc. A systematic description of greeting, which takes the socio-cultural factors into account, will do more help in the understanding of the structure of a certain society and culture.

With the quicken development of globalization, chances are inevitably arising that cultural clashes happen between people with different cultural backgrounds. So we are facing to do an urgent task to avoid or overcome the cultural clashes in cross-cultural communications. Since greetings occur among people all over the world, it is an excellent part of social behavior to study. So people should do more systematic contrastive study of greeting in cross-cultural communications and find a better way to change the scene. A better understanding of cultural differences will do people more help in daily greetings and help people to maintain and improve the relationship in cross-cultural communications.

1.3 Organization of the Thesis

The thesis is divided into five parts. Chapter One is the general introduction, including the purpose, the significance of the study, and the organization of the thesis. Chapter Two, which deals with the theories related to greetings in China and abroad, such as Leech's Politeness Principles, Brown and Levinson's Face Theory in English culture, and Gu's Politeness studies in Chinese culture. It indicates that people's behaviors in different cultures are governed by different communication rules. Chapter Three has a detailed description of the categories of greetings and the functions of greetings on the basis of an English movie, and introduce the use of greetings in people's daily life in English countries. Chapter Four describes the reasons affecting the use of greetings. Chapter Five is the conclusion of the thesis, a summary of major findings and limitation of the study being presented.

2. Literature Review

Nowadays greeting is very important for everyone in social life. So there are many linguists and sociologists did verities of researches in greeting. Following are several important views in the branch of linguistic.

2.1　Foreign Studies

2.1.1　Leech's Politeness Principles

Politeness is very important for everyone in everyday life, especially on some formal occasions. Greetings also can show if one person is polite in people's daily communication. Brown and Levinson put forward the Politeness Principle (PP) from rhetorical and stylistic viewpoints, which are later specified as six maxims by G Leech (1983:16):

① Tact maxim: minimize cost to other; maximize benefit to other.

② Generosity maxim: minimize benefit to self; maximize cost to self.

③ Approbation maxim: minimize dispraise of other; maximize praise of other.

④ Modesty maxim: minimize praise of self; maximize dispraise of self.

⑤ Agreement maxim: minimize disagreement between self and other; maximize agreement between self and other.

⑥ Sympathy maxim: minimize antipathy between self and other; maximize sympathy between self and other.

In fact, the maxims are different in their emphasis on different sides. For example, in fact, act maxim and generosity maxim express the same meaning, but from different point of view. The former emphasizes how to treat the other, while the latter emphasizes how to treat self. According to the two maxims, the difference in politeness degree is easily seen from the following two examples: A is much more polite than B.

A: Excuse me, would you please show me the way to hospital?

B: Tell me the way to hospital.

Similarly, approbation maxim and modesty maxim both are concerning with the different sides of the same question. However the former defines how to treat the other and the latter defines how to treat one self. The example following shows:

　　　　A: John, this is Jack, my baseball partner.

[greeting]B: Hello, Jack.

　　　　C: Hello, John.

[phatic communication] B: Michael tells me you're a very good baseball player.

　　　　C: Believe me, I'm not that good.

Agreement maxim demands the opinions that opposite to the other should not be expressed directly. Or it is impolite. This explains why people often say something praising the other's words in Greetings. For example:

A: You look so beautiful!

B: Oh, yes? Thank you. You are very handsome, too.

As for the last maxim in Politeness Principle, the point is to express the same feeling, with the other. Let's see an example:

A: How's your father now? He wasn't very well, was he?

B: Well, actually, he has gone to the hospital.

A: Oh, I am sorry to hear that. I didn't know.

The maxims in Politeness Principle can also be adapted to the most Chinese greetings. For example, tact maxim shows a common greeting between colleagues or friends who meet the first time in the morning: "来啦?(You have come to work.)" Colleagues in the same office meet almost every day, so greetings between colleagues or friends are usually not as formal as those upwards greeting or downwards greeting. A simple "来啦?" reflects close relationship between them. On the other hand, going to work is a part of daily life. Going to work on time implies that our life proceeds smoothly. In this sense, the greeting "来啦?" suggests politeness and concern with the person.

Sympathy maxim is embodied in another example of Chinese greetings. A man who is repairing his bicycle may be greeted as: "怎么啦? 车坏了?(What's the matter? Does your bicycle go wrong?)" Apparently, this type of greetings seems to be asking for new information and wanting to offer help. But in fact it is just a way of expressing sympathy of the addresser. It's just a kind of greeting.

It seems that Leech (1983) provides a dominating framework for politeness researches. These maxims of Politeness Principle are generally observed in communication in any language community. The speaker often offers more benefit to the speaker and leaves more cost to himself, for the purpose that both sides will feel respected and make a good impression on the other.

Although some maxims in Leech's Politeness Principle are adapted to Chinese greetings, every culture has their own features, so we cannot say that politeness means the same in all cultures. Gu Yueguo's Politeness Maxims reveal the unique features of Chinese politeness.

2.1.2 Brown and Levinson's Face Theory

Everyone wants to make himself honored while receiving respect from others. So within people's daily social interactions, they generally behave as polite as possible. It concerns about their public image and their faces. They want to be respected.

Brown and Levinson (1978) analyze greetings in different cultures. The general idea of Brown and Levinson about greetings is Face Threatening Act and Face Saving

Act. The wants related to politeness are the wants of face. If a speaker says something that represents a threat to another's face, it is described as a Face Threatening Act.

Generally speaking, if someone says something that has the possibility to threat another's face, the speaker can say something to lessen the possibility of threat happens. This is called a Face Saving Act. Generally speaking, every person involved in every communications will try to respect the face of others and there are many different ways of performing face saving acts.

According to Brown and Levinson (1978), there are two sides of face. One is "negative face," hoping their self, property and freedom of action can't be violated by others. The other is "positive face," wanting their character, profession, hobbies and dressing to be appreciated and praised by other people. In simple terms, negative face is the need to be independent and positive face is the need of faces.

For example, greetings in English such as "A nice day, isn't it?""How do you do?" are used to maintain people's positive face. In another kind of English greeting "Excuse me. Are you Professor Li?" the expression "excuse me" can be considered to be a greeting expression directed towards people's negative face. Similarly, "您好" and "你早" as greeting expressions in Chinese seem to be directed towards people's positive face. Another kind of Chinese greeting "请问您贵姓？(Excuse me. What is your noble name?)" is a kind of greeting expression directed towards people's negative face. And "请问" is used by the speaker as an apology for the interruption of someone. Chinese often greet others "你吃了吗？" or "你去哪？" to show politeness and respect to others and at the same time it maintains people's positive face. Therefore Chinese politeness has its own features.

2.2 Literature in China

Based on modern Chinese data, Gu Yueguo alters some of Leech's theories and puts forward some maxims such as the self-denigration maxim and the address maxim that are claimed to be unique in Chinese politeness. (Gu, 1990: 239)

There are basically four notions based on the Chinese conception of "li mao": respectfulness, modesty, attitudinal warmth, and refinement. "Respectfulness" is one self's positive appreciation or admiration of other concerning the latter's face, social status, and so on. "Modesty" can be seen as another way of saying "self-denigration.""Attitudinal warmth" is self's demonstration of kindness, consideration, and hospitality to other. Finally, "refinement" refers to one self's behavior to other which meets certain standards.

The four aspects are detailed telling about the politeness maxims. Gu (1990: 237—257) lists four maxims:

① the self-denigration maxim
② the address term maxim
③ the tact maxim and the generosity maxim
④ the Principle of Balance, and the Principle of Sincerity

Gu (1992: 10—17) offers further revision of them and demonstrates altogether five maxims.

① Self-denigration maxim: denigrate one self and elevate other. This maxim absorbs the notions of respectfulness and modesty.

② Address term maxim: address your interlocutor with an appropriate address term. This maxim is based on the notions of respectfulness and attitudinal warmth.

③ Refinement maxim: one self's behavior to other meets certain standards. With regard to language use, it means the use of refined lanaua—a and a ban on foul Ian—ua—e. The use of euphemisms and indirectness is also covered.

④ Agreement maxim: make efforts to maximize a—reemit and harmony and minimize disagreement.

⑤ Virtues-words-deeds maxim: minimize cost and maximize benefit to other at the motivational level, and maximize benefit received and minimize cost to self at the conversational level.

Compared with Leech's Politeness Principle, Gu's Politeness Maxims reveal the pragmatic and cultural differences between English and Chinese politeness. The difficulty in cross-cultural communication is that it is hard for native speakers of English to interpret the cultural connotation of Chinese "qianxun" (modesty) which is different from Leech's "modesty" in his "modesty maxim" in many ways. Unlike Leech's tact of maintaining, balance of cost and benefit between people, Chinese politeness is expressed especially by self and respecting other (zi qian zun ren). Seeking balance is against Chinese ethics.

However, the observation of PP or PM doesn't guarantee the appropriate use of greetings since it is more often concerned with maintaining or enhancing social relationship between people.

3. The Categories and the Functions of Greetings

Greeting ways are different in different countries and rooted in the background of different cultures. Different greeting ways have different functions on different occasions. In this part, we mostly talk about the different categories and the functions in English countries.

3.1 The Categories of Greetings

In fact, greetings can be classified into two big categories. One needs people to talk to someone, but another doesn't. The first one requires people to say "Hello!" or "Hi!" etc. The second one just requires people to nod their head, wave their hands or smile to someone. The second category is very simple and hasn't so many differences between different cultures. Thus it doesn't need to talk more. So the following categories don't involve the second one.

3.1.1 Greetings According to Time

Generally speaking, many greetings are related to time. But some greetings can be used for any day or at any time of the day whereas some cannot. Thus they can be divided into four kinds according to time:

(1) All-time greetings;
(2) Real-time greetings;
(3) Seasonal greetings;
(4) Ceremonial greetings

All-time greetings are those their usage cannot be limited by the time, and they can be used for any day and at any time of the day. The following expressions belong to this category:

In English	In Chinese
Hello! /Hi!	你好!
How are you?	你怎么样?

Real-time greetings are those used closely related to the time of the day. Each of them can only be used at a specific time of the day. The following expressions belong to this category:

In English	In Chinese
Good morning!	早上好!
Good afternoon!	中午好!
Good evening!	晚上好!

However, "中午好" and "晚上好" are seldomly used in daily conversations in China, but at the beginning of TV/ radio broadcasts, speeches and some formal occasions.

Seasonal greetings are those used only on some special days, such as Christmas, New Year's Day, and other festivals. For example:

In English	In Chinese
Happy New Year!	新年快乐!
Merry Christmas!	圣诞快乐!

Ceremonial greetings are those used at birthdays, wedding ceremonies and some other occasions. For example:

In English	In Chinese
Happy birthday!	生日快乐!

Congratulations, congratulations!　恭喜恭喜！

3.1.2　Greetings According to Formality

Greetings vary with speech styles. According to their formality of usage, Leech (1975:151) suggests that they can be classified into three kinds:

(1) Formal greetings

(2) Informal greetings

(3) Familiar greetings

Formal greetings are those used on some important occasions where maximum attention needs to be paid and speakers must be very polite. For example:

  In English   In Chinese

  How do you do!   您好！

Informal greetings are those used in ordinary conversations for creating a relaxed language environment. For example:

  In English   In Chinese

  Hello!（used as an introductory greeting）你好！（less formal or polite than "您好"）

Familiar greetings are those used between close friends to enhance relationships. For example:

  In English   In Chinese

  How is your family? 你家人怎么样？

3.1.3　Greetings According to Politeness Strategies

Greetings are linguistic routines concerned with politeness in social interactions. According to Brown and Levinson (1978,1987), politeness strategies are concerned with people's face: they are used when doing face-threatening acts to maintain people's negative face or to enhance their positive face to any degree. There are five strategies for this purpose:

(1) Bald on record

(2) Positive politeness

(3) Negative politeness

(4) Off-record

(5) Not doing the FTA

Bald on record strategy refers to starting a conversation without redressive action, that is, without greetings, as in conversations between family members, close friends. For example:

In English:

(1) A: Parker? Thought you left for work.

  B: I did.

In Chinese:

(2) A:昨天去学校图书馆了吗?(Have you gone to school library yesterday?)
　　B:没有。(No.)
　　A:啊,那太可惜了。(Oh, what a pity!)

These two dialogues may occur between two family members or two close friends. Because they are very familiar with each other, and there is no need to do those symbolic greetings.

Positive greetings are those with redress action directed towards the people's positive face. They are to please people to a certain degree. For example:

In English:

What a sweetheart you are!

You look very beautiful today.

In Chinese:

幸会幸会!(Nice to meet you!)

久仰大名,如雷贯耳!(Your name has long resounded in my ears.)

These expressions are used to show the speakers' delight of meeting people and his appreciation of people's kindness, appearance, etc. The speaker praises or flatters another people directly or indirectly, attempting to enhance the latter's positive face and their relationship.

Negative greetings are those with redress action directed towards the speaker's negative face. They are frequently used when speaker doesn't know or doesn't know well about the people talking to. The expression "Excuse me" can be considered a negative greeting expression directed towards the speaker's negative face, which means to disturb someone or to draw one's attention. For example:

In English:

Hey, excuse me, Sir. The dog out there.

In Chinese:

打扰一下,请问去医院怎么走?(Excuse me. How to go to the hospital?)

Off-record greetings are those used between close friends to enhance relationship or to create a humorous language environment. The following is an example from Irving (1974:180):

A: Still alive?

B: Alive and kicking.

It is the evidence that this dialogue is a joking greeting between close friends or colleagues with very close relations.

Not doing the FTA are those greetings used in ordinary situations to maintain the relationship between the speakers without any change of their social distance. For example:

In English:　　　　　　　　　　In Chinese:

Hello!	你好!
Morning!	早!

3.1.4 Greetings According to Social Settings

Greetings vary with the social settings in which they occur. They can be classified into the following categories according to this:

(1) Service encounter

(2) Telephone call

(3) TV/radio broadcast

(4) Other settings

Greetings of service encounters are those used by shop assistants, bank-clerks and waiters, etc. For example:

In English	In Chinese
May/Can I help you?	有什么能帮您的?

Greetings used in a telephone conversation have their own characteristics. For example:

In English

A: Hello?

B: Hello, do you put the puppy flyers?

A: The puppy flyers, yes? Are you the dog's owner?

B: No. I just wanna ask if the dog has been taken.

A: No, no one's come forward yet.

B: Ok, I want to take the dog, and do you have any requirements?

A: We just wanna make sure the dog has a good home.

B: There is no problem.

A: Could I get your number? I'm sure my husband would wanna call you.

B: Ok, ok…

A: Hold on a second, I need to find a pen. Hold on.

In Chinese

A:喂,你好,你是?(Hello! Who is that?)

B:您好,我是邮电局一名员工。请问王师傅在吗?(Hello! I'm a worker of post office. Is Master Wang in, please?)

A:我就是啊,你是老李吧?(I'm [Master Wang]. You are Lao Li, aren't you?)

B:是的是的,你好啊,老王。(Yes, yes. How are you, Lao Wang?)

A:你好,你好!(Fine! How about you?)

Greetings on TV or radio broadcast also have their own features. For example:

In English

This is BBC, North America, from Chicago a very good evening to you.

In Chinese

各位观众,晚上好!(Good evening, everyone!)

There are other social settings such as school or army camps, where special greeting expressions should be employed. For example:

In English (in a classroom)

Teacher: Good morning, class!

Students: Good morning, Mr. Smith.

In Chinese (in an army camp)

Commander: 同志们辛苦了!(Comrades, [you are] laborious!)

Soldiers: 为人民服务!(To serve the people!)

3.1.5 Greetings According to Content

Greetings vary with the content or orientation that they convey. Some greeting expressions are concerned about the person greeted, while others are related to the weather or other topics. They can be classified into the following two kinds:

(1) Personal greetings

(2) Non-personal greetings

Personal greetings are those concerned about the speaker's health, families, work, and other mentionable personal affairs or belongings. They can be further divided into the following two categories:

(a) Direct personal greetings

(b) Indirect personal greetings

Direct personal greetings are those with the personal pronoun "you" either in the surface structure or in the deep structure of the sentence, and those with the possessive pronoun "your" in the sentence. For example:

In English

How are you?

How is your family?

How is your work?

Are you all right?

In Chinese

你最近怎么样?(How are you recently?)

你吃过饭了吗?(Have you eaten?)

Indirect personal greetings are those without the possessive pronoun "you" in the sentence but understood by both speakers that the things mentioned are closely related to the person greeted. For example:

In English

Is the working properly?

In Chinese

饭菜很好吃！（What delicious meal!）

Non-personal greetings are those concerned about weather or other things which are not personal. For example：

    In English   In Chinese
    Lovely day, isn't it?   天气真好！是吗？
    Beautiful park, isn't it?   这公园真美！是吗？

3.1.6　Greetings According to Language Origin

Greetings in both English and Chinese languages vary with their language origin：most of them are native expressions, but some of them may be borrowed from other languages. They can be classified into two broad categories：

(1) Native greetings

(2) Foreign greetings

In English there are some foreign greetings, such as：

    Long long ago.   <from Chinese：(很久很久以前。)>
    Long time no see.   <from Chinese：(好久没见了！)>

In Chinese, we also have some foreign greetings. For example：

    嘿！   <from English：Hi!>
    很高兴见到你。 < from English：Very glad to see you.>

3.2　The Functions of Greetings

3.2.1　Greetings as Illocutionary Acts

As Firth (1972:30) comments, greetings are "a system of signs that convey other than overt messages." But how do people convey the covert messages (i.e. the intention or goodwill of the speaker) from this intricate sign system? Austin's Speech Act Theory is helpful for the explanation of this phenomenon.

According to Austin (1962), greeting ways can be used by particular speakers to achieve different communicative goals on different occasions, thus there are different greeting ways on different occasions by different purposes. In his theories he suggests three basic senses：

(1) Locutionary act：the actual uttering of a sentence with a particular meaning；

(2) Illocutionary act：the intent that the speaker has in uttering the sentence；

(3) Perlocutionary act：the result achieved in uttering the sentence；

Among the three acts, the second one is the act that interests linguists most. The reason is that speakers can mean more things by what they say. According to Austin (1962), there are six types of illocutionary acts：

(1) Assertives, used to express a belief (stating, admitting, concluding, etc.)

(2) Directives, used to get the hearer to do something (ordering, requesting, advising, etc.)

(3) Commissives, used to commit the speaker to do (promising, pledging, volunteering, etc.)

(4) Expressives, used to express the emotional state of the speaker (thanking, apologizing, greeting, etc.)

(5) Effectives, used to change the state of some reality (appointing, naming, arresting, etc.)

(6) Vindictives, used to determine institutional state of affairs (adjudicate, etc.)

According to the above classifications of illocutionary acts, greetings can fall into the category of "expressives." For example, when an English speaker asks you "How are you?" or "How do you do?" he may not be really concerned about your health or something, but just a kind of greeting, and make you know that he see you and care about you. It is just a kind of politeness.

The same, when a Chinese speaker greets people with "你吃了吗?（Have you eaten?）" or "去哪?（Where are you going?）," he seldom really wants to know whether you are full or hungry, or where you are going. It's just a kind of politeness, that shows friendliness. Actually such a greeting expression is not an invitation but a means to show the speaker's friendliness and care about the hearer.

The discussion above shows from pragmatic perspective, greetings can be regarded as illocutionary acts.

3.2.2 Greetings as Access Rituals to Further Communicative Interaction

Greetings also have the function of helping people to open the topic and access the further communication. In Erving Goffman's (1971) words, they "mark the transition to a condition of increased access." (Erving Goffman, 1971:107) He includes greetings in his definition of "access ritual," which marks a change in degree of accessing. For example:

Parker: Good morning, Maryann.

Maryann: How you're doing, Parker?

Parker: I'm doing great. I wonder if I can ask you for a favor.

Maryann: Sure. Anything.

…

In this example, Parker greets Maryann politely when he meets her, and Maryann replies with "How are you doing, Parker?" This indicates the relationship existing between them. These greetings are no practical meaning. Later is the point. Through these greetings, they can access the further conversation. Parker then puts forward the topic: "I wonder if I can ask you for a favor." If there aren't such greetings as "Good morning!" "How you're doing, Parker?" or "I'm doing great." etc, there probably isn't the further conversation. In this case, greetings can be considered as a necessary part of conversations.

3.2.3 Greetings as Interpersonal Functions

Greetings also have the function of indicating the position and relationship of the speakers. There are several common usages following:

First, upward greetings usually happen between the inferior to the superior, the young to the old, students to teachers or the poor to the rich. Upward greetings are defined by upward relationships, which are generally decided by people's social status, wealth, age, profession and other related variables. In upward greetings, the positional low usually takes the initiative to greet the positional high, and the addressing terms need to be an indispensable part of politeness in greetings. Furthermore, the choice of the second-person pronoun in Chinese greetings is usually "您" instead of "你," to show politeness, respect and power distance.

Example: A: Good morning, Mr. Professor! B: Jess!

Example: A:刘老师,您好! B:哎,小李。

Downward greetings are those from the superior to the inferior, the old to the young, and teachers to students. In a word, they are from the high position to the low position. In downward greetings, the superior usually expect greetings from the inferior first, which means the superior does not take the initiative to greet (except when the greeter is a little child). And the addressing terms are no longer the norm of politeness. Meanwhile the greetings initiated by the superior are usually more brief and conventional than upward greetings.

Example: A: Moira!
    B: Good morning, Parker!

Example: A: 去哪,小王?
    B:刘校长,您好!

4. Main Factors Causing the Use of Greeting in English Countries

There are many reasons that can have an effect on greetings. However, generally speaking, it can be social factors and cultural factors.

4.1 Social Factors

Human beings are social animals. And people cannot live by himself. They have to keep contacting with others. So we can't avoid that they will meet some people or contact someone. Then we need greetings. Thus greetings belong to a kind of social behavior. And the factors that can influence greetings must be the social factors. It may include the social realities and people's communicative purpose. Greetings are linguistic routines concerned with politeness in social interactions. According to Brown and Levinson, politeness strategies are related closely to people's face. They are used when doing face-threatening acts to maintain people' negative face or enhance their positive face to any degree. Neutral greetings are those used in ordinary situations to maintain the relationship between people without any change of their social distance. Many routine expressions can fall into this category. We need to consider the social factors that affect the use of greetings in the choice of appropriate strategies.

Social power and social distance are considered as two major factors that influence the use of greeting. The causes that can influence the use of greetings are numerous, including not only the characteristics of the speaker's age, sex, occupation, wealth, education, family background but also more general factors, such as the content of the conversation, the presence of the third person. And social power can include the following aspects:

(1) Power of control

(2) Social status or rank

(3) Authority or the legitimate right to exert influence

(4) A general notion of equality-inequality

When there is power difference, the use of greeting between people is mainly governed by age and occupational status. In a society, people with a higher occupational status imply more power. Thus the status relationship between people has strong influence on selecting appropriate greetings.

Age influences people's speech act strongly, too. People of different ages may have different characteristics of speech. So they greet others differently. In a society, older age implies power and higher social status.

Distance is another main factor in determining the choice of suitable greetings. According to Spencer-Oatey (1996), social distance can be divided into the following parts:

(1) Social similarity/difference

(2) Frequency of contact

(3) Length of acquaintance

(4) Familiarity, or how well people know each other

(5) Sense of like-mindedness

(6) Positive/negative affect

4.2 Cultural Factors

From the born of a child, culture formally and informally teaches him/her how to behave appropriately and what behaviors can be accepted by adults. Therefore, there is no need for members of a culture to spend much energy on thinking what each event means or how to respond to it; usually, all those who share a common culture know their habits well, so it is easy to behave correctly and suitably.

Since western culture stresses individual rights, freedom and independence, showing respect to one's liberty, rights and independence is considered polite or it will be regarded improper and even rude. So the habits of people greeting follow this idea. Individualism is deeply rooted in western culture and is highly valued by English people. In this sense, it is hard to give a satisfactory translation in Chinese for this term since in Chinese environment the term is quite often associated with egoism, hedonism and selfishness.

In English countries, people stress the individual's initiative, independence and freedom of action, and encourage competition along with personal achievement. Besides, English people are self-oriented. They strive for their own goals to promote or realize themselves. They highly value self-autonomy, self-reliance and self-realization (God helps those who help themselves). They stress directness, preciseness and self-exposure in conversation, which are perceived as the effective communication strategies. (Hu, 1999)

The individualism factor and low power distance have both a direct and an indirect effect on communicational behaviors of members of English culture and thus influence the ways English people show politeness when handling interpersonal relationships.

English speakers are known to be rather more considerable. They are particularly sensitive about their privacy as well. Questions such as "Where are you going?" or "What are you doing?" sound related to their secretary, so these greetings may not be proper, and are not be accepted by them.

5. Conclusion

5.1 Summary of the Study

Greeting is an important tool to establish and maintain people's relationships. Increasing awareness of cross-cultural differences is a key to reduce people's mistakes made in cross-cultural communication. However, it is not easy to do so. This is due to the existence of a gap between the target language and target culture in cross-cultural communication.

It is found that Leech's Politeness Principle as well as Brown and Levinson's Face Theory are not well adapted to Chinese conversation. Speakers of different languages may use different overt messages to convey politeness. And something is polite in one language. However it may not be so in another. Although the choice of linguistic routines is generally influenced by common social factors, the actual use may vary from person to person and from language to language.

In this world with a diversity of cultures, no culture may necessarily be better or worse than another. By the same, no culture may necessarily be superior or inferior to another. Yet there are real differences between groups and cultures. The participants in cross-cultural communication must become aware of their real situations, that is, the cultural communication background of each participant. They can learn to accept those differences, adopt and respect them. Respecting their culture is a kind of respecting to every human being belonging to this culture. In this way, the successful communication can be achieved.

So there is the study about greetings. In this thesis, it gets some conclusions through the research about greetings in English countries based on the English movie. Different cultures have different greeting ways. And different greetings have different functions. If people want to do correct greetings in cross-cultural communication, they must learn the target culture and know the difference between two cultures.

5.2 Limitation of the Study

As mentioned above, this thesis is a study of English greetings. Thus, there must be several limitations.

First, on the one hand, it's just a study of greetings in one movie, without plenty of other evidences; so many people perhaps cannot be convinced by it. On the other hand, it's just an American movie, no comparison with Chinese movies or other Chinese culture, so it can't figure out the differences between English and Chinese greetings clearly.

Second, due to the limited time, energy and capability, the sources (can be used) of the study is limited, so there must be many shortages. So there may be some thing that can't be found.

Third, after all, it's a study of a movie, not the real life, so there are probably some distinctions with the daily life. So people should look at it with the dialectical eyes.

Bibliography

Austin, J. L. 1962. How to Do Things with Words. Cambridge, Mass.: Harvard University Press.

Brown, P. & S. Levinson. 1978, 1987. Politeness: Some Universals in Language Usage. Cambridge: Cambridge University Press.

Clark, D. & Argyle. 1982. Conversation Sequences. Advances in the Social Psychology of Language. Fraser & Scherer. (eds.) Cambridge University Press.

Clark, D. and D. H. Schunk. 1980. Polite Responses to Polite Requests. Cognition. Conversational Routine. Columns, F. (ed). The Hague: Mouton Publishers.

Firth, J. R. 1972. Verbal and Bodily Rituals of Greeting and Parting. The Interpretation of Ritual. J. S. LaFontaine. (ed.).

Goffman, E. 1967. Interaction Ritual: Essays on Face to Face Behavior. Garden City, New York: Doubleday and col, Inc.

Irvine, J. T. 1974. Strategies of Status Manipulation in the Wolof Greeting.

Laver, J. 1975. Communicative Function of Phatic Communion. Organization of Behavior in Face-to-Face Interaction. Kendon et al (eds).

Laver, J. 1981. Linguistic Routines and Politeness in Greeting and Parting. Conversational Routine. The Hague: Mounton Publishers.

Leech, Geoffrey N. 1983. Principles of Pragmatics. London: Longman.

Levinson, Stephen C. 1983. Pragmatics. Cambridge: Cambridge University Press.

Spencer, Oatey, H. 1996. Reconsidering Power and Distance. Journal of Pragmatics.

毕继万.1999.跨文化非语言交际.外语教学与研究出版社.

陈松岑.1989.礼貌语言初探.商务印书馆.

邓炎昌、刘润清.1989.语言与文化.外语教学与研究出版社.

顾曰国,1992.礼貌、语用与文化.外语教学与研究.

胡明扬.1987.问候语的文化心理背景.世界汉语教学.

胡文仲.1988.跨文化交际与英语教学.上海译文出版社.

——.1994.文化与交际.外语教学与研究出版社.

——.2003.跨文化交际面面观.外语教学与研究出版社.

——.2004.跨文化交际学概论.外语教学与研究出版社.

胡壮麟、刘润清.1988.语言学教程.北京大学出版社.

钱厚生.1996.英汉问候语告别语对比研究.商务印书馆.

第二节 文 学 类

×× 大 学

本科生毕业论文(设计)册

题目：从生态角度解读柯勒律治的《老水手行》

学院＿＿＿＿＿＿＿
专业＿＿＿＿＿＿＿
班级＿＿＿＿＿＿＿
学生＿＿＿＿＿＿＿
指导教师＿＿＿＿＿
完成日期＿＿＿＿＿

An Ecological Interpretation of Coleridge's
The Rime of the Ancient Mariner

By
×××
Prof. ×××, Tutor

A Thesis Submitted to the Foreign Languages

Institutes in Partial Fulfillment of the Requirements

For the Degree of Bachelor of Arts at

×× University

May 2014

Abstract

Samuel Taylor Coleridge is one of the greatest Romantic poets in British literary history, but also a renowned ideologist, a literary critic and theorist. Coleridge has only a small handful of poems through his life but holds an important position in literature. Among his works melt ordinary details and poetic symbolism one, where there are some supernatural mystical tendencies. *The Rime of the Ancient Mariner* is a lengthy narrative poem, an emotional vent in Coleridge's exited state. And it is recognized as Coleridge's masterpiece. This thesis consists of three parts. The first part is the Introduction, which mainly introduces the background of the poem and literature review. The second part is the body, which includes three chapters: Chapter one makes a brief introduction of the original relationship between man and nature. At first, man and nature enjoy a harmonious relationship. Chapter two takes the view from alienation to reveal human's increasing serious damage to nature and nature's punishment. Chapter three mainly explores the salvation of the relationship between human and nature. The third part is the conclusion. Humans began to respect nature, go back to nature and protect nature. This thesis aims to interpret *The Rime of the Ancient Mariner* from the ecological point of view, to explain the significance nature exerts on human being by the break and return of the relationship between man and nature, so as to further reveal the meaning of the poem to protect nature and seek sustainable development.

Key words: Ecological relationship　Man and nature　Harmony　Alienation　Back to nature

摘　要

　　塞缪尔·泰勒·柯勒律治是英国文学史上最伟大的浪漫主义诗人之一,同时也是一位杰出的思想家和文学批评理论家。柯勒律治一生创作不多,但在文学上却有重要地位。他的作品融平凡的细节和富于诗意的象征于一体,其中也不乏超自然的神秘主义倾向。他的诗歌不仅体现了19世纪浪漫主义文学的特征,而且也反映了他个人独特的风格和高超的诗艺。《古舟子咏》是一部长篇叙事诗,是柯勒律治兴奋状态下的情感宣泄,被视为柯勒律治的代表作。论文共分为三部分。第一部分为引言,主要介绍该诗的相关背景和文献综述。第二部分包括三章。第一章首先简述人与自然最原始的和谐关系。最初,人与自然是和谐的,但这种和谐并不稳定,因而有了后来的破坏与惩罚。第二章主要从人与自然关系的割裂这一角度来看人类对自然日益严重的破坏及自然界对人类违背自然而进行的惩罚。第三章主要介绍了人与自然关系的回归与改善。第三部分是结论。人类开始尊重自然,重返自然,并且保护自然。本文从生态角度对《古舟子咏》进行解读,从人与自然关系的破裂与回归阐述自然界对人的意义,从而进一步解释诗歌寓意,保护自然,持续发展。

关键词: 生态关系　人与自然　和谐　疏远　回归自然

Contents

Abstract ··
Abstract in Chinese ···
Introduction ···
Chapter One　The Harmony Between Man and Nature ·································
　　A. Harmony Between Man and the Animal ···
　　B. Harmony Between Man and the Sea ··
Chapter Two　Conflict Between Man and Nature ··
　　A. Human's Indifference to Nature ··
　　B. Nature's Punishment on Human ···
Chapter Three　Improvement of the Relationship Between Man and Nature ······
　　A. Respect for Nature ···
　　B. Back to Nature ···
　　C. Preach for Nature ··
Conclusion ··
Notes ···
Bibliography ··

Introduction

Samuel Taylor Coleridge is one of the most fertile and versatile figures in English history. He is an influential poet, literary critic and philosopher in his time. Like his friend Wordsworth, he is also one of the Lake Poets, and one of the founders of the Romantic Movement in England.

Coleridge's works are mainly divided into three classes—the early poetic, the middle critical and the later philosophical. He is most famous for his poetry. Published in the first edition of *Lyrical Ballads* in 1798, *The Rime of the Ancient Mariner* is generally recognized as the best poem of Coleridge. Originated from a short dream told by a friend, this narrative poem is conceived by Coleridge's splendid imagination. It tells a strange story in the form of ballads. It is about an ancient mariner's sin and suffering, confession and repentance. Three guests are on their way to a wedding party, but one of them is stopped by an ancient mariner. The mariner tells his own adventure on the sea. He killed a friendly albatross who had helped him before and made the deity angry. Thus falls misfortune and he and his crew are punished by God, threatening by horrible scenes and terrified by death. Only when he realized his sin and prayed for all of God's creatures does the spell break.

In the second half of the 18th century, England has witnessed a boom of the Industrial revolution. This development has transferred England from an agricultural country to a modern nation. The foot of the economy development cannot be stopped and more and more existences have to give way to it, including nature. However, despite such a large group of supporters of this hot trend, some hold a different attitude. They leave away the noisy city to embrace and eulogize the great nature. Ecological literature comes out as a result of the worse environmental condition. The second half of the 20th century starts a new perspective for the study of this poem, that is, the ecological perspective. In order to arouse more awareness, ecological literature comes into being. Eco-criticism starts from 1970s. It flourished from America then sweeps to many European countries including England. In 1972, Joseph Meeker first put forward Literary Ecology in his book: *The Comedy of Survival: Studies in Literary Ecology*[1]. In 1992, the first journal of eco-criticism literature, *Interdisciplinary Studies in Literature and Environment* came out in America, which marks the beginning of this discipline. It advocates that all creatures are born equally, which means human is no superior than other living things. Though living in the 19th century, Coleridge really has the foresight to guide people to love and respect nature. Aiming to arouse people's awareness of environment, ecological literature stresses the importance of the harmony between man and nature. Coleridge is sensitive enough to note this, so he writes *The Rime of the Ancient Mariner*, in which the relationship between man and nature is exactly the history of man's development.

When first published in 1798, *The Rime of the Ancient Mariner* was believed a poem without a clearly definable meaning by the contemporary critics. Wordsworth once said: "From what I can gather it seems that '*The Rime Mariner*' has upon the whole been an injury to the volume. I mean that the old words and the strangeness of it have deterred readers from going on."[2] Because the meaning of *The Rime* is difficult to understand, many critics gave up studying it. This circumstance changes when the critics gradually focus more on the symbolic meaning instead of its apparent meaning. The 20th century witnessed the booming of the study of *The Rime of the Ancient Mariner*. Critics begin to explain it from different aspects. Many critics hold that the poem has a Christian moral. G. Wilson Knight comments it as various Christian symbols: "From this the albatross saves them: it is as 'a Christian Soul'."[3] George Whalley views the poem as an autobiographical of Coleridge, in which the image of the mariner is so lonely, just likes the poet himself.[4] Robert Penn Warren thinks that this poem has a profound moral and spiritual significance. In his "A Poem of Pure Imagination," he points out that "It might be said that reason shows us God, and imagination shows us how nature participates in God."[5] The last two decades of the 20th century has witnessed a flourishing trend of an ecological study of *The Rime of the Ancient Mariner*. It is recognized as "the most famous ecological fable."[6] The British scholar, biographer and critic Jonathan Bate points out in his *The Song of the Earth* that Coleridge writes this poem as "the natural ethic tragedy or land ethic tragedy, but not the destiny tragedy."[7]

In China, there are also many researches of *The Rime of the Ancient Mariner* from different aspects. In 1991, Wang Zuoliang points it as: "rely everything on imagination and make poetry and literature based on inspiration and genius."[8] He also speaks highly of its music beauty. In 2002, Zhang Lilong analyzed this poetry from a Christian perspective to reveal people's loneliness and pain under the strict fetter of the religion.[9] In 2009, Wang Li makes an analysis of the symbolic meaning of the albatross, which further reveals the excellent imagination of Coleridge.[10] Although there are many researches on this poetry, the great work still has lots to be discovered. This thesis will analyze it from an ecological aspect, to arouse people's awareness of the environment and learn to respect and love nature.

From this poem, it can be drew the following lessons from an ecological view. All creatures are equal. Human is no superior than other living things. Though living in the 19th century, Coleridge really has the foresight to guide people to love and respect nature. The mariner kills the albatross after it leads them out of the plight, which exactly alludes to human's development at the cost of damaging nature. All creatures have the right to survive; they are coexisting with human and friendly to the world. It is cruel for human to kill them and the only result for destroying nature is to draw disasters for man. Without a right ecological overlook man will no doubt fall into the vicious circle. It is time for human to awake to protect nature and build a friendly environment. Coleridge suggests human to pass this faith from generation to generation.

The history of human can be explained as a history of relationship between human and nature. Composed of seven parts, this poem can be divided into three stages, which reflects changes of human's attitude towards nature. At the beginning, human fear of nature, their relationship is harmonious but original. They respect nature because they revere it, but not for understanding. The second stage human comes to know nature and want to control everything. They seek for their own development at the cost of destroying nature. Thus nature starts to revenge human and causes the conflict between nature and human. At last, human begin to realize that all creatures are created equally. Nature is the best friend of human and human has responsibility to protect and respect nature. This ecological view lead human to improve the relationship between man and nature and in this way can human develop continuously.

Chapter One The Harmony Between Man and Nature

The relationship between man and nature is not something that is invariable. Instead, it changes a lot along with the development of man's concept of nature. It has gone through the process of the harmony, the conflict and at last reached a compromise again. At the beginning, however, man and nature enjoy a harmonious relationship; even it is a short one.

A. Harmony Between Man and the Animal

The first two parts describes an ancient mariner blocks the way of a guest who is going to attend a wedding. The ancient mariner has grey beard and skinny hands. He uses his glittering eyes to hold the guests and tells him the sailing adventure of his own. His appearance and behavior at the scene is so strange that the guests want to leave. But this old man seems stubborn and keeps telling his own story. The wedding-guest has no choice but to listen to him. So this ancient mariner slowly tells the guest how he shot a friendly albatross and caused disaster.

And now the Storm-Blast came, and he

>   Was tyrannous and strong;
>   He struck with his o'ertaking wings,
>   And chased us south along.
>
>   With sloping masts and dipping prow,
>   As who pursed with yell and blow
>   Still treads the shadow of his foe,
>   And forward bends his head,
>   The ship drove fast, loud roared the blast,
>   And southward aye we fled. [11]

At the beginning, the mariner and his crew has great difficulty in sailing, they are blocked by the severe weather. The storm forces the ship to south polar circle, their masts are sloping and their prow dipping, the storm drives them fast to the south. The south polar circle is not their direction, but they have no idea but to reduce to the storm. This cold place is really a challenge to them, it comes both misty and snowy, and it grows wondrous cold. No matter how much has the mariner sailed before, no matter what experience they may have, facing with nature's force, they only have to suffer. There, they could see nothing living, neither men nor beasts. In this cold place, the only thing they could see is ice; the only sound they could hear is the crack and growl of the ice. They are helpless at the moment. They may be trapped here for long until their death. However, thanks to a friendly albatross, who stands for the symbol of Christ, comes to help them and lead them out of the plight.

>   At length did cross an Albatross,
>   Thorough the fog it came;
>   As if it had been a Christian soul,
>   We hailed it in God's name.
>
>   It ate the food it ne'er had eat,
>   And round and round it flew.
>   The ice did split with a thunder-fit;
>   The helmsman steered us through!
>
>   And a good south wind sprung up behind;
>   The Albatross did fellow,
>   And every day, for food or play,

Came to the mariner's hollo!¹²

In this dilemma, wonder appears. An albatross comes thorough the fog. As a symbol of Christ, it brings good luck to the crew and finally they are able to get out of the plight. The ice split and they break the dilemma to find their direction. With the help of the lucky albatross, they have the right south wind which drives the ship to leave for north. The friendly albatross follows the ship to bless them, and play with them. How harmonious it is! However, this friendly atmosphere cannot be maintained longer, a more serious disaster falls soon for the ancient mariner's crime. He rudely shot the albatross.

However, this harmonious relationship between man and nature cannot exist for long. Short after the albatross helps the sailors to get out of the south polar, it is shot by the ancient mariner mercilessly. There are reasons behind this short relationship.

The first is that this original harmony between human and albatross is based on human's fear of nature. At first the crew is forced by the severe storm and trapped to the lifeless south polar. The ship is broken and the crew froze. Surrounded by the ice stretches to the horizon, the sailors could not figure out the direction. Endless snow, pervasive fog, cracked ice and chill air all depress the crew. Even the most optimistic man becomes frustrated and helpless under this circumstance. Human can be so small facing with the power of nature. Especially in the early days, when natural disaster happens, hardly can human deal with it. So when the albatross comes to them, bringing hope for the crew, the sailors are encouraged and welcome the albatross with great hospitality. But this hospitality is not from their deep heart. Instead, it is a yield to nature. When nature finishes it's roaring and turns on a peaceful look, human are grateful to accept this. They like nature only when it shows goodness. This act is like child's fear for parents, or people's blind trust for authority. They surrender not for respect from heart, but just because they could not afford the result of disobey. So the sailor's love and care for the albatross is wrong right from the beginning, which causes the tragedy later.

Secondly, because this original relationship is not pure, what man want to do is to make use of the bird. When the albatross brings luck to the crew, it is welcomed by human. But right after it finishes its mission, right after the sailors get rescued, it is shot to death. It is obvious the life of albatross is treated with indifference. When the sailors need the bird, it is lovely and well treated; when they get out of difficulty, they immediately forget it and even kill it.⁹ How cruel the sailors are! When they have established safety, they forget what albatross has done for them. When they get away from the plight, they owe all their misfortune to the dead bird.

Their attitude towards the albatross changes so quickly just because in their eyes it no longer has its value, which is used by human.

Thirdly, the relation between albatross and sailors is of great imbalance. A harmony relationship must be built on equality. However, the sailors view themselves as superior than the albatross and do not care much about the non-human life. When the albatross helps sailors, it happily flies after the ship, plays with sailors and ushers the direction blithely. It is friendly with human and helps them voluntarily. But sailors do not return the same sincerity. Because they have to rely on the bird to get out first, so they are happy to have this bird to fly with them. For this purpose, they treat it friendly, feed it, watch it, and call it. After they get what they want from the bird—the direction and good luck, they no longer view it as a friend but shoot it ruthlessly. And after its death, they even attribute their misfortune to it and believe they themselves are lucky stars. This imbalance between sailors and the albatross will incur the break doubtlessly.

From an ecological view, the above three aspects have formed every reason for the break of the relationship. Ecological thinking advocates understanding, equality, and respect. The act of the crew has violated all of these values. They do not know what the proper relationship between man and nature should be, thinking man can be separated from nature, to conquer animals, to abuse resources, to rule the whole world. So they ignore and damage nature for sake of their own development. The imbalance between man and nature makes human overlook the importance of nature, they only want to make use of it but never try to protect it. Man concentrate on themselves too much and ignore other living creatures. This decides the harmonious relationship between man and nature breaks soon.

B. Harmony Between Man and the Sea

Like the relationship between sailors and albatross, the original harmony between man and nature is also an immature one. At that time, they have not realized that human is also a part of nature. They view nature as something mysterious and capricious. They have no idea how to get along with it but to suffer. They do not know why it turns fierce or how it get calm. They just owe it to the will of God and never introspect. In fact, man is also a component of nature and for many a time it is quite human that influent nature most. It is man's action and attitude that change the climate, and many disasters are caused by human themselves.

At the first part, the appearance of the albatross drives the fog and snow away, sailors play with this bird and they get along well. For this, the weather turns clear and climate is cool, human and nature are able to share a harmonious relationship. However, this harmony is also very short due to human's crime. Man do not pay attention to maintain this harmony and in result it breaks quickly, causing a horrible result. Everyone is punished yet nobody knows why. They owe it to the killing of the bird but never do they really come to know how to get along with nature. They do not respect and they overlook other creatures. Their ignorance to life incurs the tragedy. "And the good south wind still blew behind,/But no sweet bird did fellow,/Nor and day for food or play/Came to the mariners' hollo!"[13]

Here the poet makes a contrast between the two stanzas. Comparing with the beginning, the south wind blows the same but there is no bird follows any more. It buries a foreshadowing here and explains the following plot. The same south wind blows but draws different scene. When the bird died, the tender climate soon turns to a hellish environment. No wind, no water to drink, the motionless ship and the crawl slimy things. Sailors are all too thirsty to speak and meet their death in the end. So what causes the different result? It must be the albatross. Just because of a bird's death nature makes such a huge punishment on the whole crew, to teach them a lesson to learn to love and respect life. From here it shows the harmony between man and nature is a short one because man do not understand nature. But nature will act according to man's behavior. When man are friendly to nature and love its creatures, nature will guarantee a peaceful and safe environment for them; when man offend lives and even commit a sin to threaten other creatures, nature begins to revenge. Because man have not grasped the rule of nature and still view it as a capricious mood of God, their harmony is just a flash in the pan. This ignorance will later cause bigger problem and through the continuous disaster and punishment, man will, however, finally grasp the gist and learn to establish a true harmony with nature.

Ecological holism is one of the main concepts of ecological thinking. From this perspective, there is a cause and effect behind this break. Although there is a harmony between man and nature, this is a short one for it violates the ecological view. Man tend to be self-centered and ignore the necessity to maintain this harmony. However, according to ecological holism, the whole world belongs to an integrity, which cannot be separated. No matter man or animals, life or lifeless, every part of nature is of equal position. According to Wang Nuo, "The basic presupposition of ecological holism is decentralization or no centralization."[14] If man stress too much for self-concentration, they will violate the ecological rule, thus cause damage to the ecosystem. And the only result of this is the distinction of man.

Chapter Two　Conflict Between Man and Nature

The harmony between man and nature is transient, and the conflict occurs when man offend nature and attempt to conquer it. After establishing the harmony with nature, man turn to be indifferent towards nature, and incur nature's punishment. The harmony between man and nature soon turns to a fierce conflict, which cannot be affordable for man.

A. Human's Indifference to Nature

The relationship between human and nature is not born to be harmonious. The process of human to discover and protect nature is full of conflict and exploration. Until recently there are still contradictions lying between human and nature, like resources overexploitation, environmental damage, wild animals killing, the Greenhouse effect and so on. In the same way, at that time, it is not sensible to expect a mature relationship between man and nature. Especially in the eighteenth century, there is a time when the Industrial Revolution has swept the whole Britain and later most of the western countries until the whole world. At that time, human have just taken the rocket of development. As all race are the most developed and grasp the greatest power, they are ready to grow stronger at the cost of any sacrifice. As a treasure house of natural resources, nature is reduced to being the exploiting object of man's endless desire. Living in the eighteenth century, Coleridge has viewed the whole process of human's villainy on nature. *The Rime of the Ancient Mariner* comes to express what Coleridge thinks of these behaviors. He describes human's disrespect and abuse towards nature by telling the adventure of the mariner. This narrative poem in fact is a narration of what people do towards nature at that time. In the poem, the sailors all view nature as something mysterious, nobody would consider for nature and they just do things that benefit them, no matter what their deed would cause for nature. When the albatross comes to the aid, they welcome it and treat it friendly; when they think they have got what the albatross has, they cruelly kill it. In their eyes, the bird is a bird, never can it be equal to a man. They treasure their own lives, but nobody takes pity on a bird. All creatures that nature has created are not worthy as human are, so they never put themselves on a fair position with nature.

When the albatross comes to the crew, it is in fact a friendly sign sent by nature. The bird serves a messenger of nature and comes to help people figure out the way. In this way, a short harmonious relationship is established. But this only last for a little while because when sailors have gone through the difficulties, they quickly forget the favour of nature and kill the bird. People do not treasure the harmony with nature. This plot is in fact a hint at the contemporary society. For millions of years, nature is the mother of man and has nurtured numerous people. From one generation to another generation, human worship and hold sacred ceremony to pray for safety and harvest. However, when the Industrial Revolution booms, human have found a shortcut to improve their life quality and enjoy a more luxurious lifestyle. With their hectic pace, they no longer enjoy the beautiful natural scenery; with the booming industry building, more and more coals are burned causing more and more dust in the air; with the rising of market, more and more trees fell down, lakes and stream become polluted. It is a time human abandon nature to build their own destiny. Most of them are immersed in their golden dream except seldom clear men. Among them, Coleridge is one of the representatives who made their voices heard. Human's indifference towards nature is expressed by the killing of the albatross in the poem. Also, they do not pay much attention to the reasons behind nature's changing, so never do they care how to mend their relationship, this also proves human's indifference.

To be frank, human's indifference towards nature mainly comes from their ignorance. They are narrow eyesight and do not realize that they are alike other creatures, for they all belong to nature and cannot be divided from it. The fast development of economy makes man too proud to respect other animals. As Li Min put it, "Human's intention to conquer nature goes together with the development of economy and progress in civilization."[15] After man made great progress, they try to get rid of nature. However, this is impossible because man and nature are actually bound together. This bond will be last forever until the end of world. In the poem, sailor's killing the bird is a hint at human's abandon of nature. They think they have be mature enough to live on their own so they sacrifice their relationship with nature without hesitation. Their benighted recognition surely has to be paid. The revenge comes. The crew comes to face something even more horrible, all sailors died except the ancient mariner, who had committed the crime by his own hands. Because man's indifference to nature, now it is time for nature to ignore man's lives.

> "Is it he?" quoth one, "is this the man?"
> By him who died on cross,
> With his cruel bow he laid full low
> The harmless Albatross.
>
> The spirit who bideth by himself
> In the land of mist and snow,
> He loved the bird that loved the man
> Who shot him with his bow.[16]

Human's difference to nature now incurs a horrible revenge. The Spirit is offended so punishment begins. In this line, "He loved the bird that loved the man," "he" refers to the Spirit but Coleridge actually refers to nature. Nature loves the bird of course, and it also loves human, for they are also lives created by it. But human are too self-concentrated to ignore and even kill other creatures. Even the harmless albatross who once helps human can be shot by them. Despite human themselves, they do not care much about other living things, they have no concept to love and protect nature. For this reason, nature begins to punish human at the cost of their lives. In this poem, Coleridge uses his fantastic imagination to imply what will happen if human continue to ignore and abuse nature. The horrible punishment in the poem warns people that the result of abusing nature is something man cannot afford. The poem goes to an ending of redemption, which expresses the poet's wish that this indifference can be moved one day.

B. Nature's Punishment on Human

The nineteenth century is really a critic period in human's history. It witnesses the booming Industrial Revolution and the Enlightenment. At that time people entered a faster-paced society and never have they been more self-concentrated. Human right has been highlighted than ever before, their thoughts liberated and their minds opened. Man are released from the fetters of nature, they have their own power and are considering to control and master nature. For this time, instead of yielding to nature, they decide to resist and at last, conquer it. They turn to be so confident and are no longer afraid of nature. In their eyes, facing with the stronger human, nature has no other way but to bear it passively. So they begin to abuse nature as they like, taking no care of its condition. In fact, nature is not all mighty. It is fragile and cannot afford so much. So human's abuse will quickly cause serious effect which will in turn punish them.

> Are those her ribs through which the Sun
> Did peer, as through a grate?
> And is that Woman all her crew?
> Is that a Death? And are there two?
> Is death that woman's mate?
>
> Her lips were red, her looks were free;
> Her locks were yellow as gold;
> Her skin was as white as leprosy,
> The night-mare Life-in-Death was she,
> Who thicks man's blood with cold.
>
> The naked hulk alongside came,
> And the twain were casting dice;
> "The game is done! I've won! I've won!"
> Quoth she, and whistles thrice. [17]

When human ignore and violate nature, punishment from the latter soon falls on them. Nature loves its creatures. So when human commit crime to its child, the bird, it is enraged and begins to conduct its punishment. The following stanza is the conversation between two women. One is Death; the other is Life-in-Death. They bet with lives of the crew, watching their suffering and death without any assistance or even mercy. All disasters the crew encounter is the retribution for their killing of the albatross. It is time for nature to show its power.

The first punishment is the severe climate: everywhere but undrinkable water, the moving mist, all of the scenes form a weary time. The crew are suffering, "With throats unslaked, with black lips baked/We could nor laugh nor wail,"[18] under this severe circumstance, it is almost impossible for people to get over it. Nature wields its power to teach human a lesson: without a harmonious cooperation, human can really reduce to suffering.

Second, nature punishes human by what they did to nature. When the ancient mariner killed the albatross, no body had spoken for the poor bird which reflects human's indifference to non-human life. So nature takes its revenge by killing man's lives cruelly and turns merciless towards their painful suffering. Nothing can be more vivid than this lesson that arouses human's introspection. Nature has its rule: Human have to first respect other creatures if they want to live.

The third punishment is loneliness. Being robbed of cross by his own sailors is far from enough, what makes it worse is when all other sailors died, only left the mariner himself survive. "Four times fifty living men/(And I hear nor sigh nor groan)/With heavy thump, a lifeless lump/They dropped down one by one."[19] This is the most serious punishment for the ancient mariner. Designing this plot, Coleridge makes a mockery of human's arrogance, who want to get rid of nature and rely on themselves. In the poem, without nature's mercy, no one can survive with the undrinkable water or in the endless mist. Being divided from nature, man has only one ending, the distinction of human. Because human want to abandon nature and live by their own, so nature kills all the sailors except the mariner, who commit the kill and left him to taste this loneliness, the way they want to live. "Alone, alone, all, all alone/alone on a wide wide sea! /And never a saint took pity on/ My soul in agony."[20]

Anthropocentrism is one of the misconcept that has formed for thousand years in man's mind. Man always want to conquer and rule nature and go every means to exploit it without considering its endurance capacity. They are proud of their wisdom and want to manage everything on earth. This wild ambition has offended nature's punishment. The sails drop down, the bloody sun, the motionless ship, the water every where, the rot sea, the crawl slimy things, the death-fires... all of these scenes scaring the sailors day and night. And their tongue withered, the throat chocked, they could not even speak. In the face of this threat, man have to yield to nature, and gradually man and nature begin to embrace an improvement in their relationship.

Chapter Three   Improvement of the Relationship Between Man and Nature

The conflict between man and nature is so fierce that man cannot afford it. The punishment from nature soon awakes man and teaches them how to love and respect nature. After receiving a sincere respect from man, nature forgives man and gives them a new opportunity. This time, the relationship between man and nature starts to reach a unprecedented new level.

A. Respect for Nature

The punishment from nature really makes the mariner afraid. From his deep heart he realizes that facing with nature's great power human beings are really small and helpless. His sin of killing nature's son, the albatross, incurs all of the crazy revenge from nature. He is no longer the ambitious sailor who wanted to control nature. He is desperate to get rid of this hellish scene. At this time, "The moving moon went up the sky" and "Beyond the shadow of the ship/ I watched the water-snakes."[21] Things begin to have a favorable turn. The moon beams the sea, shining the mariner with its soft moonlight, which calms down him among the burnt water and awful red. Beyond the shadow of the ship, water-snakes appears. They move in tracks of shinning white, their rich color decorates the sea, and their moving touches the mariner.

> O happy living things! no tongue
> Their beauty might declare;
> And I blessed them unaware;
> Sure my kind saint took pity on me,
> And I blessed them unaware.[22]

Here it makes a sharp contrast to the former plot. At the beginning, when the crew was trapped, it is the friendly albatross that brings luck for them. Every day, it came for food or for play; they got along with each other very well. Even like this, the mariner still killed it without sympathy. But this time when it comes to the water-snakes, the mariner blesses them unaware, and what's more, this blessing comes from his deep heart, which is a true love for nature. The mariner's different attitudes reflect his change towards nature. When he killed the bird, he had no mind to respect or love nature. But after all the suffering, he now turns to appreciate nature and respect it, not from any utility or benefit, but from a pure love in his heart. This change is the turning point of the whole poem, since the ancient mariner learns to appreciate and respect nature, the spell of nature breaks and things turn to be normal. "The self-same moment I could pray/ And from my neck so free/The Albatross fell off, and sank/Like lead to the sea."[23] The died bird, instead of the cross, hanging on the neck of the ancient mariner is the symbol of sin, so its falling here implies that he has been forgiven and the punishment may gradually end. It's obvious that the ancient mariner's respect for nature saves him. Here the theme of this poem emerges: the only salvation for human is to learn to respect and love nature. This is what Coleridge wants to express, he appeals to the public to pay more attention to nature and to learn to love and protect it.

Ecological literature advocates human's respect for nature. Harmony is based on equality, but equality needs respect to guarantee. In today's society, without respect for nature, human can do numerous damages to the whole ecosystem. Water is polluted, land is occupied, the forests are decreasing at a very high speed. It is hard to imagine what will happen if man continue to destroy nature for the sake of economy. What is sure is that man cannot exist alone without nature. Composed of many parts, nature is a fragile system. Just like other parts like animals, plants, or water, human also belong to nature. If any link breaks, the whole system will stop to work, which will directly threaten human themselves.

B. Back to Nature

The greatness of nature lies in the spirit of dedication and its broad bosom. Nature is the mother of all, no matter what man had done to it, when they repent of their sins from their deep heart, anything can be forgiven. In the fourth part, when the ancient mariner blesses for the beautiful water-snakes, the dead bird hanging on his neck falls, which symbols nature's forgiveness. And later in the fifth part of the poem, nature begins to help him. After suffering from stress and insomnia for such a long time, the mariner eventually could fall asleep; after surrounded by the undrinkable water, it finally rains. The wind is roaring, the sky lark singing. Among them, the dead bodies rise up to help the mariner to drive the sails. They are the spirits sent by nature to come to his aid. "The harbour-bay was clear as glass/ So smoothly it was strewn! /And on the bay the moonlight lay/ And the shadow of the moon."[24] From what is described here, the mariner has been back to nature. The clear harbor, so smooth, guarantees a safe environment; the silent moon, shining the peaceful moonlight to calm him down. This description of tranquility implies a favorable ending.

> This seraph-band, each waved his hand,
> No voice did they impart—
> No voice; but oh! The silence sank
> Like music on my heart.
>
> But soon I heard the dash of oars,
> I heard the Pilot's cheer;
> My head was turned perforce away
> And I saw a boat appear.[25]

When the ancient mariner reaches the peaceful harbor, safety has been established. So the seraph, the angels who have helped him to drive the boat are waving their hands to leave. They make no voice but the mariner hears it in his heart. This voice comes from gratitude. It is obvious that the kind angels are symbol of nature, and the mariner, of man. So here nature and man again, reach a harmony, a true harmony, based on man's sincere respect. Since they have reached a harmony, all the past has gone and man are back to nature. The pilot and his son turn up to lead the ship, bringing the ancient mariner to get rid of loneliness and return nature. Here shows the mercy of nature. However, since the mariner has committed the evil sin towards nature, a lesson must be taught to him. The awakening of the mariner is at a great cost: the lives of two hundred sailors. So this lesson is unforgettable enough for the ancient mariner to remember. In his afterlife, he is always pricked by his conscience, and has to keep preaching others to relieve him.

The development of the relationship between man and nature is not something casually but obeys certain rules. Man and nature belongs to a whole system, the ecosystem. Ecological critic Aldo Leopord suggests the ecosystem is a system of interdependent parts, stressing the integrity is greater than the sum of each parts.[26] Man who leave nature cannot exist, no matter how powerful they are at first. Back to nature is the only way to guarantee man's safety and development. Only when man and other parts of nature, the animals, the plants, the minerals, the sea and other things coexist better, can the ecosystem work normally and efficiently. Without any part of the system, the whole body cannot work, which will lead to a final extinction.

C. Preach for Nature

Falling prey to deep remorse, after being saved, the mariner carried on the mission of preaching others to love and protect nature. So that is the reason for his appearance at the wedding and explains why he blocks the way of one of the three guests. "I pass, like night, from land to land;/ I have strange power of speech;/That moment that his face I see/ I know the man that must hear me."[27] He has to find someone to share his adventure to give shrift of his own sin and tell him to love man and bird and beast. There is no doubt that his preach is very effective. The guest, who is impatient at the beginning, even curses at the mariner to drive him away, is gradually attracted by this true story, being curious and worried about the story teller. In the end, the guest leaves the wedding silently, and changes a lot since then.

> The Mariner, whose eye is bright,
> Whose beard with age is hoar,
> Is gone: and now the Wedding-Guest
> Turned from the bridgegroom's door.
>
> He went like one that hath been stunned,
> And is of sense forlorn;
> A sadder and a wiser man,
> He rose the morrow morn.[28]

The wedding-guest serves as the prototype of those human who are the arrogant but ignorant, attempting to conquer and rule nature. The reason why the ancient mariner chooses this man is that the poet wants to show even the most stubborn and brutal man can be persuaded to love and respect nature. So human have no reason to damage nature, and every one has the responsibility and also the ability to persuade others to stop destroying nature and learn to love and respect all the living things. It is also the theme of this poem, to arouse people's awareness for nature protection, to respect, to be friendly, and to love. The harmonious relationship between man and nature is so precious that man need to spare no efforts to make our contribution to rebuild and maintain it.

Ecological balance is fragile, and every one is responsible to establish and keep it. Nowadays, along with the rapid development of economy, more and more natural resources are being abused by man, and man's living environment has been getting worse every day. It has become an urgent mission for human to put awareness on this problem and do their best to rebuild and maintain a friendly environment. This situation makes the study of *The Rime of the Ancient Mariner* flourish, and the attention of the critics has shifted from the difficult understanding surface meaning to the symbolic meaning, which greatly promote the ecological literature.[29] Analyzing from an ecological perspective, the contemporary critics pay more attention on the harmony between man and nature instead of the Christian spirit. *The Rime of the Ancient Mariner* attaches great importance to the harmonious relationship between man and nature, which attempts to arouse people's awareness of nature protection. Today's China is developing rapidly. After learning enough heavy lessons from foreign countries which have developed at the cost of sacrificing nature, now it is time for China to seek a new approach to reach its great goal. Although *The Rime of the Ancient Mariner* is a poem of the 18th century, the inner value of this poem is still to be discovered, especially from an ecological perspective, which is of great value to today's society.

Conclusion

The Rime of the Ancient Mariner is recognized as Samuel Taylor Coleridge's best work. Except for its exquisite structure, its beauty of music, and its delicate rhyme, it boasts of an everlasting theme: the theme of nature protection and ecological balance.

Ecological civilization is one of the main tasks of today's society. After years of exploration, humanity finally comes to know that it is nature which cultivates man and guarantees human's development. Viewing from an ecological perspective, Samuel Taylor Coleridge tells us that not only man, but also the bird, the water-snakes and all other animals are equal sons of nature, which worth human's respect and love.[18] The transient harmony between man and nature draws us to think of it and teaches us a profound and everlasting lesson: If man want to survive and develop, the first thing is to establish a harmonious relationship with nature, and the second, to maintain it. For years man has been plundering nature and has no sense to protect it. By telling the story of man's sin of killing a friendly albatross and the revenge, Coleridge aims to persuade all man to respect and protect nature for the sake of man's own survivor.

There are already enough lessons that have taught us the importance of maintaining a friendly relationship with nature. Today, by attaching more and more attention to nature protection, it is acknowledged that whoever violates nature could be punished seriously. And human cannot afford the result of destroying nature. The only way for man to develop themselves is to coexist with nature.

Notes

1. Meeker Joseph, *The Comedy of Survival: Studies in Literary Ecology* (London: Macmillan, 1972) 57
2. Wordsworth William, *Coleridge: The Ancient Mariner and Other Poems* (Hong Kong: Macmillan, 1986) 47.
3. Knight, G. W., *English Romantic Poets: Modern Essays in Criticism* (New York: Oxford University Press, 1980) 181.
4. Whalley George. *The Mariner and the Albatross* (London: Macmillan Press, 1946) 65.
5. Warren Robert Penn. *A Poem of Pure Imagination: An Experiment in Reading* (Michigan: Gale Research, 1989) 79.
6. Patrick D. Murphy ed., *Literature of Nature: An International Sourcebook* (Chicago: Fitzroy Dearborn Publisher, 1998) 169.
7. Jonathan Bate, *The Song of the Earth* (Cambridge: Harvard University Press, 2000) 49.
8. 王佐良. 英国文学名篇选著[M]. 商务印书馆,1983:707.
9. 张礼龙. 基督教的寓意与人生苦难的写照[J]. 厦门大学学报:哲学社会科学版,2002(4):114.
10. 王丽. 《古舟子咏》中的信天翁意象[J]. 巢湖学院学报,2009(5):72.
11. Samuel Taloy Coleridge, *The Rime of the Ancient Mariner* (Beijing: Foreign Language Teaching and Research Press, 2013) 32. (All the quotations in this thesis refer to this book, unless otherwise stated.)
12. Ibid., 34.
13. Ibid., 36.
14. 王诺. 欧美生态文学[M]. 北京大学出版社,2003:46.
15. 李敏. 从柯尔律治的自然观看人类生态意识的演变[J]. 消费导刊文化研究,2008(3).
16. Ibid., 64.
17. Ibid., 46.
18. Ibid., 42.
19. Ibid., 48.
20. Ibid., 50.
21. Ibid., 52.
22. Ibid., 54.
23. Ibid., 54.
24. Ibid., 72.
25. Ibid., 74.

26　Leopord Aldo. *A Sand County Almanac* (New York:Oxford,1949)28.
27　Ibid. ,82.
28　Ibid. ,84.
29　孙秀兰,吴斌.人与自然关系的生态寓言[J].东北师大学报:哲学社会科学版 2008(3):132.

Bibliography

Ashton, Rosemary. *The Life of Samuel Talyor Coleridge*. Oxford: Blackwell Publishers Ltd. 1996.

Bate, Jonathan. *The Song of the Earth*. Cambridge: Harvard University Press. 2000.

Beer, John. *Coleridge's Writings*. Vol. 1. London: Macmillan Press. 1990.

Colleridge, Samuel Talyor. *Biographia Literaiar*. Oxford: Clarendon Press. 1907.

Hill, J. Spensor. *A Colridge Companion*. London: Macmillan Press. 1983.

Knight, G. W. *English Romantic Poets: Modern Essays in Criticism*. New York: Oxford University Press.

Mckusick, James. C. *Green Writing: Romanticism and Ecology*. London: Macmillan Press. 2000.

Taylor, Paul. *Respect for Nature*. Princeton: Princeton University Press. 1986.

Wordsworth, William. *Coleridge: The Ancient Mariner and Other Poems*. Hongkong: Macmillan Press. 1986.

柯尔律治.《柯尔律治诗选》.杨德豫译,北京:外语教学与研究出版社.2013.

塞缪尔·泰勒·柯勒律治,佩利.《塞缪尔·泰勒·柯勒律治》.上海:上海外语教育出版社.2008.

孙秀兰,吴斌."人与自然关系的生态寓言".东北师大学报(哲学社会科学版).2008.

王佐良.《英国文学名篇选著》.北京:商务印刷馆.1983.

张礼龙."基督教的寓意与人生苦难的写照".厦门大学学报(哲学社会科学版).2002.

罗益民."管箫婚曲声中的流浪者".国外文学.2003.

王丽."《古舟子咏》中的信天翁意象".巢湖学院学报,2009(5).

王诺.《欧美生态文学》.北京:北京大学出版社.2003.

李敏."从柯尔律治的自然观看人类生态意识的演变".消费导刊文化研究.2008.

李正栓.郭群英.《新编英国文学教程》.河北:河北教育出版社.2006.

第三节　教学法类

××大学

本科生毕业论文（设计）册

题目：由汉语负迁移引起的高中英语句法错误分析

学院＿＿＿＿＿＿
专业＿＿＿＿＿＿
班级＿＿＿＿＿＿
学生＿＿＿＿＿＿
指导教师＿＿＿＿＿
完成日期＿＿＿＿＿

An Analysis of Syntactic Errors Caused by Chinese Negative Transfer in English Learning of Senior High School Students

By

×××

Prof. ×××, Tutor

A Thesis Submitted to the Foreign Languages

Institutes in Partial Fulfillment of the Requirements

For the Degree of Bachelor of Arts at

××× University

May 2014

Abstract

  Grammar learning in senior high school is believed to be important as well as difficult. Many students owe their English test errors to the lacking of mastery of grammar. And syntax, with innumerable rules, is the one that confuses them most. The thesis aims to explore and analyze the syntactic errors in the view of Chinese negative transfer and find out the countermeasures. Language transfer theory has been studied for quite a long time, but only a few is practical and accessible to senior high school students. The thesis presents a brief introduction to language transfer theory and a detailed research of the effects of Chinese negative transfer on English syntax learning in senior high school.

  In terms of method, the thesis makes a survey of two classes in Wuqiang Senior High School, Hebei Province. Interactions with teachers in English class are observed, writing exercises are assigned and evaluated and interviews are carried out. With the help of contrastive analysis theory and error analysis theory, the thesis makes a thorough and scientific analysis of the results.

  The results show that the students depend too much on Chinese when they try to get their own output in English, producing a lot of Chinglish and other syntactic errors. The most common ones are word order errors and agreement errors. And the main cause of the Chinese negative transfer is that the students do not have a deep understanding of the differences between Chinese and English. At last, the thesis puts forward some suggestions on English teaching in senior high school accordingly.

Key words: transfer theory negative transfer syntactic errors

摘　要

　　语法学习是高中英语学习中的重点和难点。许多学生都将自己试卷中的大部分错误归结于自己语法没有掌握好。而语法中的句法，因为规则多而繁琐，成为最令高中生头疼的问题。本篇论文试图从汉语负迁移的角度调查和分析句法方面的错误并找到解决办法。关于语言迁移理论的研究由来已久，但是只有一小部分对高中生来说是实用的、切实可行的。本篇论文介绍了语言迁移理论并详尽地调查研究了汉语负迁移对高中生句法学习的影响。

　　就方法而言，本论文对河北省武强中学的高一年级两个班的学生进行了调查，其中包括观察学生在英语课堂上与教师的互动，评估学生的写作练习，采访其他英语教师等具体措施。以对比分析理论和错误分析理论为指导，本篇论文对调查结果进行了全面、科学的分析。

　　结果显示，当学生试图用英语输出时，他们过于依赖汉语以至于产生了大量的中国式英语及其他句法错误。最常见的错误是语序混乱和主谓不一致。而汉语负迁移的主要原因是学生对汉英两种语言特点差异把握不足。最后，本篇论文有针对性地对高中的英语教学提出了一些建议。

关键词：　迁移理论　　负迁移　　句法错误

Contents

Abstract ……………………………………………………………………………

Abstract in Chinese ………………………………………………………………

1. Introduction ……………………………………………………………………
    1.1 The purpose and significance of the research …………………………
    1.2 The background of the research ………………………………………
    1.3 The organization of the thesis …………………………………………
2. Theoretical Basis ………………………………………………………………
    2.1 The language transfer theory ……………………………………………
        2.1.1 Definitions of transfer ……………………………………………
        2.1.2 Classifications of language transfer theory ………………………
        2.1.3 Syntactic transfer …………………………………………………
    2.2 The contrastive analysis theory …………………………………………
    2.3 The error analysis theory ………………………………………………
        2.3.1 Definition of errors ………………………………………………
        2.3.2 Definition of error analysis ………………………………………
        2.3.3 Distinction of errors and mistakes ………………………………
3. Research Methods ……………………………………………………………
    3.1 Participants ………………………………………………………………
    3.2 Research methods ………………………………………………………
        3.2.1 Class observation …………………………………………………
        3.2.2 Writing exercises …………………………………………………
        3.2.3 Interview …………………………………………………………
4. Research Results and Discussion ……………………………………………
    4.1 Results ……………………………………………………………………
        4.1.1 Results from class observation …………………………………
        4.1.2 Results from writing exercises …………………………………
        4.1.3 Results from interview ……………………………………………
    4.2 Results analysis …………………………………………………………
        4.2.1 Conjunction ………………………………………………………
        4.2.2 Word order ………………………………………………………
        4.2.3 Agreement …………………………………………………………
        4.2.4 Omission …………………………………………………………
        4.2.5 Negation …………………………………………………………
        4.2.6 Tense ………………………………………………………………

4.3 Result discussion
 4.3.1 Failing to realize the differences between
   English and Chinese
 4.3.2 Lack of comprehensible input
 4.3.3 Lack of knowledge of English culture
5. Conclusion
 5.1 Suggestions for avoiding Chinese negative transfer
  5.1.1 Facilitating the learning environment
  5.1.2 Syntactic training
  5.1.3 E-C contrast training
 5.2 Conclusion of the research
  5.2.1 The unexpected findings
  5.2.2 A summary of the whole research
Bibliography

1. Introduction

1.1 The purpose and significance of the research

Nowadays, English has been identified its undeniable status as the world's universal language. About four million people speak English as their first language and seventy-three countries and regions in the world regard English as their official language. Whatever international issues come into your mind: politics, economy, and tourism and so on, they are all in English. Therefore, it is necessary for each "global" person to speak and understand English.

In China, millions of people begin to learn English as a foreign language when they are kids. Senior high school students, motivated by the NMET, nearly spare no efforts to learn English well. They spend plenty of time every day reading English texts, reciting English words and doing English exercises. However, the result is not as good as they expect. Errors still abound in the test papers.

The phenomenon gets countless researchers into action to find out the reasons. No doubt, the results vary a lot. The thesis has its own findings as well. The senior high school students' poor performance in English has much to do with the Chinese knowledge they have already acquired long before and practiced over and over again. To put it in other words, the Chinese knowledge, grammar in particular, affects the students negatively to some extent when they try to make sentences in English, both spoken and written.

The thesis will make a survey and analysis of the senior high school students about the negative influence Chinese cast upon their English learning. Since English learning in senior high school is quite a big topic with numerous details, the thesis will try to solve the problem that confuse the students most: the syntactic errors caused by Chinese negative transfer.

Obviously, English grammar learning is not an easy issue to many senior high school students. On the one hand, English grammar consists of too many rules, including some irregular ones which the learners have to learn one by one. On the other hand, there are a lot of differences between Chinese grammar and English grammar in spite of some similarities and these differences are easily to be neglected. Being part of cross-cultural studies, the latter has become the focus of linguists and educators. It is believed that the differences result in errors. And the errors are what the thesis will focus on.

In the end, the thesis will come up with some pedagogical suggestions about how to help and guide the senior high school students to learn English grammar efficiently regardless of Chinese negative transfer.

1.2 The background of the research

The study of language transfer theory has been under discussion for at least a century, for it is a very important topic in second language acquisition, applied linguistics and foreign language teaching (Odlin, 2001). The development of language transfer theory can roughly be divided into three stages.

The first stage, during the 1950s and 1960s, the theory enjoyed great popularity and prosperity. It played an important role in the second language acquisition theory. At the same time, it was associated with the predominant Behaviorism, becoming the theoretical basis of the contrastive analysis hypothesis.

The second stage, nevertheless, was a period that language transfer theory did not run smoothly. From the end of the 1960s to the 1970s, the universal grammar which was put forward by Noam Chomsky was largely accepted. Quite a few linguists, represented by Robert Lado (1964) and Edward Vivian Gatenby (1967), held a negative attitude towards the contrastive analysis hypothesis and language transfer theory. In the field of foreign language learning, behavioral language learning was attacked and the transfer theory was demeaned.

Then another side of the picture was presented at the third stage, which began at the end of the 1970s and the start of the 1980s. Once again, language transfer theory became a heatedly-discussed topic by linguists and was regarded as an important strategy and a complex process affected and restricted by many factors.

There are quite a few Chinese linguists who are interested in the language transfer theory and make efforts to make it practical and available to English learners. Domestic researchers find that it is a universal phenomenon in China that students usually make use of Chinese grammar to complete English translating and writing tasks. And it is believed that the more difficult the task is, the more frequently students will turn to Chinese for help (Dai Weidong & Shu Dingfang, 1994: 34—37). Errors tend to occur where the differences of Chinese and English lie (Zhu Zhongdu, 1999:28—30). And Ma Bingyi (1999:19—21) makes it clear that there exist indeed differences between English and Chinese, particularly syntactic structures with the former one being grammatical while the latter one semantic.

Nowadays, people put a lot of emphasis on transfer and make researches and studies from perspectives of psychology, linguistics and society and so on (Dai, 2002). More questions are raised and more methods are adopted. But the effects are not satisfactory. Few of the theories can be practical or helpful to English learners, senior high school students in particular, to whom learning English is not an efficient process despite both time and energy devoted. The thesis is designed as a bridge to help the senior high school students to get access to the transfer theory by analyzing the syntactic errors caused by Chinese negative transfer.

1.3 The organization of the thesis

The thesis focuses on the syntactic errors caused by Chinese negative transfer and it follows the formal layout of the thesis of TEFL, which is in orderly and logical organization.

At the beginning, the thesis makes a brief introduction to give the readers a glimpse of the whole thesis as to why the study is done and where its significance lies. Background information is presented to help the readers to know more about the research field, both its history and new discoveries. The thesis takes advantage of the previous theories and achieves its new and practical value, seeking to help senior high school students to learn English without Chinese negative transfer.

Then the thesis illustrates what is "language transfer theory." Though most people come across "language transfer problems" frequently, they may not know why it happens or how it actually works. Other theories such as contrastive analysis hypothesis and error analysis theory which support the study theoretically are also introduced.

The theoretical knowledge is followed by the research methods. The thesis makes a survey of eighty-two students in Wuqiang Senior High School, Hebei Province. After observing the students' interactions with teachers in English class, analyzing the errors of the writing exercises and interviewing the local English teachers, the thesis makes a summary and discussion of the results, according to which it puts forward the causes of Chinese negative transfer. It is surprising to know how little the students pay attention to the differences between Chinese and English and how much they rely on Chinese when they learn English.

In the end, the practical function of the thesis is presented. Accordingly, it comes up with some suggestions for English grammar teaching in senior high school, and avoiding Chinese negative transfer accounts for a large part such as facilitating the learning environment, syntactic training and E-C contrast training. The thesis also summarizes some unexpected findings.

In a word, Chinese negative transfer is one of the main causes of the common syntactic errors in English learning and it can be avoided by taking some positive measures, such as getting to know western culture and listening to native English more frequently and so on.

2. Theoretical Basis

2.1　The language transfer theory

2.1.1　Definitions of transfer

Researches and studies of language transfer abound, but a standard definition has not been achieved yet. Many linguists have their own understandings of transfer, and even some misunderstandings used to be popular.

A common one is that language transfer is the result of the formation of simple language habits. Behaviorists hold that language capacity consists of a series of habits. Learning a language is like developing a habit. When the new habit comes into being, the old habit begins to disappear, namely, the new habit takes place of the old one. But the second language people are learning will not replace their mother tongue. Actually, they coexist. "The formula of the language processing of the brain is not the simple $1+1=2$, rather, $1+1>2$" (Wang, 1990).

The behaviorists' definition does not last long. There are indeed a few authoritative definitions of transfer which have been used for guidance and evidence over and over again.

Jacqueline Schachter (1974) treats language transfer phenomenon as a kind of constraint in the language learning process. Based on a cognitive perspective, she denies that language transfer is a psychological process. She believes that the learners' previously acquired language knowledge constrains the learners' hypothesis of the target language. Transfer can be caused by all previous knowledge during the foreign language learning process. The learners will make some hypothesis of the target language, and develop its inter-language while checking the hypothesis, which is constrained by all the language knowledge acquired before.

American applied linguist Terence Odlin looks on transfer as a sort of cross-linguistic influence, which is based on the common aspects and distinct aspects between target language and mother tongue. The conclusion comes from a cognitive perspective. The original definition goes like this: "Transfer is the influence resulting from the similarities and differences between the target language and any other language that has been previously (and perhaps imperfectly) acquired (1989:27)."

Odlin names the above sentence "working definition" and it provides the theoretical basis for the thesis. More specifically, transfer refers to the phenomenon that students are affected by the acquired Chinese knowledge when they learn English. It does not necessarily mean that errors arise as long as transfer occurs. In fact, language transfer works in more than one direction. It can be beneficial as well as disturbing to language learning.

2.1.2 Classifications of language transfer theory

2.1.2.1 Positive transfer

Positive transfer refers to the phenomenon that the former experience or knowledge makes the latter easier and effortless. A common case in daily life is that how much it helps to learn to ride a motor-bike if one masters the skills of riding a normal bicycle in advance. Obviously positive transfer occurs from bicycle riding to motor-bike riding (Johnson, 2002:60).

Fortunately learners can experience positive transfer when they learn a foreign language. For instance, "journal" is both an English word and a French word with the same meaning. An English learner of French will find it easy to acquire the vocabulary. Similarly, Germans will not find the English article system complicated or confusing, because there is a roughly identical one in their native language. Chinese students, most of whom learn English for various reasons, also experience some positive transfer. The sentence pattern "S(ubject)+V(erb)+O(bject)" belongs to Chinese and English at the same time. As a result, such sentence translation task as "I like summer," "They visit museums," "Mum washes clothes" will cause few word order problems.

2.1.2.2 Negative transfer

"Transfer could also be negative in the sense that experience with one set of events could hurt performance on related tasks." (Lunchins & Lunchins, 1970: 53—54) It refers to the phenomenon that the former experience or knowledge disturbs the latter and gets the learners to make errors. In fact, almost nobody can avoid negative transfer completely in daily life. People tend to apply old rules to new things but it does not work or even provides unexpected results. For instance, the new computer's volume control takes the place of the old computer's switch control. When the owner wants to turn on/off the computer, he is actually turning up/down the computer.

In foreign language learning, negative transfer is a main cause of errors and it occurs at all levels. The first one is negative phonological transfer. Not every English sound can find its equivalent in Chinese. There is no distinction between /v/ and /w/ in Chinese, so well/wel/ can be pronounced as /vel/ (Liang, 2006).

Negative lexical transfer comes next. Examples can be found in words which have different connotations or scope in Chinese and English. In English the word "blue" refers to being "low in spirits" in addition to the sense of color. However, Chinese culture labels "blue" being serious. So there is a tendency for Chinese students to misuse the word. Negative lexical transfer can also be found in the exercises of collocation. The phrases "well beautiful" and "give you a color see see" are all typical errors.

The third one is negative cultural transfer. The ways English people greet each other are different from Chinese ones. Negative transfer occurs when Chinese students translate their own greetings literally, such as "Have you eaten yet?"(ni chi le ma?), "Where are you going?"(qu na a?) etc. English speakers treat the former one as an invitation and the latter one as an offence of privacy rather than normal greetings.

Finally it is negative syntactic transfer. It is a complicated topic and is the one that confuses the senior high school students most. Sentences like "Because I am ill, so I will not go to school today." and "Though it is raining hard, but we will still carry out our plan." abound in their test papers. The thesis will analyze the errors caused by negative syntactic transfer in details in the following chapters.

2.1.3 Syntactic transfer

When syntax comes under discussion, it is inevitable to talk about conjunction, negation, agreement, omission, word order, tense and voice and so on. Definitely, the similarities between the two languages will help Chinese students to learn English syntax and in this case the transfer is positive. In terms of word order, both Chinese and English have the basic "S + V + O" structure. Therefore, Chinese students will not find the English expression awkward. But it is the differences that result in errors. Many students attempt to mix English vocabulary with Chinese grammar, a common way resulting in negative transfer, and it usually does not work. As to agreement, verbs do not change in accordance with the subject in Chinese while it is a necessity in English. The thesis will make an analysis of the errors of conjunction, negation, agreement, omission, word order, tense and voice caused by Chinese negative transfer and attempt to help senior high school students to get rid of the negative influence of mother tongue.

2.2 The contrastive analysis theory

Learners can realize the easy points and difficult points of the foreign language learning if they make a comparison and contrast of the new language and his original language in advance (Cook, 2000:15—18). This is what "contrastive analysis hypothesis" refers to. It is Robert Lado who gives a definition first. He suggests that "those elements that are similar to [the learners'] native language will be simple for him, and those elements that are different will be difficult" (1952:2).

The theory suggests that the similarities between the two languages will make learners experience positive transfer and the differences will lead to negative transfer. Besides, when there is a lack of equivalents in the mother tongue, the learners will have trouble in understanding certain terms. For instance, most Chinese students are confused the first time they get to know the distinction between "borrow" and "lend." The theory tries to identify the differences and to predict the possible errors so that learners will be more careful and make fewer errors.

Rod Ellis puts forward two basic claims of the theory which connect the differences with the errors: the more different is target language from mother tongue, the more difficulties the learners will meet to acquire the new knowledge; and more difficulties tend to make the errors appear more frequently (1993). The significance of the claims can be explained by their frequent appearance in many researchers' studies.

However, the results of contrastive analysis state clearly that mother tongue negative transfer is by no means the only cause of errors. In fact, learners are not likely to make errors if the differences are obvious enough. They tend to make errors when they fail to recognize the differences. Therefore, contrastive analysis theory enjoys an ambiguous popularity among linguists.

Being criticized, Lado's theory has been polished over the years and it is playing an important role in language teaching. The study will take advantage of the methods of the theory, explain the causes of the errors and come up with some suggestions.

2.3　The error analysis theory

2.3.1　Definition of errors

Language learning and teaching will not be a complete topic if errors do not take part in the process. No one can avoid to make errors and the causes of errors are many. All of these are very important to researchers of foreign language learning. As to the question what is an error, different researches hold different understandings.

The most frequently adopted definition is given by Ya Dafu, who suggests that an error is "a sequence of production in which a certain constituent or combination of constituents violates any linguistic norm of standard English usage" (2000: 107).

Hu Zhuanglin treats errors as "the learner's misuse or misunderstanding of the target language may it be grammatical or pragmatic" (2001:148—225).

Although there is more than one type of definition, all the experts try to explain the same thing: errors are the results of violation of the normal rules. On one hand, making errors is inevitable. On the other hand, it has reference value. The thesis will adopt the last one as its theoretical basis.

2.3.2　Definition of error analysis

Error analysis is "the study and analysis of the ERRORS made by second language learners" (Richards & Schmidt 2002: 159—160). At the end of the 1960s, error analysis came to be accepted and nearly replaced contrastive analysis.

Researchers of error analysis described and analyzed the learners' errors in details, forming a series of effective analysis methods. The theory aims to get to know learners' real language capacity. It also tries to explain and describe all kinds of errors to find out how learners deal with second language information. Therefore, it functions in a different way from contrastive analysis which has to predict in advance the errors caused by mother tongue negative transfer.

There are five basic steps of error analysis: "collection of a sample of learner language, identification of errors, description of errors, explanation of errors and evaluation of errors" (Corder, 1967:161—169). The thesis will follow the steps to help senior high school students to reduce their errors and improve their English performance.

2.3.3 Distinction of errors and mistakes

Errors are nothing like mistakes in error analysis. Errors are caused by the learners' lack of some knowledge of certain language rules. The errors will not be diminished until the learners acquire the rules. Mistakes are occasional. They occur when the learners are absent-minded in using the rules that they have already learnt by heart. So mistakes are equal for everyone and they are committed mostly by those careful persons. The carelessness can result in mistakes even when they speak mother tongue. Error analysis is not the analysis of mistakes but the analysis of errors. For instance, the sentence "He stay awake all night to take care of the patient." goes against the rule of "subject-predicate concord" principle. It can be an interference of mother tongue because in Chinese predicates do not change morphologically with subjects. It is an error for the learner who does not know the rule at all.

The chapter has a brief review of the theoretical basis of the thesis. Language transfer theory is what the whole thesis starts with. Contrastive analysis theory, despite its drawbacks, performs an important role in providing the framework of comparing the differences of Chinese and English. Error analysis theory helps a lot with the design of the whole study. All of the above theories make the thesis meaningful, logical and reasonable.

It is obvious that the theories on language transfer are all controversial but they are developing all the time and are playing an important part in offering suggestions to foreign language studying. Till now, researches on lexical transfer and cultural transfer are many while on syntax transfer are few. The thesis will try to fill the gap, integrate the merits of the above theories and put them into practical use.

3. Research Methods

3.1 Participants

The participants of the present study are eighty-two students of Grade One from two classes in Wuqiang Senior High School, Hebei Province. It is a boarding school whose class distribution is carried out randomly so the results shall be relatively representative and persuasive.

The students, the average age of whom is seventeen, take high school English classes regularly. They finish one or two pages of exercise book every day, read or recite English words, sentences or paragraphs every other morning and do listening exercises three times a week. Time is consumed. Effort is paid. However, the students' English performance does not improve accordingly.

3.2 Research methods

3.2.1 Class observation

The first method is concerned with observing the students' interaction with teachers in English class. The method aims to find out how students behave in English class, namely how to answer the teachers' questions, how to deal with the difficulties and how to carry out the discussion tasks. Besides, the English teachers are also observed as to how much English is spoken.

The data collected is from the observation notes based on three reading classes: "The True North—from Toronto to Montreal," "A Master of Nonverbal Humor" and "Communication: No Problem?"

The method is adopted in that English classes and English teachers are of great importance to the students. The English classes are nearly the only way in which the students get access to systematic English learning and the very place where the students speak English most. Class observation can help to analyze why negative transfer occurs.

3.2.2 Writing exercises

The second method is to examine the students' writing skill. It focuses on the syntactic errors, rather than mistakes. More specifically, errors of conjunction, negation, agreement, omission, word order and tense will be paid special attention to. The interference of Chinese resulting in these errors is described and analyzed.

The students are asked to write two essays. The first is an informal narration. The students should make a narration of what has happened during last week. The second is a letter writing. The students should try to invite a foreign friend to visit their school by offering a vivid description. Both of the two essays should be written more than eighty words. Then all the essays are collected.

The method is adopted in that writing skill is a relatively difficult one compared with the skills of listening, speaking and reading. It can reflect how well the students have acquired the knowledge and how much they depend on Chinese when they want to express an idea.

3.2.3 Interview

In the end, six English teachers of the school are interviewed. The interview aims to learn about the local teachers' teaching approaches, their attitude towards their students' errors and their comments on their students, the school and themselves.

There are twelve questions being divided into three sections in total. The first section is about the teachers' teaching approaches. The second one is about how the teachers treat the students' errors, the ones shadowed by Chinese in particular. The last one is the appraisal part: How do they like the current English learning situation? Are they satisfied with their students, the school or themselves?

The method is adopted for a couple of reasons. Firstly, different teachers have different teaching approaches which affect their students in a direct way. Secondly, it is the teachers who have a full understanding of their students. They can explain why certain methods do not work and why certain phenomenon is there. Lastly, by talking to the local teachers, the students' English learning environment can be known, thus helping to find out the causes of Chinese negative transfer.

4. Research Results and Discussion

4.1 Results

4.1.1 Results from class observation

After observing three reading classes: "The True North—from Toronto to Montreal," "A Master of Nonverbal Humor," "Communication: No Problem?" conclusions are drawn and the following phenomena are what happens in local English classes every day.

As to the teachers, they tend to give priority to vocabulary and grammar in their class planning. A popular belief is that the efficiency of the class will not be achieved if too much information about the background is introduced. The teachers read the texts in English but explain the grammar rules in Chinese. And they allow the students to answer in Chinese when they meet difficulties in oral English.

As to the students, they are more active in English class when they are allowed to speak Chinese. And they show more interest in the life and culture of English countries than in the grammar rules. In the reading class of "Canada—the True North," the students are highly concentrated in the beginning when information of Canada is introduced, but their enthusiasm declines as the leading-in part moves to the comprehension part.

Besides, if the teachers and students communicate in Chinese, few problems will come in the way. But when the teacher begins to speak English, the students feel at loss. They are not confident in understanding the teachers, thus keeping seeking help from their classmates nearby.

4.1.2 Results from writing exercises

There are eighty-two students in total but actually seventy-five of them have finished the task according to the requirement. So the 150 valid essays will account for the final data. Most students write more words in narratives than in the letters. And there are fewer errors in narratives.

In the narration task, ten students have completed their essays with no obvious syntactic errors. The rest are more or less concerned with the possibility of translating their previously prepared Chinese equivalents, because they are occupied with Chinese ways of expressing ideas. And they are not aware that the stories they tell should be in past tense.

In the letter task, only eight students have not committed obvious errors. Errors of agreement abound, such as "There is two girls' dorm buildings," "The teachers here is very nice and responsible" and so on. The following tables demonstrate six types of errors and corresponding occurrence.

Types	Occurrence
Conjunction	15
Word order	11
Agreement	23
Omission	7
Negation	4
Tense	39

Table one: the result from narratives

Types	Occurrence
Conjunction	20
Word order	23
Agreement	37
Omission	10
Negation	6
Tense	17

Table two: the result from letters

4.1.3 Results from interview

In addition to the factors of the students themselves, the interview reveals a great deal of information of the learning "customs" of the school.

Firstly, five teachers confess that their teaching methods are restricted by the frequent exams. What will be tested decides what should be taught. So students can hardly get access to native English except for listening comprehension exercises. The cultural activities in class will be treated as a waste of time and they are carried out only when absolutely necessary. Chinese explanation is much more efficient in English class. Only one teacher tries to let their students know more than the language itself. All the six teachers agree that English test paper ranks first in the list of the popular types of homework.

Secondly, errors are the targets to be hated and are treated equally. All the six teachers believe that errors indicate a lack of hard working. The students' errors should be corrected immediately. And the teachers' errors will lead to embarrassment and the students' distrust. If errors of one type appear over and over again, two teachers tend to repeat the language points and the others hold that punishment is more effective. Four teachers refuse to credit self-correction or peer-correction which as a result is not likely to appear in their classes. Only two of the six teachers think that dependence on Chinese may have some uncertain negative effects.

In the end, there is a divergence among the six teachers when it comes to the appraisal part. Two teachers think that the current situation for English learning is fine. As long as the students work harder and the teachers assign more homework, they are sure to get higher marks. The rest are not satisfied with the current approaches or the students' performance. They hope that the school can help with the improvement process. More emphasis will lead to more efforts of the teachers. Furthermore, it is quite necessary for their students to get easy access to native English.

4.2 Results analysis

4.2.1 Conjunction

Among the essays, sentences in which "because" and "so" go together abound. The conjunctions "though" and "but" also appear within the same sentence in many students papers. Here are examples from the narratives.

(1) On Monday, though it was windy, but we still did morning exercise.

(2) Because the hero was dead in the end, so I did not think highly of the film.

The examples also abound in English class when students try to answer the teacher's questions or have a discussion with their classmates.

(3) Because Canada is largely covered by snow, so it is a good place to go skating.

(4) Though you have won his support, but I don't agree with you on this point.

It is a rule in English that "though" and "but" cannot exist in the same sentence, neither can "because" and "so." However, in Chinese, it is a must for each pair to appear at the same time. The students who have committed such errors must have acquired the Chinese rule and applied it to his / her English writing, leading to Chinese negative transfer.

To make a correction, all that needs to be done is to delete either "though" or "but" in sentence (1) and sentence (4) and to delete either "because" or "so" in sentence (2) and sentence (3).

4.2.2 Word order

From the students' narratives, the conclusion that some students are actually following the Chinese word order can be drawn. And it can be justified by the following examples.

(5) I by bike went to the Palace Museum.

Chinese：我骑自行车去了故宫博物院。

(6) I and Shao Ying did homework.

Chinese：我和邵颖做了作业。

(7) You how solved that chemistry problem?

Chinese：你是怎么解决的那个化学难题？

In sentence (5), the adverbial "by bike" is put in the wrong position. In Chinese the adverbial can be placed in front of the verb. But it is more common to put the adverbial at the end of the sentence in English. Sentence (6) is about the sequence of pronouns. In Chinese the order is "the second person, the first person and the third person." But it is "the second person, the third person and the first person" when the pronoun is in English singular form. Sentence (7) is an interrogative sentence but it is in Chinese word order. To obey the English grammar rule, "how" together with an auxiliary verb "did" should be placed at the beginning of the sentence.

The above-mentioned three sentences are an explanation of the distinction of Chinese and English in word order and an illustration of the influence of Chinese negative transfer.

4.2.3 Agreement

In terms of number, there is only one predicate form in Chinese but two in English, singular form and plural form. And English predicates need to change in accordance with the subjects. Failing to realize the difference and following the Chinese pattern will result in the following errors, which are from the students' letters.

(8) Wu Tong and I am satisfied to finish the work together.

(9) A new store have been opened this year.

Sentence (8) has two subjects, so the predicate should be in plural form by the English grammar rule. The word "am" should be replaced by "are." There is only one subject in sentence (9) and the predicate should be in singular form. The word "have" should be replaced by "has."

4.2.4 Omission

Both English and Chinese involve the matter of omission. However, they comply with different rules. Among the 150 essays, subject omission, object omission, conjunction omission and omission of "be" are most frequently applied by the students but errors frequently appear as well.

(10) At our school have 254 teachers and 4,300 students.

(11) I enjoyed very much in the fair.

(12) I played computer games, watched TV, visited my friends on Saturday.

(13) Our future will brighter and brighter.

All the four sentences can be literally translated into totally right Chinese sentences.

(10) 在我们学校有 254 名老师,3,000 名学生。

(11) 我在集市上很愉快。

(12) 星期六那天,我玩了电脑游戏,看了电视,拜访了朋友。

(13) 我们的未来将越来越美好。

Comparison of the two groups of sentences (10) to (13) can make it obvious that the omission errors appear owing to the Chinese negative transfer. Errors are inevitable if students try to apply Chinese rules to English writing where difference lies. The sentences should be corrected in this way:

(10) There are 254 teachers and 4,300 students in our school.

(11) I enjoyed myself very much in the fair.

(12) I played computer games, watched TV, and visited my friends on Saturday.

(13) Our future will be brighter and brighter.

4.2.5　Negation

It is the common sense that "Yes" stands for agreement and "No" stands for disagreement. But when there is divergence between English and the Chinese equivalents, errors occur. Conversation (14) and (15) take place in the reading class "A Master of Nonverbal Humor."

(14) T: Do you like Chaplin's humor?

　　　S: Yes, I do. / No, I don't.

(15) T: Don't you think Chaplin is a great person who can make the world laugh?

　　　S: Yes, I don't. / No, I do.

Conversation (14) is a right one whose translation into Chinese is "你喜欢卓别林式的幽默吗？是的,我喜欢。/ 不,我不喜欢。" The sentence structure is the same in the two languages. Few students commit errors here. Conversation (15) is different. The teacher's question is negative in itself, which means that "yes" equals Chinese "不" and "no" equals Chinese "是." But in form "not" still goes together with "no" rather than "yes." Therefore, native speakers of English will carry on the conversation in this way:

(15) T: Don't you think Chaplin is a great person who can make the world laugh?

　　　难道你不认为卓别林是一个能让世界笑的伟大人物吗？

　　　S: Yes, I do. / No, I don't.

　　　不,我这样认为。/ 是的,我不这样认为。

4.2.6　Tense

In English, the form of predicates is an indicator of the time of the happenings: in the past, at present or in the future. Actually, the English language involves sixteen tense aspects in total. However, the form of Chinese predicates has never changed at all. The contrast can explain why some students always forget to change the form of verbs. The following sentences are from the students' narratives.

(16) I go for a walk with my grandfather after supper yesterday.

(17) Guo Te washed clothes when I came to visit.

(18) I thought that I am cheated.

In sentence (16), "yesterday" is an indicator that "to go for a walk" is already done. So sentence (16) should be in simple past tense and "go" should be changed into "went." Sentence (17) should be in past progressive and "washed" should be changed into "was washing." In sentence (18), "am" needs to be changed into the past form "was" to go in harmony with "thought." The correct ones should be like this:

(16) I went for a walk with my grandfather after supper yesterday.

(17) Guo Te was washing clothes when I came to visit.

(18) I thought that I was cheated.

4.3 Results discussion

The analysis above shows how heavily students depend on Chinese when they learn English. All the learning process is a translating practice for them. They are translating all the time whether when they are answering the teachers' questions in class or when they are doing exercises out of class. When there is a group discussion on "body language," most students show interest and exchange ideas with their partners eagerly. But they communicate with each other in Chinese. Only when they need to make a summary and report their work to the class will they translate their ideas into English.

By means of the analysis of the class observation, the writing errors and the interview of the teachers, the causes of Chinese negative transfer are discovered and shown in the next sections.

4.3.1 Failing to realize the differences between English and Chinese

Chinese negative transfer is mainly caused by the students failing to realize the differences between English and Chinese. Senior high schools in China "impose" each student a tight schedule. In class, the students need to listen to the teachers who mainly explain the grammar rules. Out of class, the students are required to recite English vocabulary and do English exercises. All the work is proceeding in a mechanical way. They are made to believe that the more they practice, the better results they will receive. In fact, their errors can be consolidated as well. When they come across difficulties, they always turn to Chinese for help which is not very reliable.

Differences are easy to find by a comparison of the two languages. In addition to the six aspects that have already been discussed and stated, the following examples concerned with voice can also make the point clear.

(19) Aunt Li cleaned the sitting room.

李阿姨打扫了客厅。

(20) The sitting room was cleaned by Aunt Li.

客厅被李阿姨打扫了。

In example (19), the two sentences are both in active voice and follow the same pattern "S+V+O." In example (20), both the English sentence and the Chinese one are in passive voice. The English one is indicated by "be" and the Chinese one is indicated by "被." The sequence is different. Failing to realize the difference will result in such sentence as "*The sitting* room by *Aunt Li* was cleaned."

The two languages are also different in the mode of thinking. Chinese people tend to think in images while English-speaking people tend to think in concepts. Both habits are the results of history accumulation and are the marks of nationality. The former means that Chinese people like expressing abstract ideas by vivid and particular examples while the latter shows that English people are used to making use of abstract concepts to express concrete things. For example:

(21) 开幕式上人山人海。

(22) There were so many people in the ceremony.

If the students do not realize the distinction in thinking mode, they may translate sentence (21) into "*There were people mountain people sea in the ceremony*," which is obviously Chinglish.

4.3.2 Lack of comprehensible input

In the local school where the research is going on, English is given less emphasis not because it is not important, but in that it is difficult to the students. There are fewer English reading materials than those of other subjects in the reading room. There is multi-media equipment in the school but English films are strictly restricted and are allowed only when absolutely necessary. For example, "The Gold Rush" of Chaplin is allowed in that one of the texts in the book is a description of the film. But films like "Despicable Me," "Man of the Honor" and "Charlotte's Web" and so on are forbidden because they bear no relationship with the exam and are considered as a waste of time.

As to the teachers who spend most of the time in class explaining grammar rules, they do not regard speaking English as a necessity. The students, affected by the teaching approach and the tight schedule, have never got the habit or the interest of reading or speaking English. Apart from the local teachers, listening class is another way for the students to get access to native English. It is an efficient way to train the students' listening skill. But the teachers should have a careful design and a strict supervision of the listening class.

In high school, English is indeed a special subject. New and exotic, language learning calls for the skills of reading, speaking, listening and writing. Students will learn English better if they can get access to native English more frequently and get more comprehensible input (Krashen, 1988). However, the English learning environment of the school is not very helpful for the students to learn English or improve their scores in tests. When they cannot get enough English input, the students have to resort to Chinese and are less likely to avoid negative transfer as a result.

4.3.3 Lack of knowledge of English culture

The English language is rooted in English culture and it expresses and reflects the culture. Therefore, to understand the language better it is a necessity for the students to get to know English culture.

Astonishing differences exist between Chinese culture and English culture. For instance, "You are a lucky dog" delivers the message of praise and favor in English. But in China, it is offensive to associate a person or behavior with the word "dog" because it has derogatory connotation all along Chinese history. Knowledge of cultural background absent, the translation "你是一条幸运的狗" is easily made and misunderstanding may be caused. Indeed, the right version of the translation is "你是一个幸运儿。""Dragon" is another example that usually causes misunderstandings. Chinese people regard it as a symbol of prosperity and luck. However, it stands for evil in western culture. So it is completely forbidden to compare a westerner to a dragon.

In the senior high schools' texts, there is "Warming-up" section introducing background information in each unit. In unit 5 "Canada—the True North," general knowledge of the country including language, flag, population and natural scenes is discussed. The teachers will not give a detailed presentation of the country only to "improve" the efficiency of the class. As a matter of fact, students are more interested in the country than in the text. They can benefit from the background information which can broaden their horizon. Lack of cultural knowledge will make the students confused when there are no Chinese equivalents. And they tend to feel it awkward not to act in the Chinese customs.

5. Conclusion

5.1 Suggestions for avoiding Chinese negative transfer

5.1.1 Facilitating the learning environment

5.1.1.1 Speaking English in English class

To senior high school students, English class is the most important place where they can get access to a systematic study of English. So English rather than Chinese should be dominant in English class. Both the teachers and the students should be inspired to speak English more frequently.

In the beginning, it can be a little demanding to some students. The teachers can adopt some methods to lower the difficulty. For instance, the teachers can slow down or repeat the sentence when it is very long. The teachers can also speak English first and repeat it in Chinese when necessary.

Speaking English benefits the students in more than improving the oral English. It can also improve the students' reading speed and listening ability. Only by speaking a language can a person really acquire it.

5.1.1.2 Listening to native English more frequently

There are three listening classes every week in this school and the listening materials are all exam-oriented. It is not helpful to improve the students' listening ability. Listening exercises should not be packed and cast to listening classes only, which are easy to make students bored and exhausted.

Listening exercises can be done by dictation. The teachers can make a summary of the language points of the previous day and let the students write down the sentences or paragraphs that the teachers have read.

Listening exercises can also be done by warming-up of the reading class. Getting the students to listen to the audio of the text before reading is an adoptable method. In fact, the training is the most effective when reading, speaking, listening and writing go together.

5.1.1.3 Using English-English dictionaries

Many students have not developed the habit of looking up new words in the dictionary. Even if they have, most of their dictionaries are English-Chinese ones. Both the teachers and students think that it is efficient to consult English-Chinese dictionaries. Indeed, English-English dictionaries are more helpful and should be introduced, since no absolute Chinese equivalents of English exist at all.

Actually, when students search for words in English-English dictionaries, they can get more information than they need. By this means, students can get more comprehensible input simply. The English definition can help them to avoid wrong collocation to some extent. For instance, the explanation of "heavy" provided by an English-Chinese dictionary is "重的,沉的," on which condition students may get confused when they come across the phrases like "a heavy rain" or "a heavy smoker." But an English-English dictionary not only provides the English definition "weighing a lot / a lot or in very large numbers" but also explains the common phrases "a heavy smoker / drinker" as "someone who smokes a lot or drinks a lot of alcohol."

5.1.1.4 Introducing culture of English-speaking countries

As language is the elite part of culture, knowing about the culture of English-speaking countries, Britain and America in particular, is quite necessary. The teachers should make full use of the "warming up" part to introduce the foreign culture which can help the students understand the text better and more easily.

English proverbs which draw many students' interest are quite culture-bound and may lead to errors if the cultural background is absent. Students can barely connect "班门弄斧" with "teach fish to swim" if they know nothing about English culture. Just like Chinese, each English proverb comes from a story. Errors and misunderstandings can be avoided by learning the stories behind.

Not all the connotations of colors in western culture are the same with those in Chinese. For instance, Chinese people dress in white in funerals while westerners dress in black. Red is for happiness in China but it is the signal of blood in English culture. In a word, culture learning is absolutely necessary for the students' benefit.

5.1.1.5 Treating the errors in an effective way

Errors are unavoidable for anyone. It is the attitude towards errors that matters (James, 1998). Generally speaking, teachers tend to punish the students by more similar work. Writing the corrected sentences repeatedly or reciting them directly is favored most by the teachers. The method can function for once. But students are likely to commit the same errors again, because they have only done the work mechanically.

Teachers should hold a positive attitude to students' errors. Explanation and guidance are more efficient than punishment. The first choice of the teachers should be giving the students chances of self-correction. Peer-correction is another effective way which can facilitate mutual progress. It may be time-consuming for the moment but it will show its positive effect in the long run. The teachers had better restrict their own work to analyzing and classifying the errors and leave the rest to their students. Reflection and summary should be made by the students themselves.

5.1.1.6 Making full use of the multi-media equipment

The English knowledge that the students need to acquire is much more than what the texts can provide (Harmer, 2000). The teachers can take advantage of the multi-media equipment to show pictures, maps and even movies to the students, not only adding interest to the class, but also helping the students to understand certain knowledge better.

The English context provided by the multi-media equipment is very helpful for the students to feel the foreign culture and native English. Therefore, the teachers can make the equipment a necessary helper of their classes.

5.1.2 Syntactic training

Syntax accounts for a large part of senior high school grammar. And it reflects the most obvious influence of Chinese negative transfer. So it is of great necessity to take respective syntactic training, among which tense, agreement and word order should be paid special attention to.

5.1.2.1 Tense training

There are sixteen tense aspects in total in English. The form of the verbs indicates the time of the occurrence. So students should not only identify the tense but change the forms of the verbs accordingly.

Keeping a diary is an effective way to train the students' proficiency in past tense. It is preferable that a story should be told in past tense. Students will not get bored when they recall what has happened during the day and write it down. When the task is assigned and the emphasis is put on "the tense," the students will pay more attention and errors will drop.

Similar task can be assigned in terms of a certain tense aspect. For instance, the teachers can get the students to have a discussion based on the topic "I will become a... in ten years" to check whether they have trouble with "the future tense."

5.1.2.2 Agreement training

Agreement is another aspect that calls for special training. There are many exceptions that do not follow the common rules and need to be learnt one by one.

It is a rule that the predicate should be in the same number form with the subject, whether singular or plural. But abiding by the rule does not always result in right answers.

(23) Ten years ____ (is / are) a long time.

"Ten years" is plural in form, so in general the blank should be filled with a predicate in plural form as well, producing the sentence "Ten years are a long time." However, another rule should be obeyed here. When the expression of time, money and distance is a unity, it is regarded as a singular. Otherwise, it is a "plural." Therefore, sentence (23) should be completed as "Ten years is a long time".

In terms of agreement, such phrases as "there be," "not only... but also...," "as well as," "together with" and so on also call for intensive training because they are excluded from the common rules.

5.1.2.3 Word order training

Even though the students have mastered the basic structures of English sentences, the training is still needed in that it is the special sentence structures that are usually tested on.

Interrogative sentence structure, exclamatory sentence structure, inverted sentence structure and so on obey rules neither similar to Chinese grammar rules nor to common English ones. The underlined parts of the following sentences are what the students usually get confused with.

(24) When will she come to town?

(25) I have no idea when she will come to town.

(26) Only by studying hard can I catch up with her.

(27) Hardly had I finished the last question when the teacher collected the papers.

(28) What a kind person she is!

5.1.3 E-C contrast training

Since Chinese negative transfer is mainly caused by failing to realize the differences between Chinese and English, E-C contrast training will help a lot to reduce the negative transfer.

5.1.3.1 E-C translation training

Mostly, students learn English by taking advantage of Chinese. They naturally think in Chinese and then translate the ideas into English. It is very likely to produce Chinglish.

Students can realize the differences between Chinese and English by E-C translation training. They are expected to commit fewer errors because they are very familiar with Chinese and will feel awkward if they do the translation work literally.

(29) The girl sitting in the car is my sister.

Few students will translate sentence (29) into "女孩坐在车里是我姐姐。" Most students can realize that the sentence order should be rearranged and the Chinese equivalent should obey the Chinese rule that the modifier should be placed in front of the noun. Therefore, the right version of translation is "坐在车里的女孩是我姐姐。" In this way, E-C translation gives the students a lot of chances to correct the possible errors by themselves.

Through E-C translation training, students can avoid negative transfer consciously owing to their Chinese knowledge.

5.1.3.2 E-E paraphrasing training

It is probably a little demanding for students to paraphrase English sentences. However, it is a very effective way to help the students to think in English and avoid Chinese negative transfer. The teachers should adopt paraphrasing as a major way of explaining the difficult points rather than translating them into Chinese.

For example, a teacher needs to explain the following sentence which contains three new words to the students.

(30) "... they see a penniless young man wandering on the pavement outside their house."

Instead of translating it, the teacher paraphrases the sentence into "they see a young man without money and he is walking without a direction on the sidewalk outside their house." The students can understand the new words without the interference of Chinese so that they can avoid the negative transfer.

Students should be inspired to do such exercises. Learning English by English is the most effective way so that the teachers and the students should work together to acquire new knowledge based on the previous.

5.2　Conclusion of the research

5.2.1　The unexpected findings

In addition to what has been presented in the main body of the thesis, there are other findings which have not been predicted in the very beginning.

Firstly, there exists intense competition among the teachers. During the interview, all the six teachers show great desire for the progress of their students. They are afraid to fall behind and are busy with checking the students' papers all the time. Obviously, the competition is mainly caused by the exam-oriented educational system. The orientation also explains why the teachers refuse to spend too much time on background information or group discussion. So the local teachers should work together to shift their focus.

Secondly, the students trust their teachers very much and tend to imitate their teachers. Though the students' English performance is not very good, they adore their English teachers a lot. They totally trust their teachers and correct the errors according to the teachers' instructions. They attempt to imitate their teachers as well, not only the way in which they speak and write English, but also other aspects they show in class. The reason may be that the English teachers are almost the only source of their English learning and foreign culture. To them, the English teachers are persons of authority. Definitely it is harmful on condition that the teachers make mistakes. But it can be very helpful if the teachers have developed good habits themselves.

Lastly, the students have acquired a number of "popular" English words and expressions. It is astonishing to find out that even the students who are poor at English have a relatively "large vocabulary" of "popular" English, such as "high tea, microblog, housing funds, fake fans, idol type, soul infidelity..." The phenomenon provides strong evidence for the motto that "Interest is the best teacher." The motto, in turn, shows the necessity to provide the English culture background which attracts the students more than the words and rules.

5.2.2　A summary of the whole research

The research is carried out in Wuqiang Senior High School by analyzing the syntactic errors in perspective of Chinese negative transfer. It attempts to help senior high school students to improve their English grammar learning. The subjects are eighty-two students from two classes. Their behavior in English class has been observed and notes have been made accordingly. They have also been asked to write two essays: one is a narration and the other one is a letter. In addition, an interview of six local teachers has been carried out. They have talked about their teaching approaches, their attitudes towards the students' errors and their comments on the English learning environment.

Then errors of the students have been classified and analyzed. The causes of Chinese negative transfer have been discussed. The main cause is that the students fail to take the differences between Chinese and English seriously, believing that Chinese rules can also be applied to English. The other two causes are lack of comprehensible input and knowing little of foreign culture.

In the end, suggestions come up to reduce Chinese negative transfer and improve the students' syntax learning, including facilitating the learning environment and strengthening syntactic training and E-C contrast training. Overall, the whole research has fulfilled its purpose to help local students to learn English syntax effectively and efficiently.

Bibliography

Brown, H. Douglas. 2007. *Principles of Language Learning and Teaching*. Beijing: Foreign Language Teaching and Research Press.

Cook, Vivian. 2000. *Second Language Learning and Language Teaching*. Beijing: Foreign Language Teaching and Research Press.

Corder, S. P. 1967. "The significance of the learner's errors". *International Review of Applied Linguistics* NO.5, 160—170.

Ellis, Rod. 1993. *The Study of Second Language Acquisition*. Oxford: Oxford University Press.

Faerch, Claus & Gabriele **Kasper**. 1983. *Strategies in Interlanguage Communication*. New York: Longman.

Harmer, Jeremy. 2000. *How to Teach English*. Beijing: Foreign Language Teaching and Research Press.

James, Carl. 1998. *Errors in Language Learning and Use: Exploring error analysis*. Harlow, Essex: Addison Wesley Longman Limited.

Johnson, Keith. 2002. *An Introduction to Foreign Language Learning and Teaching*. Beijing: Foreign Language Teaching and Research Press.

Krashen, Stephen D. 1981. *Second Language Acquisition and Second Language Learning*. New York: Pergamon Press.

Lado, Robert. 1957. *Linguistics across Cultures: Applied linguistics for Language Teachers*. Ann Arbor, Michigan: University of Michigan Press.

Lunchins, A. S. & E. H. **Lunchins**. 1970. *Wertheimer's Seminar Revisited: Problem Solving and Thinking* (Vol. 1). Albany, NY: State University of New York.

Odlin, Terence. 2001. *Language Transfer—Cross-Linguistic Influence in Language Learning*. Shanghai: Shanghai Foreign Languages Education Press.

Richards, Jack. & Richard W. **Schmidt**. 2002. *Longman Dictionary of Language Teaching and Applied Linguistics*. Beijing: Foreign Language Teaching and Research Press.

Richards, J. C. & Theodore S. **Rodgers**. 2001. *Approaches and Methods in Language Teaching*. Cambridge: Cambridge University Press.

Schachter, Jacquelyn. 1974. "An Error in Error Analysis". *Language Learning* No.1, 2.

戴炜栋,束定芳. 1994. 对比分析、错误分析、中介语研究中的若干问题. 外国语 (5), 1—2.

戴炜栋. 2002. 语言迁移研究:问题与思考. 外国语(6), 1.

胡壮麟,姜望琪. 2002. 语言学高级教程. 北京:北京大学出版社.

梁海英. 2006. 英语口语中的母语负迁移现象. 外语教学(13), 2.
马秉义. 1999. 英汉句子结构常式比较. 解放军外国语学院学报(2), 19—21.
王初明. 1990. 应用心理语言学. 长沙：湖南教育出版社.
雅达复. 2000. 英语错误形式分析. 西安：陕西人民出版社.
朱中都. 1999. 英语写作中的汉语负迁移. 解放军外国语学院学报(2), 28—30.
http://en.wikipedia.org/wiki/Error_analysis#Error_analysis_in_second_language_acquisition

第四节 翻 译 类

××大学

本科生毕业论文(设计)册

题目：功能加忠诚理论视角下论文摘要英译

学院＿＿＿＿＿＿＿＿
专业＿＿＿＿＿＿＿＿
班级＿＿＿＿＿＿＿＿
学生＿＿＿＿＿＿＿＿
指导教师＿＿＿＿＿＿
完成日期＿＿＿＿＿＿

C-E Translation of Abstracts in Academic Papers Under the Perspective of Function Plus Loyalty

By
×××
Prof. ×××, Tutor

A Thesis Submitted to the Foreign Languages

Institutes in Partial Fulfillment of the Requirements

For the Degree of Bachelor of Arts at

×× University

May 2014

Abstract

The academic paper is the authors' achievements in scientific and technological research or their opinions which is an important part of undergraduate education in universities. And the abstract is an essential part of an article in a journal paper. A well-prepared abstract guides authors into summarizing more explicitly the contents of their articles, and help readers to judge whether it is worthwhile to read the whole article. The English abstract of an academic paper plays a crucial role in international academic communication. This paper tries to introduce the theory of Functionalism, especially the "function plus loyalty" theory put forward by Nord as the theoretic framework. And this paper also analyzes the research methods and some kinds of problems of abstract translation in lexicology, sentence and text. As a tentative study in exploring the abstract of an academic paper translation, this paper intends to provide some perspectives and be of certain value for future research on developing a further approach for the translation of the abstract of an academic paper.

Key words: the abstract of an academic paper   translation   theory of function plus loyalty

摘 要

　　撰写毕业论文是我国高校本科生学业的重要一环,用以简单表明作者在科学研究中取得的成果或提出的见解。论文摘要是学术论文中的重要组成部分。好的摘要要清楚完整地总结出文献内容的梗概,可以帮助读者迅速判断文章的内容并决定是否有必要阅读全文。英文摘要对在国际进行知识的传播交流有着重要的作用。本文将尝试以诺德提出的功能加忠诚理论作为理论依据,分析论文摘要翻译的研究方法,并举例从词汇、句法、语篇层面分析目前高校论文摘要翻译存在的问题,本文作为论文摘要英译的一个尝试性研究,旨在为未来关于摘要翻译提供某些角度及参考价值。

关键词: 论文摘要　翻译　功能加忠诚理论

Contents

Abstract …………………………………………………………………

Abstract in Chinese ……………………………………………………

1. Introduction …………………………………………………………
   1.1 Aims of the research ………………………………………………
   1.2 Significance of the research ……………………………………
   1.3 Methodology of the research ……………………………………
   1.4 Organization of the thesis ………………………………………

2. Theoretical Framework ……………………………………………
   2.1 An Overview of functionalism in Germany ……………………
   2.2 Christiane Nord: function plus loyalty …………………………

3. C-E Translation of Abstracts in Academic Papers ………………
   3.1 Definition of C-E translation of abstracts ………………………
   3.2 Classification of C-E translation of abstracts …………………
   3.3 Development of C-E translation of abstracts …………………
   3.4 Features of C-E translation of abstracts ………………………
   3.5 Function of C-E translation of abstracts ………………………
   3.6 Common errors of C-E translation of abstracts ………………
      3.6.1 Errors of Lexical Level ………………………………………
         3.6.1.1 The first letter case and number errors ……………
         3.6.1.2 Spelling errors
         3.6.1.3 Punctuation errors ………………………………………
         3.6.1.4 Person errors
      3.6.2 Errors of syntactical level …………………………………
         3.6.2.1 Tense errors ………………………………………………
         3.6.2.2 Voice errors ………………………………………………
         3.6.2.3 Other errors ………………………………………………

4. The Application of Function Plus Loyalty in C-E Translation of Abstracts of the Academic Papers ……………………………………
   4.1 Analysis of sentence level ………………………………………
      4.1.1 Adjustment of the words order ……………………………
      4.1.2 Omission of the subject ……………………………………
   4.2 Analysis of text level ………………………………………………

5. Conclusion ……………………………………………………………
   5.1 Finding ………………………………………………………………
   5.2 Contributions ………………………………………………………
   5.3 Limitations and suggestions for further researches …………

Bibliography ………………………………………………………………

1. Introduction

1.1 Aims of the research

The academic paper is the authors' achievements in scientific research or their opinions which is an important part of undergraduate education in universities. And the abstract is an important part of an academic paper. The abstract of an academic paper plays a crucial role in international academic communication which can help readers to judge whether it is worthwhile to read the whole article. With the globalization of economy and the China's entry into the WTO, an increasing number of countries enter into the international academic communication, and English, as the language of international communication, is necessary for Chinese to translate our achievement into English.

In order to communicate well, it is no doubt that the translation of abstract should also achieve the original effect and express the author's real intention. Only by doing this can we spread our achievements to other countries. Translation, in nature, is a process of information transferring between two languages and transformation from one kind of language codes and symbols to another kind. The language in abstract is formal, refined, specific and complete, so that the abstract translation is such a difficult work. Therefore, how to make the exquisite language and scientific and rigorous attitude in the original text reappear in the translation work needs to be explored.

As the abstract of an academic paper features scientific and rigorous attitude, formal and refined language, and profound scientific conception, translators are required to deal with it from the perspective of special scientific field when translating abstract. This thesis intends to find the errors that students make in three levels: vocabulary, sentence and text.

This thesis, with the theory of functionalism, especially the "function plus loyalty" theory raised by Christiane Nord as its theoretical framework, intends to explain and prove the necessity of abstract translation and to discuss its application by analyzing the translation work of some students' paper from three aspects, namely lexicology, sentence, and text.

1.2 Significance of the research

The author, by making a research on the combination of loyal translation in the abstract translation work with the functionalism as the theoretical guidance, attempts to find the approach in abstract translation and help the future translators achieve the communicative effect in the translation of abstract.

This research can help undergraduates improve the quality of academic English abstract, in order to increase the chances of paper to be used, and promote domestic academic achievements in international exchange and communication.

Previously, the general research of abstract is mainly on the published academic papers, while the analysis of unpublished graduation thesis of the non-English majors is few.

1.3 Methodology of the research

Compared with studies on the translation of other literary genres, the analysis of unpublished graduation thesis of the non-English majors is few. The reason is that the translation of abstract has not aroused people's attention. Both teachers and students who are non-English majors do not think that English abstract is important for their thesis. But in recent years, international academic exchange and cooperation is increasing exceedingly. China, as a large developing country, should participate in activities actively. Consequently, in order to enhance our influence in the international market, we should not only master the skill of writing Chinese abstract of graduation thesis but also learn to translate their Chinese abstract into English.

Functionalist approach towards translation has emerged in Germany since 1970s. As an important breakthrough of traditional translation theories, it has been attracting increasing attention in recent years. Generally speaking, the development of modern functionalism has gone through four stages: 1) text typology; 2) Skopostheorie; 3) translation action; 4) function plus loyalty.

Here, function means the factors that make a target text work in an intended way in the target language and in abstract translation. It refers to the translation of the original meaning from the source language to the target one and the need to achieve the practical and academic effect of the original abstract in the target reader; loyalty refers to the interpersonal relationship between the translators, the source-text sender, the target-text addressees, and the initiator, and in abstract translation, it means the loyalty to the original author when transmitting the meaning in the thesis. The present thesis intends to use the "function plus loyalty" theory as the theoretical direction or methodology of the research on the abstract translation.

1.4 Organization of the thesis

This paper consists of five chapters. Chapter one is an introduction in which the aims of the research, significance of the research, methodology of the research and organization of the thesis are presented. In Chapter two, the theoretical framework of this thesis is introduced. In Chapter three, C-E Translation of abstracts in academic papers is introduced from five aspects, definition, development, features, function and some kinds of errors of English abstract in non-English major's academic paper. In Chapter four, the application of function plus loyalty in C-E translation of abstracts of academic papers, the translation work of different kinds of disciplines as cases study is exploring from four aspects, sentence level, word order, omission and text level. The last chapter is the conclusion, in which some findings, contributions, limitations and suggestions for further studies are included.

2. Theoretical Framework

The functionalist approaches originated in Germany in 1970s and sprang up in 1980s, opened up a new perspective to translation studies. Christiane Nord is the lead scholar of German translation research field. Due to the culture barrier, many readers cannot get the essence of some works and views of writing by language which is not his or her mother language. Sometimes, they even misunderstand the meaning. Christiane Nord, as a leader of the German functionalism theory, is aware of the importance of communicative activity. So she designed translation-oriented discourse and translated the German work *Text Analysis in Translation: Theory, Methodology, and Didactic Application of a Model for Translation-Oriented Text Analysis* into English whose purpose is to provide type classification criterion for translation teaching and guidance for the evaluation of translation quality.

Christiane Nord's functionalism translation approach was mainly influenced by her teacher Katharina Reiss, who expressed great loyalty to the Skopostheorie theory put forward by Hans J. Vermeer, and appreciated Justa Holz-Manttari's translational action theory. At the same time, she also has her own opinions about it. She has made great contributions to German functionalist approaches to translation research. It even can be said that without Christiane Nord, the time English community comes to acquaintance with German functionalism would be postponed (Wu Lili, 2009: 14). She introduced the loyalty principle into German functionalism; put forward the "function plus loyalty" theory, in order to solve the problems of essential functionalism in translation. In this theory, loyalty means the interpersonal relationship between the translator, the original author, the receiver and translation initiator. Nord states that the theory of functionalism can cover all types of translation, and has an important meaning to translation teaching and practice. In order to well understand the essence of the Nord's theory, the author will make an overview of the representative views, and then focus on the review of the "function plus loyalty."

2.1 An overview of functionalism in Germany

The equivalence theory is the main theory in the German academic translation field followed by the functionalism, and its representatives are Wolfram Wilss and Werner Koller. Equivalence theory focuses on the original text, and claims that the characteristics of the original text must be presented in the target language. But when translating practical texts, translators think if they base their opinion on this theory, they will pay too much attention to the equivalence and translate it word by word.

Consequently, some translators point out that this theory is far away from the translation practice.

The German functionalist theory emerged in the 1980s and 1990s. And Katharina Reiss, Hans J. Vermeer, Justa Holz-Manttari and Christiane Nord are the four main representatives of the theory who have made great contribution to the development of the functionalist translation theory. And their landmark theories are: the text typology theory of Reiss, the Skopostheorie theory of Vermeer, the theory of Translation Action of Holz-Manttari and Nord's Function plus Loyalty theory.

2.2 Christiane Nord: function plus loyalty

Christiane Nord is contributed to many kind of respects about translation, here, this part just recommends her "function plus loyalty" theory. Nord's "function plus loyalty" theory is deeply influenced by the text typology theory of her teacher Reiss. While accepting the text typology theory totally, Nord is also loyal to the Skopotheorie. In Vermeer's opinion, the translator sets the Skopos of translation based on the initiator's instructions, however, in Nord's opinion, she does not think that the translator has the freedom to set the Skopos by themselves. She indicates that the Skopos should not be determined by the translator but by the initiator.

Nord introduced the concept of "function plus loyalty" firstly in her book *Text Analysis in Translation*. At that time, she was mainly talking about the Translation Action Theory of Justa Holz-Manttari. In Manttari's view, the text is a tool of realizing the communicative action and its essential value. So the translator only need to be responsible to the environment and the target text can be completely independent of the original text. But Nord believes that the free writing does not belong to the scope of translation, so she points out that "no original text, no translation." The translator should be responsible both for the original text and the target environment, as well as for the initiator and the target reader. This kind of responsibility is what she calls "loyalty."

The loyalty principle limits the scope of the translation function of the original text and increases the negotiations about translation task between the translator and customer. Nord said that "loyalty" enabled the translator two-way loyal to both the source and target goal, but the loyalty should not be confused with fidelity or faithfulness. Because fidelity or faithfulness refers to the relations between source and target text, loyalty is an interpersonal concept which refers to the social relationships between individuals. The function plus loyalty is Nord's unique translation theory, more specifically, it is her ideal.

3. C-E Translation of Abstracts in Academic Papers

With increasing number of academic paper appearing, people find it difficult to seek some relevant data from so many genre of academic paper, as they do not have so much time to read the whole article. Consequently, we need the help of abstract. A well-prepared abstract guides authors into summarizing more explicitly the contents of their articles, help readers to judge whether it is worthwhile to read the whole article. The abstract of an academic paper plays a crucial role in international academic communication.

In China, all of the undergraduate students are required to finish a graduation thesis before they get the degree certificate. And in order to adapt to international communication environment, every abstract in scientific and technological journal paper needs to be translated into English. The scientific and technology academic paper is the author's own opinion, when translate it, we should not only consider the readers' reading level and requirements but also the author's original opinion. Therefore, how to make the exquisite language in the original abstract text reappear in the translation work is a study which needs to be explored. In this chapter, the author intends to introduce the definition, development, features, function and some errors of C-E translation of abstracts.

3.1 Definition of C-E translation of abstracts

Many definitions about abstracts have been given by scholars or institutes. *The Oxford Advanced Learner's Dictionary of Current English* defines abstract as "a short account of the contents of a book, etc." International Organization for Standardization(ISO) 214—1976 (E) defines abstract as "an abbreviated, accurate representation of the contents of a document, without added interpretation or criticism." Educational Resources Information Center(1980:3)defines it as "an abbreviated representation of a document, without added interpretation or criticism." *The Arrangement of Social Science of Institutions of Higher Learning* points out that abstract should objectively reflect the main information of the paper, and also be independent and self-contained. *The National Standard of the Abstract Writing Rules of the People's Republic of China* (GB 6447—86)indicates that the abstract is the concise narrative essay without the author's own comments and additional explanation whose purpose is to provide literature content. These definitions indicate that an abstract is a concise summary of an academic paper.

3.2 Classification of C-E translation of abstracts

Types of abstracts are different according to different purposes and structures. There are two types of abstract: traditional abstracts (or non-structured abstracts) and structured abstract. According to the degree of detail, the structured abstract can be divided into full-structured abstracts and semi-structured abstracts. And the traditional abstracts can be divided into three types: informative abstract, indicative abstract (sometimes called descriptive abstract) and informative-indicative abstract.

Abstracts could be of different lengths according to the purpose or requirements. An abstract could be as short as 20 or 30 words, or as long as about 2000 words. For a B. A. thesis, an abstract has usually 200 to 300 words. It is usually one page and written in a single paragraph, or no more than 3 paragraphs.

3.3 Development of C-E translation of abstracts

Broadly speaking, researches on abstract in domestic can be divided into three stages: the first stage from 1980 to 1985 is called exploratory stage. In this period, lots of researches are to summarize previous translation experiences, especially for the abstract writing methods and skills. Although the depth of these researches, to some extent, is not so deep, it guides the researchers of this area understand knowledge of abstract writing, and laids a solid foundation for the later researches. The second stage from 1986 to 2001 is known as gradually the standard stage. In this period, there are two kinds of research at the same time, one is based on GB 6447—86、GB 7713—87 and Translation principles (Ma Jinlong, 2001; Zhu Fan etc., 2001). The other is introduction, introduce and gradually promote structured abstract on the biomedical journals (Qian Shouchu, 1990; Pan BR, 1994; Liu Xueli, 1999). The third stage from 2002 to the present is called diversified development. In this period, research center is developing from the lexical and syntactic level to text level.

3.4 Features of C-E translation of abstracts

The academic paper is the authors' achievements in scientific research or their opinions which is an important part of undergraduate education in universities. And the abstract is an essential part of an article in a journal which is a short description, or an accurate condensation, of the contents of a piece of paper. So on the stylistic characteristics, it has these four features: formal, refined, specific and complete.

Firstly, abstract should be in formal style, whose syntactic structure is precise and specific. In this paper, not only the sentence is complete, but also words are precise and specific. Secondly, abstract is concise, so there should be no example and no contrast with other research, seldom sentence repetition. And the main cohesive device is word. Thirdly, every concept and argument in abstract should be specific and accurate. So it is not usual to write papers in general "what it is about," but write a paper directly "what it is." Finally, abstract should be complete. For some readers using the abstract magazine or index cards for research work, it is not likely for them to read the full thesis before they think the abstract is useful for them. Consequently, do not cite a certain section or pictures in the thesis instead.

3.5 Function of C-E translation of abstracts

ISO 214-1976(E) points out the three functions of abstract: to determine correlation, be easy to search and used in computer automatic retrieval. And Sang Liangzhi

(1993) sums up five major functions of the digest which is appropriate for abstract: the first is signal in address function (only the retrieve abstract has this function). Second is the index function which is the foundational feature of the index abstract. Readers can get their interesting information in different respects. Third is spreading function, as abstract is applicable and spreading widely. Fourth, advertising function: abstract can improve the reading efficiency which plays an important role in advertising indirectly. Fifth is intelligence function, as a formal abstract (no matter what type) can faithfully and accurately report the main information of original literature.

3.6 Common Errors of C-E translation of abstracts

There are many mistakes in abstract of graduation thesis. Generally, the mistakes can be divided into two kinds: lexical level and syntactical level. In this part, the author intends to analyze some examples to find the reasons of them and present the improvement opinions. The examples of common errors of C-E translation of abstracts presented here are authentic. That is, although some of them have been simplified for instructional purpose, none are invented. Most were graduation thesis writing by the author's schoolmates.

3.6.1 Errors of lexical level

The first letter case errors, spelling errors, person and number errors, and punctuation errors are about all basic mistakes that can be avoided if they check the thesis carefully. In this part, the author takes some graduation thesis abstracts as cases to analysis those kinds of mistakes.

3.6.1.1 The first letter case and number errors

(1) Vigorously developing animal husbandry mechanization is a necessary condition for the development of modern agriculture in china, only to make the animal husbandry mechanization.

(2) At present our country is the largest country in the global solar water heater production and usage, but there are some problems in most of the solar water heater. therefore, The research and development of advanced solar water heater control system is becoming more and more important.

In the first example, according to the context, the "china" in the sentence means The People's Republic of China not the porcelain. So the first letter of china should be capital.

In the second example, the "therefore" should be capital and the "The" should be lowercase.

Through these two examples, we can find that the office software cannot find this kind of errors that meaning is not right, but the spelling is right. Consequently, in order to reduce this kind of error the author should check the text carefully.

(3) Key words: Sewage treatment automation kingview

(4) Keywords: Kernel function feature extraction Statistical Learning Theory Kernel Principal Component Analysis(KPCA) Support Vector Machine (SVM)

The requirements of writing key words: 3 – 5 words, no punctuation mark, lowercase letters. In the third example, "Sewage treatment" means "污水处理," is not a proper noun. According to the rules of writing key words, it should be lowercase letters "sewage treatment." But the "kingview" which means "组态王" is a kind of proper noun in this field, the first letter can be capital. (The colon in this example will discuss in the following examples.) In the next example, there are both proper nouns and non proper nouns. And the translator realizes this kind of problem, he or she lowercases the non proper nouns and capital the proper nouns. In the practice of translation, this kind of errors cannot be found and marked by the office software. So the translator must pay much attention to this kind of problem and tries his or her best to avoid it by not only learning the specific knowledge but also checking the translation text carefully when finish the translation practice.

One of the reasons causing this kind of error is that the author does not know the principle that every word of key words in abstract of academic paper, except for proper word, should be lowercase letters. The other reason is that they do not care whether it is lowercase or capital. The only way reducing this kind of errors is to check the text carefully.

(5) This paper use the method of analogy to gauss theorem form to electromagnetic fields in the form of gauss theorem in the gravitational field and through the example of application of gauss's law in the gravitational field, the calculation is more convenient.

(6) Points out the PLC design which is the key to satisfy the basic control function, improve the intelligence of the system, and the security, convenience, etc.

In the fifth example, the writer of this sentence failed to notice that "this paper" is a singular noun, according to the subject-predicate consistency principle, he or she should add a "s" behind the "use." So the right version is "uses." In the sixth example, it is an imperative sentence, so the predicate verb should be "Point."

(7) This paper first discuss the research and development of the lawn mower cutting theory, expounds the development process of foreign mower, lists the performance characteristics of the research in recent years, as well as new mower, and puts forward the problems and development trend of mower technology in China.

In this example, the writer of this sentence failed to notice that "this paper" is a singular noun, according to the subject-predicate consistency principle, he or she should add a "s" behind the "discuss." So the right version is "discusses." But in the following sense-group the "s" behind the "expound," "list" and "put," shows that the translator realizes the subject "this paper" is a singular noun. According to this phenomenon, we can infer that the translator knows the subject-predicate consistency principle, but in the translation practice he or she does not pay much attention on this kind of problem.

These kinds of errors are common in students' work, which are subject-predicate consistency problem. Chinese who learn English knows the principle of subject-predicate consistency, but it usually appears in abstract writings, as Chinese do not have this type of grammar. The only way reducing this kind of errors is to check the text carefully.

3.6.1.2 Spelling errors

(1) to the phenomenon of stuff which is commom in nearly all existing machines to solve the existing problem

(2) Key word: The solar water heater PLC sensor

In the first example, according to the context, the author intends to express the phenomenon is usual, so the "commom" is spelling wrong, it should be "common."

This kind of errors can be found and marked by the office software, so we can find it easily through the red line under the word. But in the second example, there is more than one key word, so it should be in plural form, that is to say, plus a "s" behind the "Key word." The right version is "Key words." This kind of error cannot be marked by the office software, because it is not a spelling wrong word.

3.6.1.3 Punctuation errors

(1) Key words biomass; briquetting; flat-molding; modification

The requirements of writing Key words in abstract of academic paper are: 3—5 words, no punctuation mark, and lowercase letters. So in the first example above, the semicolon between the keywords should be deleted. There is something about the colon behind the "key words"—different school have their own requirements about the academic paper, so whether it is need to plus the colon behind the "key words," it depends on the school.

(2) In today's poor marine market which cargo transportation increase very slowly, the one who can reduce the cost of running a company can last longer!

Another requirement for abstract is that the author should convey information in the original document accurately and concisely, with an absence of any attempt emotion. The exclamation mark "!" is never used in an abstract, and question mark "?" is seldom used. So in this example, the exclamation mark "!" should be deleted.

(3) Design and material selection in the process... focus on the use of mechanical design knowledge, in addition to using the drawing tools AutoCAD……

In Chinese, there are six points in the punctuation of apostrophe, like "……" But in English there are three points, like "..." So the right version in the example is "..."

3.6.1.4　Person errors

The abstract is a kind of formal writing, so it is better to use the third person. That is, the word "I," "we," and "you" will not normally appear in the text (though of course they may appear in quoted materials). Besides, the focus has to remain on what you have to say (rather than on you, the person who is saying it). Writing in the first person (I) focuses on the author, and writing in the second person (you) draws the attention of the audience. Therefore, by using the third person the author directs the reader's entire attention to what you have to say. For instance, instead of saying, "In this thesis I want to discuss," the author can write "The present thesis attempts to discuss." Instead of saying, "Now I want to conclude that..." the author can write "It is concluded that..."

(1) We first introduce kernel principal component analysis into feature extraction of the gene expression data analysis, studied on kernel principal component analysis' Gaussian kernel function parameter's selection.

(2) We obtain a more satisfactory result by targeting the experimental results analysis, we found that the introduction of kernel function greatly improves the performance of learning methods... we supply a certain reference value.

In these two examples, when the author intends to present the research content, he use the word "we" as the subject. He or she can write "This thesis intends to introduce kernel principal component analysis into feature extraction of the gene expression data analysis..." or "This research found that the introduction of kernel function greatly improves the performance of learning methods..."

But at present, as for the first person in academic paper, the first person plural, we, is accepted gradually by increasing number of scholars. They claim that "we" is more faithful and accurate than "I." Because "we" stands for a group of people who do the research and "I" only stands for the author only.

For these kinds of errors, maybe they are not the errors; it is not objective to use the first person in this kind of paper. The reader who reads the paper definitely knows the fact that it is the author's work, so he or she does not need to emphasize the subjection by using the first person. The author who needs to write a thesis should learn the principle of abstract writing to solve this problem.

3.6.2　Errors of syntactical level

The syntactical problem in abstract translation may be concerned with tense errors, voice errors, sentences order and tactics in dealing with the relations between these sentences. To avoid the poorly constructed sentences, the author needs to be careful in the forms of sentences, the logics of sentences and the connections of sentences.

3.6.2.1 Tense errors

Tense is one of the most difficult things for Chinese students, because Chinese language has no strict tense system, while English has concrete and complicated tense requirements for each sentence. Tense choice in reviewing research is subtle and somewhat flexible. It may not be the "rules" you have been taught in English classes. The following, therefore, are only general guidelines for tense usage. Several studies have shown that at least two-thirds of all citing statements fall into one of these three major patterns.

Past refers to the researcher's activity as agent. For example, "Jones (1987) investigated the causes of illiteracy." or use another sentence pattern like "The causes of illiteracy were investigated by Jones (1987)."

Present perfect refers to the researcher's activity not as agent. For example, "The causes of illiteracy have been widely investigated (Jones 1987; Ferrara 1990; Hyon 1994)" or "There have been several investigations into the causes of illiteracy (Jones 1987; Ferrara 1990; Hyon 1994)" or "Several researchers have studied the causes of illiteracy (Jones 1987; Ferrara 1990; Hyon 1994)."

Present refers to no reference to the researcher's activity. For example, "The causes of illiteracy are complex (Jones 1987; Ferrara 1990; Hyon 1994)" or another sentence pattern "Illiteracy appears to have a complex set of causes (Jones 1987; Ferrara 1990; Hyon 1994)."

In short, use the present tense to describe the conclusion of the author, and use the past to describe the work of the author.

3.6.2.2 Voice errors

There is a proposition emphasizing that it is better to use passive voice and the third person singular in writing abstract. Because using the passive voice cannot only omit the action practitioner, but also can emphasis the subject which is the important thing, which is helpful to highlight their status in this sentence and explain the facts clearly and concisely. Though using passive voice can avoid mentioning executives, and can make the style of the article appear objective. But at present, increasing number of people advocate the usage of the verb in the active voice as it is beneficial to the clearness, conciseness, and powerful expression of the text. Current international organization stresses that the tense of the verb is based on not only the features of abstract but also the need of expression, and cannot say that paper should try to use the active voice or use the passive voice usually.

(1) 本文建立了柔轮原始曲线的数学模型。

The expressions of the original curve of the flexspline are derived in this paper.

In this example, the author uses passive voice to emphasis the subjective—the original curve of the flexspline. And it is alright to translate the sentence like this "This paper intends to derive the expressions of the original curve of the flexspline." which can also express the same meaning. Using what kind of the sentence depends on the author.

3.6.2.3 Other Errors

When forming a parallel structure, the author should pay attention to a basic rule, that is, all the paired elements must belong to the same grammatical category. But this rule has been failed to focus in some abstract translation.

(1) 在航海实践中,经验丰富的船长在靠离泊无拖轮协助下,通常会根据船舶的吨位、泊位状况及船舶操纵性能使用锚进行靠离泊。

In marine practice, master who own rich experience berths without tugs, he can use anchor to berth according ship's tonnage, conditions of berth and ship's maneuverability, and so on.

The parallel structures in the example are composed of several single words. The translator lists most of them in the form of "A's B," while "conditions of berth" is not in this form. So the revision should be "berth's condition."

Incomplete sentences also appear in some articles.

(2) 尤其在工艺规程设计中,运用了大量的科学加工理论及计算公式,对它进行了精确地计算。

Especially in the process of design, use of scientific processing theory and a large number of formulas, the accurate calculation of.

The author translates the Chinese sentence word by word. This sentence "运用了大量的科学加工理论及计算公式,对它进行了精确地计算" has no subject in Chinese, but in English, the author should add the subject for it. The reversion is "Especially in the process of design, this paper uses lots of scientific processing theory and a large number of formulas to calculate it accurately."

4. The Application of Function Plus Loyalty in C-E Translation of Abstracts of the Academic Papers

4.1 Analysis of sentence level

Due to the differences between Chinese and western about culture and the way of thinking, sometimes, it is very different in language expression way. According to Nord's "function plus loyalty," loyalty is a interpersonal concept which refers to the social relationships between individuals. And the translator does not have the freedom of the translation Skopos. So the translator should pay equal attention to the function of the text and the interpersonal relationship. Consequently, the translator has to understand English and Chinese deeply, understands the essence of the original text thoroughly, and only by doing this can he or she overcome these translation obstacles caused by these differences and make the translation conform to the target language readers' way of thinking and expression habit.

4.1.1 Adjustment of the words order

Word order refers to the combination sequence of language composition according to the grammatical relation between linear and horizontal sequence. Word order is an important means of expressing grammatical relations. In Chinese and English, word order plays a decisive role in determining the sentence structure insuring the internal grammar. English and Chinese have many differences in grammatical structure. In the process of translation, if the translator only based on the word order of the original copy, ignoring the habits of the translation, the translation will not be. So when doing translation practice, the translator should follow the language habits, and adjust the word order of the original, make the translation smooth.

Therefore, the target readers can get the same meaning with the original readers. For example：

在航海实践中，经验丰富的船长在靠离泊无拖轮协助下，通常会根据船舶的吨位、泊位状况及船舶操纵性能使用锚进行靠离泊。

In marine practice, master who own rich experience berths without tugs, can use anchor to berth according ship's tonnage, conditions of berth and ship's maneuverability, and so on.

In this translation, the main trunk of the sentence is "船长使用锚进行离泊." And the other part modifying the predicate—"靠离泊," which we call it adverbial. In Chinese, the adverbial always set between the subject and the predicate. But in English, in order to avoid the top-heavy sentence, the author always sets the adverbial before or behind the sentence, in this way, the sentence will be balanced in structure. So in the example, "... master who own rich experience berths without tugs, can use anchor to berth according ship's tonnage and so on." the translator advances the predicate "berth."

4.1.2 Omission of the subject

There are two or more verbs, in Chinese sentences, with only one subject, and other verbs follow, this kind of structure is called the gearing type predicate, that is to say two or more verbs act as predicate of the sentence. In Chinese, for example, "本文介绍了……总结了……综述了……" Such sentence structure is common in the natural science paper. When translating them into English, we have two kinds of method: the first is that translate them into side-by-side predicate, and there should be an "and" before the final predicate. The second is that, analyze the semantic relationships between verbs, and then use one of the verbs to be the predicate, and others using the participles, infinitive verb or preposition to express.

(1) 本文首先介绍了课题的背景和意义，总结了四臂螺旋天线的发展历程和研究现状。综述了全球导航卫星系统(Global Navigation Satellite System,GNSS)的发展历史、现状及相关天线的技术要求和形式。

This paper presents the background and significance of the topic, summarizes the development history and current research status of the QHA. And introduce the history and current status of the development of the GNSS (Global Navigation Satellite System).

(2) 本文讨论了割草机切割理论的研究和进展,阐述了国外割草机的发展历程,列举了近几年国内的研究情况以及新型割草机的性能特点,最终提出我国割草机技术的不足与改进意见。

Through discussing the research and development of the lawn mower cutting theory firstly, expounding the development process of foreign mower, and listing the performance characteristics of the research in recent years, this paper puts forward the problems and improvement suggestions of mower technology in China.

In the first example, it is easy for the author to translate it without analyzing the logical relationship of the verbs. But not all of the verbs have logic. According to the theory of function plus loyalty, the translator is loyal to the original text and the target reader can understand the meaning of the translation. Thus both of these two types of version are all right.

4.2　Analysis of text level

Cohesion is one of the core content of linguistic research. The language of the abstract of academic paper is independent. Authors achieve the communicative purpose by using the right words to form grammatically correct sentences and using some logical connectives to make the discourse coherent. In English, there are some connective words like:"in other words," "namely," "as well as," "furthermore" to express the Chinese meaning "也就是说" "如" "也,还,而且" "此外" and so on.

Based on the theory of function plus loyalty, the author provides the ways to grasp the original meaning and convey it to the target readers in the process of the translation with some examples.

(1) 首先,将核主成分分析引入基因表达数据分析特征提取中,对核主成分分析中的高斯核参数选择问题进行了研究……

其次,将支持向量机引入基因表达数据分类问题中,研究了在不同的特征提取方法下支持向量机中高斯核函数的参数选择问题。

最终通过针对实验结果的分析,我们发现核函数的引入很大程度上提升了学习算法的性能……

We firstly introduce kernel principal component analysis into feature extraction of the gene expression data analysis...

And then we introduce the support vector machine into a gene expression data classification problem, studied on support vector machines' Gaussian kernel function parameter selection in different feature extraction methods.

Finally, by targeting the experimental results analysis, we found that the introduction of kernel function greatly improves the performance of learning...

In this example, the author uses the connection cohesive devices, including "firstly," "then" and "finally" which belong to the overt way.

(2) 正确使用会有利于船舶安全高效地靠离泊；如果使用不当，不但不利于安全，还会造成丢锚及断链等事故。

It can improve ship's safety and efficiency when ship berths and unberths; On the contrary, anchor used improperly, it will be harmful for vessel.

In this example, in Chinese version, the meaning of the two sentences forms a contrast, but if the author just looks at the surface, it is like a kind of the conditional sentence because of the "如果" in the second sentence. But in the English version, the author tries to convey the contrast of the two sentences by using "on the contrary."

In conclusion, the first example is connecting based on time, and the second is based on logical. According to the theory of function plus loyalty, both of them are loyal to the original text. Besides taking the purpose of the target into consideration, the translator does not have to translate the literal meaning "如果" into English and takes "On the contrary" instead.

5. Conclusion

5.1 Findings

The abstract is an essential part of an article in a journal paper. The author attempts to provide another perspective to the translators on the C-E translation of abstracts of academic papers by using the "function plus loyalty" theory.

Firstly, this thesis introduces the functionalist translation theories by listing some leading theories: the text typology theory of Reiss, the Skopostheorie theory of Vermeer, the theory of Translation Action of Holz-Manttari and Nord's Function plus Loyalty theory. And then it introduces the function plus loyalty theory in detail.

Secondly, it makes a brief introduction to the definition, classification, development, feature, and function of the English abstract. In this part, it also focus on the common errors that students always make in their abstract translation, such as, number errors, spelling errors, punctuation errors, and person errors, and so on. For each situation, the author analyzes the reason of errors and gives the solution. Some errors in the students' paper can be avoided by checking the text carefully. Some can be avoided only by learning some special principle of abstract writing.

Thirdly, this paper analyzes the application of the functionalist approach to the translation of the abstract especially the "function plus loyalty" theory by the case study of some students' abstract of their graduation thesis in two aspects: sentence level and text level. In the sentence level, avoiding the top-heavy sentence, the translator should adjust the order of words to make the sentence balanced. And in Chinese, there is more than one verb with only one subject, but in English, it is not allowed. So the translator needs to analyze the logic between the verbs and then use one of the verbs to be the predicate, and others using the participles, infinitive verb or preposition to express. In the text level, the author mainly stresses the cohesion of the text. Some belong to the overt way, like time and logic, but others belong to the recessive way. For the first example in 4.2, the translator can use "firstly or finally" to express the chronologic order. But for the second example, the translator should understand the real meaning of the original text and take the purpose of the target into consideration. For instance, Chinese may use "假如" or "如果" to express an opposite meaning. When translate this kind of sentence, "if" is not right. The translator need take "on the contrary" instead. Only in this way can the translator be loyal to the original text. In a word, the translation of the abstract is a kind of interpersonal and communicative action. So when translate the Chinese abstract into English, the translator should know the characteristics of the abstract and the differences of the Chinese and English.

According to the analysis of this paper, it is easy to see that in abstract translation, the translator should not only understand the deep meaning of the original text, but also understand and comprehend both original and target language. And then, be loyal to the original text style and the purpose of the target reader. So that he or she can convey the original meaning, by choosing proper words and right sentence patterns.

5.2 Contributions

Firstly, the author, doing a research on the application of "function plus loyalty" theory in C-E Translation of abstracts of academic papers of some students' graduation thesis, contributes to the future study of the translation of abstract. And he suggests that the translator should understand the original text and the target purpose and then consider the two sides' elements when doing the translation. Secondly this paper provides some perspectives and be of certain value for future research on developing a further approach for the translation of the abstract of an academic paper. Finally, this paper analyzes some abstract of students' graduation thesis combining with the "function plus loyalty" theory, which is good for the future English abstract writing and C-E Translation of abstracts. And the results of this research can be applied to undergraduate teaching of writing graduation thesis in colleges and universities and can also be applied to college English teaching, such as English-Chinese translation, reading, English writing, which can improve students' translation ability and better reflect the real scientific research level.

5.3　Limitations and Suggestions for Further Researches

At the end of this paper, I have to admit that abstract translation is a complicated issue which needs to be explored further in the future. And because my knowledge of this study is limited, this study has the following deficiencies: firstly, the author has not understood the functional translation theory totally, especially the "function plus loyalty" theory which is put forward by Nord. Secondly, the acquisition of English abstract is inadequate. Finally, the evaluation about the examples may not professional. The abstract translation still needs further research. Yet, this thesis is an attempt to offer translators another viewpoint on the C-E translation of abstracts of academic papers by using the "function plus loyalty" theory.

Bibliography

Bassnett, Susan. (2004). Translation Studies (Third Edition). Shanghai: Shanghai Foreign Language Education Press.

Catford, J. C. (1965). A Linguistic Theory of Translation London: Oxford University Press.

Koller, W. 1979. An Introduction to the Science of Transition. Heidelberg.

Nord, Christiane. (2001). Translating as a purposeful activity: Functionalist Approach Explained. Shanghai: Shanghai Foreign Language Education Press.

Nida, Eugene A. (1982). The Theory and Practice of Translation. The Netherlands: E. J. Brill, Leiden.

Nida, Eugene A. (1993). Language Culture and Translation. Shanghai: Shanghai Foreign Language Education Press.

Robinson, D. (2000). Western Translation Translation Theory. Manchester U. K. : St. Jerome Publishing.

Reiss, Katherina. (1971). Possibilities and Limitations of Translation Criticism. Munich: Hueber.

Reins, Katherina. (1977). Text Types, Translation Types and Translation Assessment. In Andrew Chesterman. Readings in Translation Theory (pp. 112). Helsinki: Oy Finn Lectura.

Shuttleworth, M & M. Cowie. 1997. Dictionary of Translation Studies. UK: St Jerome Publishing.

Vermeer, Hans J. (1989). Skopos and Commission in Translational Action.

Vermeer, H. J. 1987. What does it mean to translate?. Indian Journal of Applied Linguistics (2): 25—33.

Wilss, W. 2001. The Science of Transition: Problems and Methods. Shanghai: Shanghai Foreign Language Education Press.

卞建华. 对诺德"忠诚原则"的解读. 中国科技翻译, 2006(8): 34—35.

陈小慰. 翻译功能理论的启示. 中国翻译, 2000(4): 10.

戴东丁. 功能加忠诚原则及其在官方文件英译中的应用. 上海: 上海外国语大学, 2007.

方梦之. 应用翻译教程. 上海: 上海外语教育出版社, 2004.

冯庆华. 实用翻译教程. 上海: 上海外语教育出版社, 2002.

高健. 翻译中的风格问题. 外国语, 1995 (3).

侯宝晶. 从德国功能派翻译理论的角度研究. 哈尔滨: 哈尔滨理工大学, 2008.

胡壮麟. 语篇的衔接与连贯. 上海: 上海外语教育出版社, 1994.

胡作友. 德国功能派翻译理论述评. 学术界, 2008(6): 249.

贾文波. 翻译理论对应用翻译的启示. 上海翻译, 2007(2).

黎敏. 浅谈德国功能主义翻译理论. 湖北教育学院学报, 2006(12).
李正栓. 实践、理论、比较: 翻译教学的几个重要环节. 河北师范大学学报(教育版), 2003(4).
潘炳信, 李正栓. 翻译研究. 保定: 河北大学出版社, 2007.
石磊. 功能对等理论与其在英语新闻翻译中的应用. 上海: 上海师范大学, 2009.
胥瑾. 英汉对比与翻译教程. 北京: 化学工业出版社. 2010.
张培基、喻云根、李宗杰、彭谟禹. 英汉翻译教程. 上海: 上海外语教育出版社. 1983.
张道真. 现代英语用法词典. 上海: 上海译文出版社, 1983.

第五节　商务英语类

××大学

本科生毕业论文(设计)册

题目:会话含义在商务英语中的应用

学院＿＿＿＿＿＿
专业＿＿＿＿＿＿
班级＿＿＿＿＿＿
学生＿＿＿＿＿＿
指导教师＿＿＿＿＿＿
完成日期＿＿＿＿＿＿

A Study of Conversational Implicature in Business English

BY
×××
Prof. ×××, Tutor

A Thesis Submitted to the Foreign Languages

Institutes in Partial Fulfillment of the Requirements

For the Degree of Bachelor of Arts at

×× University

May 2014

Abstract

Pragmatics, as an area of linguistics, has received considerable attention from linguists. Abundant efforts have been made to study pragmatic phenomena and different theories have been established. The cooperative principle is one of the most important concepts in pragmatics. Cooperative principle is proposed by the Oxford philosopher Herbert Paul Grice in 1967.

Conversation is an important means to deliver and obtain information. In conversational exchange people usually try to reach a common goal by mutual efforts or at least make the conversation develop in the direction of their expectation. It is H. P. Grice who finds some rules working in human conversations and establishes his theory of conversational implicature. Conversations in business English are the most common way to build business relations or make a deal. By conversing, each side can get the useful information and understand the intention of the other, so it is meaningful to study business English conversations. The selected examples are classified into different categories according to the violation of each maxim of cooperative principle; meanwhile the factors of context and politeness principle are also taken into consideration. It is found that, in order to produce implicatures or obtain business goals, people in business English conversations often violate maxims. And usually, people flout the conversational maxims and convey their real intention indirectly in order to damage or save face.

The writer, by analyzing business conversations in a pragmatic approach, believes that this thesis can make certain contribution to correctly understand the conversational implicatures in business English conversations and help people in business English conversations and shed light on the application of pragmatics.

Key words: conversational implicature   cooperative principle   business English conversations   context and politeness principle

摘 要

　　语用学作为语言学中的重要领域已经引起许多语言学家的极大关注。这些语言学家倾心研究各种语用现象,现已创建了许多理论。合作原则是语用学中最重要的概念之一,此理论是格赖斯于1967年提出的。

　　会话是一种获得和承载信息的重要方式。在会话交流当中,人们通常会共同努力达成某种共同的目标或者努力让会话向期望的方向发展。格赖斯发现了人们的会话中存在某些规律,借此他提出了会话含义理论。会话是商务运作中建立关系或达成一致的最常见的方式,通过会话商务合作双方可以相互理解对方并取得有利信息。这就是研究商务英语交流活动的意义所在。本文所选用案例按照合作原则项下的四项准则进行分类。与此同时,作者还对语境原则及礼貌原则进行了考量。在商务英语对话中,合作原则项下四项准则极大地解释了人们的预期和目的。另一方面,人们通常利用这四项准则间接地表达自己的真实意思,以此来撕破或者保全面子。

　　本论文旨在帮助从事商务英语会话的人正确理解商务英语会话中的含义。此外,本文也对语用学在商务英语中的应用做了相应阐释。

关键词: 会话含义　合作原则　商务英语会话　语境和礼貌原则

Contents

Abstract ....
Abstract in Chinese ....
1. Introduction ....
   1.1 Background of the study ....
   1.2 Purpose and significance of the study ....
   1.3 Framework of the study ....
2. Conversational Implicature ....
   2.1 The definition of conversational implicature ....
   2.2 The cause of conversational implicature ....
   2.3 Identifying features of conversational implicature ....
3. The Language Features of Business English ....
   3.1 The definition of business English ....
   3.2 The classification of business English ....
   3.3 The language features of business English ....
4. The Application of Conversational Implicature in Business English ....
   4.1 Key points for drawing conversational implicature ...
   4.2 Conversational implicature by violating cooperating principle ....
5. Conclusion ....
Bibliography ....

1. Introduction

1.1 Background of the study

Pragmatics is a new subject in the study of the linguistics, which has been paid much attention by the linguists. They have made a large number of researches on it, among which Herbert Paul Grice has enjoyed fame for his conversational implicature together with his cooperative principle and its four maxims in his "Logic and Conversation." He has been trying to "explain how a hearer get from what is said to what is meant, from the level of expressed meaning to the level of implied meaning" (Thomas, 1995:56). Grice also presents that people produce conversational implicature by observing or violating the cooperative principle and its maxims. From the study on the cooperative principle from the text book of Linguistic, the writer finds that Grice H. P. makes a large number of researches on daily communications between people. While nowadays, Business English is becoming a more and more important subject in international business activities. Concerning that Business English is a sub-subject of English, and business conversation occurs every day. But there is little studies on the conversational implicature in business activities, and the importance of the conversational implicature in international business activities has been neglected by people. So the writer will take a great effort to have a study on the application of the conversational implicature in business interactions. Just like Grice, we will look into why businessmen generate conversational implicature and what's their original intention.

Grice, in his "Logic and Conversation," thinks that there is some regularity in conversations. He writes like this, "Our talk exchanges do not normally consist of a succession of disconnected remarks, and would not be rational if they did. They are characteristically, to some extent, a common purpose or set of purposes, or at least a mutually accepted direction." (Hu Zhuanglin, 1975: 45) That is to say, we seem to follow some principle like the following: "Make your conversational contribution such as is required, at the stage at which it occurs, by the accepted purpose or direction of the talk exchange in which you are engaged." (Hu Zhuanglin, 1975: 45) This is the cooperative principle we are going to talk about in this thesis. Since 1967 William James lectures, cooperative principle begins to attract the very attention of the linguists, and it has become the research object of many scholars majoring in Linguistics. Grice has centered his research in the cooperative principle in his study of the conversational implicature. Since the publication, the cooperative principle has contributed a lot to human communicative activities, whose purpose is to explain human communication's realization process.

1.2 Purpose and significance of the study

This thesis tries to analyze Business English with Grice's cooperative principle and its four maxims to find out how conversational implicature is generated. The writer wants to get some insights into the application of pragmatics in Business English as well as help readers get the meaning of conversational implicature in another way. The writer also expected to know more about the application of pragmatics.

This thesis has the following major significance.

First of all, the thesis can show in what ways the business partners generate conversational implicature and the true purpose of their intention.

Secondly, the thesis can conclude the common strategies which businessmen use when they convey the conversational implicature to the other side.

Thirdly, through applying pragmatics to Business English, the thesis is aiming to make the readers have a better understanding on Business English interactions in business activities.

Fourthly, the thesis can enrich the studies of conversational implicature and provide more materials for the future study on it.

1.3　Framework of the study

This thesis is composed of all together five chapters, all of which are working for the study of the conversational implicature in Business English. The following order is the order by which the thesis runs.

In chapter one, the introduction part, the writer will show the background study, research purpose and its significance in a general point of view.

In chapter two, the basic theory of the thesis will be introduced, that is, Grice's conversational implicature. The definition and identifying features of conversational implicature will be covered. And the cooperative principle, together with its four maxims, and the politeness principle will be introduced as the basic theory of producing conversational implicature.

In chapter three, the thesis will move on to the second most important theoretical part, that is, the theories of Business English. They are the definition, the characteristics, and the classifications of Business English in international business activities.

In chapter four, the conversational implicature will be talked about together with Business English, which constructs the most important part of the paper. In the front part of this chapter, the key points of drawing conversational implicature will be showed first. And then, we will find out how conversational implicature is generated by violating the four maxims of cooperative principle.

In the conclusion part, the writer will present the findings of the study.

2. Conversational Implicature

2.1　The definition of conversational implicature

"Conversational implicature is a type of inference, referring to the meaning which a speaker intends to convey, but does not explicitly express. Conversational implicature was proposed by Oxford philosopher Herbert Paul Grice. There is evidence that Grice began to formulate his ideas of this theory in the fifties, but it was through the William James lectures he delivered at Harvard in 1967 that this theory first became known to the public. Part of the lecture was published in 1975 under the title of 'Logic and Conversation'."(Liu Runqing, Wen Xu, 2006:154)

Here is an example of a conversational implicature. Suppose Alice asks Bill "Where is my chocolate?" and Bill replies "The cat just now jumped down from the desk and ran out." On the face of it, this is an idiotic response to a simple question: Bill has declined to mention a specific person at all, and has instead brought up the cat, the desk and what the cat did, none of which was being asked about. And yet this is a perfectly normal and satisfactory answer to the question: providing that Alice knows that the cat likes to eat chocolate, she can reason as follows: "Bill doesn't know who has eaten the chocolate, or he would simply have told me, but Bill tells me he saw the cat jump down from the desk and run out; doubtless he wants to show that it is the cat rather than him who has eaten the chocolate, or Bill wouldn't have mentioned it." Alice's conclusion that Bill is not the one who has eaten the chocolate is an example of a conversational implicature, or CI.

2.2 The cause of conversational implicature

Implicature is usually caused by observation or violation of the Cooperative Principle or the Politeness Principles.

2.2.1 Grice's cooperative principle

Usually, people would mean more than what he says or writes. In this case, the problem would be that how the speaker succeeds in conveying extra meaning and at the same time, how the hearer manages to apprehend the speaker's actual meaning. H. P. Grice suggests that there is a set of assumptions guiding the conduct of the conversation. "Our talk exchanges do not normally consist of a succession of disconnected remarks, and would not be rational if they did. They are characteristically, to some degree at least, cooperative efforts and each participant recognizes in them, to some extent, a common purpose or set of purpose, are at least a mutually accepted direction."(Hu Zhuanglin, 1975:45) To specify the assumptions, Grice introduces the cooperative principle and it's for maxims like the following:

Make your conversational contribution such as is required, at the stage at which it occurs, by the accepted purpose or direction of the talk exchange in which you are engaged.

To specify the CP further, Grice introduced four categories of maxims as follows:

The Maxim of Quality

Try to make your contribution one that is true, i.e.

1. Do not say what you believe to be false;

2. Do not say that for which you lack adequate evidence.

The Maxim of Quantity

1. Make your contribution as informative as is required (for the current purpose of the exchange);

2. Do not make your contribution more informative than is required.

The Maxim of Relation

Be relevant.

The Maxim of Manner

Be perspicuous, i.e.

1. Avoid obscurity of expression;

2. Avoid ambiguity;

3. Be brief (avoid unnecessary prolixity);

4. Be orderly. (Hu Zhuanglin, 1975:45)

In order to be cooperative and make the interaction go smoothly, Grice thinks that people ought to obey the four maxims of the CP when they interact with each other. However, the fact is that the participants constantly violate one or more maxims at one time and then Grice's conversational implicature theory works.

2.2.2 The politeness principle

In the last part of the thesis, we point out that the cooperative principle is a rule for a successful conversation. But we have realized the fact that the CP alone could not fully explain how people make a successful interaction with each other. The CP explains how conversational implicature is given rise to but it doesn't explain at the same time why people do not say directly their actual intension. Here, it's necessary for us to notice another principle which also works in people's interactions just like the cooperative principle, which is the politeness principle.

The politeness principle is put forward by Leech so as to "rescue the cooperative principle" for the reason that it can satisfactorily explain exceptions to and apparent deviations from the CP and it can be regarded as a necessary complementary for conditions where the CP fails to work.

Leech's politeness principle runs as follows:

Minimize (other things being equal) the expression of impolite beliefs and maximize (other things being equal) the expression of polite beliefs.

The six maxims of the PP:

Maxim of Tact (in directives and commissives)

1. Minimize cost to other

2. Maximize benefit to other

Maxim of Generosity (in directives and commissives)

1. Minimize benefit to self

2. Maximize cost to self

Maxim of Approbation (in expressive and assertives)

1. Minimize dispraise of other

2. Maximize praise of other

Maxim of Modesty (in expressive and assertives)

1. Minimize praise of self

2. Maximize dispraise of self

Maxim of Agreement (in assertives)

1. Minimize disagreement between self and other

2. Maximize sympathy between self and other

The politeness principle explains "why people are often so indirect in conveying what they mean" and why certain forms are more acceptable than others.

2.3 Identifying Features of Conversational Implicature

Toward the end of his "Logic and Conversation," Grice mentioned briefly some features of conversational implicature. They are as follows.

(1) They are not entailments, that is, they do not follow logically from what is said. For instance, we can infer from "Pete has a cousin" that "At least one of Pete's parents is not an only child," but since this is an entailment it is not a conversational implicature. On the other hand, in the following example:

A: Can I talk to Jane?

B: Jane is in the shower.

Here the inference that Jane is not able to take a telephone call, is not an entailment.

(2) They are cancelable, that is, they are relatively weak inferences and can be denied by the speaker without contradiction. For instance, B's reply in the following would normally be taken into meaning "I don't intend to tell you":

A: How old are you?

B: That's none of your business.

If B added "But I'll tell you, anyway." this would cancel the inference, but B would not be guilty of self-contradiction. This is characteristic of conversational implicatures.

(3) They are context sensitive, in that the same proposition expressed in a different context can give rise to different implicatures:

A: I think I'll take a shower.

B: Jane's in the shower.

This implicates that you can't take a shower just yet, rather that Jane can't accept a phone call.

(4) They are non-detachable, that is, in a particular context the same proposition expressed in different words will give rise to the same implicature. In other words, the implicature is not tied to a particular form of words. For instance, if B above had said "That doesn't concern you." The implicature would be the same.

(5) They are calculable, that is to say they can be worked out using general principles rather than requiring specific knowledge, such as a private arrangement between A and B that if one says X it will mean Y.

3. The Language Features of Business English

3.1 The definition of Business English

Business English is the English that people use when dealing with the affairs in areas such as international trade, international economy, international finance, etc. It is the kind of English which is often used by people when dealing with international business activities and the English which is involved in international business subject. These activity areas include: international trade, international economy, international finance, international business law, international accounting, international marketing, international logistics, international payment, international investment, business administration, human resources management, bank, insurance, custom affaires, check item, quarantine, tourism, commercial service, etc. Briefly speaking, Business English is General English plus special vocational English.

3.2 The classification of Business English

Business English can be classified into different types from different perspectives. First of all, Business English has the writing form and the speaking form. Because of the limited space of the thesis, and the time it is used, the writer only talks about written forms of Business English. Here the study of Professor Liao Ying will be put out to support the thesis. And the following eight categories are classified from the perspective of pragmatical use.

(1) Letters: Letters are most often used in international business interaction. No matter within or outside the company. They are widely used in formal or informal business affairs and they consist of private letters and official letters.

(2) Commercial documents: They are widely used in the areas of economy and trade. Commercial documents consist of special commercial documents and general business letters.

(3) Etiquette documents: They are constituted of congratulatory documents and condolatory documents, etc.

(4) Contracts or deeds: They consist of sales confirmation, the intention agreement, agency agreement, contract, cultural exchange agreement, letter of appointment,

stipulations of agreement, etc.

(5) Informative and revelational documents: They are used in business activities to inform or to bring something into a public notice, such as announcement, notification, memos, posters, notice, found, advertisement, report, proposal so on and so forth.

(6) Expository writing: It is used to explain or illustrate a certain problem or matter, containing instructions of products, trademark, caption, certificate of quality, etc.

(7) Bills and vouchers: They consist of bills, certificates, shipping documents, policies, forms, receipts, I.O.U., order, and so on.

(8) Documents for meeting affairs: They contain those signed or issued before, during and after the meeting.

Besides the above, we could also classify Business English according to the areas it involves. For example, Business English involves many areas, such as finance, insurance, bank, international trade, tourism, business law, accounting, logistics, advertising and so on, so it can be classified as legal English, advertising English, insurance English, financial English, technical English, etc.

3.3 The Language features of Business English

As a kind of language, Business English is a kind of communication tool and a carrier of communicating knowledge and information, which has the obvious feature reflecting the area of the international business subject. So, compared with the general English, Business English has its own particular language features. The core of Business English is English. Its background is business activities, so its language is realistic. Or in the other words, the most important feature of Business English is objective and realistic. We will discuss the language features of Business English in terms of its vocabulary, discourse construction, linguistic stylistic style, etc.

3.3.1 Style diversification

Because Business English covers a large number of areas, it grows a characteristic of style diversification. According to the division of English function, the style of English can be divided into the following kinds: English literature, English advertising, English news, English technology, and English laws.

Concerning the professional areas which Business English involves in, among the above five style, English advertising and English laws (mainly referring to international business laws and English regulation) belong to Business English style. Besides, Business English style also includes practical English writing style. Having knowledge on the features of Business English is benefit for distinguishing different styles in Business English teaching, translation and study.

3.3.2 Practical applicability

Business English has the feature of practical applicability, because the areas of the international business have relatively strong practicalness. There are foreign scholars looking from the uses of international business who think that the features of Business English are: it's related to business background knowledge; it has clear purpose; it is based on need analysis; it has pressure of time.

3.3.3 The productivity of vocabulary derivation

Business English has a strong ability of deriving vocabulary. Some collocations of some vocabularies are endless. For example, the word "free" can construct many phrases with international business meaning in collocating with many other words, such as free goods, free loan, free on board, free time, free trial, etc. Another example is the word "short," the collocations are short bill, short delivery, short-landing, short sale, short-time working, etc. And there are many other words like these two.

3.3.4 A large number of industry-specific terminologies

Business English involves in many industrial areas, in which there are many terms with very obvious industrial features. The teaching and study of Business English must concern these terms, such as force majeure, target market, market segmentation, counter-offer, balance sheet, etc.

With the fast development of international business, new words and phrases with the industrial feature of Business English will keep appearing. For example, after the establishment of the international logistic subject, the vocabulary 3PL (Third Party Logistics) appeared, and after the establishment of electronic business, the vocabulary B2B (Business to Business) appeared, and so on.

3.3.5 A large number of abbreviations

The abbreviations appear with the convenience of the language use. The use of abbreviations can avoid the complex language use. With the fast development of society and technology, we today do all things efficiently. All businessmen focus on efficiency, which starts from having the concept of time. "Time is money or efficiency" will never be out of date. So it is normal that there are many abbreviations in Business English. Abbreviations are welcomed for their briefness and terse. Abbreviations are so concise that it is easy to be remembered. These abbreviations are usually the English with industrial features. For example, 4Ps (Product, Price, Place, Promotion), CEO (Chief Executive Officer), R&D (Research and Development), etc.

3.3.6 A large number of common sentence patterns

There are many common sentence patterns in Business English, for example, when we introduce the company, we usually say: ABC Company, located in Shijiazhuang,

Hebei, specializes in paper import and export. When we introduce the products, we usually say: Our products are good in quality and reasonable in price. Another example is that we often see sentences in business laws and English regulations like this: Upon the terms and conditions hereinafter set forth... unless otherwise stipulated... it is agreed that... There are more common sentence patterns in business letters. For example, enclosed please find... we could very much appreciate it if you could... further to our conversation on the phone yesterday, I'd like to... The appearance of sentence patterns is due to the regular working procedures in international business activities. And compared with English literature, Business English changes little in daily use.

3.3.7 The ABCs of Business English

We have already known that Business English is realistic from the above discussion, so its language is plain without exaggeration and ornament. On the basis of the study on its linguistic feature and stylistic feature, we can make a conclusion about the characteristics of Business English as ABCs.

(1) A: Accurate

Because Business English objectively describes the reality, so it is required that the language of Business English is accurate and no vague language is allowed to appear. For example, the description of the technical index in the product manual must be accurate. And the language in international business laws must be accurate, too. The terms of business law involve the stipulation of the buyer and seller's right and obligation. In order to avoid the disputation, the writ of business law must function efficiently. Its vocabulary and meaning must be accurate enough to avoid the ambiguity caused by vague vocabulary and sentences. Take this sentence as an example: This contract is signed by and between Party A and Party B. In this sentence, by and between are repeatedly used with the purpose to avoid misunderstanding, which defines that the contract is signed by the two parties of the business. Another case is that when we broadcast our new products, we need to introduce their special functions in detail. The language must be accurate enough so that the customers will get the right information about the product, otherwise, they may not buy the products. Besides, when introducing the new products, if you tell your customer that the manufacture technology is brought from Japan, rather than only telling that the technology is brought abroad, it will work better. The language is also be required to be accurate when writing business report. The degree of the accurateness depends on the choice of language. For example, the sentence "I wouldn't be surprised if our sales in Shijiazhuang drop" shows the possibility is 75 percent. While the sentence "I doubt whether we will make any sales in Shijiazhuang" shows the possibility is only 25 percent. If you want to present a 100% possibility, you can change the sentence into "I am sure that we will make no sales in Shijiazhuang." From the above all, we can see that accurateness is the most notable feature of Business English.

(2) B: Brief

Business English is brief in language. In other words, if we can express our intension in one sentence, then we will not say more than one sentence, which will make the discourse complex and dilatory, both in oral English or written English. For example, when communicate with customer, we need to avoid complex dialogues, we often see the following case: A: Hello, I am so pleased to see you again. B: Hello again. B's answer is very clear, so here, if B answers: I am so pleased to see you, too. It will not have an effect of briefness. Business English is also brief in written language and it doesn't have to be exaggeration and ornament like English literature. Here an exception is with the advertising. As a kind of Business English, English advertising has its particular language feature. English advertising attracts the customers with its language, so its language needs to be modified, but still to be brief, for example, the choice is yours, and the honour is ours.

All businessmen focus on time efficiency. So the interact language in business activities needs to be brief and terse, no matter in the daily memo within the company or in the email with the customer. Only in this way, the working efficiency can be improved. Just because international business activities pursue the efficiency, Business English is characterized by its briefness.

(3) 3Cs

① The first C: Concrete. Business English describes reality, which is concrete rather than abstract. Otherwise, it will arise unnecessary disputation. For example, when offering, we always say, "This offer is valid by the end of April 2014." In this way, we will not need to worry that the other party will censure beyond the validity. If there is no acclaim like this, a misunderstanding may occur between two parties. Another case is in the reply letter, we write like this, "Thank you for your letter dated April 7th, 2014, concerning your order our papers." We must note that which letter this reply refers to, if we only write like this, "We have received your letter." Then confusion may happen.

② The second C: Clear. That Business English is clear means that the information it carries is clear and easy to understand. The language of Business English is clear and easy to be understood, and there is no extra information. In the activities of international business, people like to be direct in conversation, although sometimes connotation is needed. The following is an example which contains both clear and complex expression.

Eg. You will notice that every single one of our products is made from 100% natural ingredients—we use no artificial addictives at all.

Eg. I should like to take this chance of drawing your attention to the fact that all our products are manufactured from completely natural ingredients and that we do not utilize any artificial addictives whatsoever.

The first sentence is very clear, while the second one is not that satisfactory.

Another case is when writing to your superior, especially in proposal or report, the language must be clear enough. Sometimes, graphs will be used to bring a direct effect. Businessmen have no patience and interest to study what you mean in your report.

③ The third C: Courteous. This character is reflected in the interaction among people, for instance, in business conversations and business letters. In the interaction of international business, even in oral form, the language should be polite and courteous, even when you are quarreling with the others. There is an old saying in China "Harmony brings wealth" which also notes the importance of politeness in business conversation. Take the following case as an example, if the buyer keeps delaying the loan, we can reply to him in this way, "If you don't pay the rest of the outstanding bill to us within this month, we will be forced to take court action." Although the discourse is a little tough, it is still with politeness. The phrase "be forced to" means that we are not willing to do so, but we have to do it without any other method. If we reply in another way, "You must pay the rest of the outstanding bill to us within this month; otherwise, we will take court action." Then the discourse has lost its politeness. Courteousness is a feature of Business English; after all, harmony is valued in business. Only in this way can the parties of the business build a friendly relationship with each other, which will bring profit for the company in a long run.

4. The Application of Conversational Implicature in Business English

4.1 Key points for drawing conversational implicature

The reduction of conversational implicature has three key elements: Context includes prompt context and cognitive context. The former context refers to the prompt contextual element when the discourse occurs. The latter one refers to the shared knowledge of the participants of the interaction. Indirect speech act refers to the speech act in which the speaker uses its surface meaning to realize another deep meaning. Relevance refers to the cognitive logical connection between the actual speaking and the true intension.

4.1.1 Context

Context is an essential factor in the interpretation of utterances and expressions. The most important aspects of context are: (a) the immediate physical situation, (b) knowledge shared between speaker and hearer.

(1) We draw conversational implicature from immediate context.

Eg. Pete: Coming down to the pub tonight?

Bill: I've got to finish a piece of work.

Here we can come up with a question like this, "What are the physical contexts relevant to the implied meaning intended by Bill?" And the answer is "Coming down to the pub and finishing a piece of work cannot happen at the same time."

(2) We draw conversational implicature from cognitive context.

Eg. Student: I want to write a thesis on the comparison between the expression of French and English.

Teacher: If you success, you will win the Nobel Prize.

Here we can also raise a question like this, "What is the cognitive consumption that is relevant to the implied meaning intended by the supervisor?" And the answer here is "There is no Nobel Prize for linguistics at all."

4.1.2 Indirect speech act

We use an utterance to perform an act. This is an utterance that has the typical form of one kind of speech act, but which functions, either typically or in specific contexts, as a different type of speech act?

Many instances of indirect speech acts are highly conventionalized. (This leads some scholars to maintain that their "indirectness" is only of historical relevance.) The following are typical: (1) "You will do as I say" has the form of an assertive (i.e. tries to get someone to do something). (2) "Would you mind if I opened the window?" superficially is a question inquiring about the hearer's attitude to a hypothetical event, but is a frequent way of questioning permission. (3) "Could you lend me a hundred pounds?" literally is a question regarding the hearer's ability to do something, but is conventionally used as a (relatively polite) directive. (4) "What did I tell you?" is a question, but conventionally functions as an equivalent to "I told you so!"

4.1.3 Relevance

If the maxim of relation is violated, conversational implicature arises. We find it necessary to seek the cognitive-logical connection between what is said and what is implicated. This was first suggested by the philosopher Grice as the basis for an explanation of how conversational implicature arise. Grice portrayed a conversation as a co-operative activity in which participants tacitly agree to abide by certain norms. Grice spelled out the norms in greater detail in the forms of a set of maxims of conversation, one of which is that of relation, which says that what is actually said must be relevant to the topic at hand. If the maxim of relation is violated, conversational implicature arises.

4.2 Conversational implicature by violation of cooperative principle

In the actual verbal business conversational activities, observing the cooperative principle strictly sometimes will cause embarrassment and even lead to business termination. So in some cases, people often violate the cooperative principle and its four maxims to avoid embarrassment and misunderstanding of each other, and finally succeed in a successful communication.

The following examples are grouped into four categories according to the four maxims of the cooperative principle. They are all with rich conversational implicature in the actual use.

4.2.1 Violation of the quantity maxim

In Grice's opinion, people should be polite by cooperating with each other during the interaction so as to make the interaction go smoothly. However, in the actual case in business activities, such as in negotiations, the participants often flout cooperative principle on purpose and deliberately. People violate the maxim of quantity by offering more or less information than is required, which leads the hearer to calculate the reasons of the violation of the principle. With the information of the context and the background knowledge of the business activities, the hearer may know the actual intension implicated in the interaction.

4.2.1.1 Less information

The first submaxim of the maxim is to make your expression as informative as is required (for the current purposes of the exchange). In other words, a speaker may offer less information to convey extra meaning. In business activities, if one part doesn't provide enough information, he is probably trying to conceal something or disclose more than the literal meaning. Some cases are as follows:

Discourse Context: Kim is a new employee of a company selling A4 papers. Kim's company has cooperated with Jim's company for a long time. In order to promote Kim's ability in business activities, his company sends him to Jim's company to have a negotiation with them. Jim is appointed as the representative of his company.

Situational Context: It is on a meeting, and it's time for them to talk about the payment.

Kim: What about payment?

Jim: Er, D/P.

In this conversation, we can see that Jim hasn't given the sufficient information about the specification of the payment that Kim wants. So here Jim has violated the submaxim of the quantity maxim and he is supposed to offer more information to Kim. The word Er and Jim's appearance have shown that he is sending some conversational implicature. His extra utterance is that "You don't know you are required to pay by D/P, you surprise me." While Jim doesn't say the words directly, as a matter of fact, Jim may then have a sense that Kim is a new employee of his company. According to the context, it is understandable for Jim to say so because the two companies have cooperated with each other for a long time so that they do not need to mention the payment like this. We can also see from the conversation that Kim hasn't prepared well for the negotiation without an overall understanding of his business partner.

4.2.1.2 More information

In business activities or daily communications, people sometimes offer more information than is required just like the less information case. The extra information, sometimes, can be described as "supportive move" (Ran Yongping, 2006: 127). The extra information can help the speaker support his own utterance. The following is an example.

Discourse Context: Alice is the representative of the trading company, and Mary is the representative of the trust company. Now Alice wants to give the cargo trust on Mary's company.

Situational Context: In common case, Alice would not give her trust on one trust company easily. She would make the decision after having an overall understanding of the credit situation of that company.

Alice: What about your company's credit standing?

Mary: For our credit standing, please refer to the Bank of China, Shijiazhuang Branch. Our enterprise credit is also known to all.

From the conversation, we can know that aiming for Alice's question, Mary has given more information than Alice wants by adding "our enterprise credit is also known to all" to her answer. Here Mary has violated the second submaxim of quantity maxim. And here Mary's implied meaning is that "our company's good credit can be proved not only by the bank, but also by other companies in business." Here although Mary has violated the quantity maxim, she succeeds in this conversation for the reason that she knows how to play to the customer.

From the case, it can be concluded that in business negotiations, the participants may offer more information than what the other side wants, which will help the other side understand their situation in a more multi-faced, multi-angled way. Interacting like this can develop the trust with each other and at the same time can express their sincerity in cooperation.

4.2.2 Violation of the quality maxim

The quality maxim requires the speaker to make the contribution one be true. If the speaker says something which is false or for which he has no enough evidence, then he violates the quality maxim and he is implicating something. And here the conversational implicature appears. The several categories of this kind are as follows.

4.2.2.1 Irony

Irony is a common example which flouts the quality maxim. The following is an example.

Discourse Context: Kitty and Mary are two employees from two trading companies separately. They are both applying for the bank credit. And finally Kitty succeeds and Mary doesn't. So Mary is not happy because of this. She talks with Tom on their way back to the company.

Situational Context:

Mary: I have never failed like this before.

Tom: It doesn't matter. We still have chance.

Mary: They might have painted the city red!

Here the expression "paint the city red" means that someone is extremely happy and excited and so that he paints the city red to celebrate. And obviously it cannot be true so Mary has violated the quality maxim. Here the implied meaning is that Mary is angry at it which is concluded from the discourse context.

4.2.2.2 Hyperbole

Leech describes hyperbole as "a case where the speaker's description is stronger than is warranted by the state of affairs described" (Leech, 2003:86).

Discourse Context: Mr. Liu's employees make some mistakes with their work. And it is not the first time that they have made the same mistake, which made Mr. Liu angry with them. One of the employees Mark comes to him to ask for the solution.

Situational Context:

Mark: We have sent the false good to the customer, and the customer wants to return the goods.

Mr. Liu: What! You guys drive me up a wall!

Here Mr. Liu expressed his disappointment for the employees. And through the usage of hyperbole, he wants to deliver the message that the employees has brought the company another big trouble which needs to be dealt with by them together. And Mark may get the information that they have to work harder to coordinate with the customer and decrease the loose of the company. So the point here is that effective business conversations require the speaker to have a complete understanding of the listener and be well-prepared to act properly to the speaker.

4.2.2.3 Metaphor

Metaphor is also be often used to produce conversational implicature by violating the quality maxim. The following is the example.

Discourse Context: Mark is in a trading company selling A4 papers and Bill is in a stationary company. The two companies have cooperation with each other for a long time. Now Mark's company met with financial trouble, and he plans to borrow some money from Bill's company.

Situational Context:

Mark: Can you lend my company MYM300,000?

Bill: I'm sorry to hear that, but it is the last straw of my company.

Here Bill uses the method of metaphor to refuse Mark's ask by expressing that the money is so important for Bill's company and he cannot lend it to Mark. Bill expresses his intension clearly and in this way avoids the embarrassment caused by direct refuse.

4.2.3 Violation of the Relation Maxim

The relation maxim requires people to speak things that are related to the topic of the conversation. When the speaker speaks something which is unrelated to the topic, he may want to express conversational implicature. In this case, a hearer who can have an understanding of the implied meaning will make the conversation successful.

Discourse Context: Mary and Mark are both the employees in Morning Stationary Company, but they are in separate departments. That day, Mary and Mark have lunch together in the dining hall of the company.

Situational Context:

Mary: I have heard that one of your new employees has been guilty for stolen. Is it true?

Mark: Do you think that the new cook in our company has done a good job?

Usually, people in different departments have different duties even in one company. They all have the duty to keep secret for their own department. Here, Mark says something unrelated to Mary's question and he violates the relation maxim. In this way, Mary may get the idea that Mark doesn't want to talk about that issue. Mark by doing this is keeping the fact and leaving Mary get an impression that he has good management skills. So Mark violates the relation maxim.

4.2.4 Violation of the manner maxim

Avoid obscurity of expression and ambiguity is the first and second submaxims of the manner maxim. We will talk about them separately.

4.2.4.1 Ambiguity

In Grice's opinion, "We are concerned only with ambiguity that is deliberate or that the speaker intends or expects; it is expected to be recognized by his hearer." (Jiang Wangqi, 2000:51) Here are the examples.

Discourse Context: Mark is in a trading company selling A4 papers and Bill is in a stationary company. Mark's company is suffering a financial crisis. Mark wants to borrow some money from Bill to come through the difficult time. But the money is of great importance for Bill's company which may cause themselves a financial crisis. When they two talk, Jim, Bill's colleague comes to discuss the matter with them.

Situational Context:

Mark: Can you loan me MYM300,000? I would return it within 3 months.

Bill: OK.

Jim: If there's no return, we will suffer some difficulty in finance.

Bill: I know. But I trust Mark, he will do as he promises.

Jim: You trust people very easily.

Bill: How can you cooperate with people who you don't trust on?

Actually the use of the word "people" makes Jim violate the relation maxim and manner maxim. And Jim is trying to tell Bill not to lend the money indirectly. From Bill's answer, we can see that Bill has got his implied meaning. He also uses the word "people" to reply to Jim. They both have succeeded in saving the face of all the three people.

4.2.4.2　Obscurity

Sometimes, the speaker will say something obscure to generate conversational implicature. The hearer with a good knowledge of the context and background will complete a successful conversation with the speaker. Here is an example.

Discourse Context: Circle is a new employee of a trading company selling A4 papers. Helen is the manager of that company. Helen is asked to take Circle to become familiar with the affairs in the company.

Situational Context:

Helen: Our papers have two kinds of packages. When communicating with the customer, make sure which package he would choose. My paper or the green one. Some customers may use their own package.

Circle: What do you mean by saying my paper?

Helen: My Paper is the N-A-M-E of the package.

Here Helen uses the separate letters of the words to answer Circle's question, which violates the manner maxim by being obscure. She is producing the conversational implicature like this: She is surprised that Circle even doesn't know My Paper is the brand name of the package. And she is expressing that she is disappointed that Circle hasn't become familiar with the basic knowledge about the product of the company.

From the above discussion we can see that in order to reach a successful conversation, people may observe or violate the cooperative principle. Observation or violation, the speaker needs to make a choice to make the conversation successful. Either observing or violating the cooperative principle and its maxims blindly will bring the business into the end. So it requires the participants to make the proper choice depending on the certain context. In some cases, producing conversational implicature by violating the maxims may have a good effect on the business and contribute to the smooth running of business activities.

5. Conclusion

The thesis makes a comprehensive review of the researches on Grice's theory. From the thesis, it can be looked out that it is of great significance and necessity to have a study on the rich conversational implicature in Business English interactions from pragmatic perspective. Here, Grice's conversational implicature theory is constituted of cooperative principle and its four conversational maxims which function as the theoretical basis of the study. Grice uses his conversational implicature theory to explain for us why people don't cooperate and why conversational implicature is generated. In the above discussion of this thesis, different categories of Business English examples are sorted to analyze the conversational implicature by employing Grice's cooperative principle and its four conversational maxims, meanwhile context and politeness are taken into consideration.

There are four categories of violation of the maxims, each of which has been discussed in detail. By studying how the four maxims are observed or violated, this thesis presents how pragmatics is capable to reveal the implicated meaning and the real intention of the participants in international business activities.

In international business activities, people may flout the conversational maxims based on the consideration of politeness principle and politeness maxims should be regarded as politeness strategies to reach conversational goals. It is found that people in business activities may choose to flout conversational maxims with the purpose of upholding politeness maxims and perform the FTA (face-threatening acts) indirectly. Besides, the context is also an important factor for the study of the thesis. Without specific context—the common context or background knowledge, the hearer may fail to figure out the implicature or neglect the implicature.

In a word, this thesis explores how and why the implicatures are generated from business interactions and what the implicatures are in specific context. It finds that business interaction can also be interpreted within the scope of the conversational implicature theory and cooperative principle. With the guidance of conversational implicature theory, businessmen can finish their English conversational work more smoothly.

Bibliography

Baldoni, John. 2009. *Make Your Place Proud of You* [J]. Harvard Business Review.

Doug, E. & Hagen, S. 1992. *Language in International Business* [M]. London: Hodder & Stoughton Ltd.

Ellis, M. & Johnson, C. 2002. *Business English Teaching* [M]. Shanghai: Shanghai Foreign Education Press.

Ellis, R. 2003. *Task-based Language Learning and Teaching* [J]. Oxford: Oxford University Press.

Gates, B. 1999. *Business at the Speed of Thought* [M]. Penguin Graded Readers Level 6.

Hutchinson, T. & Water. 1984. A. *How Communicative is ESP* [J]. ELT Journal.

Harmer, Jeremy. 2000. *How to Teach English* [M]. Beijing: Foreign Teaching and Research Press.

Keenan, E. O. 1976. *The University of Conversational Postulates* [A]. *Language in Society* [C], Vol. 5. Cambridge: Cambridge University Press.

Mikhial, Bakhtin. 1981. *The Dialogic Imagination* [M]. Texas: University of Texas Press.

Novak, Candice. 2008. *7 Ways Your E-mail Can Get You Fired* [J]. U. S. News and World Report.

胡壮麟. 2011.《语言学教程》. 北京大学出版社.

刘润清. 文旭. 2006.《新编语言学教程》. 外语教学与研究出版社.

盛小利. 2007.《商务英语谈判口语》. 中国宇航出版社.

翁凤翔. 2009.《商务英语研究》. 上海交通大学出版社.

周保国. 2007.《商务交际英语听说教程》. 武汉大学出版社.

附录1 《中国图书馆图书分类法》基本类目表

A 马克思主义、列宁主义、毛泽东思想
B 哲学
C 社会科学总论
D 政治、法律
E 军事
F 经济
G 文化、科学、教育、体育
H 语言、文字
I 文学
J 艺术
K 历史、地理
N 自然科学总论
O 数理科学和化学
P 天文学、地球科学
Q 生物科学
R 医药、卫生
S 农业科学
T 工业技术
U 交通运输
V 航空、航天
X 环境科学
Z 综合性图书

附录2 《中国科学院图书馆图书分类法》基本类目表

00 马克思列宁主义、毛泽东思想
10 哲学
20 社会科学(总论)
21 历史、历史学
27 经济、经济学
31 政治、社会生活
34 法律、法学
36 军事、军事学
37 文化、科学、教育、体育
41 语言、文字
42 文学
48 艺术
49 无神论、宗教
50 自然科学(总论)
51 数学
52 力学
53 物理学
54 化学
55 天文学
56 地球科学(地学)
58 生物科学
61 医药、卫生
62 中医、中药学
63 临床医学
63.3 药物学
65 农业科学
71 工程技术
72 能源学、动力工程
73 电工技术、电子技术
73.9 计算机科学技术
74 矿业工程
75 金属学(物理冶金)
76 冶金学

77 金属工艺、金属加工
78 机械工程、机器制造
81 化学工业
83 食品工业
85 轻工业、手工业及生活供应技术
86 土木建筑工程
87 运输工程
90 综合性图书

附录3 科学技术报告、学位论文和学术论文的编写格式

1 引言

1.1 制订本标准的目的是为了统一科学技术报告、学位论文和学术论文(以下简称报告、论文)的撰写和编辑的格式,便利信息系统的收集、存储、处理、加工、检索、利用、交流、传播。

1.2 本标准适用于报告、论文的编写格式,包括形式构成和题录著录,及其撰写、编辑、印刷、出版等。

本标准所指报告、论文可以是手稿,包括手抄本和打字本及其复制品;也可以是印刷本,包括发表在期刊或会议录上的论文及其预印本、抽印本和变异本;作为书中一部分或独立成书的专著;缩微复制品和其他形式。

1.3 本标准全部或部分适用于其他科技文件,如年报、便览、备忘录等,也适用于技术档案。

2 定义

2.1 科学技术报告

科学技术报告是描述一项科学技术研究的结果或进展或一项技术研制试验和评价的结果;或是论述某项科学技术问题的现状和发展的文件。

科学技术报告是为了呈送科学技术工作主管机构或科学基金会等组织或主持研究的人等。科学技术报告中一般应该提供系统的或按工作进程的充分信息,可以包括正反两方面的结果和经验,以便有关人员和读者判断和评价,以及对报告中的结论和建议提出修正意见。

2.2 学位论文

学位论文是表明作者从事科学研究取得创造性的结果或有了新的见解,并以此为内容撰写而成、作为提出申请授予相应的学位时评审用的学术论文。

学士论文应能表明作者确已较好地掌握了本门学科的基础理论、专门知识和基本技能,并具有从事科学研究工作或担负专门技术工作的初步能力。

硕士论文应能表明作者确已在本门学科上掌握了坚实的基础理论和系统的专门知识,并对所研究课题有新的见解,有从事科学研究工作或独立担负专门技术工作的能力。

博士论文应能表明作者确已在本门学科上掌握了坚实宽广的基础理论和系统深入的专门知识,并具有独立从事科学研究工作的能力,在科学或专门技术上做出了创造性的成果。

2.3 学术论文

学术论文是某一学术课题在实验性、理论性或观测性上具有新的科学研究成果或创新见解和知识的科学记录;或是某种已知原理应用于实际中取得新进展的科学总结,用以提供学术会议上宣读、交流或讨论;或在学术刊物上发表;或作其他用途的书面文件。

学术论文应提供新的科技信息,其内容应有所发现、有所发明、有所创造、有所前进,而不是重复、模仿、抄袭前人的工作。

3　编写要求

报告、论文的中文稿必须用白色稿纸单面缮写或打字;外文稿必须宜用 A4(210mm×297mm)标准大小的白纸,应便于阅读、复制和拍摄缩微制品。

报告、论文在书写、打字或印刷时,要求纸的四周留足空白边缘,以便装订、复制和读者批注。每一面的上方(天头)和左侧(订口)应分别留边 25mm 以上,下方(地脚)和右侧(切口)应分别留边 20mm 以上。

4　编写格式

4.1　报告、论文章、条的编号参照国家标准 GB 1.1《标准化工作导则标准编写的基本规定》第 8 章"标准条文的编排"的有关规定,采用阿拉伯数字分级编号。

4.2　报告、论文的构成(见附表 2-1)

5　前置部分

5.1　封面

5.1.1　封面是报告、论文的外表面,提供应有的信息,并起保护作用。

封面不是必不可少的。学术论文如作为期刊、书或其他出版物的一部分,无需封面;如作为预印本、抽印本等单行本时,可以有封面。

附表 2-1　报告、论文的构成

前置部分 { 封面、封二(见 5.1、5.2,学术论文不必要)
题名页(见 5.3)
序或前言(见 5.6,必要时)
摘要(见 5.7)
关键词(见 5.8)
目次页(见 5.9,必要时)
插图和附表清单(见 5.10,必要时)
符号、标志、缩略词、首字母缩写、单位、术语、
　名词等注释表(见 5.11,必要时)

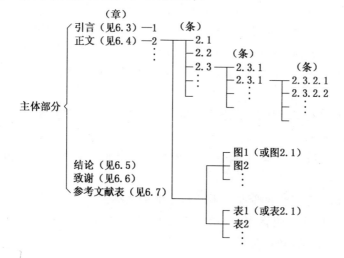

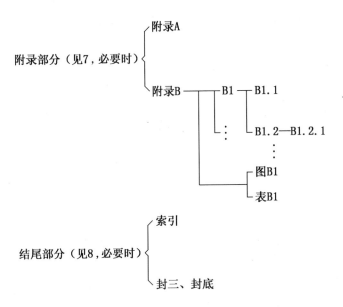

5.1.2 封面上可包括下列内容：

a. 分类号 在左上角注明分类号，便于信息交换和处理。一般应注明《中国图书资料分类法》的类号，同时应尽可能注明《国际十进分类法 UDC》的类号。

b. 本单位编号 一般标注在右上角。学术论文无必要。

c. 密级 报告、论文的内容，按国家规定的保密条例，在右上角注明密级。如系公开发行，不注密级。

d. 题名和副题名或分册题名 用大号字标注于明显地位。

e. 卷、分册、篇的序号和名称 如系全一册，无需此项。

f. 版本 如草案、初稿、修订版等。如系初版，无需此项。

g. 责任者姓名 责任者包括报告、论文的作者、学位论文的导师、评阅人、答辩委员会主席以及学位授予单位等。必要时可注明个人责任者的职务、职称、学位、所在单位名称及地址；如责任者系单位、团体或小组，应写明全称和地址。

在封面和题名页上，或学术论文的正文前署名的个人作者，只限于那些对于选定研究课题和制订研究方案、直接参加全部或主要部分研究工作并作出主要贡献以及参加撰写论文并能对内容负责的人，按其贡献大小排列名次。至于参加部分工作的合作者、按研究计划分工负责具体小项的工作者、某一项测试的承担者以及接受委托进行分析检验和观察的辅助人员等，均不列入。这些人可以作为参加工作的人员一一列入致谢部分，或排于脚注。

如责任者姓名有必要附注汉语拼音时，必须遵照国家规定，即姓在名前，名连成一词，不加连字符，不缩写。

h. 申请学位级别 应按《中华人民共和国学位条例暂行实施办法》所规定的名称进行标注。

i. 专业名称 系指学位论文作者主修专业的名称。

j. 工作完成日期 包括报告、论文提交日期，学位论文的答辩日期，学位的授予日期，出版部门收到日期（必要时）。

k. 出版项　出版地及出版者名称,出版年、月、日(必要时)。

5.2　封二

报告的封二可标注送发方式,包括免费赠送或邮购以及送发单位和个人;版权规定;其他应注明事项。

5.3　题名页

题名页是对报告、论文进行著录的依据。

学术论文无需题名页。

题名页置于封二和衬页之后,成为另页的右页。

报告、论文如分装两册以上,每一分册均应各有其题名页。在题名页上注明分册名称和序号。

题名页除5.1规定封面应有的内容并取得一致外,还应包括下列各项:

单位名称和地址,在封面上未列出的责任者职务、职称、学位、单位名称和地址,参加部分工作的合作者姓名。

5.4　变异本

报告、论文有时适应某种需要,除正式的全文正本以外,要求有某种变异本,如:节本、摘录本、为送请评审用的详细摘要本、为摘取所需内容的改写本等。

变异本的封面上必须标明"节本、摘录本或改写本"字样,其余应注明项目,参见5.1的规定执行。

5.5　题名

5.5.1　题名是以最恰当、最简明的词语反映报告、论文中最重要的特定内容的逻辑组合。

题名所用每一词语必须考虑到有助于选定关键词和编制题录、索引等二次文献可以提供检索的特定实用信息。

题名应该避免使用不常见的缩略词、首字母缩写字、字符、代号和公式等。

题名一般不宜超过20字。

报告、论文用作国际交流,应有外文(多用英文)题名。外文题名一般不宜超过10个实词。

5.5.2　下列情况可以有副题名:

题名语意未尽,用副题名补充说明报告论文中的特定内容;

报告、论文分册出版,或是一系列工作分几篇报道,或是分阶段的研究结果,各用不同副题名区别其特定内容;

其他有必要用副题名作为引申或说明者。

5.5.3　题名在整本报告、论文中不同地方出现时,应完全相同,但眉题可以节略。

5.6　序或前言

序并非必要。报告、论文的序,一般是作者或他人对本篇基本特征的简介,如说明研究工作缘起、背景、主旨、目的、意义、编写体例以及资助、支持、协作经过等;也可以评述和对相关问题研究阐发。这些内容也可以在正文引言中说明。

5.7 摘要

5.7.1 摘要是报告、论文的内容不加注释和评论的简短陈述。

5.7.2 报告、论文一般均应有摘要,为了国际交流,还应有外文(多用英文)摘要。

5.7.3 摘要应具有独立性和自含性,即不阅读报告、论文的全文,就能获得必要的信息。摘要中有数据、有结论,是一篇完整的短文,可以独立使用,可以引用,可以用于工艺推广。摘要的内容应包含与报告、论文同等量的主要信息,供读者确定有无必要阅读全文,也供文摘等二次文献采用。摘要一般应说明研究工作目的、实验方法、结果和最终结论等,而重点是结果和结论。

5.7.4 中文摘要一般不宜超过 200—300 字;外文摘要不宜超过 250 个实词。如遇特殊需要字数可以略多。

5.7.5 除了实在无变通办法可用以外,摘要中不用图、表、化学结构式、非公知公用的符号和术语。

5.7.6 报告、论文的摘要可以用另页置于题名页之后,学术论文的摘要一般置于题名和作者之后、正文之前。

5.7.7 学位论文为了评审,学术论文为了参加学术会议,可按要求写成变异本式的摘要,不受字数规定的限制。

5.8 关键词

关键词是为了文献标引工作从报告、论文中选取出来用以表示全文主题内容信息款目的单词或术语。

每篇报告、论文选取 3—8 个词作为关键词,以显著的字符另起一行,排在摘要的左下方。如有可能,尽量用《汉语主题词表》等词表提供的规范词。

为了国际交流,应标注与中文对应的英文关键词。

5.9 目次页

长篇报告、论文可以有目次页,短文无需目次页。

目次页由报告、论文的篇、章、条、附录、题录等的序号、名称和页码组成,另页排在序之后。

整套报告、论文分卷编制时,每一分卷均应有全部报告、论文内容的目次页。

5.10 插图和附表清单

报告、论文中如图表较多,可以分别列出清单置于目次页之后。

图的清单应有序号、图题和页码。表的清单应有序号、表题和页码。

5.11 符号、标志、缩略词、首字母缩写、计量单位、名词、术语等的注释表

符号、标志、缩略词、首字母缩写、计量单位、名词、术语等的注释说明汇集表,应置于图表清单之后。

6 主体部分

6.1 格式

主体部分的编写格式可由作者自定,但一般由引言(或绪论)开始,以结论或讨论结束。

主体部分必须由另页右页开始。每一篇(或部分)必须另页起;如报告、论文印成书刊等出版物,则按书刊编排格式的规定。

全部报告、论文的每一章、条的格式和版面安排,要求划一,层次清楚。

6.2 序号

6.2.1 如报告、论文在一个总题下分为两卷(或分册)以上,或分为两篇(或部分)以上,各卷或篇应有序号。可以写成:第一卷、第二分册;第一篇、第二部分等。用外文撰写的报告、论文,其卷(分册)和篇(部分)的序号,用罗马数字编码。

6.2.2 报告、论文中的图、表、附注、参考文献、公式、算式等,一律用阿拉伯数字分别依序连续编排序号。序号可以就全篇报告、论文统一按出现先后顺序编码,对长篇报告、论文也可以分章依序编码。其标注形式应便于互相区别,可以分别为:图1、图2.1、表2、表3.2;附注1);文献[4];式(5)、式(3.5)等。

6.2.3 报告、论文一律用阿拉伯数字连续编页码。页码、由书写、打字或印刷的首页开始,作为第1页,并为右页另页。封面、封二、封三和封底不编入页码。可以将题名页、序、目次页等前置部分单独编排页码。页码必须标注在每页的相同位置,便于识别。

力求不出空白页,如有,仍应以右页作为单页页码。

如在一个总题下分成两册以上,应连续编页码。如各册有其副题名,则可分别独立编页码。

6.2.4 报告、论文的附录依序用大写正体A,B,C,……编序号,如:附录A。

附录中的图、表、式、参考文献等另行编序号,与正文分开,也一律用阿拉伯数字编码,但在数码前冠以附录序码,如:图A1;表B2;式(B3);文献(A5)等。

6.3 引言(或绪论)

引言(或绪论)简要说明研究工作的目的、范围、相关领域的前人工作和知识空白、理论基础和分析、研究设想、研究方法和实验设计、预期结果和意义等。应言简意赅,不要与摘要雷同,不要成为摘要的注释。一般教科书中有的知识,在引言中不必赘述。

比较短的论文可以只用小段文字起着引言的效用。

学位论文为了反映出作者确已掌握了坚实的基础理论和系统的专门知识,具有开阔的科学视野,对研究方案作了充分论证,因此,有关历史回顾和前人工作的综合评述以及理论分析等,可以单独成章,用足够的文字叙述。

6.4 正文

报告、论文的正文是核心部分,占主要篇幅,可以包括:调查对象、实验和观测方法、仪器设备、材料原料、实验和观测结果、计算方法和编程原理、数据资料、经过加工整理的图表、形成的论点和导出的结论等。

由于研究工作涉及的学科、选题、研究方法、工作进程、结果表达方式等有很大的差异,对正文内容不能作统一的规定。但是,必须实事求是,客观真切,准确完备,合乎逻辑,层次分明,简练可读。

6.4.1 图

图包括曲线图、构造图、示意图、图解、框图、流程图、记录图、布置图、地图、照片、图版等。

图应具有"自明性",即只看图、图题和图例,不阅读正文,就可理解图意。

图应编排序号(见6.2.2)。

每一个图应有简短确切的题名,连同图号置于图下。必要时,应将图上的符号、标记、代码以及实验条件等,用最简练的文字,横排于图题下方,作为图例说明。

曲线图的纵横坐标必须标注"量、标准规定符号、单位"。此三者只有在不必要标明(如无量纲等)的情况下方可省略。坐标上标注的量的符号和缩略词必须与正文中一致。

照片图要求主题和主要显示部分的轮廓鲜明,便于制版。如用放大缩小的复制品,必须清晰,反差适中。照片上应该有表示目的物尺寸的标度。

6.4.2 表

表的编排,一般是内容和测试项目由左至右横读,数据依序竖排。表应有自明性。

表应编排序号(见 6.2.2)。

每一表应有简短确切的题名,连同表号置于表上。必要时,应将表中的符号、标记、代码以及需要说明事项,以最简练的文字,横排于表题下,作为表注,也可以附注于表下。附注序号的编排,见 6.2.2。表内附注的序号宜用小号阿拉伯数字并加圆括号置于被标注对象的右上角,如:"X X X",不宜用星号" * ",以免与数学上共轭和物质转移的符号相混。

表的各栏均应标明"量或测试项目、标准规定符号、单位"。只有在无必要标注的情况下方可省略。表中的缩略词和符号,必须与正文中一致。

表内同一栏的数字必须上下对齐。表内不宜用"同上""同左"……和类似词,一律填具体数字或文字。表内"空白"代表未测或无此项。"—"或"…"(因"—"可能与代表阴性反应相混淆)代表未发现,"0"代表实测结果确为零。

如数据已绘成曲线图,可不再列表。

6.4.3 数学、物理和化学式

正文中的公式、算式或方程式等应编排序号(见 6.2.2),序号标注于该式所在行(当有续行时,应标注于最后一行)的最右边。

较长的式,另行居中横排。如式必须转行时,只能在 $+,-,\times,\div,<,>$ 处转行。上下式尽可能在等号"="处对齐。

示例1
$$W(N_1) = H_{0,1} + \int_{\tau^{-1}}^{\tau^{-1}+1} L_a^r e^{-2\pi i a N_1} d\alpha$$
$$= R(N_0) + \int_{\tau^{-1}}^{\tau^{-1}+1} L_a^r e^{-2\pi i a N_1} d\alpha + O(P^{r-n-v}) \tag{1}$$

示例2
$$f(x,y) = f(0,0) + \frac{1}{1!}\left(x\frac{\partial}{\partial x} + y\frac{\partial}{\partial y}\right)f(0,0)$$
$$+ \frac{1}{2!}\left(x\frac{\partial}{\partial x} + y\frac{\partial}{\partial y}\right)^2 f(0,0) + \cdots$$
$$+ \frac{1}{n!}\left(x\frac{\partial}{\partial x} + y\frac{\partial}{\partial y}\right)^n f(0,0) + \cdots \tag{2}$$

示例3
$$-\frac{8\mu}{Nz}\frac{\partial}{\partial S}\ln Q = -\left[\left(1 + \sum_1^4 z_v\right) - \frac{2\mu}{z}\right]\ln\frac{\theta_a(1-\theta_\beta)}{\theta_\beta(1-\theta_a)}$$
$$+ \ln\frac{\lambda_a}{\lambda_\beta} - z_1\ln\frac{\varepsilon_1}{\zeta_1} + \sum z_v\ln\frac{\varepsilon_v}{\zeta_v}$$
$$= 0 \tag{3}$$

小数点用"."表示。大于 999 的整数和多于三位数的小数,一律用半个阿拉伯数字符的小间隔分开,不用千位撇。对于纯小数应将 0 列于小数点之前。

示例:应该写成 94 652.023 567;0.314 325

不应写成 94,652.023,567;.314,325

应注意区别各种字符,如:拉丁文、希腊文、俄文、德文花体、草体;罗马数字和阿拉伯数字;字符的正斜体、黑白体、大小写、上下角标(特别是多层次,如"三踏步")、上下偏差等。

示例:I,1,1,i;C,c;K,k,K;○,0,O,( );S,s,5;Z,z,2;B,β;W,w,ω。

6.4.4 计量单位

报告、论文必须采用1984年2月27日国务院发布的《中华人民共和国法定计量单位》,并遵照《中华人民共和国法定计量单位使用方法》执行。使用各种量、单位和符号,必须遵循附录B所列国家标准的规定执行。单位名称和符号的书写方式一律采用国际通用符号。

6.4.5 符号和缩略词

符号和缩略词应遵照国家标准(见附录B)的有关规定执行。如无标准可循,可采纳本学科或本专业的权威性机构或学术团体所公布的规定;也可以采用全国自然科学名词审定委员会编印的各学科词汇的用词。如不得不引用某些不是公知公用的、且又不易为同行读者所理解的、或系作者自定的符号、记号、缩略词、首字母缩写字等时,均应在第一次出现时一一加以说明,给以明确的定义。

6.5 结论

报告、论文的结论是最终的、总体的结论,不是正文中各段的小结的简单重复。结论应该准确、完整、明确、精练。

如果不可能导出应有的结论,也可以没有结论而进行必要的讨论。

可以在结论或讨论中提出建议、研究设想、仪器设备改进意见、尚待解决的问题等。

6.6 致谢

可以在正文后对下列方面致谢:

国家科学基金、资助研究工作的奖学金基金、合同单位、资助或支持的企业、组织或个人;

协助完成研究工作和提供便利条件的组织或个人;

在研究工作中提出建议和提供帮助的人;

给予转载和引用权的资料、图片、文献、研究思想和设想的所有者;

其他应感谢的组织或个人。

6.7 参考文献表

按照 GB 7714—87《文后参考文献著录规则》的规定执行。

7 附录

附录是作为报告、论文主体的补充项目,并不是必需的。

7.1 下列内容可以作为附录编于报告、论文后,也可以另编成册:

a. 为了整篇报告、论文材料的完整,但编入正文又有损于编排的条理和逻辑性,这一类材料包括比正文更为详尽的信息、研究方法和技术更深入的叙述,建议可以阅读的参考文献题录,对了解正文内容有用的补充信息等;

b. 由于篇幅过大或取材于复制品而不便于编入正文的材料;

c. 不便于编入正文的罕见珍贵材料;

d. 对一般读者并非必要阅读，但对本专业同行有参考价值的资料；

e. 某些重要的原始数据、数学推导、计算程序、框图、结构图、注释、统计表、计算机打印输出件等。

7.2 附录与正文连续编页码。每一附录的各种序号的编排见4.2和6.2.4。

7.3 每一附录均另页起。如报告、论文分装几册，凡属于某一册的附录应置于该册正文之后。

8　结尾部分（必要时）

为了将报告、论文迅速存储入电子计算机，可以提供有关的输入数据。

可以编排分类索引、著者索引、关键词索引等。

附录4 修改符号 Correction Symbols
（摘自美国汤姆森集团出版的
Discoveries of Academic Writing）

符号 SYMBOL 修改建议及例子 BEANING. CORRECTION ADVICE. AND EXAMPLES

FRAG fragment；使句子完整 complete the sentence
　Example
　　　Original Sentence：I went to the doctor. Because I was sick.
　　　Revised Sentence：I went to the doctor because I was sick.

R-O run-on；使用句号、分号或连词断句 divide the sentences with a period or semicolon, or use a conjunction
　Example
　　　Original Sentence：He will go to school he will make good grades.
　　　Revised Sentence：He will go to school, and he will make good grades.

P punctuation；添加、省略或改变标点 add, omit, or change it
　Example
　　　Original Sentence：I'll call you, after I get home.
　　　Revised Sentence：I'll call you after I get home.

∧ article；使用 a, an, the 等冠词或去掉冠词 or no article use a, an, the, or no article
　Example
　　　Original Sentence：Learn about the culture as well as language.
　　　Revised Sentence：Learn about the culture as well as the language.

∧ missing text；添加词或词组 add a word or group of words
　Example
　　　Original Sentence：Please speak to me before leave.
　　　Revised Sentence：Please speak to me before you leave.

Φ omit；删除冗余词汇 take out unnecessary words or phrases
　Example
　　　Original Sentence：I like the my teacher.
　　　Revised Sentence：I like my teacher.

F form；变换词性 use another form of the same word or verb
　Example
　　　Original Sentence：The U.S. and Japan used to be very difference.

Revised Sentence: The U. S. and Japan used to be very different.

V   **voice**；正确使用主动和被动语态 use active and passive voice correctly

   Example

      Original Sentence: Advances in technology are making.

      Revised Sentence: Advances in technology are being made.

W   **word choice**；变换选词 use a different word or phrase

   Example

      Original Sentence: I have been knowing English for two years.

      Revised Sentence: I have been studying English for two years.

S   **spelling**；检查拼写，使用拼写检查功能或词典，正确断词 check spelling, using a spelling-check feature or a dictionary; divide words correctly

   Example

      Original Sentence: I dicided to study at MU.

      Revised Sentence: I decided to study at MU.

WO   **word order**；使用符合英语表达习惯的语序，移动词或词组的位置 use English word order; switch or move words or groups of words

   Example

      Original Sentence: Hot and spicy food Korean is delicious, such as kimchi.

      Revised Sentence: Hot and spicy Korean food, such as kimchi, is delicious.

C   **capitalization**；单词大小写的转换 change to capital or lowercase letter

   Example

      Original Sentence: The united states is a big country.

      Revised Sentence: The United States is a big country.

**number agreement**；正确使用可数、不可数名词和名词的单复数形式 use countable/noncountable and singular/plural nouns correctly

   Example

      Original Sentence: The equipments in the lab will help me do my researches.

      Revised Sentence: The equipment in the lab will help me do my research.

↖AGR   **agreement**；使用正确的主谓或代词—先行词的搭配 use correct subject-verb or pronoun-antecedent agreement

   Example

      Original Sentence: John do not like sports because it is boring.

      Revised Sentence: John does not like sports because they are boring.

T   **verb tense**；变换时态 change the verb tense

   Example

      Original Sentence: When I come to the U. S., I was surprised by many things.

      Revised Sentence: When I came to the U. S., I was surprised by many things.

↖REF   **reference**；明确指代关系 change the sentence to clarify what word this word refers to

Example

Original Sentence: John called Bill when he finished eating.

Revised Sentence: When John finished eating, he called Bill.

⌒ **join**;将两个词合而为一 combine two words into one

Example

Original Sentence: Does any one know the answer to this question?

Revised Sentence: Does anyone know the answer to this question?

COMBINE **combine**;连接句子或短语 join these sentences or phrases

Example

Original Sentence: I have a brother. He lives in Ohio. He has two children. They are cute.

Revised Sentence: My brother, who lives in Ohio, has two cute children.

DIVIDE **divide**;断句或将其缩写 this sentence is too long; divide or shorten it

Example

Original Sentence: My brother, who lives in Ohio, has two cute children, who like to go swimming in the city pool even though one of them almost drowned last summer, a very frightening experience.

Revised Sentence: My brother, who lives in Ohio, has two cute children. They all like to go swimming in the city pool even though one of the children almost drowned last summer. It was a very frightening experience.

/ **separate**;分成两个单词 separate into two words

Example

Original Sentence: Joe was injured in the accident, and he maybe in the hospital for a while.

Revised Sentence: Joe was injured in the accident, and he may be in the hospital for a while.

// **parallelism**;使用平行结构 make structures parallel

Example

Original Sentence: I like to cook, sleeping late, and when I work out.

Revised Sentence: I like to cook, sleep late, and work out.

¶ **paragraphing**;将段落综合或分开 combine or separate the paragraphs

? **unclear, unreadable, doubtful, awkward**;将此部分表述清楚 reword this part so that it is clear and effective

参 考 文 献

陈妙云.《学术论文写作》.广州：广东人民出版社,1998.
陈仕持.《文史哲类学生论文导写》.重庆：中南大学出版社,2001.
程晓麟,王晓路.《当代美国小说理论》.北京：外语教学与研究出版社,2001.
邓炎昌,刘润清.《语言与文化——英汉语言文化对比》.北京：外语教学与研究出版社,1989.
冯幼民编著.《高级英文写作教程：论文写作》.北京：北京大学出版社,2002.
郭群英,段晓英,姬生雷主编.《二十世纪英美文学研究》.天津：花山文艺出版社,2001.
何康民编.《英语学术论文写作》.武汉：武汉大学出版社,2007.
胡庚申主编.《英语论文写作与发表》.北京：高等教育出版社,2000.
胡文仲.《跨文化交际面面观》.北京：外语教学与研究出版社,1999.
黄国文.《英语学术论文写作》.重庆：重庆大学出版社,2009.
黄继昌.《自考毕业论文写作教程》.北京：北京大学出版社,2003.
黎宏,荀露玲等.《写作与实践》.成都：四川大学出版社,2004.
刘新民主编.《英语论文写作规范》.北京：高等教育出版社,2003.
李炎清.《论文写作导引》.福州：福建教育出版社,2000.
陆道夫主编.《英语专业学士论文写作教程》.广州：暨南大学出版社,2009.
穆诗雄等编.《英语专业毕业论文写作》.北京：外语教育与研究出版社,2002.
漆权,王检军等.《自考毕业论文写作教程》.北京：北京大学出版社,2001.
祁寿华,William W. Morgan.《回应悲剧缪斯的呼唤》.上海：上海外语教育出版社,2001.
覃先美等.《高等学校英语专业毕业论文导写》.长沙：湖南师范大学出版社,2001.
《外语教学与研究》Vol. 36, No. 6, 2004, 6.
王嘉陵编著.《毕业论文写作与答辩》.成都：四川大学出版社,2003.
王俊芳."撰写文献综述的基本要求".《教育科学研究》,2004年第6期.
王林海,董洪学.《英语教学中的学术研究与写作》.上海：复旦大学出版社,2007.
王首程编著.《论文写作》.北京：高等教育出版社,2002.
武德春.《高等职业(专科、本科)教育管理类专业毕业论文写作教程》.北京：人民交通出版社,2001.
徐融等.《毕业论文写作》.北京：中国商业出版社,2002.
徐振宗,唐伯学主编.《学术论文》.北京：教育科学出版社,1992.
杨纪针,汪林,张树发编著.《地道英语写作技巧——系统实践》.汕头：汕头大学出版社,1992.
张纪英主编.《英语专业毕业论文写作教程》.武汉：华中科技大学出版社,2007.
张盛彬主编.《文科论文写作》.北京：北京大学出版社,1989.
《中国英语教学》2004年10月第27卷,第5期.
郑裕福,徐威编著.《英文科技论文写作与编辑指南》.北京：清华大学出版社,2008.

Beidler, Peter G. *Writing Matters*. Chengdu：Sichuan University Press, 2003.
Carole. *Slade Form and Style：Research Papers, Reports and Theses*. 北京：外语教学与研究出版社 & 汤姆森出版社,2000.
Fabb, Nigel and Alan Durant. *How to Write Essays, Dissertations and Theses in Literary Studies*.

Chengdu: Sichuan University Press, 2003.

Frank Austermühl.《译者的电子工具》(*Electronic Tools for Translators*).北京：外语教学与研究出版社，2006.

Gibaldi, Joseph.《MLA 科研论文写作规范》.上海：上海外语教育出版社，2001.

Harlen Seyfer,吴古华.《英语学术论文写作》.北京：高等教育出版社，1998.

Joseph Gibaldi.《MLA 文体手册和学术出版指南》(第二版).北京：北京大学出版社，2001.

罗伯特·戴,芭芭拉·盖斯特尔.《如何撰写和发表科技论文：第六版》(影印版).北京：北京大学出版社，2007.

罗薇娜·莫瑞.《如何为学术刊物撰稿：写作技能与规范》(影印版).北京：北京大学出版社，2007.

麦科马克,斯莱特著,清华大学外语系改编.《新世纪标准大学英语学术英语写作教程》(学生用书).北京：高等教育出版社，2006.

Moore, Brooke Noel and Richard Parker. *Critical Thinking*. California: Mayfield Publishing Company, 1986.

American Psychological Association. *Publication Manual of the American Psychological Association, Fifth Ed*. 2001.

Robert A. Day, Barbara Gastel. *How to write and Publish a Scientific Paper, Sixth Edition*. Cambridge: Press of the University of Cambridge, 2006.

Stanley Wells.《莎士比亚研究》.上海：上海外语教育出版社，2000.

The Journal of Asia TEFL Volume 1, Number 2, Autumn 2004.

Watson, George. *Writing a Thesis: A Guide to Long Essays and Dissertations*. Chengdu: Sichuan University Press, 2003.

汤姆森集团. *Discoveries of Academic Writing*.

论文格式网：http://www.lunwengeshi.com/lunwengeshi/166.html

芝加哥论文格式：http://www.Chicagomanualofstyle.org